Christian Ethics

Christian Ethics

An Introduction

Edited by Bernard Hoose

continuum
LONDON • NEW YORK

Continuum

The Tower Building, 11 York Road, London SE1 7NX

370 Lexington Avenue, New York, NY10017 – 6503

First published 1998
Reprinted 1999, 2000, 2002

British Library Cataloguing-in-Publication Data
A catalogue record for this book is available from the British Library.

ISBN 0-304-70263-3
ISBN 0-8264-4968-9

Contents

Part II Applied ethics

Social ethics

Interpersonal and sexual ethics

Medical ethics

The contributors

Charles E. Curran is the Elizabeth Scurlock Professor of Human Values at Southern Methodist University in Dallas, Texas. His latest books are *History and Contemporary Issues: Studies in Moral Theology* and *The Origins of Moral Theology in the United States: Three Different Approaches*.

Tom Deidun is a lecturer in New Testament studies at Heythrop College, University of London, as well as being editor of *The Heythrop Journal*. His writings include *New Covenant Morality in Paul* and numerous articles concerning New Testament themes.

Timothy J. Gorringe taught theology and ethics in India and Oxford before moving to the University of St Andrews, Scotland, where he is Reader in Contextual Theology. Recently published works are *Capital and the Kingdom* and *God's Just Vengeance: Crime, Violence and the Rhetoric of Salvation*.

Richard M. Gula is professor of moral theology at the Franciscan School of Theology at the Graduate Theological Union in Berkeley, California. Recent publications include *Euthanasia: Moral and Pastoral Perspectives*, *Ethics in Pastoral Ministry* and *Moral Discernment*.

Patrick Hannon is professor of moral theology at St Patrick's College, Maynooth, Ireland and a member of the Irish Bar. He is the author of *Church, State, Morality and Law* and *Knowing Right from Wrong*.

Bernard Hoose is a lecturer in Christian ethics at Heythrop College, University of London. He is the author of *Proportionalism: The American*

Debate and Its European Roots and *Received Wisdom? Reviewing the Role of Tradition in Christian Ethics.*

Gerard J. Hughes is vice principal and lecturer in philosophy at Heythrop College, University of London. His writings include *Authority in Morals* and *The Nature of God.*

Richard G. Jones, who previously taught Christian ethics in Manchester, England, is a former President of the Methodist Conference and is currently editor of the *Epworth Review*. He is also the author of *Groundwork in Christian Ethics.*

James F. Keenan is associate professor of moral theology at Weston Jesuit School of Theology in Cambridge, Massachusetts. His books include *Virtues for Ordinary Christians*, *The Context of Casuistry* and *Goodness and Rightness in Thomas Aquinas'* Summa Theologiae.

David F. Kelly is professor of theology and health care ethics at Duquesne University, Pittsburgh, Pennsylvania and Director of the Duquesne University Health Care Ethics Center. He is the author of *Critical Care Ethics: Treatment Decisions in American Hospitals*, *The Emergence of Roman Catholic Medical Ethics in North America* and *A Theological Basis for Health Care and Health Care Ethics.*

Kevin T. Kelly combines his pastoral work as a priest with writing and lecturing. He is part-time Senior Research Fellow in Moral Theology at Liverpool Hope University College. His writings include *Divorce and Second Marriage, New Directions in Moral Theology* and *Life and Love: Towards a Christian Dialogue on Bioethical Questions.*

Thomas R. Kopfensteiner is associate professor of theology at Fordham University in New York. His writings have appeared in various journals, including *Theological Studies*, *The Heythrop Journal* and *New Theology Review.*

Karen Lebacqz is Robert Gordon Sproul Professor of Theological Ethics at the Pacific School of Religion in the Graduate Theological Union in Berkeley, California. Her publications include *Professional Ethics: Power and Paradox, Six Theories of Justice*, and *Word, Worship, World and Wonder.*

Vincent MacNamara teaches theology at the Kimmage Mission Institute, Dublin. He is the author of *Faith and Ethics: Recent Roman Catholicism* and *The Truth in Love: Reflections on Christian Morality.*

Gareth Moore taught Old Testament and philosophy at Blackfriars, Oxford before moving to Belgium, where he is currently living and working. He is the author of numerous writings, including *The Body in Context: Sex and Catholicism*.

Aureliano Pacciolla is a clinical psychologist and moral theologian who teaches moral theology, psychology of religion, general psychology and hypnosis at various institutes in Rome and Turin. His writings include *La comunicazione metaforica: diventare adulti, Ipnosi, Esperienze pre-morte* and *I nostri figli*.

Susan F. Parsons is Principal of the East Midlands Ministry Training Course in Nottingham, England. She is the author of *Feminism and Christian Ethics* and of *The Ethics of Gender* (forthcoming).

Joyce Poole initially trained in paediatric surgery but moved into family practice. Her professional involvement with seriously ill and handicapped children kindled an interest in medical ethics. She is the author of *The Harm We Do: A Catholic Doctor Confronts Church, Moral and Medical Teaching* and of numerous articles on medical ethics.

Joseph Selling, a US citizen, is professor of moral theology at Katholieke Universiteit in Leuven, Belgium. He co-edited *The Splendor of Accuracy: An Examination of the Assertions Made by 'Veritatis Splendor'*. He has also written a number of commentaries on Church documents and articles on various other topics.

Introduction

In recent years there has been something of an upsurge of interest in the study of Christian ethics. To those who enter into this field, however, much of what is written can appear confusing or beyond reach. One of the reasons for this is the fact that a good deal of what is produced by scholars is part of 'in house' debates: the theologians and philosophers concerned are really writing for other theologians and philosophers and for those of their students who are already sufficiently well versed in such matters to be able to understand. Clearly worded introductions to the various elements of Christian ethics are not many in number. This volume is an attempt to improve matters.

It is sometimes stated, rather simplistically, that Protestants base their ethics solely on the Bible, whilst Roman Catholics ground theirs only in natural law. It is at least debatable that either of these stereotypes presents a complete picture of what was truly the case even in earlier centuries. Today, however, few Christian ethicists would even make the claim. Advances in biblical scholarship in more recent times have led most scholars – Protestant and otherwise – to conclude that Scripture alone does not provide a sufficient basis for Christian ethics. On the other hand, during the last three or four decades, there has been a tendency within Roman Catholicism to pay more attention to the contribution of Scripture than was previously the case.

Nowadays, in fact, there is a good deal of agreement among scholars of various denominations that there are several sources of which we can make use in our journey towards ethical wisdom. These include the Bible, various insights of philosophers (some of whom are, of course, natural law thinkers), and our own reasoning powers and sensitivities. We can also add the findings of the various sciences to this list. Sciences such as biology and psychology do not normally tell us directly what is morally right or wrong activity. However, they do help us to ensure that our ethical decisions are based on correct factual information. An additional item is found within one branch of Christianity, for, within Roman Catholicism, there is also an official teaching body which is claimed to be a privileged source of information and guidance. It is sometimes claimed that certain moral norms emanating from this last mentioned teaching body and from some other sources apply always and everywhere, regardless of circumstances. Not all scholars agree about the validity of such absolute norms. It is hardly surprising, therefore, that there has been an enormous amount of debate concerning this matter in recent decades. Some Christian ethicists, however, have observed that many of the contributions on both sides of this debate have concentrated too much upon the rightness or wrongness of acts and have given insufficient attention to the person acting. They believe that this imbalance can be overcome by turning to virtue ethics.

All that has been said so far explains, to some extent at least, the presence of the first five chapters in Part I of this book. The sixth is dedicated to a discussion of the human person. The revival of virtue ethics, the development of a dynamic approach to natural law and a growth in the influence of personalism in Christian ethics have led numerous scholars in recent times to accentuate the importance of trying to understand the various aspects or dimensions of human personhood, whilst seeing them all in the unity that is the person.

Clearly, it is the person, the acting subject, who takes into account the various sources of ethical wisdom indicated above and who is ultimately responsible for his or her freely taken decisions in the moral arena. Here we come to the role of conscience, but the term 'conscience' can mean different things to different people. This concept too, then, needs to be examined in some detail, and this is done in Chapter 7. Closely connected to the subject of conscience is that of the goodness or badness of the person. In this regard, chiefly among Roman Catholic scholars, a theory about the basic moral orientation of the individual has been developed: the theory of the fundamental option, which forms the subject matter of Chapter 8.

There are two other chapters in this first part. For many centuries, works on moral theology or Christian ethics were written almost exclusively by males from a male point of view. Women, moreover, were in many ways subordinated to men and undervalued. Clearly, an important dimension of what it is to be human was missing. As part of the ongoing attempt to redress the balance, we need to consider the impact and importance of contributions made in recent years in the field of feminist ethics, a task undertaken in Chapter 9.

Finally, having taken all of these matters into account, we do well to ask if there is any such thing as *Christian* ethics. If it is indeed the case that the Bible cannot fulfil the role that some early Protestants tried to ascribe to it, what, if anything, is specifically or distinctively Christian in the discipline we call 'Christian ethics'? This is a question we have to deal with in the final chapter of Part I.

In Part II we apply some of the general principles to specific matters in the fields of interpersonal and sexual ethics, social ethics and medical ethics. In order to keep the book to a reasonable size and an affordable price, we have been necessarily restrictive in the choice of subjects examined. Important contemporary moral problems in such fields as environmental ethics, business ethics and genetic engineering have not been covered. It is, however, hoped, that readers will feel encouraged to pursue their studies concerning not only the matters dealt with in this book but also others such as those just mentioned.

The contributors to this volume were chosen to write specific chapters because of their expertise in those fields. Many of them are scholars of international renown. The idea of producing such a volume which would permit the contributors to specialize in areas in which they are strong came from Michael Walsh, the librarian at Heythrop College. My sincere thanks go out to him, to Joe Selling who gave me valuable advice and encouragement, and to my wife Jayne, who is a constant source of sound counsel and support.

Bernard Hoose

PART I
Basic Christian ethics

1

The Bible and Christian ethics

Tom Deidun

Most Christians believe that the Bible has, or should have, a special role in Christian living. Ethicists in the Protestant tradition have generally been more alert than Roman Catholic moralists to the need to take this belief seriously in the conduct of their discipline. However, since the decades leading up to Vatican II, and especially after that Council's call for moral theology to be revitalized through more contact with the Bible, Roman Catholic moralists have increasingly acknowledged the need to give the Bible a higher profile in their reflections. In a 1971 article[1] Charles Curran was able to review several significant benefits brought to Catholic moral theology in the 1960s by what he called the 'Scriptural renewal'.

However, it is sobering to note that Curran then went on to warn about certain 'limitations' or difficulties inherent in the use of the Bible in moral theology – limitations and difficulties relating especially to the Bible's diversity and to its historical and cultural distance. More sobering still is the thought that the 'Scriptural renewal' whose benefits Curran applauded had owed its success largely to its failure to notice such difficulties. It was, in fact, the tail-end of a movement (the so-called 'Biblical theology movement' in its 1940s/1950s form), whose scientific naïvety had already been amply exposed by the time Catholic theology began enjoying its benefits.[2] This is not to say that these benefits were not real as far as moral theology was concerned; only that they appear to have been made possible by methods of biblical interpretation which are now widely regarded as inadequate for scientific purposes. Hence, the 'Scriptural renewal', while it may have prevented Roman Catholic moral theology from ever reverting to its traditional mould, offers no satisfactory way forward today.

My aim in this chapter is not to add substantially to what Curran wrote in 1971 but only to describe in more detail, for the benefit of students who are new to the discussion, the problems that may arise from the standpoint of biblical scholarship when Christian ethicists look to it for some contribution to their discipline. Only by way of postscript, as it were, do I venture a suggestion for a possibly constructive 'use' of the Bible in Christian ethics which respects the nature of the biblical writings.

Two distinct steps: interpretation and appropriation

If we are to apply 'what the Bible says' to our own ethical concerns (that is, if we are to pass from text to life), then we must first do our best to establish 'what the Bible says'. This prior task involves trying to discover what a given biblical writer understood himself to be saying. There are two distinct steps, therefore, in any attempt to apply biblical material in Christian ethics: interpretation of biblical texts and some kind of appropriation or contemporization.

Obvious as that last remark may sound, many modern hermeneutical theorists would argue that far from these two steps being distinguishable, the merging of the interpreter's horizons with those of the text is integral to any act of interpretation. There is no such thing as a 'presuppositionless' interpretation. Interpretation involves a circular, or spiral, movement of interaction between interpreter and text, and this interaction is itself constructive of meaning. In that sense, the reader is the text's co-author.

But it is one thing to say that there is no interpretation without some involvement of the interpreter, and quite another to make the interpreter's involvement a methodological imperative. It may be true at some level that 'the theologian is ... an exegete simultaneously of Scripture and existence';[3] but in what follows I take the old-fashioned view that in so far as the theologian is an exegete of biblical texts, his or her only remit is to explain the text in its historical and literary context. This entails doing one's utmost to prevent one's 'exegesis of existence' colouring one's interpretation of biblical texts. Experience surely teaches us (if common sense failed to do so) that interpreters who turn to biblical texts in search of 'relevance' will surely find what they are looking for, but only after imposing on the texts their own notions of what counts as relevant.

This is not to say that interpretations of biblical texts which operate on modern hermeneutical theories will have nothing to contribute to Christian ethicists' appropriation of biblical texts. Quite the opposite, for such interpretations might, given certain conditions, turn out to be peculiarly enriching, not least because of their inevitable pluralism and their ability to bring to the ethicist's use of the Bible a faculty which often remains unexercised in biblical interpretation, namely, imagination.[4]

Interpretation

Historical-critical exegesis

The method (or cluster of methods) of interpretation which professes to concern itself with discovering what the biblical writers understood themselves to be saying, and which claims to provide the least fragile defence against the imposition of gratuitously subjectivizing elements on biblical texts, is commonly described as the 'historical-critical method'. This operates on the principle that a prerequisite for discovering what any given biblical writer understood himself to be saying is a careful use of all available critical tools (historical, linguistic and literary), joined with an honest effort to be objective and an openness to unfamiliar ideas.

As implied above in my references to current hermeneutical theories, the historical-critical method has not gone unchallenged in recent decades, and in some quarters has given way to, or been supplemented by, methods which start from very different hermeneutical premises. Still, most biblical scholars continue to regard it as irreplaceable, and as a necessary first step, at least, in the interpretation of all, or almost all, biblical writings. The Roman Catholic Church, having gradually become less fearful of it than it once notoriously was, has recently given it its official blessing (even if that blessing perhaps evokes, in uncharitable minds, reminiscences of the blind Isaac).

A recent official Roman Catholic Statement about the historical-critical method

The Pontifical Biblical Commission's remarkable 1993 Statement, *L'Interprétation de la Bible dans l'Église*,[5] declares at the outset that 'The historical critical method is the indispensable method for the scientific study of the meaning of ancient texts' (§I, A), proceeds to evaluate it with the words 'It is a method which, when used in an objective manner, implies of itself no *a priori*' (§I, A, 4), and concludes that 'To attempt to by-pass [historical criticism] would be to create an illusion . . .' (Conclusion). In his address on the occasion of the presentation of this Statement (23 April 1993), Pope John Paul II told his audience that 'The Church . . . attaches great importance to the "historico-critical" study of the Bible', and went on to remind them that his predecessor Leo XIII had approved of it 'vehementer'.[6]

A premiss and some implications of the historical-critical method

A premiss of the historical-critical method is that biblical texts are *wholly* human products (it has nothing to say about whether they are *only* human products). This means that '[the historical-critical method] studies the biblical text in the same fashion as it would any other ancient text and comments upon it as an expression of human discourse' (*L'Interprétation*, §I, A, 2). Of the many areas of broad consensus about the implications of this among those who practise historical-critical exegesis, I shall highlight those which anyone hoping to make a scientific use of the Bible in Christian ethics will especially need to come to terms with.

The biblical writings are 'culture-bound'

It is no disparagement of the Bible to say that its writings are 'culture-bound', for the Bible would not be a human product if they were not.[7] This does not mean that biblical texts cannot speak out of their own culture in ways that may be vitally relevant to us; but it does mean that they speak out of *their* own culture, not ours. They therefore have to be read with an eye to what can be known of the particular author's (and his readers' or hearers') historical, cultural and theological horizons, which, common sense tells us, are likely to be quite different from our own.[8]

For example: Christian ethicists need to be alert to, and to make allowance for, the 'apocalyptic' mindset of early Christianity, with its tendency to devalue 'this world' and with its general unconcern for, and pessimism about, society at large. Early Christians could never have come up with anything like a 'social encyclical'. They had no interest in the social justice concerns which preoccupy many Christian ethicists in our day, and no inkling that the gospel required them to defend – and still less that it was essentially about defending – 'human rights'. They never thought it was their business to try to transform social and political structures by working for, say, the abolition of slavery, the social equality of women or a more just distribution of wealth in society at large; and this, presumably, because restructuring the ballroom will not be high up on the agenda of people who believe the ship is sinking.[9]

It is not that New Testament writers looked critically at a range of possible moral priorities and consciously opted for the other-worldly ones. It was simply that their cultural and mental horizons excluded a fundamental assumption of our theology and ethics, namely, that the world is important. Hence any dialogue between modern Christian ethicists whose reasonings mostly presuppose that the world is here to stay, and first-century Christians who thought maybe it will end at tea-time tomorrow, is likely to be at cross-purposes. Christian ethicists need to be alert to this. It is easy to be alert to it in instances where biblical writers expressly indicate that their ethical statements are bound up with their imminentist eschatology (e.g., Paul in 1 Cor 7:25–31); but such instances are few.

Admittedly, appeals to the eschatological colouring of ethical teachings in the New Testament writings can be overdone. It may be significant that in an epistle which very clearly reflects the 'imminentist' expectations of one Pauline community (1 Thessalonians: cf. 1 Thess 1:10; 5:1–5), Paul includes what appears to be routine exhortation (1 Thess 4:3–12); and several sayings in the 'Sermon on the Mount', which is often said to be markedly 'eschatological' in character, can be paralleled by sayings in rabbinic and other Jewish writings which had no thought of an imminent End.[10] The problem for those who wish to find something relevant in New Testament ethical teachings is to determine, from case to case, the *extent* to which those teachings are tied up with a bygone eschatology.

I remarked above that common sense tells us that the biblical writers' cultural and theological horizons are likely be different from our own. A less common sense will warn us that this may be so especially where the horizons of biblical writers appear to coincide with ours. For example: we may too easily assume that underlying the statements about sexual matters to be found in the Bible there is a universal, perennial rationale which must, therefore, make them directly relevant to us.[11] This appears to be the assumption of those who advocate a 'return to "Biblical morality"' as the solution to all sexual-ethical controversies in our day (and for whom, in fact, 'Biblical morality' appears to be synonymous with 'sexual morality'); and also of those who, less combatively, just take it for granted that the Bible must tell us something about God's rules on sex.

But this may be an assumption induced in us by our failure to enter into the cultural worlds of the biblical writers. For regarding, first, the Old Testament (and the Old Testament, in matters sexual, has probably burnt deeper into the Christian psyche than the New), the factors which typically underlie sexual prohibitions in certain well-thumbed pages have more to do with cultural taboos (where 'purity' is, from our point of view, non-moral and where, for example, menstruation, contact with a corpse, cross-dressing, same-sex relations and intercourse with animals are all deemed equally to be dreaded, and apparently for the same kind of reason), than with anything that most Christians nowadays would admit to thinking had anything to do with sexual *morality*; or else were based on considerations of 'property rights', such as may be quite foreign or even morally unacceptable to us. Then, with regard to New Testament writers, we need to enquire (from case to case) to what extent their attitudes towards sexual matters derived from the same cultural sensibilities as those of Old Testament writers.[12]

However one explains the sexual attitudes of the New Testament writers, the fact is that none of them (with the possible exception of the author of Eph 5:28ff.) comes anywhere near suggesting that sex might contribute to the spiritual enrichment of the person and of a personal relationship, or that there might be some connection between sex and Christian love. Vatican II (e.g., *Gaudium et Spes*, n. 49) came up with some positive reflections on the Christian dimensions of sex; but such reflections were only possible through a giant leap away from New Testament perspectives.

The following random reflections might alert us to the distance between present-day Christian convictions about sexual morality and those of New Testament writers: (1) In the whole of 1 Corinthians 7, where Paul discusses sex, marriage and celibacy, he never once mentions *agape*. This is especially odd from our point of view if (as many interpreters believe) Paul's purpose in that chapter was precisely to correct wrong-headed views on those subjects. (2) In 1 Corinthians 6:12–20 Paul exhorts the Corinthians not to go with prostitutes. He uses several different motivations. Some of these are not easy to interpret, but respect for the other is definitely not one of them. Paul is apparently not at all concerned for the prostitute's well-being, and *agape* is conspicuously absent from the passage. What would surely be a paramount consideration of most Christian ethicists today in any discussion of sexual morality simply has no look-in with Paul in this passage. Perhaps it is also significant (3) that the subject of sexual morality was nothing like as fascinating to New Testament writers as it is to us, and the Gospel traditions are almost totally silent about it.

Then, in how many other areas would we need to query whether the ethical perspectives of some or all New Testament writers coincide with the best of ours? It may be significant that in the very area where Christian ethicists have taken it for granted that they do – namely, neighbour love – there may in fact be a radical divergence or only a partial overlap. We should not assume that everywhere in the New Testament the 'love' that Bible readers warm to really measures up to our own best Christian appraisals of love. In some places it does; and sometimes it surpasses all that we might have thought love to be capable of. But this is not always so. The love that is fervently commended in the Johannine epistles turns out to be a sectarian-type love, whose flipside is fear and hatred. Raymond E. Brown says of it:

> No more eloquent voice [than that of the author of 1 John] is raised in the NT for love within the brotherhood and sisterhood. . . . Yet that same voice is extremely bitter in condemning opponents who had been members of the community and were no longer. They are demonic,

antichrists, false prophets, and serve as the embodiment of eschatological lawlessness and iniquity. . . . Those who believe that God has given His people the biblical books as a guide should recognize that part of the guidance is to learn from the dangers attested in them, as well as from their great insights. . . . [I]n a passage like II John 10–11 [the author] supplied fuel for those Christians of all times who feel justified in hating other Christians for the love of God.[13]

Even in cases where New Testament notions of love are not vulnerable to such strictures, we should not assume that they coincide with ours. For New Testament writers are typically concerned with the perfection of the subject who loves, and only obliquely, if at all, with the interests and needs of the one loved. From this one might infer that the New Testament writers seem not to know of the altruism that is cherished in the best of our own culture, and arguably, in the most really Christian souls; and that the love they commend is in the last analysis (albeit ever so spiritually) self-centred;[14] or, alternatively, one could take the difference in perspective as a cue for critical self-questioning about possible deficiencies in our own culture's evaluation of love. But all that aside, the point I am concerned to make here is that there *is* a difference in perspective, and Christian ethicists need to be aware of it.

The Bible's diversity

The Bible is a *collection* of writings produced in many different cultural contexts over a very long period of time (even the New Testament writings, in the judgement of most historical-critical scholars, are assignable to a sixty- or seventy-year period). These writings are not like so many chapters of a catechism produced under editorial direction but, for the most part, free-standing literary works, whose authors held a wide range of theological viewpoints and who each chose one or more of a variety of literary genres through which to express them. Even among New Testament writers, alongside a small number of fundamental beliefs held in common, there is a considerable diversity of theological and ethical viewpoints, extending even to the manner in which those fundamental beliefs are understood and articulated.[15]

The Bible's diversity does not worry historical critics. Problems arise only for dogmaticians and ethicists who link the Bible's normativity with its canonical status and who, in addition, care about theoretical consistency. For if canonicity renders the Bible normative, it must render all of it normative, even when elements in it stand in tension with each other or are mutually exclusive.

A first major problem for the canonically-minded is that of the dissonance between 'Old' Testament and 'New' in the Christian canon. For ethicists, this problem presents itself perhaps most acutely in the New Testament writers' repudiation of at least some of the purity laws, which lie at the heart of Torah.[16] Appeals to New Testament texts like Romans 14:14, Mark 7:14–23 or Acts 10:9–16 do not solve this problem; they only compound it. For, as canonical texts they invite Christians to accept that at a very convenient point in time (i.e., the beginnings of the gentile mission) God suddenly decided to 'cleanse' precisely those things which throughout tedious pages of the same canon the same God had stridently pronounced abominable. When Peter heard the voice from heaven telling him 'What God has cleansed, you must not call common [defiling]', it is not surprising that he was 'inwardly perplexed' (Acts 10:17).

Purity laws apart, there still remains the problem what canonically minded ethicists are to make of those Old Testament passages which, for example, command or commend the ideology of holy war, or which speak of polygamy or adultery without batting an eyelid. Most Christians, I imagine, now regard such texts as belonging to an irretrievably distant moral world. But on the logic of canonicity the discarding of 'obsolete' elements (including the purity laws) is possible only by way of arbitrary selectivity, or by appeals to some kind of progressive divine pedagogy, which comes to the same thing.

For the notion of 'pedagogic progressivity' cuts more ways than one. If it justifies our discarding some elements in the Old Testament, does it not by parity of reasoning justify our discarding the lot (à la Marcion)? But to discard all Old Testament ethical teachings as but yellowed records of some elementary stage of the divine pedagogy, now superseded, would be to deprive ourselves of many inspiring ethical perspectives which are lacking in the New Testament, and without which Christians' moral vision would be very much the poorer. For example, the Old Testament exhibits imaginations of God, creation and the future which differ markedly from those of the New Testament, but are not, surely, for that reason less to be cherished. May not Psalm 128, for example, or the Song of Solomon, and all those Old Testament texts which celebrate joy in *this* creation be 'meant' as a counterpoint to the world-shunning attitudes of most New Testament writers?

In any case, theories of progressivity beg the question as to where the progressivity is supposed to end. The usual view is that it ends with the revelation of the New Testament, seen as definitive (Heb 1:1f., etc.). But we need to be discriminating about New Testament ethical teachings too; and we can only be thus discriminating on some theory of progressivity which extends *into* the New Testament. In reality, theories about a progressive divine pedagogy provide no honest way out of the problems which confront canonically-minded Christian ethicists.

Even if there existed some plausible means of harmonizing the Old Testament and the New such as does justice both to their dissonance and to their co-equal canonical status, the troubles of the canonically-minded would only be just beginning. For even within the two collections taken separately there are a variety of ethical perspectives, and different or even plainly incompatible stances on some quite specific ethical issues.

To confine ourselves to examples from the New Testament:[17] The ethical stances of Matthew and Paul are quite different (which is not surprising, given that these writers were addressing two quite different forms of Christianity). To his (Jewish Christian) community looking for ethical guidance, Matthew recommended Torah reinterpreted and reprioritized in the light of his Christology and his appreciation of the Jesus tradition, and accommodated, so it seems, to his community's needs and to the requirements of an incipient gentile mission; whereas Paul wanted his gentile communities to put Torah out of mind,[18] and to look rather to the Spirit, to community discernment and to traditional Christian baptismal catechesis (supplemented by selective endorsements of current Jewish and Hellenistic moral standards) as an adequate guide to conduct.[19]

Further, 1 Corinthians 7 – for whatever reason – presents a dismal and trivializing view of marriage and sex, whereas Ephesians 5 is theologically profound about it. (And let us not complicate matters by noting that the Song had got lyrical about erotic love.) Then, attitudes towards society at large differ markedly as between Paul's epistles and Acts; the ethical evaluation of the state and of civil authorities expressed in Romans 13:1–7 is hardly compatible with Revelation 13, or even with 1 Corinthians 6:1–11; and the evaluation of the moral condition of humankind *extra evangelium* is very different in Romans from what it is in Acts 17, and very different in Romans 2:14f. from what it is in Romans 1:18ff. and 7:14ff.

Then, even regarding such a particular issue as divorce:[20] In the Gospels of Mark and Luke, Jesus' prohibition is presented as absolute, whereas Matthew has Jesus include an 'exceptive clause' (which has caused some exegetes, especially Roman Catholics, to engage in endless exegetical gymnastics aimed at showing that Matthew's Jesus after all admits of no exceptions to the divorce prohibition); and Paul in 1 Corinthians 7:12–16, as it seems to some (including, traditionally, the Roman Catholic Church in its canonical-legal practice),[21] allows for some accommodation of, or departure from, Jesus' prohibition in certain circumstances.

The diversity of the New Testament writers' moral teachings calls into question any use of the Bible which relies in one way or another on being able to speak of 'what the Bible says', or of 'biblical morality' or of '*the* New Testament teaching'.[22] This stricture will apply as much to the methods of the 'Biblical theology movement' as to more recent and more cautious positions, such as that of Richard B. Hays,[23] who recommends interposing an act of 'synthesis' between the 'descriptive' and 'hermeneutical' tasks. Hays acknowledges that such a synthesis will require bold selectivity. But any selectivity is bound to end up with a canon within the canon, which is a flight from the logic of canonicity and a common ploy of canonically-minded interpreters who want to have their cake and eat it.[24]

The situational character of the biblical writers' ethical statements

Most biblical writings are contextual in a far narrower sense than their simply being historically and culturally conditioned, for they addressed very particular situations, or they were occasioned by very particular circumstances. (I leave aside for now the question whether it is possible to establish connections, parallels or analogies between the situations addressed by particular biblical writers then, and situations which typically confront us now – supposing that establishing such connections, etc., might be useful.) In the case of Paul's letters, for example (with the possible exception of Romans), and in the case of, say, the Johannine epistles, so much is obvious. It is perhaps less obvious in relation to the Gospels. They too, however, almost certainly had in view the circumstances of particular communities. (A careful study of each Evangelist's redactional strategy suggests so much.)

So it will not do to bring to the interpretation, say, of Matthew, only the general knowledge that he speaks out of the culture of some kind of first-century Jewish Christianity (fatal as it would be to overlook this fact). One would need also to establish, in so far as this is possible, what Matthew's community's relationship was with this or that sector of contemporary non-Christian Judaism, what the latter were up to at that time, whether there was interaction between Matthew's community and the non-Christian Jews in the 'synagogue over the road' ('*their* synagogues'!); whether there was debate between them, and if so, over what issues; whether and to what extent Matthew's community still observed the whole or part of Torah, and, if so, whether some or all of its members interpreted it in ways which distinguished them from their non-Christian kinsfolk, and in what ways; and whether this gave rise to problems, and how Matthew's community appears to have handled these problems, and whether, and how, and for what reasons their belief in Jesus messiah aggravated such problems; then, further, whether Matthew's community was engaged in, or was contemplating, a gentile mission, and, if so, how this might have complicated (or even created) those problems – to say nothing, finally, of the sociological profile of Matthew's community and the light that this might throw on his Gospel. On historical-critical principles, it would be illegitimate to seek to appropriate Matthew's text, not to say miscellaneous bits of it, without first considering at least these questions.

So also, regarding, say, 1 Corinthians, one would need to try to discover the mindset, beliefs and problems of the Corinthian community, if only to decide whether what Paul says about marriage in 1 Corinthians 7 is to be read as timeless wisdom, or whether that chapter was not rather addressed to very particular needs, for example, those of a community of semi-converted Christians with hang-ups about sex and celibacy.[25] It could make all the difference.

As readers of the Bible we are first of all eavesdroppers. This means that a proper interpretation of the biblical writers' ethical statements presupposes the prior task of reconstructing the situation which a given biblical writer was addressing there and then. We may need to reconstruct the unrecorded side of the interchange to stand any chance of understanding what is being said in the biblical text, and with what nuances or emphases, and in order to be reasonably sure that we are not getting the wrong end of the stick altogether. In the case of a few biblical writings the quest for a reconstructed dialogue partner may be misguided; in the case of others it may be desirable, but impossible for lack of clues; but in most cases the clues are there, and it would be disingenuous to ignore them.

Attempts at reconstruction will inevitably involve varying degrees of conjecture and provisionality. Doubtless, the very idea of conjecture and provisionality will cause hilarity or annoyance among those born or reborn to see the Bible as the word of God *tout court*; and may be regarded with suspicion by those who, while not holding a fervent view of biblical inspiration, still see the Bible as a repository of straightforward truths, and scholarly conjecture as an evasion of those truths. But the alternative to scholarly conjecture is to risk getting it all wrong, and perhaps with dire consequences.[26]

The Bible's literary genres

The biblical texts demand to be read with an eye to the particular literary genre(s) which a given biblical writer chose to employ, and therefore with an understanding of the conventions governing literary genres in the cultural worlds of the Bible.[27] These conventions might be quite different from those governing what at first sight appear to be straightforwardly comparable genres in more familiar literatures. To complicate matters further, any given biblical writing (say, Genesis, or a prophetic book, or a Gospel) might embrace a variety of genres or 'forms', each requiring its own canons of interpretation – a fact which may be confusing to us moderns, who take it for granted that, say, a law report, or *Spitting Image*, or *Budgie the Little Helicopter* are each patient of a uniform and predictable set of interpretational criteria from beginning to end; and quite baffling to those of us who come to the Bible with ears attunable to only two modes of expressivity, namely, factual reporting and legal responsa.[28]

In regard to some parts of the biblical literature the fact that different genres (or 'forms') require different interpretational postures is now widely appreciated. Christians who persist in taking Genesis 1 – 3 literally (with or without the Hebrew-speaking serpent) are now widely seen – at least outside some circles in Tennessee and kindred intellectual milieux – as daft; and those who take the Book of Revelation as a preview of things to come are also widely regarded as daft (or as weird and possibly dangerous). Most Christians are less prone, however, to be hermeneutically cautious about apocalyptic language when it is attributed to *Jesus* (e.g., Mark 13); or about the Jewish or Jewish apocalyptic images which Jesus used in referring to the coming of the Son of man, or about the Judgement, and gehenna. Then, when it comes to Jesus' reported *ethical* sayings, Christians are inclined to drop their hermeneutical guard altogether, for something tells them that the genre of such sayings *must* be Sinaitic. But why should it be? And if it has to be, why are some of those sayings (e.g., the one about self-mutilation, or the one about not resisting the evil one) serenely accepted by the mainstream churches as all-too-obvious instances of prophetic hyperbole, whereas others of them are pounced on as timelessly valid moral norms, and, in the case of one of them – the prohibition of divorce – as an unalterable statute?

Respect for context and for the author's textual strategy

Critical interpretation demands that a biblical text, like any other text, be read in the light of its immediate and broader *literary* (as well as historical) context. Even the smallest components of texts should be read with regard to their function within their contexts. We mostly do this as a matter of course when reading, say, an advertisement, a school report or a Lionel Blue anecdote, but it is strange how doctrinal and other preoccupations incline us to atomize *biblical* texts and to isolate those elements in them that, for altogether extraneous reasons, especially appeal to us.[29] One still meets (or, more usually, is met by) a certain type of earnest Christian eager to puzzle one with questions like 'What do you make of Romans 1:18?' They never ask 'What do you make of Romans?' (which might make such encounters marginally more educative).

The temptation to home in on what is merely transitional in, or incidental to, the text's internal logic is hard to resist; for in every biblical interpreter there is something of the little boy who, on being asked by his RE teacher, after a reading of the Parable of the Prodigal Son, 'Now *who* was very sad to see the younger son return?', replied 'Please, Miss: the fatted calf!' There is no biblical interpreter who has wholly resisted the temptation to bring to the text fascinations that have come to them from elsewhere (whether from cherished dogmatic or apologetic concerns, or some paramount life concern or some all-consuming pastoral/socio-political commitment).[30]

Manifestations past and present of the fatted-calf syndrome are beyond counting, so examples must be chosen at random. Classic are: the (second-think) Augustine's – and then, more disturbingly, Luther's – misuse of Romans 7:14ff.; the Roman Catholic tradition's cultivation of the Mat-thean 'Petrine text'; the same tradition's use of the New Testament texts which speak of marriage and divorce (though with curious disregard for Matthew's 'exceptive clause', cf., e.g., *Veritatis Splendor*, n. 22);[31] the Lutheran tradition's fascination with the verb 'to reckon' in Romans 4; *Veritatis Splendor*'s refocusing of Matthew's account of the Rich Young Man (Matt 19:16–22) on verses 17–18; and the feminist exegete Elisabeth Schüssler Fiorenza's discovery, in those resurrection narratives which omit mention of the women, evidence of a calculated suppression of an earlier women-oriented tradition.[32] The little boy need not have worried, for in one form or another the fatted calf is alive and well.

A hermeneutic of suspicion

A corollary of all this is that exegetes, by training if not by temperament, will be suspicious of texts that look like they demand to be read at face value.[33] The wisdom of regarding 'obvious' readings as at least pro-visionally suspect could be supported by countless illustrations taken from the history of interpretation. Here are just two, the first 'doctrinal' and the second more directly 'ethical'.

(1) In Galatians 4:4–5 Paul wrote: 'When the fullness of time came, God sent his son, born of woman, born under Torah, to redeem those under Torah, [and] so that we might receive adoption as sons.' Now no one doubts that by 'born of woman' Paul meant that Jesus was human. The question is, why he drew attention to the fact. Interpreters have normally assumed that he wanted to say that Jesus was human *as well as divine*. Is it not just possible, though, that he meant, rather, that Jesus was human *and not just a Jew* (and because he was human and not just a Jew, people have direct access to his blessings just because they are human, i.e., they do not have to become Jews first)? The literary context of these verses, and the situational context of Galatians (where Paul was opposing rival missionaries who sought to persuade his converts to embrace elements of Judaism as a precondition of access to Jesus) overwhelmingly support this latter interpretation. Yet traditionally interpreters, doubtless assum-ing that New Testament writers shared their doctrinal preoccupations,

have taken it for granted that Paul's intention in this passage was to assert the doctrine of incarnation and the two natures of Christ. (Never mind that any preoccupation with the idea of incarnation, and, arguably, even the idea itself, arose several decades later than Paul.[34])

(2) In 1 Corinthians 7 Paul writes about marriage and sex. He seems to be saying that whereas celibacy is preferable ('it is good for a man not to touch a woman'), marriage and normal conjugal relations are advisable for most Christians as a safeguard against the temptation to engage in non-marital sex. Throughout the centuries Christian interpreters have assumed that Paul in this chapter is calling his own tunes, and that a straight-forward reading conveys his considered assessment of marriage, viz., that marriage is a regrettable necessity for those Christians who cannot control themselves; and that the best that can be said of it is that it is no sin. A very common view of interpreters nowadays is that Paul's agenda in this chapter was determined not by himself but by those in Corinth whose dualistic disdain of the body and pursuit of spiritual elitism had led them to advocate (or even seek to impose) an eccentric sexual asceticism. If this view is correct, then 1 Corinthians 7 tells us more about the Corinthians' evaluation of marriage (which Paul vigorously opposed) than it does about Paul's.

The pitfall of the 'obvious meaning' claims most victims from among those who are ignorant of the connotations of words in biblical texts – as is often the case when these texts are approached through translation. For example, it is wrong to suppose that the Hebrew terms generally translated 'holy', 'sin' or 'abomination' have the same semantic resonance as their 'equivalents' in modern languages; or that *mysterion* in Ephesians 5:32 (translated as *sacramentum* in the Latin versions) says anything at all about marriage being 'a sacrament'. Then: it is wrong to equate Paul's *sarx* with 'the flesh' as this term is used in later ethical discourse; or to interpret his *soma* ('body') in the light of anthropological perspectives which were not his; or to assume that his *nomos* ('law') has any simple equivalent in our own conceptuality, or any necessary overlap with our own uses of 'law' (e.g., '"natural" law'). Similarly, the RSV is wrong to translate the Greek *episkopos* and *diakonos* (e.g., Phil 1:1) respectively as 'bishop' and 'deacon'; and is at least misleading when it renders the Greek *malakoi* and *arsenokoitai* (1 Cor 6:9) as 'sexual perverts'. Germain Grisez has written that according to *Veritatis Splendor* 'passages such as 1 Cor 6:9–10 mean exactly what they say: those who do certain kinds of acts, such as adultery and sexual perversion, will not inherit the Kingdom . . .'.[35] Whether or not such passages mean exactly what they say, or what Grisez says they say, one must first establish what they say. A sure way of aborting this task *ab ovo* is to ignore the Greek text and to neglect to ask what the terms used in it would have meant to Paul and his hearers.[36]

Some areas of controversy in biblical scholarship

As if the areas of general *agreement* among exegetes were not cautionary enough for Bible-keen Christian ethicists, there are also unending *controversies* among exegetes, and a wide variety of views precisely in those areas which might have been expected to provide the most promising points of departure for a Christian ethical use of the Bible: namely, the ethical teachings respectively of Jesus and Paul. These subjects continue to be storm centres in historical-critical debate.

Jesus

In non-scholarly views of 'Christian morality', and in much scholarly Christian ethical discussion as well, Jesus' ethical sayings are accorded unique authority. (Even those who hold that the Bible's words are the very words of God somehow manage to maintain that Jesus' words are uniquely authoritative.) However, those who wish to appeal to Jesus' ethical teachings are faced with a number of difficulties. There is, first, the unsolvable problem of how to distinguish what Jesus said from what the Evangelists, often variously, say that he said.[37] Several methods have been used in the course of this century to retrieve Jesus' words from underneath the layers of later encrustations. None of these methods has escaped criticism, nor have all of them together come up with more than tentative findings, with the result that many scholars have concluded that what Jesus actually said is now beyond retrieval (intermittent waves of scholarly optimism notwithstanding). For New Testament scholars as such this is not at all worrying, and in any case it does not diminish the value of the Gospels as testimonies to traditions which were surely shaped by the impact of the historical Jesus. But it offers no encouragement to those whose use of the Bible in Christian ethics depends above all on an appeal to the authority of Jesus' 'actual words'.

In spite of the difficulties of establishing Jesus' 'actual words', there is now some measure of consensus on the core themes of Jesus' preaching, namely, the kingdom of God; God reaching out to the alienated as never before; the call to *metanoia* (repentance). But what consensus there is has hardly brought an end to the debate. For even granted that 'the kingdom' was a central theme in Jesus' preaching, it is still not clear what he meant by it, or what his religious outlook was, and how, therefore, his supposed utterances on ethical matters are to be understood. This unclarity has given rise to a host of reconstructions, some of them more or less plausible and all of them conjectural.[38]

For the 'kingdom of God' has turned out to be an endlessly debatable concept. Did it refer to some ideal order of society for which people were to strive, or to an apocalyptic intervention of God? Was Jesus a teacher of the inwardness of religion and of 'the infinite value of the human soul', or was his whole endeavour aimed rather at liberating the Jews from Roman occupation? Was Jesus above all (or at all) intent on opposing a religious attitude which makes law a surrogate for God, or was he rather God's witness *par excellence* to the centrality of law?

At least some of the 'historical' reconstructions which seek to provide answers to such questions are clearly attempts to invest this or that modern stance with the authority of the historical Jesus. They show a Jesus refashioned in the enquirer's own theological image and likeness. Liberal Protestants found in Jesus the prototype of Liberal Protestantism – a Jesus who, having been rescued from underneath the abstruse dogma of Paul and ecclesiastical tradition, could at last speak pertinently to the modern world. Albert Schweitzer in his *Quest of the Historical Jesus* (1906) finally put paid to the notion that Jesus was a Liberal Protestant, with his powerful restatement (or overstatement, as it turned out) of the view that Jesus' whole outlook was dominated by his expectation of an imminent apocalyptic irruption of the kingdom of God in this world. Jesus never intended to provide an ethical guide for Christians living in an on-going history, but only to recommend emergency measures appropriate to the days leading up to the impending crisis (an 'interim ethic'). Schweitzer thus came up with a Jesus who was foreign not only to Liberal Protestantism but also to all who would look to Jesus for ethical relevance. Henry Cadbury, similarly, in his *The Perils of Modernizing Jesus* (1937), stressed the historical 'distance' of Jesus, in protest against the ease with which the proponents of the 'social gospel' (heirs to Liberal Protestantism) claimed the historical Jesus' support for their cause. More recently (1991), Nicholas Harvey has argued that even our assumption that Jesus was preoccupied with morals says more about ourselves than about Jesus.[39]

While most New Testament scholars are now very much more alert to the perils of modernizing Jesus, and most take from Schweitzer at least the point that Jesus' ethical teaching, or some of it, was intertwined with his eschatological beliefs, there is a still unresolved debate about the extent to which, and the senses in which, Jesus' 'ethics' were conditioned by his 'eschatology'.[40] There is, first of all, debate over what Jesus' eschatological beliefs actually were. Did his preaching focus entirely on the *coming* 'kingdom', as Schweitzer maintained; or was it not rather concerned with the *present* inauguration of the 'kingdom' in his person and ministry (as C. H. Dodd's *The Parables of the Kingdom* [1935] maintained); or was it concerned, paradoxically, with both in equal measure?

Suppose, first, that Schweitzer was right to maintain that Jesus' ethical teaching was wholly conditioned by his expectation of an imminent end. (This view is no longer widely held, though as recently as 1986 Jack

Sanders vigorously defended it.[41]) On this view, Jesus' ethical teaching turns out to be as irrelevant to us as his eschatology was mistaken. Arguably, it might still be legitimate to *reinterpret* his imminentist eschatology, perhaps in the sense that all of us are living on borrowed time, or in the sense that any one moment of our lives is just as close to eternity as any other.[42] But however impressive such reinterpretations might be, perhaps in some pastoral or homiletic inculcation of moral urgency, they will not solve the historical problem of the relationship between Jesus' ethical teachings and his eschatological beliefs; and they will in any case be unhelpful to those Christian ethicists (most of them, I assume) who would not be satisfied with an ethic devoid of material content.[43]

If, then, *contra* Schweitzer, Jesus intended to promulgate 'the law of the [*present*] kingdom of God' (Dodd, *Parables*), then what are we to make of such seemingly unrealistic injunctions of Jesus as 'Do not resist the evil one', or of his demand (Luke 14:33) for complete abandonment of material possessions as a condition of discipleship? Dodd (*Gospel and Law* [1951]) argued that Jesus' 'precepts' must be understood precisely as precepts, but then went on to say that they were intended to specify the 'quality and direction' which acts must have if they are to be genuine expressions of Christian love. What Dodd meant is unclear to me, since, surely, precepts by their very nature do not prescribe only the 'quality' or 'direction' of actions but enjoin or prohibit this or that particular set of concrete actions. How might I tell my bank to ensure that my deposit and current accounts have the 'quality' or 'direction' of being closed, short of instructing it to close them forthwith and credit the balance to Oxfam?

Then, if it is neither Schweitzer's 'imminentist' eschatology nor Dodd's 'realized' eschatology which must determine the interpretative horizons of Jesus' sayings, but rather an eschatology of present *and* future ('already' *and* 'not yet'), held together somehow paradoxically, then the question presents itself, just how this paradox is to be maintained in ethical theory. By taking literally those of Jesus' demands which seem realizable, and the rest of them with a hermeneutical pinch of salt? But then the paradox collapses into prosaic categorization. And who is to do the categorizing? It might just as well be maintained that *all* of Jesus' reported sayings are to be taken as hyperbole in the service of paradox (which seems a bit of an overkill); or that *all* of them are to be taken literally (which won't work).

The debates surrounding the teaching of the historical Jesus, his religious outlook and the thrust of his mission as he understood it continue unabated, and are no nearer clarity.[44] If these debates matter, then Christian ethicists who claim special authority for the teaching of the historical Jesus will need first to reconstruct that teaching and then to interpret it. In neither of these tasks will they be able to rely on any broad consensus among New Testament scholars.

Paul

Christian ethicists have traditionally had recourse to Paul on two levels: on the level of the content of his moral exhortations, and at a deeper doctrinal/ethical level, where he wrestles with such questions as the relationship between sin and the law, or the relationship between faith and 'works'. Recent controversies in Pauline studies affect not so much the legitimacy of appeals to his moral exhortations (though these are often problematic enough, for other reasons), as traditional interpretations (typically the Lutheran one) of the import of Paul's doctrinal/ethical statements. Such interpretations have been massively challenged especially since the 1970s by a thoroughgoing application of historical-critical methods to Paul in the context of the Judaism of his day, motivated by a determined effort to free the exegesis of Paul's epistles from doctrinal presuppositions. (I refer to E. P. Sanders and what James Dunn has called the 'new perspective' on Paul.[45])

The essence of this critique of traditional interpretations is that (a) Paul's opposition to Torah observance has been misinterpreted (it had nothing to do with the Lutheran antithesis between gospel and law, but concerned only the demands to be made of gentile converts), and (b) Paul's statements linking Torah with sin reflect not a phenomenological critique of contemporary Judaism, nor any profound theological or anthropological analysis, as Lutheran interpreters have always supposed, but rather Paul's own 'tortured' attempts to extricate himself from the theological difficulties which arose from his 'dogmatically' motivated repudiation of Torah.

The dilemma into which the 'new perspective on Paul' has led Pauline studies[46] may dismay those Christian ethicists who look to Paul for support in their advocacy of a gospel that is allergic to law, and, more particularly, may challenge some theologians in the Lutheran tradition who appeal to Paul for support not so much in this or that ethical stance as in their aversion to ethics altogether.

I said at the beginning of this chapter that Christian ethicists intent on 'using' the Bible in their discipline must consider the two steps of exegesis and appropriation. Having reviewed the chief difficulties which they will need to face in relation to the first step, I now move on to the question of appropriation, and some of the difficulties which that step involves.

Appropriation

Under this heading I first indicate the ways in which the Bible has commonly been used by Christian ethicists, with some critical comments on each of them; and then I make some tentative recommendations.

Some standard approaches

Although there can be no altogether tidy means of classifying the various approaches to the Bible by Christian ethicists, the classification proposed by Edward LeRoy Long Jr in 1965 and adopted by Charles Curran in 1971[47] seems as good as any. There are basically (1) *prescriptive* approaches, which focus on individual biblical *'commands'* and which typically appeal to proponents of a deontological ethic; (2) *principles/ideals* approaches, which deal with the Bible's individual ethical statements with a high degree of selectivity and seek rather to encapsulate the Bible's ethical teachings in one or more basic principles or ideals (e.g., love) – such approaches appeal rather to exponents of a teleological ethic; and (3) *response/relational/contextual approaches* which focus on the biblically proclaimed *indicative* (what the Bible tells us God is like and about how God acts) and take that as a point of departure for recommending how the Christian, in freedom and responsibility before God, should best respond to God in present circumstances (the basic ethical *imperative*).

Curran observed that this classificatory scheme meshed with the one adopted by James F. Gustafson (1965/1971),[48] who had chosen a basically twofold scheme, that is, (1) ethicists who looked to the Bible as 'revealed *morality*' (= Long's and Curran's [1] and [2] above), and (2) those who looked to the Bible as 'revealed *reality*' (= Long's and Curran's [3] above).[49] Allen Verhey[50] covered the same ground under different heads but on generally comparable criteria. I follow this broad classification, with modifications here and there, and offering my own critical comments.

The Bible as a repository of divine commands

This position holds that the Bible gives us 'objectively revealed precepts' and that

> . . . the criterion of our standing in the Kingdom of God and of reward in the age to come is nothing else than meticulous observance of the commandments of God in the minutial details of their prescription and the earnest inculcation of such observance on the part of others.[51]

Gustafson attributed this position to 'evangelical conservative Protestants'. In fact, it is not limited to one particular Christian mindset, since nearly all Christians, more or less consciously and more or less selectively, subscribe to it, having been brought up on it; and the mainstream churches have traditionally made a carefully selective use of it (e.g., when focusing on 'the Ten Commandments' or Jesus' prohibition of divorce).

Whether thoroughgoing or selective, this approach is highly problematic, for a number of reasons. It must first side-step, or turn a blind eye to, most of the difficulties hitherto described in this chapter.[52] Especially in the matter of the Bible's diversity, ethicists beholden to the oracular authority of individual biblical injunctions are faced with enormous difficulties. First of all, do 'Old Testament' injunctions count, as well as those of the 'New'? If yes, then do all of them or only some of them? If only some of them, who is to decide which? What reliable criteria have we for discriminating between such injunctions as 'You shall do no injustice in judgement' (Lev 19:15), and such as 'You shall not mar the edges of your beard' (Lev 19:27)? Or by what logic do some participants in the debate over homosexuality appeal to Leviticus 18:22, while discarding as no longer relevant Leviticus 19:7ff. (the sin of not observing a cultic regulation, punishable, like the 'abominations' mentioned in the context, by being 'cut off from among the people') and, presumably, Leviticus 18:19 (prohibition of intercourse during the woman's period), both of which latter prescriptions appear to belong to the same code as Leviticus 18:22, and certainly belong to the same canon? Or: why does *Veritatis Splendor* (n. 91), when looking for Old Testament examples of heroic fidelity to 'God's holy law', seize on the example of Susannah (sex) and not rather (or not also) on that of Eleazar (pork)?[53]

Or should norm-hunting Christian ethicists perhaps take on board 'Old Testament' law only in so far as it can claim the New Testament's endorsement? But then, how will they handle the diverse attitudes of New Testament writers to 'Old Testament' law? Paul thought it was finished with (e.g., Rom 10:4), whereas a view 'canonized' by Matthew's Gospel (Matt 5:18f.) held that every detail stands.

Or should they accept that Old Testament prescriptions are obsolete, and that only the New Testament provides timelessly valid ethical norms? If so, then on what canonical authority are they to distinguish between such New Testament injunctions as bid a person not to tell lies or gratuitously condemn their fellow, and those which forbid women to teach, or have authority over males, or be heard in church, or to attend church without a head-dress; or those which bid slaves be obedient to their masters, or which make women's salvation conditional on childbearing? Are *Matthew*'s versions of Jesus' words on divorce (with their 'exceptive' clause) to be taken as normative, or not rather those of Mark and Luke? Does Paul's injunction to 'judge those inside the church' (1 Cor 5:12) override Jesus' injunction not to judge? Should Paul's exhortation to respect civil authorities as God's ministers (Rom 13) take priority over his recommendation that we should consider secular courts 'unrighteous' (1 Cor 6 [he means: in the biblical sense])? Should we take it that the non-Christian partner in a 'mixed' marriage is 'consecrated' by the Christian (1 Cor 7:14), or should Christians recoil from any union with non-believers on pain of being defiled (2 Cor 6:14–18)?

Then, even if there were some acceptable criteria for separating off those biblical injunctions that are still 'valid' from those which are no longer so, on what criteria are Christian ethicists to decide how to interpret this or that still valid command, and to determine what its status and function must be? Origen thought that Jesus' commendation of those who 'make themselves eunuchs' ought to be taken literally, but afterwards (too late) changed his mind. Others, while acknowledging that these words of Jesus, if indeed they were his words, were meant metaphorically, still differ on how the metaphor is to be interpreted.[54] Again, to return to a point made above: what authorizes some to interpret Jesus' words on divorce as a non-negotiable juridical norm, while serenely interpreting others of Jesus' sayings as hyperbole?

As well as having to come to terms with the above difficulties, and others not mentioned for lack of space, people who see the Bible as a repository of divine commands run the risk of trivializing the Bible by isolating elements of it at whim, or by arbitrarily privileging one particular mode of biblical discourse over all others ('norm reductionism'). This can lead to a restricted number of biblical texts exerting a mantra-like influence upon their devotees. And in so far as this kind of approach to the Bible is typically accompanied by the conviction that the Bible is the sole authority in ethical matters, its advocates surely suffer the evil of having their whole ethical vision narrowed down to scattered biblical prescriptions, being left to their own imagination, or prejudices, in those vast areas of present-day ethical concern to which the Bible speaks not at all. (Which, conceivably, is part of the appeal of that kind of approach.)

The Bible as an expositor of ethical ideals

This approach consists in choosing a biblical or New Testament ethical or ethically relevant master theme (e.g., neighbour love; the kingdom; justice; the beatitudes; freedom; the imitation of Jesus) to be used as the divinely authoritative framework of a Christian ethics which draws also on other sources of ethical knowledge. As is often observed, this approach has been more commonly adopted by people with a 'looser' view of biblical inspiration and who correspondingly bring to the Bible a less literalist mode of interpretation – and who, in addition, are alert to the limitations of the 'divine command' model described above. As Gustafson and Long pointed out, this approach characterized Liberal Protestantism and the 'social gospel' movements.[55] But it was also typical of Roman Catholic moralists during the period of 'Scriptural renewal'.[56]

The main objection to this approach is that the pursuit of a biblical or New Testament master theme is perilous in the extreme, for it is bound to end up ignoring the diversity of biblical writings in favour of its pet relevancies.[57] Typically vulnerable to this objection is John Howard Yoder's claim that 'a social style characterized by the creation of a new community and the rejection of violence of any kind is a theme of New Testament proclamation, from beginning to end, from right to left'.[58] This does not work, for even if it were true that non-violence is a dominant or recurrent theme throughout the New Testament (which it is not), that would not justify our singling it out as *the* New Testament's central ethical message, rather than, say, almsgiving, prayer or speaking the truth.[59]

The same will apply to *Veritatis Splendor*'s tendency to assimilate the biblical writers' various perspectives on 'law' to a traditional Catholic understanding of 'natural law' (law = the decalogue = what Jesus insisted on, and perfected = what the Spirit empowers Christians to obey = natural law → exceptionless norms) in order to claim scriptural support for a condemnation of consequentialist and proportionalist positions among some contemporary moralists.

Even the most modest applications of this synthesizing approach – the kind that settles for a reduction of New Testament ethical teaching to 'love' – will have difficulties from the point of view of critical exegesis. For, first, it is not the case that New Testament writers always give 'love' the unique ethical status that many moderns are inclined to give it (New Testament writers were under no pressure to come up with a single, self-validating ethical principle); and it is doubtful whether either Jesus' or Paul's ethical teachings are reducible to, or deducible from, the single principle of 'love'.[60]

Then, even when New Testament writers acknowledge the paramountcy of love, we should not assume that they all mean the same thing by it. Jesus in the Synoptics speaks of love of God and neighbour, whereas Paul speaks almost exclusively of neighbour love (love for everyone, especially fellow Christians). The Fourth Gospel seems to understand neighbour love as love within the Johannine community, and the Johannine epistles as love within one's own narrower group.[61] These various slants on Christian love may give rise to very different, even opposing, Christian ethical stances, so that blanket statements about love in the New Testament really lead nowhere.

A similar critique will apply, finally, to Richard B. Hays's suggestion that if the Bible is to be useful for Christian ethics, there is a 'synthetic' task to be accomplished between exegesis and application, in order to 'describe a unity of ethical perspective within the diversity of the canon'.[62] Hays seems to be over-confident about the usefulness of the results of his proposed synthesis, which are (a) the primary addressee of God's imperatives is the community as counter-cultural community of discipleship; (b) Jesus' death on the cross as a paradigm of God's faithfulness; (c) the eschatological framework of Christian life (the new creation is already but not yet). For, first, it is not true that New Testament writers are only secondarily concerned with the individual's moral choices; second, many passages of the New Testament reflect attitudes which are not at all 'counter-cultural' (e.g., much of Paul's and the Deutero-Paulines' moral exhortation consists of thinly Christianized borrowings from Judaism or Hellenism); and, finally, the principles that are supposed to emerge from Hays's suggested 'synthesis' are too general to be useful. Would not *Humanae Vitae*, for example, qualify as biblically-based under them?

The Bible as providing analogies or precedents for action

On this approach, biblical writers' moral assessments of situations which confronted them are used as the basis for judging comparable or analogous situations today. As has often been remarked, the main problem with this approach is that of control, for the tendency will be to choose biblical analogues which support one's prior stance. Gustafson noted the necessity of often having to choose between biblical situations (e.g., between the Israelites' liberation from oppression in Egypt and their aggression in Canaan – both of which are judged positively by biblical writers) as 'normatively proper' analogues to this or that political-ethical situation today. His recommendation was that those biblically described situations should be preferred which were 'more nearly consistent with certain central tendencies of the biblical, theological, and moral witness' and '"truer" to the central themes of biblical morality'.[63]

I take the point that the choice of 'biblical analogies' can be biased, and consequently that caution and control are necessary. However, in my view Gustafson's quest for '*normatively* proper' analogues makes this approach more hazardous than it need be. As I shall argue below, the quest for 'normativity' in the Bible is probably the greatest single obstacle to a constructive Christian-ethical use of the Bible. Conversely, I think that an imaginative and relaxed use of biblical 'analogies' (especially given the fascination of historical critics with the situational contexts of biblical writings) might be one useful area of shared insight between biblical scholars and Christian ethicists.

Tom Deidun

The Bible reveals not a morality but a reality: the character of the living God

Although in some respects this approach is similar to the one just described, it differs from it in that it is not concerned with the biblical writers' *moral* reactions to particular situations but with their description of what God is like and how God acts. Gustafson described this approach thus:

> ... The primary question became not 'How ought we to judge this event?' nor even 'What ought we to do in the event?' But 'What is God doing in this event?' 'What is he saying to us in this event?' Three articles published by H. Richard Niebuhr during World War II have titles which illustrate this: 'War as the Judgment of God', 'Is God in the War?' and 'War as Crucifixion'.[64]

This approach[65] looks not to biblical *imperatives*, interpreted in a more or less simple fashion, but to generalized descriptions of the biblical *indicative*. Christian morality is about response to a person, not a rule. The Bible draws us away from fascination with God's laws and calls us instead to a discerning and responsible relationship with God. According to this approach, we are not looking to the Bible for normativity, but for partial insights. By considering (among other things) what sort of God the Bible reveals to us, we discern how best we can fulfil our role as responsible moral agents responding to the living God who now acts in contemporary events (a response that may entail more radical and more demanding action than is ever required by the directly ethical imperatives to be found here and there in the Bible). As the interpretative key to what God is like and how God acts, practitioners of this approach typically rely on what they consider to be *the* central or all-embracing biblical theological theme, for example, 'liberation'; 'crucifixion and resurrection'; 'hope'; 'God's doing humanizing work'.

The main problems with this approach are, first, the basic theological one of whether it makes sense to say that God is 'doing' *anything* in this or that event (does not Job protest against simple-mindedness in this matter?); and, second, its over-confidence in its ability to discover in the Bible a central theological theme, or a dominant portrayal of God. For who is to say where in the Bible we must look to discover what God is like and how God acts? Should we look to the jihad God of some Old Testament passages or to a God who looks approvingly on all of creation? To the Deuteronomist's God, or to Job's? To Paul's gospel about God's limitless outreach to sinful humanity, or to the Book of Revelation? To the God of Sinai or to the God of Luke 15? To passages which speak of God's 'wrath', or to passages which portray God as endlessly forbearing? The Bible simply does not give us a uniform portrayal of what God is like, since different biblical writers have different theological viewpoints, and many of them hold together within their several writings images of God which are not uniform and often stand in tension with one another. One's diagnosis of contemporary events will depend on which biblical portrayal of God one brings to it, so that for all its apparent theological sophistication, this approach, like the rest, may end up simply canonizing prejudice.[66] In a word, we are here in the thick of the 'Biblical theology movement', with its naïveties and its dangers.

Still, given these caveats, I think that this approach to Christian ethical uses of the Bible might be fruitful, provided that it is used sensitively, is humble enough to remain interrogative and does not seek to impose itself as *the* way to the appropriation of biblical wisdom.

The Bible as formative of character

Bruce Birch and Larry Rasmussen suggested that 'the role of the scriptures in the nurturing of a basic orientation and in the generating of particular attitudes and intentions is a central one'[67] – that is, that the Bible's most effective contribution to Christian ethics is to form the character of the ethical decision maker. These authors also make the important point that the Bible's contribution to Christian ethics will be greatly impoverished if we look only to its nomistic statements, ignoring the far greater potency of its images, stories, historical narratives, rituals and paradigms.

I have a lot of sympathy for Birch and Rasmussen's stress on the Bible's potential for character formation and for their (and Gustafson's) stress on the variety of types of biblical discourse, and will return to these topics later. Here, suffice it to say that my sympathy for Birch and Rasmussen's view ends at the point where they say that the Bible's central contribution to Christian ethics (i.e., its character-forming role) may dispense with 'biblical scholarship' (p. 325). I would have thought that critical control was especially necessary if the Bible is to be used in the formation of character. Surely Birch and Rasmussen are aware that some of the most virulent forms of bigotry in our own day are promoted by people who have been formed from mother's knee on the Bible unencumbered by biblical scholarship.[68]

Gustafson's 'great variety' approach

Gustafson (1970, 1974) favoured a 'loose' approach to the methodology of Bible use in ethics, which took account of the great variety of moral values, norms and principles expressed in the Bible through a multiplicity of literary forms – from laws to visions and from parables to allegories –

and of the fact that they were addressed to a variety of particular historical situations. Ethical judgements are to be made

> *in the light of* appeals to this variety of material as well as to other principles and experiences. Scripture is one of the informing sources for moral judgments, but it is not sufficient in itself to make any particular judgment authoritative.[69]

I consider Gustafson's approach to be probably the most honest and most circumspect of them all. Perhaps my own recommendation would differ from his only in worrying less about questions of authority and methodology and in being less concerned to find *some* (however qualified) normative use of the Bible in the consideration of contemporary ethical issues. Was Gustafson prompted to bring together the Bible and the Cambodian invasion (pp. 168ff.) by the prior assumption that the former *must* have something authoritative to say about the latter? I doubt whether we need constrain the Bible even to that extent. Gustafson clearly had moral objections to the invasion, but his objections to it seem to me to be just such as would arise in any humane and Christian conscience, regardless of the Bible.

Some principles that should govern Christian ethicists' approach to the Bible

Acceptance of the often tentative results of exegesis

The Biblical Commission's 1993 view that 'to attempt to by-pass [critical exegesis] would be to create an illusion' means in effect that Christian ethicists who want both to make use of the Bible and to be intellectually honest must be prepared to accept the uncertainties of exegesis, and to rest content with exegetical findings that are often only tentative.

Christian ethics – ethics practised by Christians

I sympathize with those Christian ethicists who maintain that basically they are Christians engaged in the business of ethics, and as such are concerned to uphold the autonomy of that discipline. Charles Curran insisted that the methodology appropriate to Christian ethics is just an extension of that which is appropriate to ethics in general; and Gerard J. Hughes maintained that neither Scripture nor tradition could ever be the ultimate authority for deciding any moral issue, since both Scripture and tradition are subject to the discrimination of reason. Gustafson, in mildly Protestant vein (though here reflecting a position which, on the surface at least, is not too far removed from the traditional Catholic one), spoke of a 'dialectic between principles of judgement which have purely rational justification and which also appeal to the tradition expressed in scripture and developed in the Christian community'.[70] All this must mean that the premisses on which Christian ethicists work are falsifiable, and the methodology they use is subject at every stage to rational scrutiny. Christian ethicists are not gnostics who work on first principles that are unavailable to outsiders.

The Bible's 'authority'

All the various approaches to Bible use reviewed above presuppose that the Bible is authoritative, whether in a strict, nomistic sense, as often among interpreters who hold to high notions of biblical inspiration, or in a looser sense, as among those who feel that however sophisticated we need to be in discovering and interpreting 'the Bible's teaching', that teaching is in the end normative.

The question of the Bible's authority for Christian ethics is part of the more general question of the Bible's authority and its relation to other sources of authority – a question that can only be settled dogmatically (hence with no regard for the interpretation of texts).[71] Although some Christians would see the authority of the Bible (or parts of it) as foundational, in reality such a view represents a dogmatic claim which always more or less avowedly involves a 'dialectical' (or, put less charitably, a circular) relationship between an authority claimed for the Bible and the authority claimed by a Church, or by some other kind of orthodoxy. Others would regard the Bible's authority as always at best secondary, since reason, precisely as the arbiter of whether or not it is being addressed authoritatively, is always primary. (Even religious claims for a 'sacrifice of the intellect' must address themselves to the intellect.) Still others, on ostensibly theological or philosophical grounds, would make *experience* the arbiter of the Bible's authority, as well as the heuristic guide to its meaning, whether this experience is described in traditional religious terms (e.g., the continuing experience of the Spirit or allegiance to some ecclesial tradition) or in pastoral and socio-political terms (e.g., the experience of oppression).[72]

Bestriding these views is the Roman Catholic position, with its four-focal view of moral authority: right reason, Scripture, tradition, magisterium, not necessarily in that order. Nowadays the magisterium tries hard to highlight Scripture. Vatican II modified the traditional formula about the sources of divine revelation being '*partly* Scripture, *partly* tradition' to one which seemed to give Scripture co-equal status: '*both* Scripture *and* tradition'. *Veritatis Splendor* (e.g., n. 5) even endeavoured to ground moral obligation in biblical texts. It seems clear, however, that the magisterium, as authentic interpreter of right reason, Scripture[73] and tradition, wants to remain decisive. A consequence of this is a marked tendency to assimilate Scripture to its own tradition, determining which elements in the Bible are to be considered 'authoritative', or at least denying the Bible a critical function *vis-à-vis* tradition. From a scientific point of view, those who use the Bible with these presuppositions, however extensive their coverage of biblical material, will not have progressed beyond the traditional Roman Catholic use of the Bible as a source of proof texts; which is a pity, because the Roman Catholic tradition, which generally has no hang-ups about biblical authority, is better placed than most to make an imaginative and creative use of modern biblical studies.

One's view of the Bible's authority will condition the ways one uses the Bible in Christian ethics. As became apparent in the above review of the various methods of Bible use, those who hold to a high doctrinal view of the Bible, and who typically opt for a correspondingly straightforward interpretation of biblical texts, will pass from text to existence without much hermeneutical fuss (though not without a great deal of arbitrary selectivity). After that, the more supple one's view of the Bible's authority, the less straightforward one's ways of approaching the Bible will be. Although some ways of approaching the Bible may be less fraught with difficulties than others, nevertheless, so long as the Bible is seen as normative, no approach to it is problem-free, and in most cases the same fundamental problems arise from one or more of the factors that have been illustrated in the bulk of this chapter.

This might be an appropriate place to comment on the view of those who advocate turning to the Bible's authority as a refuge from the impasses of philosophical ethics or as a supplement to a less than adequate human reason. Biblical authority, so it is claimed, provides a degree of clarity and reliability which rational discourse can never hope to attain to.[74] A principal aim of this chapter has been to illustrate the naïvety of such optimism. The tasks of interpreting the Bible and using it in ethics involve just as much complexity, and are subject to just as much opaqueness and provisionality, as any debate in philosophical ethics. Christians who seek refuge in the Bible from the impasses of philosophical debate put me in mind of the man in Amos who took refuge in a house and leant with his hand on a serpent.

In what sense 'authoritative'?

Perhaps the whole problem of the relationship between Bible and Christian ethics derives precisely from our preoccupation with the Bible's *authority*.[75] This preoccupation was born of past controversies, and to the extent that much present-day Christian theology in the West is still worried about positions taken up in those controversies, it is perhaps understandable. But past controversies were embedded in past cultures; and as Nineham reminded us, 'The desire to settle things by an appeal to authority is itself a culturally conditioned phenomenon'.[76] Preoccupation with the question of the Bible's authority may not be the way forward now, and indeed may be the best way of depriving ourselves of the Bible. Why, after all, do we need to speak of the Bible's authority, and not, rather, of its potency or fecundity? Are potency and fecundity less 'divine' than 'authority'?

If the Bible is now to be creative rather than destructive for Christians, we need a far more mature view of its 'authority'. The value of the Bible for Christian ethics is perhaps more to be compared with the value, for the human spirit, of the imbibing of a great foreign culture than with, say, the authority of common law for deciding legal cases in England, or with the authority of *The Lancet* for making decisions about appropriate surgical procedures. We do not (except by conscious metaphor) speak of the 'authority' of classical Greek literature or of the 'authority' of Renaissance art. The 'law' in Christianity is, after all, not a legal code or an authoritative document but the fertile Spirit of God.[77]

A recommended non-method

The approach to the Bible which I favour will not lend itself to any 'methodology', but will instead be free and unpredictable. Since one of its main concerns will be to respect the principles and methods of exegesis, it will not be vulnerable to the criticisms which show other – apparently more tidy – approaches to be either inconsistent in theory or unworkable in practice. It might be more enriching than any of the methods reviewed above, while remaining hospitable to elements of most of them. It will seek to stimulate rather than terminate Christian-ethical discussion. Its strength will lie in being inventive, rather than in seeking to settle issues on its own biblical say-so. Its attention to biblical texts will be versatile and imaginative. It will be disdainful of biblical one-liners, and suspicious of 'favourite' biblical texts or 'themes', such as are nowadays cherished by all manner of ideologues. Since it will make no blanket judgement about the 'authority' of biblical texts, it will not need to be consistent; and selectivity will be its virtue. Because it will want to take biblical writings seriously, it will not use them woodenly. It might on occasion put forward the opinion that the ethical insight of this or that biblical writer is wonderfully intuitive, while accepting with perfect equanimity that this or that other biblical writer's ethical stance is irrelevant or distasteful. Similarly – and consistently with its refusal to be compelled to be relevant – it will not feel that it has something special to say on every contemporary ethical issue or ethically significant event.[78] It will not feel obliged to come up with a 'biblical' explanation of Auschwitz, or with a 'biblical' verdict on Cambodia. It might decide that 'the Bible' has nothing directly relevant to say about AIDS, and nothing beyond the broadest generalities to bring to certain huge areas of contemporary Christian ethical debate.

This is not to say, however, that such a 'non-method' will not be able to make solid contributions to Christian ethics, nor that, for all its lightness of touch, it will be less concerned with the serious business of praxis than other approaches which give the impression of being more earnest. On the contrary, it might perform a myriad useful functions, and contribute solidly to Christian ethics in unexpected ways. Such contributions might be either initially 'subversive' or directly constructive. The following examples must necessarily be rather scattered.

Some 'subversive' functions

On this level, an important aim of this approach would be that of seeking to 'defamiliarize' Christian ethicists with biblical texts. For example, it might call into question the supposed 'biblical basis' of traditional beliefs or practices; or invite ethicists to look again, in the light of modern criticism, at texts which became 'standard' in a pre-critical era. In the context of Roman Catholicism, it might urge the magisterium to seek a greater convergence between its official statements about biblical interpretation and its actual use of biblical texts.

More particularly: it might query how a contributor to the *Catechism of the Catholic Church*, in a section devoted to the Ten Commandments, could virtually invest the whole traditional Roman Catholic moral catechism with Sinaitic authority.[79] Or: it might prompt us to ask to what extent traditional Roman Catholic Church practice in the matter of marriage and divorce still labours under a pre-critical understanding of New Testament texts, or relies on tendentious exegesis, and what modifications of this practice a critical reading of biblical texts might suggest. (Which, I suspect, might lead to marriage being taken more, not less, seriously.) Or: it might put to us the question, whether Paul's alarm in 1 Corinthians 7 at the fact that the Corinthians, or some of them, were opting for celibacy under pressure from (some in) the community, and the theological and prudential reasons Paul gives for vigorously opposing this, might not have some bearing on present-day discussion about mandatory – albeit 'freely opted-for' – celibacy for Roman Catholic diocesan clergy. (As far as I know, this fascinating text – as opposed to bits of it, taken out of context – has never been brought to bear on any such discussion.)

Or again: it might raise the query whether a properly contextualized interpretation of Matthew 5 – 7 might challenge nearly every interpretation of 'The Sermon on the Mount' that has hitherto been proposed, in that nearly all of them regard the 'Sermon' as a source of *law* (binding on some or all), without ever asking about the genres of Jesus' sayings, or about Matthew's understanding of Jesus *vis-à-vis* Torah, or whether Matthew considered law (and not rather the character of Jesus as wisdom-Torah in person) to be the prism of God's will for Christians (cf., e.g., Matt 11:28ff., with Sirach 24:19–23; 51:23–26).

Some more directly constructive functions

On a more directly constructive level, the kind of approach I favour would seek to stimulate unfamiliar reflections, perhaps turning the very 'foreignness' of the Bible to our advantage. As L. William Countryman put it:

> ... one of the primary contributions which Scripture makes to the work of the Spirit in the life of the Christian community is that it stands outside our present and therefore prevents us from reading our contemporary world as an inevitability.[80]

For we too are culture-bound, and where shall we turn for something to jolt us out of our domesticity?

The kind of approach I favour might stimulate fresh discussion on specific ethical issues, or, more generally, urge on Christian ethicists the need to expand their horizons of relevance; or at least it might call attention to possible imbalances in their agenda: for example, by posing the strange question, why Christian ethical discussion is intensely concerned with questions of sexual morality, social justice, bioethics, business ethics, human rights, gender issues and the like, and not also with what was a major preoccupation of many biblical writers – what the psalmist calls 'truth in the heart' or what, obversely, the Fourth Gospel saw as the hidden depths of mendacity in human behaviour (e.g., John 2:25b; 3:19f.). Similarly, while the insights of biblical writers may be hopelessly pre-Freudian, they might none the less invite us to query whether our post-Freudian 'therapeutic ethos'[81] has got it right in all respects.

More bittily: Such an approach might, for example, bring to bear biblical texts about *adam* as steward of creation (also in the Christological sense) on environmental ethics and the 'futurity problem';[82] or some prophetic texts which condemn the practice of 'religion' without social justice on current social-justice issues (perhaps a useful point of encounter between the Judaeo-Christian tradition and humanists); or a consideration of the thrust of Romans to a discussion of religious (including Christian) particularism; or an analysis of the dialogue between Paul and the Corinthians (in 1 Corinthians) to a discussion of contemporary inner-Church issues, for example, pluralism, conflicting rights, the dangers of spiritual elitism, the co-equal sharing of spiritual gifts and the correlative functions of community members (e.g., magisterium/theologians; lay/ordained; males/females) in 'building up' the Christian (and wider) community; or, say, a consideration of the situation which occasioned Galatians to a discussion of the relationship between faith and behavioural conformity; or the implications of Hebrews to a critical discussion of the place of cult in religion. Or, it might draw on this or that psalm, this or that section of wisdom literature, this or that parable of Jesus, to suggest to us unfamiliar insights.

This is not to say that the Bible will be able to contribute to Christian ethics only when it is presented as 'foreign', or only when its interpreters come visibly armed with historical-critical tools. Doubtless, to dispense with such tools would be 'to create an illusion'. But even when we have heeded the strictest caveats of historical criticism, we cannot ignore certain recurrent emphases in most New Testament writings which surely go to the heart of their authors' perception of what we still regard as central Christian values: for example, the emphasis on innocence, love, compassion, forbearance, humility, and so forth. Even while acknowledging even here the danger of arbitrary selectivity, we can hardly deny that there *is* a recognizable set of ethical attitudes (seen as profoundly Christian and authentically human) which span the gap between then and now. Scholars who spend their days poring over the Bible, for all their technical sophistication, must surely think it part of their contribution to Christian ethics to recall to its practitioners such central Christian values, in case *their* technical sophistication causes them to lose sight of them.

Further: an approach to the Bible that wants to be free and creative will welcome every insight, even those not born of historical-critical parentage. The approach I favour would be warmly welcoming of modern hermeneutical insights, such as those which highlight the importance of the reader's involvement in the interpretation of texts, or the transformative potency of story, or which seek to go behind the text to unmask negative ideologies. At the same time, there must be *some* means of identifying and excluding the plainly aberrant. Dennis Nineham spoke of the distinction between 'insight' and 'vagary', and took comfort in the assurance of Graham Hough that 'the consensus of those qualified to judge seldom has much difficulty in deciding where the area of legitimate and illuminating interpretation ends and the lunatic fringe begins'.[83] Nineham must have written that in one of his rare trusting moments; at all events, our own day has surely taught us that consensus is not necessarily a safeguard against lunacy. Still, in order for hermeneutically sophisticated interpreters of biblical texts to contribute, and to contribute richly, to Christian ethical reflection, it will be sufficient that they include in their point of departure a consideration of what can be known of the original authors' contexts of thought, and also that they give an account of themselves, to assure us that they are not off on a frolic of their own, or not all along plotting to invest their readerly co-authorship of biblical texts with 'biblical authority'.

It is interesting to observe that the kind of unprogrammatic (yet still, I believe, fruitful) approach to the Bible which I favour was the one that early Christians instinctively adopted and freely employed. New Testament writers were convinced of the fecundity of Hebrew scriptures, but never thought them to be independently binding and never felt the need to apologize for the theoretical inconsistency in the way they 'used' them. Although some New Testament writers often use formulae which show that they considered parts of these writings authoritative, or often argue on the basis of their supposed authority, none of them interpreted that authority nomistically, for all of them were uninhibitedly selective. For example, as mentioned above, kashrut rules were jettisoned quite early on in some quarters (admittedly after much squabbling); and Paul regarded the whole prescriptive function of Torah – in ethical matters too – as obsolete. To judge from the uses made of the Old Testament by most New Testament writers, Paul and the Pauline tradition were quite typical when they said that the Scriptures were there to be *'useful'* – to give us 'teaching', 'admonition', *'paideia'* (instruction) and 'encouragement' (2 Tim 3:16; Rom 15:4; 1 Cor 10:11). They did not think they were there to regulate their lives or to provide a divinely authorized point of departure for an ethical 'methodology'.

Also, the approach I favour, which seeks to allow the Bible to animate and nourish Christian ethics, rather than requiring it to legislate (in however loose a fashion) seems splendidly to accord with the best insights of Vatican II, which invited theologians to make the Scriptures the *'soul'* of all theology', and recommended that the scientific exposition of moral theology be 'magis *nutrita'* by them – not to enable traditional moral theology to mesh methodologically with the Bible, but so that moral theology might 'throw light on the exalted vocation of the faithful in Christ and their obligation to bring forth fruit in charity for the life of the world' (*Optatam Totius*, n. 16). 'Soul', 'nourishment', 'charity' and 'life' seem to me to reflect a rather more expansive mindset than one which still looks to the Bible primarily as written evidence of God's eternal preoccupation with exceptionless norms.

Contributions in broad brush

In case my description of the approach I favour has given the impression that it is rather too disorganized or too desultory to contribute solidly to Christian ethical reflection, I conclude with just three examples (chosen from a whole range of possible ones) of very general, though still important, insights which biblical studies might bring to Christian ethics.[84]

Coinherence of 'imperative' and 'indicative'

For all the diversity and historically conditioned character of the New Testament writers' ethical teachings, these writers shared a more or less explicit awareness that the Christian 'ought' now flowed from a specifically Christian indicative. This does not mean that Christian ethics has now become estericized; only that for Christian ethicists the ethical imperative is henceforth grounded not simply in right reason and/or consideration of the sovereignty of the creator, but in the new action of God in Christ and the continuing action of the Holy Spirit. New Testament writers, in varying degrees of generality, thought their ethical thoughts in the context of this novel indicative.

This is perhaps clearest in Paul. It is well known that in the content of his moral exhortations Paul is jackdaw-like – choosing whatever appeals to him, from (so it seems) Jesus' stress on the paramountcy of love, through traditional baptismal catechesis, to standard Jewish allergies or the moralizing platitudes of Hellenism. But on a deeper level, Paul's ethics are an integral part of his theology, for, as he sees it, the fundamental imperative of right living flows from the indicative; indeed, *is* the indicative becoming dynamic in human freedom. So, for example, he often, paradoxically, juxtaposes indicative and imperative: 'You have put on Christ' – 'Put on Christ!'; 'You have life in the Spirit' – 'Walk in the Spirit!'; 'For freedom Christ has set you free' – 'Be free!' Or, he characteristically introduces his moral exhortations with a *'Therefore . . .'*, referring back to his exposition of the divinely-wrought indicative. (Classic are Rom 6:12; 8:12 and 12:1.) Then, in answering the charge that his dispensing with Torah must lead to antinomianism (Rom 3:8; 6:1, 15), he turns not to some alternative set of prescriptions, but to the indicative of the Christian's sharing in Christ's destiny (Rom 6). One could say that Paul's insistence on the imperative is simply a function of his proclaiming the indicative.

We may be on less secure historical ground regarding *Jesus'* teaching: but in so far as the moral demands which Jesus made of his disciples flowed from the indicative of the kingdom, and had to do with responding to it, we may say that Jesus always at least implicitly introduced his ethical teaching with a *'Therefore'*.

An enhanced awareness that the context of 'Christian' ethical thought and action is always the Christian indicative might greatly benefit Christian ethics. In fact, it must be this that makes Christian ethics

Christian. The difference between the ethical stances and values of Christians and those of non-Christians is not that Christians have an ethical agenda that could not be cherished by others, but that the context in which they seek to realize this agenda is that of the gospel's indicative, which in practice means a personal experience of Christ. The *Christian* part of Christian ethics comes in when the people wrestling with ethics have a faith-experience of Christ, are formed by the ethos and values of Christian tradition, are sensitive to the insights and concerns of Christian communities and, in a word, see the world with eyes which are (by their best endeavours) both human and Christlike; and, finally, that their insights are intended to benefit Christian communities, and the world through them.

Put differently: if Christian ethics has any Christian specificity, it must surely be one that derives from the *faith* dimension of its practitioners' experience. But the faith element in Christian ethics means more than (and surely other than) accepting 'in faith', say, a particular interpretation of a biblical text or, in the case of Roman Catholics, a particular pronouncement of the magisterium. The faith element comes in when Christian ethicists, while striving critically to bring to bear on ethical issues right reason, whatever scientific knowledge is currently available, biblical insights, and the wisdom of their own church teaching and traditions, and in dialogue and debate with their non-Christian colleagues, see their efforts and integrity in all of this procedure as their personal response to a transcendent calling.

In practice, the New Testament writers' view of the co-inherence of imperative and indicative in Christian living, if taken seriously, might have very significant effects in Christian ethics. It might, first, encourage Christian ethicists to say their prayers.[85] Less dauntingly, it might encourage them to review the relationship between their own and other theological disciplines, and maybe to think back to the coinherence of Christian ethics with dogmatic and spiritual theology of once upon a time. Roman Catholics generally deride the days when seminary moral theology was indistinguishable from canon law. Those days are said to have gone; but is it not still the case that in some university theology faculties students are admitted to postgraduate courses in Christian ethics without a thorough grounding in theology (including biblical studies)? This may be a way of ensuring an eventual return to legalism in Christian ethics, in however modern a dress.

A *biblical paradigm for the process of ethical discernment*

In Paul's communities it appears that the most important factor in shaping both the general ethical attitudes of Christians and their stance on particular issues was community discernment. 1 Corinthians 14 provides a good window onto this process. In the church gathering *all* members of the community have 'some teaching' (no doubt Paul means in ethical matters too); and if 'prophetic' utterances were somehow privileged, this was almost certainly because they were judged to be prophetic, not because they came from an elite group of prophets. *All* members of the community were potentially prophets, and indeed should be keen to exercise the gift of prophecy (1 Cor 14:1). We can only guess at the criteria which the community used (or argued about) in ethical discernment; but if Paul's own 'methodology' is anything to go by, we can be pretty sure that they looked not to a code of prescriptions but to whatever sources of wisdom they deemed to express the mindset of the Spirit (Rom 8:6) and to be relevant in the circumstances.

We cannot assume that the Pauline communities were typical in this. But does that matter? There was a way of Christian ethical discernment which has become foreign to some Christian traditions today, or even regarded as perilous. Christian ethicists in traditions where a *sensus fidelium* has come to be regarded as a threat rather than the Spirit's way of going forward might at least pause to reflect on the strange ecclesial setup of the Pauline communities. This might then lead them to ask whether the structures for ecclesial discernment perpetuated by their own tradition need to be in some kind of continuity with those of churches in the New Testament period and if so, and in so far as they are not, where the discontinuity came from, and whether it can be defended by an honest Christian conscience. Perhaps that line of questioning would take Christian ethicists into historical and theological depths which may be outside their remit; though, come to think of it, perhaps it *is* part of their essential remit.

Progressivity

I recalled above a common ploy of canonically-minded Bible interpreters in handling the problem of the (to us) obvious provisionality of much Old Testament moral teaching. To be consistent with the logic of canonicity, it was enough to assert that God was educating God's people through a progressive pedagogy, whose earlier stages were to be revealed as merely provisional at the time of New Testament graduation. We saw then that this did not work, for even within New Testament ethical teachings we need to separate off the obsolete from the potentially enduring; so that it appears that the progressive divine pedagogy continues *into* the New Testament period.

But this is not to say that *some* notion of progressivity (or at least of provisionality or corrigibility) might not encourage useful reflection among Christian ethicists. For what if the divine pedagogical process continues even *beyond* the New Testament period? If some such notion were applied in a thoroughgoing manner, that is, to provisionalize not only the Old Testament, and not only the New Testament, but also, and perhaps most importantly, on-going Christian ethical reflection, it might turn out to be a luminous, liberating concept – one perhaps that was worthy of God. For maybe the ethical perceptions of every age are but provisional stages in the divine pedagogue's teaching strategy. As Leonard Hodgson expressed it:

> So far from having given us a full and final explanation of the meaning of our faith [the New Testament writers] were taking the first steps towards its discovery, initiating a process which under the guidance of the Holy Spirit has been continuing ever since and is still going on. . . . [W]e have to take into account how the understanding of it by the New Testament Christians has been deepened and enriched in the experience of their successors, and is still being deepened and enriched by our experience of life in the world of today.[86]

If that is true, then a court-jester-like reminder about the provisionality of ethical reflection might be not the least of the broader contributions which historical-critical biblical studies have to offer students of Christian ethics.[87]

Summary

Any use of the Bible as a methodological starting-point for Christian ethics, or as a source of self-authenticating raw material, is impossible to maintain in theory and in practice is bound to impoverish both the Bible and Christian ethics; whereas a relaxed and imaginative approach to the Bible – such as refrains from burdening it with our own preoccupations, and especially our preoccupation with 'authority' – might be endlessly enriching. Such an approach might have nothing to offer by way of text-generated ethical norms, be they ever so loose, nor anything that is satisfyingly amenable to system or which could conveniently be set out in a textbook. Still, it might have the potential of enriching our ethical imagination in unexpected ways. And even if it fails in all that, it will at least be honest; and on that minimal basis alone, it might spare Christian ethicists a lot of theoretical angst – and Christians at the coalface some unnecessary misery.

Tom Deidun

Notes

1 Charles E. Curran,'The role and function of the Scriptures in moral theology', first published in *Proceedings of the Catholic Theological Society of America* (1971); reprinted in Charles E. Curran and Richard A. McCormick, SJ (eds), *The Use of Scripture in Moral Theology* (Readings in Moral Theology, no. 4; Ramsey, NJ: Paulist Press, 1984), pp. 178–212.

2 'In academic circles, this ephemeral movement was by 1960 in a state of terminal decline': Robert Morgan, 'Biblical theology' in R. Coggins and J. L. Houlden (eds), *A Dictionary of Biblical Interpretation* (London: SCM Press, 1990), p. 89. See Brevard Childs, *Biblical Theology in Crisis* (Philadelphia: Westminster Press, 1970). This is by no means to deny that many Catholic exegetes at that time were employing proper scientific methods in their study of the Bible. Some of them paid for it dearly.

3 James H. Cone, *God of the Oppressed* (London: SPCK, 1977), p. 8.

4 See, e.g., Robert Murray, *Exegesis and Imagination* (University of London, The Ethel M. Wood Lecture, 1988).

5 ET and commentary in Joseph A. Fitzmyer, *The Biblical Commission's Document 'The Interpretation of the Bible in the Church'* (Rome: Pontifical Biblical Institute, 1995).

6 After vigorously commending the historical-critical method ('which implies of itself no *a priori*'), the Biblical Commission's Statement went on to speak of 'Catholic exegesis'. I cannot understand this incongruity. Fitzmyer, who was a member of the Commission, tries hard to explain it (*The Biblical Commission's Document*, p. 47), but, as it seems to me, makes matters worse when he speaks of 'the way the Bible must be interpreted in the Church'. On p. 133, with reference to 'Catholic exegesis', Fitzmyer speaks of 'risks', 'dangers' and the need for 'caution', especially regarding the temptation to 'attribute to the Bible what is only a product of a later development'. Thirteen months after Pope John Paul had blessed the Commission's Statement, the Apostolic Letter *Ordinatio Sacerdotalis* put forward the (ostensibly historical) judgement that 'the Blessed Virgin Mary [did not receive] . . . the ministerial priesthood' (n. 3).

7 The Biblical Commission's Statement sees a denial of this as a failure to accept fully the 'consequences of the Incarnation' (Conclusion).

8 See Dennis Nineham, *The Use and Abuse of the Bible* (London and Basingstoke: Macmillan, 1976), esp. ch. 1.

9 The point being made in this paragraph does not depend entirely on the view that Jesus and the New Testament writers believed that the End was imminent (*pace* Nigel Biggar and Donald Hay, 'The Bible, Christian ethics and the provision of Social Security', *Studies in Christian Ethics* 7.2 [1994], pp. 43–64 [44f.]). I personally think that Jesus and some New Testament writers did. But even if they did not, it seems certain that their negative evaluation of the world was influenced by apocalyptic elements in Judaism. Cf. J. L. Houlden, *Ethics and the New Testament* (London and Oxford: Mowbray, 1975), pp. 8ff.

10 Cf. Eduard Schweizer, *The Good News According to Matthew* (London: SPCK, 1976), pp. 117–36; E. P. Sanders, *The Question of Uniqueness in the Teaching of Jesus* (University of London, The Ethel M. Wood Lecture, 1990).

11 Edouard Hamel is confident that the Bible presents 'a fundamental sexual anthropology' and 'the fundamental significance of sexuality': 'Scripture: the soul of moral theology?' in Curran and McCormick, *Use*, pp. 105–32 (p. 113).

12 I am not convinced by the arguments of L. William Countryman, in his thought-provoking *Dirt, Greed and Sex* (London: SCM Press, 1989), that early Christians abandoned Hebrew purity considerations over sex as resolutely as they eventually did over foods. Regarding Paul (who is important here): those places where the Jew in him prompts him to accompany condemnations of sexual impurity with derogatory remarks about gentiles (1 Thess 4:3ff.; 1 Cor 5:1, etc.) do not support that view. Nor am I convinced that Paul collapsed 'impurity' into 'greed' (Countryman, p. 108), though admittedly he and the tradition after him some-times associated the two.

13 Raymond E. Brown, *The Community of the Beloved Disciple: The Life, Loves and Hates of an Individual Church in New Testament Times* (London: Geoffrey Chapman, 1979), pp. 132, 135.

14 Cf. H. Cadbury, *The Perils of Modernizing Jesus*, pp. 86ff.; Nineham, *Use*, p. 204 (Hodgson).

15 See James D. G. Dunn, *Unity and Diversity in the New Testament* (London: SCM Press, 1977); also Nineham, *Use*, ch. 7.

16 The view that the purity laws have nothing to do with ethics mystifies me. They may have nothing to do with *our* ethics; but that is because we have, for one reason or another, chosen to exclude them. On the logic of canonicity our exclusion of them is arbitrary.

17 And to examples of diversity in directly *ethical* matters. There is also a kaleidoscope of views within the New Testament relating to eschatology, soteriology, Christ, the Church, church order, and every area of theology one can think of (see n. 15 above), all of which areas may have some bearing on ethical matters.

18 *Pace* E. P. Sanders (*Paul, the Law and the Jewish People* [London: SCM Press, 1985]), ch. 3, who argues that once Paul got off the subject of 'entry requirements' for gentiles, he took it for granted that Christians would continue to defer to the moral prescriptions of Torah. I am not convinced that texts like Romans 8:4; 13:8–10 offer any support for that view. (By this I do not mean that Paul intended members of his communities to feel free to commit adultery, steal, bear false witness, etc.)

19 John Drane, *Paul: Libertine or Legalist* (London: SPCK, 1975), argued that Paul, having at an early stage (Galatians) entertained the view that the Spirit was an adequate ethical guide for Christians, later (1 Corinthians) saw the error of his ways and adopted a law-ethic. The view that Galatians is early is debatable; and what Drane calls a 'law ethic' is already present in 1 Thessalonians 4:1–12. It is commonly held that 1 Thessalonians (which Drane's book omits to mention) is the earliest extant letter of Paul.

20 On divorce, cf., e.g., Houlden, *Ethics*, pp. 73–80; John R. Donahue SJ, 'Divorce: New Testament perspectives', *The Month* (April 1981), pp. 113–20.

21 I refer to the so-called 'Pauline privilege'.

22 Or, in Houlden's phrase, on 'the diversity of New Testament teaching [being] pulped into a plausible uniformity' (*Ethics*, p. 115). This approach characterizes the use of the Bible in the documents of Vatican II: e.g., *Lumen Gentium* (nn. 18–21) punctuates its exposition of the standard Catholic account of the historical origins of the hierarchical Church with references to the most diverse New Testament texts, all of which it sees as witnesses to a single point of view.

23 Richard B. Hays, 'Scripture-shaped community: the problem of method in New Testament ethics', *Interpretation* 44 (1990), pp. 42–55.

24 'If these texts [sc., New Testament texts that advocate incompatible ethical stances] are allowed to have their say, they will force us to choose between them –

or to reject the normative claims of both' (Hays, art. cit., p. 47). Why not *both* choose between them *and* reject the normative claims of both?

25 Cf. H. Chadwick, '"All things to all men": (1 Cor. 9:22)', *New Testament Studies* 1 (1954–55), pp. 261–75; W. E. Phipps, 'Is Paul's attitude towards sexual relations contained in 1 Cor. 7:1?', *New Testament Studies* 28 (1982), pp. 125ff.

26 For an example, see the articles referred to in note 25 above, and Peter Brown, *The Body and Society: Men, Women and Sexual Renunciation in Early Christianity* (New York: Columbia University Press, 1988), pp. 53ff.

27 Pope John Paul, in his address on the occasion of the presentation of the Biblical Commission's Statement (see Fitzmyer, *The Biblical Commission's Document*, note 5 above, pp. 5f.), reminded his audience that Pius XII's *Divino Afflante Spiritu* laid particular emphasis on Bible interpreters' need to understand literary genres. See also Vatican II, *Dei Verbum*, n. 12. The papal magisterium's interest in literary genres, and its criticism of the 'illusion' of those who refuse to 'make distinctions that would relativize the significance of the words [of biblical texts]' (Pope John Paul in Fitzmyer, p. 5), seem not to envisage the biblical writers' *ethical* language.

28 Cf. A. N. Wilder, cited by Nineham, *Use*, p. 206: 'the stultifying axiom that genuine truth or insight or wisdom must be limited to that which can be stated in discursive prose'.

29 Cf. Nineham, *Use*, pp. 47ff.

30 Cf. Houlden, *Ethics*, p. 11: 'Even the most biblically-minded Christian makes artificial patterns with the texts.' (Did he mean *especially* the most biblically-minded?)

31 Cf. Gareth Moore, 'Some remarks on the use of Scripture in *Veritatis Splendor*' in Joe Selling and Jan Jans (eds), *The Splendor of Accuracy: An Examination of the Assertions Made by 'Veritatis Splendor'* (Kampen: Kok/Pharos, 1994), pp. 71–98. Moore argues that the encyclical's preoccupation with a commandment-centred ethic induced it to home in on the text's transitional reference to 'the commandments', thus missing the whole point of the passage, which is about the 'inadequacy of thinking of a person's relationship to God in terms of law and commandment' (p. 80).

32 Cf. Anthony C. Thiselton, *New Horizons in Hermeneutics: The Theory and Practice of Transforming Biblical Reading* (London: HarperCollins, 1992), pp. 444ff. See also Thiselton's comments on Rowland and Corner's assessment of the use of biblical material in liberationist communities in Brazil, and on Cardenal's research into comparable groups in Nicaragua (the Magnificat shows that '[the Virgin] was a communist. . . . That is the Revolution'): *New Horizons*, pp. 411f.

33 Feminist and liberationist exegetes, in the wake of Gadamer, claim a 'hermeneutic of suspicion' as their preserve. In fact, most second-term students in biblical studies work on the principle that they can't trust anyone. (This is by no means to discourage feminist and liberationist exegetes from becoming even more hermeneutically suspicious.)

34 Cf. J. D. G. Dunn, *Christology in the Making: A New Testament Enquiry into the Origins of the Doctrine of the Incarnation* (London: SCM Press, 1980). (On Gal 4:4, see pp. 38ff.)

35 *The Tablet* (16 October 1993), p. 1331. Grisez continues: ' . . . assuming, that is, that the sin, committed with full awareness and deliberate consent, remains unrepented'. From the list of types who, according to 1 Cor 6:9f., will not inherit the kingdom, Grisez picks out those characterized by sexual misbehaviour and then directs his attention to particular acts. This preoccupation with certain (intrinsically evil) sexual acts he shares with the encyclical: cf. Nicholas Lash,

'Crisis and tradition in *Veritatis Splendor*', *Studies in Christian Ethics* 7.2 (1994), pp. 22–8.

36 For examples of such an enquiry, see Countryman, *Dirt*, pp. 117ff. and Robin Scroggs, *The New Testament and Homosexuality* (Philadelphia: Fortress Press, 1983).

37 Even the 'Sermon on the Mount' – often regarded as Jesus' answer to Sinai, or at least as the classic compendium of his ethical teaching – was never a sermon of Jesus, but is rather a 'veritable chorus of voices, some bearing the stamp of Jesus, the others assembled by the evangelist to form a single whole that makes certain specific points' (Schweizer, *Good News*, p. 197).

38 On the wide range of views, see, e.g., Allen Verhey, *The Great Reversal* (Grand Rapids: Eerdmans, 1984), ch. 1; or Tom Wright in Stephen Neil and Tom Wright, *The Interpretation of the New Testament 1861–1986* (Oxford: Oxford University Press, 1988), ch. 9. Perhaps we should bear in mind Henry Cadbury's observation that the idea that Jesus will have worked out any overall plan for his 'ministry', and that the 'kingdom of God' was a single, thought-out conception, may well be anachronistic. If this is true, then any attempt at a (to us) plausible 'reconstruction' will be misguided from the start.

39 '. . . the thrust of Jesus' life and teaching was at most oblique to anything that could reasonably be called morality and not infrequently subversive of it. . . . The view that Jesus offers distinctive and superior moral teaching, and the notion that he confirms and expands the highest agreed moral wisdom, are different forms of the attempt to say the best we can of him in terms of the *prior* assumption that morality is all-important. This assumption is being allowed to dictate the interpretation of Jesus': Nicholas Peter Harvey, *The Morals of Jesus* (London: Darton, Longman and Todd, 1991), pp. 32f.

40 Cf. Thomas W. Ogletree, *The Use of the Bible in Christian Ethics* (Oxford: Blackwell, 1984), pp. 177ff.; E. Clinton Gardner, 'Eschatological ethics' in John Macquarrie and James Childress (eds), *A New Dictionary of Christian Ethics* (London: SCM Press, 1986), pp. 201–5.

41 Jack T. Sanders, *Ethics in the New Testament* (London: SCM Press 1975, 2nd edn 1986): '[Jesus'] ethical teaching is interwoven with his imminent eschatology to such a degree that every attempt to separate the two and to draw out only the ethical thread invariably and inevitably draws out strands of the eschatology, so that both yarns only lie in a heap. Better to leave the tapestry intact' (p. 29).

42 'The underlying message of the New Testament is that the emergency is now, for us all': J. L. Houlden, *Bible and Belief* (London: SPCK, 1991), p. 171. Cf. Richard Hiers, 'Jesus, ethics and the present situation' in Curran and McCormick, *Use*, pp. 1–20.

43 Cf. Jack Sanders's appraisal of Bultmann's attempt to reinterpret Jesus' imminentist eschatology in terms of existential urgency (*Ethics*, pp. 11–14).

44 'Whereas twenty-five years ago a consensus had emerged, there appears now to be only confusion': Morna D. Hooker, 'Kingdom of God' in Coggins and Houlden, *Dictionary*, pp. 374–7 (p. 377).

45 See E. P. Sanders, *Paul and Palestinian Judaism: A Comparison of Patterns of Religion* (London: SCM Press, 1977); *Paul, The Law and the Jewish People* (see note 18 above). This challenge has not yet been effectively answered. At least, the only extended response to it I have seen from the Lutheran tradition (Timo Laato, *Paulus und das Judentum* [Åbo: Åbo Akademis förlag, 1991]) goes no further than an unabashed rehearsal of standard Lutheran exegesis.

46 Cf. Tom Deidun, 'James Dunn and John Ziesler on Romans in new perspective', *The Heythrop Journal* XXXIII (1992), pp. 79–84.

47 Edward LeRoy Long Jr, 'The use of the Bible in Christian ethics', *Interpretation* 19 (1965), pp. 149–62; Charles E. Curran, art. cit., note 1 above, pp. 178–212.

48 James F. Gustafson, 'Christian ethics' in Paul Ramsey (ed.), *Religion* (Englewood Cliffs, NJ: Prentice-Hall, 1965); see also Curran and McCormick, *Use*, pp. 133–50.

49 In a later article (1974), reprinted in Curran and McCormick, *Use*, pp. 151–77, Gustafson suggested some specifications of his earlier classification.

50 Verhey, *Great Reversal* (see note 38 above).

51 John Murray, quoted by LeRoy Long Jr, 'The use of the Bible', p. 150.

52 To typical practitioners of this use of the Bible, this is no problem.

53 Cf. Moore, art. cit., note 31 above, p. 86.

54 Especially in Roman Catholic tradition these words of Jesus are interpreted as a commendation of celibacy. But they are open to other quite plausible interpretations: cf., e.g., A. E. Harvey, *Eunuchs for the Sake of the Kingdom* (University of London, The Ethel M. Wood Lecture, 1995).

55 Long locates its origin in Harnack, with his 'infinite value of the human soul', and in Albert Knudson, who did much to perpetuate Harnack's view. He also cites, more recently, Paul Ramsey, Andrew Osborne and Reinhold Niebuhr.

56 Cf. Charles Robert, 'Morale et Écriture: Nouveau Testament', *Seminarium* NS 11 (1971), pp. 596–622. This kind of approach influenced Bernard Häring's *The Law of Christ* (German original 1954), commonly acknowledged to have marked a turning-point in Catholic moral theology; and it appears to be what Vatican II had in mind when it recommended that 'biblical *themes* should have first place' in dogmatic theology (*Optatam Totius*, n. 16; my italics).

57 '... the canonizing and harmonizing impulse which longs to produce "*the* New Testament view"' (Houlden, *Ethics*, p. 121). Even such (supposed) 'master themes' as the 'kingdom' or the imitation of Jesus leave most of the New Testament out of account.

58 John H. Yoder, *The Politics of Jesus* (Grand Rapids: Eerdmans, 1972), p. 250; cited by Verhey in Curran and McCormick, *Use*, p. 226.

59 In any case, it is questionable whether the New Testament references to non-violence can be so easily generalized, either into a principle of personal conduct (for we simply do not know what action Jesus or the New Testament writers might have taken had they chanced on a rape or a mugging), or into a socio-political programme (for we do not know what advice they might give to, say, British conscripts when war was declared on Hitler's Germany).

60 Here re-enters the whole problem of the historical Jesus. In Mark's Gospel, at least, neighbour love is mentioned in only one passage; and Matthew's Jesus is capable of a long tirade on the question of ethical priorities without once mentioning love (Matt 23). Regarding Paul: notwithstanding those texts which speak of the paramountcy of love, he is quite capable of bringing to moral questions criteria which have nothing obviously to do with love (cf., e.g., 1 Cor 6:12–20; 1 Cor 7; Rom 13:1–7).

61 See pp. 8–9 above.

62 Richard B. Hays, art. cit., note 23 above, p. 44.

63 Gustafson in Curran and McCormick, *Use*, pp. 163f.

64 Gustafson in Curran and McCormick, *Use*, p. 166.

65 Its origins are attributed especially to Barth. As well as in H. R. Niebuhr it is exemplified in Paul Lehmann, Joseph Sittler, Jürgen Moltmann and others. Curran, art. cit., note 1 above, p. 182, judged that it had beneficial influence in the 'Scriptural renewal' in Roman Catholic circles. It is still at the heart of

liberation theologians' use of the Bible. Cf. Gustafson in Curran and McCormick, *Use*, pp. 166f.

66 E.g., some biblically-minded people 'know' what God is 'doing' in the AIDS crisis.

67 Bruce Birch and Larry Rasmussen, 'The use of the Bible in Christian ethics' in Ronald P. Hamel and Kenneth R. Himes OFM (eds), *Christian Ethics: A Reader* (New York: Paulist Press, 1989), pp. 322–32 (p. 324), extracted from their *The Bible and Ethics in Christian Life* (Minneapolis: Augsburg, 1976). For the place of character and virtue in contemporary Christian-ethical discussion, see Chapter 5 in this book.

68 A similar caveat must apply to those who insist that 'the believing community' is the indispensable context for the appropriation of the Bible in Christian ethics. Cf. Verhey in Curran and McCormick, *Use*, p. 216: ' ... the importance of the believing community as the context for the authority and appropriation of biblical materials seems to be part of a developing consensus'. But *which* believing community? The Bob Jones University (which still, on biblical grounds, prohibits interracial dating)? The Nederduitsch Hervormde Kerk (which still, on biblical grounds, limits its membership to whites)?

69 Gustafson in Curran and McCormick, *Use*, p. 165.

70 Curran, art. cit., pp. 198, 206; Gerard J. Hughes in *The Heythrop Journal* XIII (1972), pp. 27–43; Gustafson in Curran and McCormick, *Use*, p. 172.

71 For starting-points for reflection on the Bible's 'authority', see, for example, L. William Countryman, *Biblical Authority or Biblical Tyranny? Scripture and the Christian Pilgrimage* (Philadelphia: Fortress Press, 1981); and John Barton, *People of the Book? The Authority of the Bible in Christianity* (London: SPCK, 1988).

72 ' ... the revelatory canon for theological evaluation of biblical androcentric traditions ... cannot be derived from the Bible itself but can only be formulated in and through women's struggle for liberation from all patriarchal oppression': E. Schüssler Fiorenza, *In Memory of Her* (New York: Crossroad, 1983), p. 32; quoted by Hays, art. cit., note 23 above, p. 51.

73 For the magisterium as authentic interpreter of the Bible in Roman Catholic thinking, see Vatican II, *Dei Verbum* n. 10, quoted by *Veritatis Splendor*, n. 27. For reflections on the relationship between this claim and the commitment of Roman Catholic exegetes to historical critical exegesis, see R. E. Brown in R. E. Brown *et al.* (eds), *The New Jerome Biblical Commentary* (London: Geoffrey Chapman, 1990), pp. 1163f.

74 Cf. Hughes's discussion (art. cit., note 70 above, pp. 37f.) of Keith Ward's *Ethics and Christianity* (London, 1970); Hamel, art. cit., note 11 above, pp. 109f.: 'Human reason is not infallible. ... The light provided by Scripture will be added to the light of human reason, supporting it, guiding its reflections, keeping it out of impasses and indicating to it the sure paths to be followed.'

75 Similarly, it appears to be a preoccupation with biblical normativity that has prompted Christian ethicists to speak of the 'function' of the Bible in Christian ethics, or of an appropriate 'methodology' for using the Bible in Christian ethics.

76 Nineham, *Use*, p. 268.

77 See the splendid quotation from Chrysostom in *Veritatis Splendor*, n. 24; cf. also Aquinas, *Summa Theologiae*, I-II, q. 106, a. 1, also quoted there. Aquinas (ibid., a. 2) also made the point, citing Augustine, that 2 Cor 3:6 was as applicable to the New Testament as it was to any other writing. Cf., among moderns, Houlden, *Ethics*, p. 120: 'It is arguable that to be true to the deepest convictions of the leading New Testament writers, and more, to be faithful to the Lord who lay

behind them, we need to be emancipated from the letter of their writings.' All this means, surely, that Christians are not in any nomistic sense a 'people of the Book'. Cf. Barton, *People of the Book?*

78 I second Nineham's wish when he says: 'I should like to see Christians nowadays approach the Bible in an altogether more *relaxed* spirit, not anxiously asking "What has it to say to me immediately?", but distancing it, allowing fully for its "pastness" . . .' (*Use*, p. 196).

79 *Catechism of the Catholic Church* (London: Geoffrey Chapman, 1994), Part 3, Section 2.

80 Countryman, *Dirt*, p. 237. His discussion in this book is an excellent example of what I mean here.

81 The phrase is Brian Mahon's: *Dictionary of Ethics, Theology and Society* (London and New York: Routledge, 1996), p. 59.

82 The phrase is Gregory Kavka's: 'The futurity problem' in Ernest Partridge (ed.), *Responsibilities to Future Generations* (Buffalo: Prometheus Books, 1981), pp. 109–22. For a Christian-ethical discussion of some of the issues involved, see William P. George, 'Thomas Aquinas and concern for posterity', *The Heythrop Journal* XXXIII (1992), pp. 283–306.

83 Nineham, *Use*, pp. 195ff.

84 Admittedly, the first of the following examples is not derivable only from modern exegesis; though the point would certainly be missed by ethicists who turned to the Bible on the look-out for directly ethical concerns.

85 Nineham saw fit to conclude his *Use* with a homily on prayer (p. 269).

86 Leonard Hodgson, *Sex and Christian Freedom: An Enquiry* (London: SCM Press, 1967), p. 42; quoted by Nineham, *Use*, p. 75.

87 The image is cribbed from J. L. Houlden's 'The status of origins in Christianity' in his *Bible and Belief* (London: SPCK, 1991), pp. 74–81 (pp. 80–81), used there in connection with the relationship between historical studies and systematics.

2

Natural law

Gerard J. Hughes

When it is used in connection with ethics, or with Christian ethics, the phrase 'natural law' in its broadest sense refers to the view that morality derives from the nature of human beings. The controversies surrounding this view can be traced, again in broad outline, to one of two sources, the first concerned more with method, and the second more with content. They might be summarized roughly as follows:

(1) Different views about the use of reason to discover God's designs for human beings.

(2) Different accounts of what human nature is, and about how, or indeed whether, there is any way of deriving morality from such an account.

In a broad sense it would be fair to say that almost all the classical Western philosophers, from Aristotle to Bentham, tried in some way to show that morality had its basis in human nature. Many of them would contrast morality as derived from human nature itself with the moral customs and legislation of particular groups of human beings, and would on occasion appeal to the natural law as a basis for assessing and on occasions rejecting the legitimacy of particular customs or laws. In our own day, documents like the United Nations Declaration on Human Rights propose a set of rights which belong to human beings because of what human beings are, and which ought to be respected for that reason. It can be appealed to precisely to challenge the customs or legislation of particular countries. The many difficulties encountered in attempting to elaborate what the natural law is have at least until comparatively recent times not deterred philosophers from holding that some such basis for morality there must be. However, the difficulties are serious enough. I shall in this chapter try to outline and assess them by elaborating on the two types of issue mentioned above.

Human nature and God's design

Human nature as an embodiment of God's design

A comparatively uncomplicated view of human nature which a religious believer could hold is that human nature, as we find it, reflects the wisdom and goodness of the creator God. To the extent that we can understand ourselves, to that extent we can understand God's designs in creating us as we are, just as to the extent that we can understand anything else in creation we can to that extent understand how the creator God intended things to be. In principle, then, and leaving aside for the moment any of the difficulties under (2) above, if we can show how to base morality upon human nature, we will come to understand how God intended us to live. Thomas Aquinas is typical of many Christian writers who accepted this position. His term for God's creative designs was the 'eternal law'; and under that term he included God's designs for the non-human parts of creation as well as the human. The non-human parts of creation reflect the eternal law in a deterministic way: they inevitably behave according to the natures they have. The laws of nature, discovered by scientists, describe the behaviour of things. Aquinas is willing to use the terminology of law and obedience even here, and to say that these parts of creation obey the laws of their natures; but 'obey' here is a metaphorical expression. The laws of physics do not require things to behave in a particular way, they simply describe how they by nature do behave. This is true, in part, also of human beings, since we are also part of the natural world; our bodies behave according to the laws of physics and chemistry like any other bodies in the universe. Aquinas contrasts this way of embodying God's designs with the specifically human way in which we might do so. Unlike rocks or trees, human beings can come to understand the kinds of beings they are, and are free to live in a way which corresponds to that understanding, or to refuse to do so. We are not naturally determined to exhibit God's designs in our lives. Of course, our understanding of ourselves and hence of how we should live is in all probability limited. In this respect it is no different from our understanding of physics or astronomy or any of the other natural sciences. Still, as with the other sciences, there is no limit in principle to how much we can learn; and the more we do learn, the more God's design for us will become clear.

In the eyes of some theologians, however, this comparatively simple view is altogether too simple. In particular, it fails to take into account the theological doctrine of the Fall. They would argue that human nature, as we know it now, is very far indeed from expressing the way God intended us to be; it has been distorted by our own wrongdoing at every period in human history. Theologians did, and to some extent still do, differ considerably in their estimate of the extent of this moral distortion of human nature. Views range widely. Some would argue that while indeed we are weakened, both in our minds and in our constancy in seeking the good, this weakness is not such as to invalidate the view that, reflecting on ourselves even as we are, we can still see how God intends us to live. The most they would concede is that this reflection might be more difficult than it ideally should have been. At the other extreme, it has been held that we are so weakened that, left to our own devices, we are simply not capable of seeing in ourselves anything but our own distortions; there is therefore no secure way in which reflection on ourselves as we are can tell us anything about how God intends us to be.

To give a proper account of these differences would take us too far into issues which are more properly the concern of systematic theology. But perhaps some brief points can be made which might at least help to pinpoint where the real disagreements lie. A convenient place to start is with the famous slogan of the sixteenth-century reformers, *sola fide, sola gratia, sola Scriptura*, 'only by faith, only by grace, only from Scripture'. It is the last two of these which are of immediate importance. Going back to the time of Augustine, there was a controversy in the Christian churches about the need for divine assistance, 'grace', to enable us to know what God's will is and to follow it. Pelagius and his followers were thought to deny this, and to say that with our own unaided powers we could do a great deal; and this view (whether Pelagius really did hold it or not) was rejected as heretical. It remains a further, and separate question, to whom and how God's grace becomes available. Is God's grace in fact available to everyone who sincerely seeks God, whether they are Christian believers or not? It is possible to hold that God's grace will always assist the sincere moral reflections of human beings, so that in practice human reason need never be unaided human reason, while still maintaining that the natural law can be known without appeal to the specifically Christian revelation in Jesus, as interpreted in the biblical and later Christian tradition. One might, therefore, accept *sola gratia*, without accepting *sola Scriptura*. Those theologians who insist upon *sola Scriptura* will generally reject the usefulness of a natural law approach to Christian ethics.

In any event, theologians have often found it difficult to be consistent, either in their proclaimed trust in, or in their clear distrust of, the use of reason in ethics. Reformed theologians like Karl Barth, despite their rejection of a natural law approach, have in practice used reason to reflect on human nature as we know it, partly in order to interpret Scripture

Gerard J. Hughes

itself, and partly to supplement its moral teachings to deal with issues which are not mentioned in Scripture at all. At the other end of the theological spectrum, some Catholic theologians, despite their theoretical insistence that we can in principle discover God's designs by using our reason to reflect upon human nature, have in practice shown a good deal of distrust for such purely philosophical reflections, and have insisted that they be corrected or supplemented by revelation, or by the Church as the proper interpreter of revelation.

Natural law as a counter to theologically based ethics

From the time of the Enlightenment until our own day, people have been impressed with the progress of the natural sciences. In particular, the methods of the natural sciences seem to have proved themselves beyond all doubt, simply by being so helpful in enabling us to understand, and to some extent therefore to control, the world in which we live. For this reason, it became fashionable to contrast the steady progress of science with the unsolved disputes between divided theologians, and to suggest that if human nature were studied scientifically, discoveries about human morality would rest on a more secure basis than they ever could by being left to theologians and divines. In consequence, proponents of what was at least in some sense a natural law theory of ethics saw themselves as for the first time providing a good scientific grounding for morality, a grounding which hitherto had been sadly lacking. Along with Aristotelian science, now regarded as totally discredited both in its conclusions and in its method, Aristotelian ethics, whether in its original form, or in the medieval version of it adopted by Aquinas, was also thought ripe for replacement. Strong elements of this approach are to be found in thinkers as different in many other respects as Thomas Hobbes, David Hume, Immanuel Kant and Jeremy Bentham.

Not, indeed, that the ethical conclusions reached by most of these writers were either surprising or radical. By and large, they endorsed the moral codes of their day. Hobbes said that the problem with earlier writers (among whom he very likely had Aristotle in mind) was that they had indeed given lists of moral virtues, but they had totally failed to explain why these character traits should be thought of as virtues. He therefore set out to show how those same virtues could be derived from a secure basis in physics, and human psychology. Hume, too, explicitly tried to show how it is that ethics can be explained by studying human nature, using the methods of the new sciences. His intention was not to offer revolutionary moral views, but to explain how ethics arises from the workings of human nature. Kant endeavoured to provide ethics with the same kind of philosophical justification as he believed he had provided for the natural sciences. It was not so much the conclusions of traditional ethics which these writers called in question, as the lack of any scientifically justifiable basis. Traditional ethics (as it so happened, largely Christian ethics) was rejected as methodologically unsound. Somewhat in contrast, Jeremy Bentham was much more of a social reformer, as were the utilitarians who followed him. They tried to give unarguable reasons for criticizing those who resisted the reforms which they saw as absolutely necessary in the wake of the industrial and political upheavals of the late eighteenth century. Once again, they tried to achieve this by providing ethics with a scientific foundation which could not be gainsaid. John Stuart Mill, a disciple of Bentham, once said that Bentham was not a great innovator in moral philosophy, but he was a great innovator in philosophical method in ethics.

In various ways there has long been a tension between those philosophers who insist (sometimes with hostile intent, sometimes not) on using human reason to reach conclusions about God and about how we should live, and those who insist on the primacy of revelation and theology. This tension has been evident in many areas, from astronomy to the origins of the world, from the theory of evolution to ethics. Now, truth is one, and the truths established by rational means cannot conflict with God's revelation. In trying to resolve discrepancies between what we believe we have established on philosophical or scientific grounds and what we believe to be the correct interpretation of God's revelation, we have to admit in advance that in principle either or both sets of beliefs may be mistaken. Human reasoning can go wrong and often does; and the Christian community has not infrequently misinterpreted God's revelation in Christ and in the Scriptures. It is rationally indefensible to assume in advance of any inquiry either that there can be no such thing as divine revelation, or that it can have nothing to teach us about ethics; and it is theologically irresponsible to insist on a particular interpretation of God's revelation which cannot be shown to be rationally defensible and consistent with all that we have learnt by other means about ourselves and our world.

Human nature and the basis of ethics

Human nature has been understood in many different ways. In the opinion of Plato, of Augustine and of Kant, human reason, or the human rational soul, was regarded as defining what a human being essentially was, and the human body was regarded either as an unavoidable hindrance, or at least as an irrelevance so far as the moral self was concerned. The British philosophers from Hobbes to Mill believed that ethics depended on human psychology, and that human psychology could be explained in terms of some very simple desire(s) – for pleasure, or self-preservation, or power. All these views are still in varying degrees influential. But in fact the most enduring version of the natural law tradition in Christian thought draws its inspiration from Aristotle as interpreted by Thomas Aquinas. Aristotle rejected the body/soul dualism of Plato in favour of a much more unified view of the human self in which physical and mental powers were more closely inter-related. Human beings are animals who can think. As a result, his ethical views stressed the importance of the emotions (which for Plato, and later for Kant, were simply to be tamed or excluded as motives in ethics). Aristotle would also have regarded the 'scientific' psychology of Hobbes or Hume or Bentham as grossly over-simplified. Human needs and desires are irreducibly complex; and while, doubtless, simplicity is indeed a desirable feature of any theory, whether in the human or in the natural sciences, it must not be bought at the price of distorting the facts. It was in all essentials this Aristotelian view which Aquinas adopted, modifying it only to the extent that he was prepared to supplement it with specifically Christian beliefs about the law of the Holy Spirit written in our hearts, and to adapt the Aristotelian notion of a fulfilled life (*eudaimonia*) to accommodate the Christian belief in the vision of God in heaven.

To understand the predominant Christian view of the natural law, then, one must begin with what has become known as the 'Function Argument' which Aristotle sets out in his *Nicomachean Ethics*, Book 1, ch. 7. Of course, to understand it fully one has to read it against the background of Aristotle's philosophy as a whole. Here, then, is a commentary on its main elements.

Aristotle held that human beings have a variety of activities which by nature they are capable of performing: growing, reproducing, sensing, feeling emotions, thinking and choosing. Each of these can be performed well or badly, and each one in the list depends upon the preceding ones, in the sense that for the 'higher' activities the required bodily infra-structures have to be in place and properly functioning. Some of these are activities we share with other animals, others are characteristically human. He believes that for a human being to live a fulfilled life, all these activities must be functioning well. Though a fulfilled life will, of course, involve keeping healthy, and sleeping, and digesting and so on, what makes it fulfilling are not these background activities, but the activities of intellectual understanding and contributing to society. Human beings are thinking social animals.

All thinking involves an insight into particular cases in the light of which we can formulate general laws. In scientific theories, we can then use these general laws to explain individual events. This is how Aristotle understands reason to function in its purely speculative activities, as we try to understand the world around us, and God. But, as he somewhat ruefully says, a life devoted entirely to such speculative activity is 'too high for man'. But something of this vision of the grasp of all truth being the pinnacle of human fulfilment was taken over by Aquinas and interpreted in terms of the Christian doctrine of the beatific vision. In practice, though, Aristotle accepted that human beings must also live a life of contribution to the community; and this requires us to turn our reason to practical decisions.

We will, if we have been well brought up, have already grasped connections between actions which have been described to us as wrong, or as cowardly, or dishonest, generous or mean. We can formulate general rules about what it takes to be brave, or dishonest, or generous. But, says Aristotle, practical wisdom (we might say, 'moral discernment'; his term is *phronesis*) requires that we be able to read individual situations in a morally correct way, since morality requires us to make particular decisions. We already have at our disposal many moral concepts which we have learnt to use: but we have simply to see what is required of us here and now: whether, for example, to say 'That's very good' to someone would be a lie, or a proper piece of encouragement, or a raising of false expectations of progress. There are no rules which will tell us how to do this, no arguments which can be used: what we need is long experience of life, and emotional balance.

Aristotle points out that being liable to over-react, or under-react, emotionally does not destroy someone's ability to do theoretical mathematics; but, in his view, it certainly does undermine one's judgement in making moral decisions. To make good moral decisions, and to be able also to trust our moral insight, we need to come to individual decisions with a solid emotional balance; and that, in turn, requires that our emotional responses have been properly trained. (Here, the contrast with Plato is evident.) To have appropriate emotional responses is to have all the moral virtues.

All this Aquinas takes over. He speaks, as does Aristotle, of the first principles of practical reasoning. What are these? They include two different types of principle: (1) purely formal principles: The most basic of these is the principle of Non-contradiction, which should govern all our reasoning, whether speculative or practical: another purely formal principle is 'Good is to be done and evil avoided', which should govern all practical reasoning. These formal principles as it were set the ground rules for how we should think, in science or in ethics; but they do not in themselves tell us what to think. (2) Other 'first principles' have substantive content. In science, they contain fundamental truths about the natures of things in the physical world; and in ethics, such truths as that life and health are good things, as are education, and honesty, and the virtues generally. He also points out that there are many other more detailed 'good things'; examples might be open heart surgery, or nursery schools, or confidentiality, or giving to Oxfam. I have chosen these more specific examples as indicative of ways in which we might seek to promote health, or education, or honesty; but Aquinas points out that these more detailed good things are less clear, and less likely to be truly good in all cases, than the more fundamental ones. He, like Aristotle, does not believe that it is possible in ethics to have anything like the precision one might hope for in the natural sciences. And, just as Aristotle appeals in the end to the insight of the person of practical wisdom and emotional balance, so Aquinas stresses the importance of *prudentia* (his translation of Aristotle's *phronesis*), which presupposes fortitude and temperance (the balanced emotional response in the areas of aggression and desire).

What neither Aristotle nor Aquinas believes is that from general moral principles we can simply deduce what we ought to do in individual cases. Part of the reason for this is that there is no way of logically deducing the desirability of open heart surgery from the desirability of health, even though the desirability of open heart surgery may be based upon the desirability of health; and, second, though it is true in all cases that health is a good thing, it is not true that open heart surgery will be a good thing in every case. There is no substitute for seeing, in the circumstances of each situation, what is to be done. Of course, one can explain one's decision afterwards, by stating the good ends at which it was aimed. But that does not in itself justify one's decision. For example, I could decide to say 'That's very good!' to someone, and explain that by saying that they needed encouragement at this point; but equally, I could decide to say 'Really, that could be a lot better' by saying that what was required was honest criticism. Each decision can thus be explained in terms of the good at which it aimed. But the explanation does nothing to justify one decision rather than the other. Aristotle and Aquinas agree that the person of practical wisdom will just have to see what is to be said to the person; and that 'seeing' cannot be further justified by argument. And were someone to object that saying 'Well done!' was simply a lie, and therefore wrong, the reply would be that in the circumstances, it was an act of kindness, not a lie, and if the critic does not see that then he is simply lacking in practical wisdom.

As will be seen, then, Aquinas's view of natural law combines the conviction that what one ought to do is based upon what is good for human beings given how human nature functions, with a remarkably flexible account of what people ought to do in practice. Consistency requires that we treat similar situations in the same way, and the injunction that we should do good and avoid evil requires that in explaining our choices we have to be able to explain the good at which we were aiming. But neither these requirements, nor any of the more specific statements about what things are good for human beings, will of themselves settle how particular decisions have to be taken.

Therein lies both the strength and the weakness of natural law theories, whether those of Aquinas and Aristotle, or the views of such writers as Kant, or Hobbes, Hume and Bentham.

Their strength lies in the basic contention which is common to them all, that ethics ought to be firmly rooted in what human beings are like, and how they interact with their various environments. Although in more recent times views of ethics have been propounded which are explicitly value-neutral, it is perhaps more generally accepted that we cannot just decide what we will count as a human good. What is good for us depends upon our natures, not upon our decisions. And, in theological terms, it seems more consonant with the wisdom of God that he wills us to be fulfilled individuals, fulfilled according to the nature with which we have been created. Moreover, natural law theories have always been committed to the view that there is room in ethics for truth and falsity: we can be mistaken, less easily with regard to very general aims like health, or education, or freedom, but more and more easily in more specific types of case, about what genuinely is fulfilling for ourselves or others. We can get things right, but also get things wrong. We have to discover what truly fulfils a person, we cannot simply decide what we will count as fulfilment. Moreover, these theories all insist on the connection between ethics and the human sciences. Aristotle and Aquinas were no exceptions to this, despite their lack of modern scientific knowledge, and despite the strictures of the Enlightenment critics. What has changed is the conception of scientific method, rather than the basic view that in order to understand ethics, let alone to make good ethical decisions, one has to understand human beings in a scientific way. The more we can understand medicine, or psychology, or sociology, the better placed we will be to understand what we are actually doing to ourselves and one another, and hence the better placed to see what we ought to be doing.

Their weakness, if weakness it is, lies in the difficulty of relating complex decisions to basic principles. For example, whether to spend more money on the health service than on education, or whether to insist on doctor–patient confidentiality where minors are concerned, or whether to allow genetic research, and if so under what limitations. These decisions obviously affect different people, for good and for ill, and at least often make it only too clear that it is just not possible to achieve everything we would wish all the time. Philosophers and theologians have wrestled with these issues, and have tried to give theoretically consistent accounts of why they advocate looking at them one way rather than in some other, as indeed they are intellectually bound to do. It has often been said, with some justice, that most moral philosophers and theologians, including those who are sympathetic to this overall approach, in the end are unwilling to depart very far from the received wisdom of the society or Church with which they identify, and that their theoretical accounts are tailored to defend the status quo. Aristotle, as is well known, failed to see anything wrong with slavery, or with allotting a subordinate place in society to women. Hobbes seems to us altogether too wedded to an absolutist form of government, Bentham and Mill not sufficiently sensitive to the fact that some people's desires might be morally perverse. Though in principle natural law theories are geared to the critical assessment of the received moral wisdom of any particular time or place, they have in practice not always succeeded in providing such criticism, precisely because the very flexibility of the theory can make it hard to demonstrate that a mistake is being made in its application. We tend to identify human fulfilment with what we have learnt is human fulfilment, for men, or women, Europeans or Amazonian villagers. Gross moral mistakes can be identified readily enough; but even if they can easily be spotted, there is still much room, perhaps too much room, for more detailed, but no less important, disagreement.

The temptation at this point is to use authority rather than a painstaking return to fundamental methodology to achieve greater consensus. Appeal can be made to theology, or to long-standing custom, or to the impossibility of stepping outside the moral consensus in which one has been brought up, a consensus which must therefore in its broader outlines be allowed to go unchallenged. There are many authorities to which appeal can and has been made, some with more claim to credibility than others. The mistake is to use the appeal to authority rather than reasoned argument, or to insist on the total primacy of what we take to be reasoned argument while paying no heed whatever to the accumulated wisdom of our own and past generations.

Select bibliography

Thomas Aquinas, *Summa Theologiae*, I-II, qq. 91–94; II-II, qq. 47–52.

Karl Barth, *Church Dogmatics*, II, 2 (Edinburgh: T. & T. Clark, 1957).

John Finnis, *Natural Law and Natural Rights* (Oxford: Oxford University Press, 1980).

Paul Helm (ed.), *Divine Commands and Morality* (Oxford: Oxford University Press, 1981).

Richard Kraut, *Aristotle on the Human Good* (Princeton: Princeton University Press, 1989).

3

Authority and moral teaching in a Catholic Christian context

Joseph Selling

The issue of authority and the sources of morality is a far-ranging one that will inevitably be treated differently by the different Christian churches. Some churches regard the Scriptures as the sole authority in every matter religious, others recognize the role played by philosophy and/or consensus in the formation of fundamental principles. Since there is a great deal of literature dealing with each of these perspectives, I will limit myself here to treating the issue of authority and moral teaching as it is perceived within the Roman Catholic community.

The question of authority and its role in the lives of individuals and groups of persons is not an exclusively ecclesiastical one. This simple observation points immediately to a rather significant problem that will plague any attempt to write about authority from a theological or moral perspective, namely that differing concepts of authority will be confusingly mingled in the mind of the reader. Police authority and parental authority might be posed as examples of different concepts of authority that most of us take for granted in our daily speech (although far too many parents exercise their authority as if they were police officers). We can add to these examples the notions of scientific authority (competence), judicial authority and political authority, none of which necessarily connote *moral* authority.

Using the word 'authority' will inevitably conjure up associations that can obscure moral theological discussion. When that discussion is carried out within the specific ecclesiological context of the Roman Catholic Church, we must exercise further caution for, although moral teaching certainly occupies an important place in church offices, this particular exercise of authority does not function in exactly the same way as other offices in the ecclesial body.

The teaching of Vatican II, especially that contained in the Dogmatic Constitution on the Church, *Lumen Gentium*, makes it clear that the episcopal pastors occupy the threefold office (mandate) to sanctify, to teach and to rule. In all three of these areas, the bishops exercise an authority that calls for different responses. The authority to rule addresses the question of jurisdiction which in turn calls for the response of obedience and possibly the threat of sanctions. The ruling function considers primarily the protection and the maintenance of the common good of the People of God. The authority to teach, on the other hand, addresses the question of truth, and even more specifically the truths of the faith. It primarily considers the integrity of the faith, and its aim is to convince the faithful to grasp and to accept the truths of the faith. The proper response here is not obedience but attentiveness.[1]

Too frequently people, even bishops, expect that obedience is owed to the teaching authority in an unqualified manner, neglecting the possibility that if one is not convinced of the truth – or relevance – of a teaching then the insistence on obedience may simultaneously oblige one to violate one's conscience.

Of course one will immediately object that not all teachings are of equal importance or equally binding with regard to acceptance, not just attentiveness. We will suspend the question whether this objection applies to moral teaching in particular and grant the fact that there are different levels of authority when it comes to the exercise of the teaching office in the Church. Unfortunately, these different levels, sometimes referred to as a 'hierarchy of truths',[2] are not always made clear to the faithful, perhaps because the distinction between the levels and the proper assignment of various, individual truths to one of these levels remains in dispute.

Dogma, doctrine and discipline (teaching)

I suggest that the traditional distinction that has been made between the primary and secondary objects of authoritative teaching[3] should be extended to encompass a third category. What has generally been referred to as the primary object of authoritative teaching is held to be coextensive with revelation, that is, the deposit of faith contained in Scripture and (apostolic) tradition. These constitute dogmas and they are essential to the faith, pertaining to salvation, and frequently put forth with a christological focus. With the Orthodox churches we could easily extend this general body of truths to the teachings of the first seven ecumenical councils and to the creeds, most of which are synonymous with conciliar teaching.

The secondary objects of authoritative teaching constitute a more problematic area that was not clearly defined either at Vatican I or Vatican

II. There is a general consensus, however, that this 'class of truths' includes those things which are indispensable for the maintenance of revelation, such as the condemnation of propositions that would contradict revelation or a statement of those things that would necessarily flow from revelation.[4]

It seems rather clear that there are a great number of items that would fall into neither of these categories and which, up until now, have been given no clear designation. Whereas dogmas are understood to be the object of authoritative definitions and must be accepted by one who considers oneself to be a member of the Church, and doctrines are generally considered to be 'theologically certain' if not actually irreformable, there are a significant number of 'teachings' that may be more or less important but for which there is no clear measure. My suggestion is that we attempt to delineate a category of teachings that would not so much seek to exhaust what should be contained in this body of statements or propositions as it would, by default, exclude an entire range of things that have nothing to do with ecclesiastical pronouncement.[5]

I propose that the majority of church teaching that fits this category has traditionally been referred to as *discipline*, meaning practices, habits or a manner of living, sometimes associated with the Latin term *mores*. In a theological context, these practices or disciplines frequently have an explicitly religious character. One thinks, for instance, of sacramental and liturgical practice. Sacramental discipline would include factors ranging from the time, style and manner of celebrating a sacrament to the determination of conditions necessary for its reception. Most of these elements have little or nothing to do with revelation, yet they do enjoy a certain level of importance, for both the individual and the community, and are thus the object of authoritative teaching. That said, it is clear that being the object of authoritative teaching does not *ipso facto* imply absoluteness, certainty or unchangeability.

There is also an entire range of things, however, which are not explicitly or evidently religious in character but which are relevant to what we could call the object of authoritative teaching (i.e., that which falls within the competence of the office to teach). This encompasses that broad field we call 'morality' and, at first sight, touches upon just about every facet of our lives.

'Levels' of moral teaching

Some aspects of the moral life enjoy virtually universal consensus among Christians and are thus taken for granted. It is not merely coincidental that these areas of consensus are congruent with Christian dogmas and church doctrine, intimately tied up with revelation. The most obvious example are the dictates of the Decalogue. Most people would be startled to hear us say that the Church teaches the Ten Commandments authoritatively, even infallibly. Yet the fact is that even the Decalogue needs to be *taught*, something that constitutes a primary function of the Church, exercised not only by the hierarchy but by every member of the faithful.

Less obvious examples of moral teaching that would constitute church doctrines are those things that are essential to, flow from or are necessary to protect revelation. The doctrine of free will, for example, is not explicitly stated in revelation, nor is the doctrine of grace, and the entire question of justification remains a lively debate among the Christian churches. The rejection of predestination is a doctrine that has great, if subtle, significance for Christian morality. Yet few of us ever think about any of these issues that continue to be taught – authoritatively – by the Church. We take for granted that the pastors of the Church, the hierarchy, can, do, and must continue to exercise this teaching office, lest the community of the People of God drift away from the truth (integrity) of revelation.

Church *doctrine* in the area of morality, therefore, contains statements, propositions, or more accurately *convictions* that are widely, if unconsciously, taken for granted among the faithful and are even frequently recognized by non-members as characteristic of the Christian community. Christians, for instance, are expected to pray together and worship at some fairly predictable regularity, although how and when this is actually done is a matter of practice (discipline). Christians are the kind of people who marry for life, although again how this doctrine is applied to particular situations is again a matter of practice. It is Christian *doctrine* that forgiveness and reconciliation are essential aspects of justice, but how this is worked out in practice remains very much under the influence of social, cultural, political, economic and ideological factors.[6]

All these aspects of Christian (church) doctrine contribute to the very character of the community and hence to its individual members who are expected to be attentive to and to accept what we might here call the basic tenets of that community. While these tenets together define the community, or more properly describe the community we call the Church, they are not necessarily exclusive to the Christian churches, especially as individual elements. There are those, for instance, who would subscribe to the notion that marriage is a life-long commitment but who would experience no tendency or compulsion to pray in community. That is, even in the area of doctrine, Christians do not have an exclusive claim to the individual aspects of what may constitute moral life.

Natural morality

The idea that persons can live morally without having an explicit knowledge of revelation comes as no surprise to the Christian who already has the benefit of that revelation. Following Jesus' own teaching, St Paul observes that all persons are capable of doing what is prescribed 'in the law' even if they have never known 'the law', because what is essential to the law is written in their hearts (Rom 2:14–15). It is part of Christian doctrine that human persons are capable of coming to a knowledge of what is true and what is good, that they can recognize truth and goodness because of their very being.[7]

This is sometimes referred to as natural morality because it is available to all human beings, regardless of their culture, faith or religious convictions. The leaders of the Catholic community have always claimed a competence to teach *about* natural morality or the conviction *that there is* a natural morality. Some have even gone so far as to claim a competence to expound upon the *content* of natural morality. This, however, appears to be taking a step too far, and the countless historical examples of the overextension of such claims should make us very cautious. What has been 'taught' (as a matter of discipline, not doctrine, according to the distinction proposed) about slavery, usury, or the divine right of kings is now recognized as being culturally and historically specific. At some time, it was important for everyone, including institutions such as the church, to have some position on these issues. Taking a position on something, however, was not equivalent to, nor should it be confused with, incorporating that position into the essence of what it means to be a believing person (dogma and doctrine). Even more fundamentally, as long as any given position with respect to natural morality has no demonstrable connection with revelation, there is no guarantee that such a position exhibits any inherent truth value. In most areas of natural morality, church leaders enjoy no more – or less – competence than any other intelligent or wise persons on most issues.

The exception to this observation rests in any possible connection that an issue of natural morality might have with revelation. There are some who hypothesize that the Decalogue represents the specific revelation of (the) propositions of natural morality that *a fortiori* now enjoy the status of certain truth. This is a convenient argument for those who are wedded to the notion that morality must be deductive in argumentation from some set of first principles. Nevertheless, the burden of proof still rests with those who claim that their conclusions are contained in the principles themselves.

At various times in history, claims have been made for virtually absolute certainty being attached to some interpretations of natural morality. Using the Decalogue as a starting point, taking for instance the sixth commandment, 'Thou shalt not commit adultery', enthusiastic logicians have deduced the moral status of everything from non-marital sexual encounter to dress codes to in-vitro fertilization. Few have questioned the warrant for this type of reasoning, presuming a kind of blanket authority exercised by the hierarchy of the Church to explain and pronounce upon natural morality. The reasoning goes that as God is the creator, God is the author of natural morality; those who do the work of God are therefore somehow authorized to interpret this natural morality. Occasionally this argument goes so far as to claim complete competence with regard to what it calls the 'natural law'.

If one reasons from a position that is unaware of being immersed in a relatively specific culture at a particular time in history, it is easy to overlook that the vast majority of so-called interpretations of what is 'natural', and hence somehow proper or fitting for the natural law, are little more than the expressions of a particular ethos or even a political ideology.[8] Through history, church leaders have condemned as 'unnatural' such items as using an umbrella, eating with utensils, giving vaccinations or even practising democracy, not to mention more sinister positions that have been taken on the inequality of the races or the 'natural subordination' of women to men.

Appealing to the 'natural law' in order to construct a moral position will always be at best questionable and open to the accusation of self-justification. Such an approach is typical of legalism and rationalism, both of which have infected Catholic moral theology since its delineation as a separate discipline during the counter-reformation.[9] Furthermore, it contradicts the philosophical and political roots of natural law theory that was, somewhat ironically, instigated as an argument against authority. In ancient Greek philosophy, the 'natural law' was invoked as a 'higher authority' to challenge reigning political structures.[10] In medieval philosophy it became an argument for the possibility of the universal knowledge of good and evil, very close to the Pauline text referred to above. Thomas Aquinas defined the natural law as the person's 'rational participation in the eternal law' and set forth its definition with the simple dictum, 'do good and avoid evil'.[11]

Up to this point, the 'natural law' functioned as a court of appeal or a stimulus for investigation. It had no content, *per se*, and needed to be 'fleshed out' with reason; in Thomas's scheme guided by the virtue of right reason itself, prudence.[12] In fact, I would suggest that the position of Aquinas was very close to what is today referred to as 'autonomous ethics', although the lack of cultural pluralism in his environment still makes it difficult to picture him within this school of thought.

Only slowly did 'the natural law' become a repository for moral norms. As stated above, the content usually assigned to this 'law' very much resembled dominant ethnic practices. This does not disqualify the validity or even the normative character of that content, because the aggregate of social expectations within which we live more or less constitutes, or at least reflects, the concrete material (descriptive) norms that are operative on the moral level. What is distressing about assigning these things to the 'natural' law is that it invests these norms with a character of unchangeability and absoluteness that is not only inappropriate but actually antithetical to their purpose. This is compounded by the assignment of authoritative status when these norms are taken up into a body of 'official' teaching, such as that proposed by the hierarchical magisterium of the Church.

The problem of the relationship between authoritative teaching and natural morality remains a delicate one. It is, furthermore, a problem that will not be solved by 'authoritative pronouncement'.[13]

Non-propositional moral teaching

Especially since the first Vatican Council in 1870, there has been a tendency to think of the exercise of authority in the Church as concentrated in the hands of the hierarchy alone, the pope and the bishops. This is so pervasive that even the term 'magisterium', a term that was traditionally used of learned persons and teachers,[14] has come to be virtually identified with membership in the hierarchy. Some correction to this idea was accomplished at Vatican II which restored a more balanced understanding of the Church as the 'People of God'. The Church is first and foremost a community; God relates to and reveals to a community. Therefore, no amount of papal or episcopal hegemony can claim exclusive access to the truth about God and the mystery of the relationship of God to humankind, an experience that is primarily set in the context of the entire People of God.

The exercise of authority in the Church as the People of God, therefore, does not rest solely in the hands of the episcopacy, although as we shall see the bishops remain the only persons in the Church who can lay claim to being *official* teachers. The authoritativeness of any deed or statement, furthermore, is inextricably tied up with the nature and the mission of the Church as the People of God, formed by the Word of God and shaped by apostolic tradition. Therefore, any claim to authoritative action or teaching in the Church is bound up with revelation. It 'extends as far as extends the deposit of divine revelation, which must be religiously guarded and faithfully expounded' (*LG*, n. 25).

One must carefully distinguish various degrees of connection with revelation before one can assign any level of authority to a given statement of the magisterium. Before we look at that, however, it is good to remind ourselves that the entire issue of exercising authority within the Church has tended to become highly intellectual. When one refers to the exercise of authority, one almost spontaneously thinks of members of the hierarchy making statements or issuing decrees (encyclicals, constitutions, exhortations, instructions, and so forth). Our notion of authoritative gestures has become highly propositional and almost one-sidedly preoccupied with intellectual content. Authority is exercised by making statements. This is not so much a wrong concept of the exercise of authority as it is a much too narrow one. It looks exclusively at the content of our faith without looking at its meaning and implications.

Jesus exercised authority, recognized even by his opponents and sceptics, not by formulating propositions or issuing statements. More often than not, his verbal communication was in the form of parables and exhortations that puzzled and challenged rather than explained. His most profound impact was made by what he did and how he lived. His 'authority' was expressed and exercised with actions: performing miracles, casting out devils, dying and rising from the dead. His primary means of communication we would today call his *witness* to the truth rather than his 'statement of truths'. This witness was and is constituted by the way in which one lives. For how one lives reflects what one truly believes, and the style of living one exhibits testifies to one's commitment to those beliefs.

We must not forget the intimate connection between the exercise of authority and the convincing power of one's witness through action. At the same time, when it comes to the exercise of authority in matters of morality, we should not forget that the issues being addressed also have to do with how one lives, the development of a lifestyle. An authoritative statement about Christian morality, that is, one that draws its convincing character from its connection with revelation (Scripture and tradition), addresses the question of the appropriateness of particular lifestyles – as a whole and in their individual aspects – for a person or persons who claim to believe in the message of the gospel and the revelation that is Jesus Christ.

To ask the question 'What is an appropriate way of living or an appropriate way of doing things for one who professes and shares faith with the People of God?' then, it is first necessary to consult the meaning of that faith as it is carried through time and place by the believing community – the Church. This necessitates a twofold sensitivity, one to the roots of our faith in Scripture and tradition and the other to the contemporary expression of that faith in our historical and cultural context.

Both elements must be present if our faith is to be visible through our lifestyle and our particular gestures. It is this question of appropriateness that is addressed with and through authority within the community we call the Church.

To authoritatively make an assessment, formulate a judgement, or pronounce a statement about the way of doing things must be traceable to the life of Jesus as reference point for the entire community, the *whole* People of God (Matt 5:17: 'I come not to abolish the law and the prophets but to fulfill them'). All authoritative statements are somehow tied to revelation: Scripture and tradition. This does not mean that we have to find identical or even similar events or gestures in the Scriptures before we can have a competent opinion about a particular issue; nothing in the life of Jesus or the early Christian community even came near the question of organ donation and transplantation. Nor does it mean that if we happen to find a particular gesture in the Scriptures we need to imitate it slavishly; to implement St Paul's teachings about slaves or women would be rather imprudent, to say the least. Tracing our moral stance back to revelation means that it must reflect that spirit or attitude of the teaching (witness) of Jesus. We are called to live in the love of God and love of neighbour. Thus, when a statement or judgement demonstrates that a particular manner of acting is compatible or not with the all-encompassing commandment to love, it takes a stand on what would be considered 'appropriate' for those who call themselves Christians.

By the same token, to authoritatively pronounce on the appropriateness of a given lifestyle or gesture, we must be sensitive to the cultural and historical context within which we express ourselves. The missionary zealotry that took place during the colonial period of Western civilization should have taught us a lesson about separating out moral demands from cultural expectations. How much of Western European culture was spread throughout the world in the name of Christianity? Even 'at home' however, we must be careful to be sensitive to the historical evolution of concrete behavioural prescriptions. One need only think of the teaching of Pius XI in his famous encyclical 'On Christian Marriage', *Casti Connubii* (1930). The roles of man and woman described for married life in that document may have been appropriate for the pre-war North Atlantic world, but they would hardly be appropriate teaching today.

Authority and normative ethics

The twofold sensitivity that is necessary for carrying on the enterprise of moral teaching is reflected in the practical distinction between formal, attitudinal norms that point to the exercise of virtue in moral life, and concrete, behavioural norms that describe human activity and signal the real or potential presence of good and evil. The authority of the formal or fundamental norms is the most certain because of its link with the core of Christian faith itself that specifically addresses attitude or disposition. Called to love God and love our neighbour as ourselves, we recognize this call to love being applied in the many facets of human life, especially life in community. Love applied to human relations is commonly referred to as justice; love applied to human sexuality is chastity. Love applied to communication is called honesty and a loving attitude toward commitment is called faithfulness. In other words, love applied to all sorts of human endeavour reveals the virtues: be kind, generous, patient, and so forth (1 Cor 13). The authority of the fundamental norms is the authority of revelation itself and those who pronounce such statements can claim this authority with confidence, knowing that they are servants of the source and not its creator. Those who hear the exhortation to a virtuous life respond not to the speaker but to the source itself, for 'God is love' (1 John 4:7–8).

It is quite a different story for the more explicit, concrete norms that describe specific human behaviour which always takes place in a cultural and historical context. Exactly what authority such statements might carry is dependent not simply on a demonstrable connection with the faith but also upon a consensus within the (Christian) community about the appropriateness of various forms of behaviour. Here it is clear that we need to use the utmost caution lest we overextend the claims to authoritative pronouncement or underestimate the importance of some behaviours purely on the basis of their representing cultural conventions. These are two of the dangers to be avoided in elaborating material norms.

On the first count, we could offer the example of some interpretations of the so-called natural law that claimed a hierarchy of persons based upon non-specifying differences within the human condition. As we read in *Gaudium et Spes*, 'every type of discrimination, whether social or cultural, whether based on sex, race, colour, social condition, language or religion, is to be overcome and eradicated as contrary to God's intent' (*GS*, n. 29). There have been some instances in the past in which the pretence of religious authority was used to enforce discriminatory practices as though they were willed by God.

On the other side, we should be wary of complacency toward some form of behaviour simply because it constitutes 'common practice'. One could again refer to many forms of discrimination in social living, but a good alternative would be the way in which various societies tolerate the violation of social expectations. Tolerance shown to political corruption, the practice of avoiding reasonable taxes, or the negligent breaking of traffic laws all constitute specific forms of behaviour that have an important relevance to the whole of social living. Arguing that such behaviour is 'commonplace' does not justify its perpetration. The believer must always ask whether such behaviour is really appropriate for one who claims to believe in and live the good news of the gospel.

Teaching authority and morality

Clearly, however, it is neither realistic nor possible for each and every member of the faithful – not to mention every member of society – to assess every possible form of behaviour or even come to grips with the appropriateness of a given attitude or disposition. (How, for instance, does one distinguish righteous anger from revenge, especially when one is the victim of injustice?) Fortunately, it is not necessary for us to approach the vast majority of moral issues from scratch, as it were, because we have available to us a tremendous heritage of moral wisdom. This wisdom contains insights, observations, practical rules, and tools for moral assessment and calculation that help us develop lifestyles and guide us in making moral decisions that are appropriate for living out the faith.

A person who considers himself or herself to be Christian will define their life at the most fundamental level as being a child of God, redeemed by Christ and participant in the entire People of God. A Catholic Christian (NB: not to the exclusion of others) further recognizes that the means for encounter with God encompass not only the written Scriptures but also the apostolic – episcopal – tradition, transmitted through the ages via the entire community of believers.

It resides in the office of the bishop as apostolic successor in communion with all other bishops to safeguard and teach the faith. To the extent that the bishops teach the faith on behalf of the community of the People of God, this teaching is rightly referred to as authoritative. The authority that this teaching carries is not the personal authority of the individual exercising the office but rather the authority of the source of this teaching. Insofar as various teachings can be related to the (deposit of) faith,[15] they call upon the faithful to accept these teachings as essential for membership in the community of the People of God.

When the bishops teach *dogma*, the very essentials of the faith itself, the authority they exercise is the same as the dogmas: every member of the faithful must accept these dogmas if they are to count themself as members of the faithful. When the bishops teach *doctrines*, they enunciate items that have been found to be dependent upon, flowing from or necessary for the protection of the faith, and the authority of these teachings is proportionate to their essential connection with the faith.

However, when the bishops teach about *discipline* or the practices of

Christians deemed to be appropriate for followers of Jesus Christ, they enter a realm of statements and gestures that may or may not have a significant connection with the gospel. Before one can assess the authority of any specific instance of this form of teaching, one is obliged to assess and/or demonstrate its connection with what it means to call oneself a Christian.

The area of day-to-day teaching or discipline (*mores*) is so vast that it is nearly impossible to predict the 'authoritative' value of any specific teaching in advance. While some positions taken by the Church echo a clear consensus not only among the vast majority of the faithful but also throughout significant periods of history, other areas of human conduct are so new and some so complex that it is difficult to discern any clear consensus even within the episcopacy. One thinks immediately about issues in bioethics, but I suggest that there are even larger areas of conduct that exhibit subtle but extremely complex issues about which it is extraordinarily difficult to achieve any clear consensus, especially when social, cultural, political and economic factors continuously and interactively influence human behaviour.

A typical example of such an issue would be the stewardship of human fertility. Since the human community has acquired a significant if not yet comprehensive knowledge of the intricacies of human fertility, not only the respect for this God-given gift but its management becomes the object of human responsibility. This responsibility applies not only to the individual couple but also to the whole community: the medical community, demographers, social scientists, socio-economic policy makers, educators, even agriculturalists.

Clearly the Church as the People of God has something to say about these issues; but, because of the broad scope of the issues themselves, what it says cannot be limited to the behaviour of the individual (couple). Any statement about the regulation of fertility that does not take sufficient account of the multi-dimensionality of this vital human issue will be less than credible because such a statement will not reflect the complexity of the real question at hand.

It is not our purpose to investigate a particular question of moral teaching, although some may recognize here one of the more intense issues in recent Roman Catholic moral teaching that has failed to achieve consensus among a meaningful portion of the faithful. The crisis caused by the controversy over the teaching of *Humanae Vitae* (1968) has burdened the teaching authority of the Church with a legacy it has not been able to overcome for nearly thirty years. Many have suggested that the greatest setback that resulted from the controversy over fertility regulation is the harm done to the credibility of the teaching authority itself.

Be that as it may, I propose that the authority to teach in the area of morality within the context of the believing community is intimately tied to the matter being taught. When this matter involves the fundamental truths of the faith, dogma, that authority extends as far as the truths themselves which constitute what we call revelation, Scripture and tradition. When the matter of teaching involves non-revealed truths, doctrine, its authority is proportionately related to the degree of connection with revelation or the need for such a teaching to protect the integrity of revelation. It goes without saying that already at this level we should be aware of the real possibility for change to take place through time and culture.

When it comes to questions that exhibit little or no clear connection with the content of revelation – what is essential for the faith – we must admit of a very broad scope to the claims for authoritativeness on particular issues. Especially when this competence (skill) is applied to the huge area of what is called 'natural morality', extreme caution should be exercised by the subjects (holders, authors, instigators) of authority lest they mistake as a 'vital issue' something that is little more than a social, cultural, or anthropological phenomenon. To cite a now ridiculous example, arguing whether or not it may be natural for a human being to fly is only a little removed from whether or not it is natural for kings to control the lives of their peasant subjects, and actually not very much further removed from claims for any 'natural' way in which human persons 'should' pursue and live out human relationships.

With respect to what have been referred to above as behavioural (material) norms, the crucial question appears to be whether the development and maintenance of particular lifestyles (including their component parts) are indeed appropriate for one who calls oneself a Christian, a follower of Jesus Christ and participant member of the People of God. The answer to this question cannot be found in official statements or rulings of the hierarchy alone, for these have been shown to be influenced by historical and cultural factors that militate against absolute claims to certainty. In order to determine the appropriateness of human behaviour to the message of the gospel it would seem inescapable that we need to consult those who are committed to living their lives in the faith – the People of God.

Finally, what can be taught 'authoritatively' in these areas (discipline, teaching, natural morality) needs to exhibit the three characteristics of credibility, communicability and conviction. These are the pillars that support the authoritativeness of common (day-to-day) moral teaching, even within the Church. Without these elements, no amount of insistence will render something credible, make it more communicable or ensure its ability to convince. Especially in the area of 'natural morality' we must realize that the argument from authority is always the weakest.

Notes

1 See Charles E. Curran, 'The teaching function of the Church in morality' in C. E. Curran (ed.), *Moral Theology: Challenges for the Future – Essays in Honor of Richard A. McCormick* (New York: Paulist Press, 1990), pp. 155–78 (p. 162).

2 See Avery Dulles, 'The hierarchy of truths in the Catechism', *The Thomist* 58 (1994), pp. 369–88.

3 See Francis A. Sullivan, *Magisterium: Teaching Authority in the Catholic Church* (New York: Paulist Press, 1983), pp. 127–52.

4 An example of the former would be the condemnation of certain philosophical categories being applied to Christian doctrine, such as gnosticism. An example of the latter would be the notion of the efficacy or merit of human action.

5 I have developed this idea historically and in more detail in 'The authority of church teaching in matters of morality' in F. Vosman and K. Merks (eds), *Aiming at Happiness: The Moral Teaching of the Catechism* (Kampen: Kok/Pharos, 1996), pp. 194–221.

6 Note that we can make a distinction between forgiveness and pardon, neither of which necessarily implies the other. We can forgive a murderer but refuse to pardon the murderer from punishment. Contrarily, we can pardon someone – dismiss the consequent punishment 'due' to their crime – without forgiving them, say for the sake of the peace of the community.

7 Some would say that this characteristic of being human is attributed to our being created in the image and likeness of God; others say it has to do with human nature. The verbal and philosophical vehicles of expression are mere variations of what must be a primary human experience.

8 An interesting review of some specific topics that have been dealt with as moral issues in the past can be found in Bernard Hoose, *Received Wisdom? Reviewing the Role of Tradition in Christian Ethics* (London: Geoffrey Chapman, 1994).

9 The legalism of classical textbook moral theology was introduced by the canon lawyers who became the first, predominantly Spanish, 'moral theologians' after the Council of Trent. Rationalistic influences were introduced later, as the textbook tradition underwent a revival in the second half of the nineteenth century.

10 The classic example of this appeal is found in Sophocles' *Antigone*.

11 *Bonum est faciendum et prosequendum et malum vitandum*: *Summa Theologiae*, I-II, q. 94, ad 2.

12 The way in which Thomas described the work of prudence would today be familiar to a number of theories of conscience. For Thomas himself, 'conscience' was not very important, signifying merely an act of the intellect giving assent to the findings of reason informed not only by faith but by syndereisis – an anomalous concept that has disappeared today because of our richer understanding of the human mind and our greater appreciation for what we now call conscience.

13 It is perhaps interesting to note that when the encyclical of Pope Paul VI on the regulation of births, *Humanae Vitae*, was issued in July 1968, the press officer of the Vatican who introduced the papal letter to the world, Msgr Lambruschini, was careful to point out that the 'more fundamental questions of natural moral law' are neither discussed nor resolved by this decision. See 'Conférence de presse de Mgr. Lambruschini, tenue à Rome le 29 juillet 1968' in P. Delhaye, J. Grootaers and G. Thils, *Pour Relire Humanae Vitae: Déclarations épiscopales du monde entier* (Gembloux: Duculot, 1970), pp. 183–4.

14 Very important work has been done in this area by Yves Congar OP, who has written two virtually classic articles on the subject in *Revue des sciences philosophiques et théologiques* 60 (1976): 'Pour une histoire sémantique du term "Magisterium"', pp. 85–98, and 'Bref historique des formes du "magistère" et de ses relations avec les docteurs', pp. 99–112. These have been translated into English in Charles E. Curran and Richard A. McCormick (eds), *Readings in Moral Theology*, no. 3: *The Magisterium and Morality* (New York: Paulist Press, 1982) as 'A semantic history of the term "Magisterium"', pp. 297–313, and 'A brief history of the forms of the "Magisterium" and its relations with scholars', pp. 314–31. For a wider background to these studies, see also Congar's *Tradition and Traditions: An Historical and Theological Essay* (London: Burns & Oates, 1966), originally published in two parts as *La Tradition et les Traditions: Essai Historique* (1960), *Essai Théologique* (1963).

15 The classical phrase 'deposit of faith' refers to the totality of what we as the People of God believe. As it stands, this expression gives the impression of being almost entirely propositional and hence not entirely apt for a description of the moral life which includes more 'gestures' than statements.

Select bibliography

Charles E. Curran and Richard A. McCormick (eds), *Readings in Moral Theology*, no. 3: *The Magisterium and Morality* (New York: Paulist Press, 1982), especially articles by Yves Congar, 'A semantic history of the term "Magisterium"', pp. 297–313, and 'A brief history of the forms of the "Magisterium" and its relations with scholars', pp. 314–31.

Piet F. Fransen, 'A short history of the meaning of the formula *fides et mores*', *Louvain Studies* 7 (1979), pp. 270–301.

Joseph A. Selling, 'The authority of church teaching in matters of morality' in F. Vosman and K. Merks (eds), *Aiming at Happiness: The Moral Teaching of the Catechism* (Kampen: Kok/Pharos 1996).

Francis A. Sullivan, *Magisterium: Teaching Authority in the Catholic Church* (New York: Paulist Press, 1983), pp. 127–52.

4

Absolute moral norms

Charles E. Curran

Are there moral norms that are always and everywhere obligatory? Human beings in general and Christians, as well as philosophers and theologians, have continuously grappled with this issue but the question has become more intense in the last decades as some previously accepted moral norms have been questioned.

The question needs to be nuanced and put into proper perspective. Almost all would agree that some absolute and universally binding norms exist. For example, those against murder, lack of respect for persons, cheating, harming another merely to indulge one's own sense of superiority. Such absolute norms are either formal (murder by definition is unjustified killing) or very general (justice is to be done) or quite qualified and include relatively few actions (harming others to indulge one's own sense of superiority is unacceptable). The controversy today in the churches often involves concrete, specific, unqualified absolute norms.

Most often ethicians discuss this question of absolute norms from the perspective of personal morality but this study will also consider the social dimensions of the issue. However, these two aspects should never be totally separated.

The Christian approach has generally recognized four different sources of moral wisdom and knowledge – Scripture, tradition, reason and experience. Norms have been grounded in these sources with most emphasis going to the Scriptures and human reason. Protestant approaches have given greater emphasis to the role of Scripture whereas Roman Catholic authors have appealed primarily to reason, with the Anglican tradition often appealing to both Scripture and reason.

Personal perspectives

The Scriptures have often served as the basis for absolute moral norms and laws for Christians. The Ten Commandments constitute the best known moral teaching found in the Bible. Many catechisms and discussions of Christian morality have followed the schema of the Ten Commandments. Although all Christians accept the Ten Commandments, diversity exists in the numbering of the individual commandments. The differences concern the first commandments and the last commandments. The Greek tradition and most Protestants make the prohibition of false gods the first commandment and the prohibition of false images the second commandment while combining in the tenth commandment the coveting of the neighbour's wife and goods. The Catholic and Lutheran traditions follow a slightly different version putting the prohibition of false images under the first commandment's prohibition of false gods and making the coveting of the neighbour's wife the ninth commandment and the coveting of the neighbour's goods the tenth commandment. Not all the Ten Commandments constitute absolute prohibitions as illustrated in the commandment against killing. Christians generally recognize some circumstances in which killing can be accepted albeit reluctantly. However, some absolute norms such as the prohibition of adultery have been based on Scripture.

Before the critical study of the Bible in the nineteenth century most Christians understood the moral teaching of the Bible as the commands of God for all times and places. Fundamentalists still interpret the Bible in this way. Scripture scholars and moral theologians in the mainstream Protestant and Catholic churches today recognize that the teachings of the Bible are historically, culturally and socially conditioned. We live in different circumstances and situations and consequently what was accepted as true in a particular book of the Bible written in different times and places might not be true in our changed situation today.

One good illustration concerns the submission and obedience of wives to husbands as found in the 'household codes' best illustrated in Galatians 3:18 – 4:1 and Ephesians 5:22 – 6:9. Fundamentalists and some conservative Christians still see the obedience and submission of the wife as a biblical norm continuing to be true in our day. Those who accept the more critical approach to the Scriptures see these household codes as expressions of the patriarchy of the time and no longer binding in the changed circumstances of our times.

The present controversy about homosexuality in practically all the Christian churches illustrates the different ways in which Christians interpret the Scriptures. Until the late 1960s Christian churches were unanimous in their condemnation of homosexual acts and in their recognition of a biblical basis for this condemnation. The 'holiness code' in Leviticus (18:22 and 20:13) twice condemns homosexual acts. Christians generally interpreted the famous story of the town of Sodom related in Genesis 19:4–11 as the destruction of the city by God because of its great sinfulness as shown in homosexuality. The Christian Scriptures contain three apparently direct condemnations of homosexuality (Rom 1:27; 1 Cor 6:9–10; 1 Tim 1:9–10).

Today, however, some Christians do not see in the Scriptures a condemnation of homosexual acts between a committed homosexual couple. Homosexual acts within the context of a loving relationship between two homosexually oriented persons can be morally good. In dealing with the scriptural evidence, supporters of such a position first point out that the Sodom story does not understand the destruction of the city as caused by the sin of homosexuality, thus lessening the great heinousness which had supposedly been connected with homosexual acts. The Scriptures do assume that homosexual acts are wrong but this does not seem to be a major concern of any biblical writer in either the Old or the New Testament. In addition, no arguments are given of a theological or ethical nature to explain why these acts are wrong. In the New Testament there is also a problem in the translation of the Greek. The Greek in 1 Corinthians 6:9 and 1 Timothy 1:10 probably does not refer to general homosexual behaviour but may mean only male prostitution connected with idolatry. In interpreting the meaning of the Scriptures for us today one recognizes the great cultural, historical and social differences between the biblical times and our own. The biblical traditions and writers knew nothing about homosexuality as an orientation or a condition. They were thus talking about heterosexual persons engaged in homosexual acts. Consequently, the Scriptures do not necessarily condemn homosexual acts between two homosexually oriented persons in a committed relationship.

This is not the place to enter into the discussion of the merits of both sides, the purpose is merely to show the difficulty some Christians have today in finding in the Scripture a law forbidding homosexual acts between committed homosexual persons. Some evangelical Christians (e.g., Richard Mouw) still insist on seeing the moral life primarily in terms of the commands of God as found in the Scriptures but these commands constitute *prima facie* obligations. Precisely because of the differences between the biblical times and our own circumstances other aspects come into play that may override the presumption in favour of the biblical command. Thus at the very minimum, many Christian ethicists today recognize the difficulty of grounding specific, concrete, absolute moral norms in the teaching of the Scriptures.

Experience and especially human reason have often supported the grounding of absolute norms for philosophers (e.g., Immanuel Kant with his famous categorical imperative saying that I ought never to act in such a way that I could not also will that my maxim should be a universal law) and for Christian theologians and churches. The Roman Catholic tradition more than any other Christian tradition has developed its moral positions in the light of human reason and from this perspective has insisted on some absolute norms. The Catholic tradition has employed the theory of natural law to ground its norms. This theory is developed in greater detail in Chapter 2.

For our purposes natural law maintains that human reason reflecting on human nature can arrive at moral wisdom and knowledge. The Roman Catholic Church has recently been the scene for much discussion about the theory and practical conclusions of natural law. The official hierarchical teaching continues to employ a natural law method and defends absolute moral norms. With regard to very concrete, specific and unqualified norms the official Catholic teaching insists on the absolute condemnation of contraception, masturbation, direct sterilization and direct killing, on the basis of its natural law theory. So-called revisionist Catholic theologians and many non-Catholics object to many of these very specific and unqualified absolute norms.

The question of absolute norms has arisen especially in Roman Catholicism with regard to universally condemned actions which are described in terms of the physical structure of the act; for example, masturbation, contraception, and direct killing are always wrong. The condemnation of contraception by the pope insists that human beings can never interfere with the physical conjugal act. The sexual faculty has a twofold purpose – love union and procreation. Every sexual act must always be open to and expressive of these two purposes. Direct killing according to official Catholic teaching is an act which by the very nature of the act or the intention of the agent aims at killing either as a means or as an end. Note that 'direct' is determined by the physical structure and causality of the act. In the case of the dilemma of taking either the life of the mother or the life of the foetus (a case which in practice is very rare indeed) one cannot directly kill the foetus to save the mother. Such a killing is direct because the act is specifically aimed or targeted at the foetus as a means to save the mother. One can, however, remove a cancerous uterus which contains a foetus because here the physical act is aimed at the cancerous uterus and does not directly kill the foetus. The instances where the moral act is described solely in terms of the physical structure of the act concern mostly sexual and medical ethics.

The question arises why such cases seem to be so different from other areas of morality. For the most part the Catholic moral tradition like other

Christian moral traditions has not identified the physical structure of the act with the moral act. Killing is a physical act. But not every killing is wrong. Not every act of false speech is a lie. The lying example provides helpful insight into the question under discussion. In this century some theologians began to question the accepted understanding of the malice of lying and proposed a solution which actually has roots in an even earlier Christian tradition. The accepted understanding in the beginning of the twentieth century understood the malice of lying to consist in the violation of the God-given purpose of the faculty of speech. The purpose of the faculty of speech is to put on my lips what is in my mind. To put on my lips what is in contradiction to what is in my mind is perverting the faculty of speech and is therefore going against its God-given purpose. Such an approach developed an elaborate casuistry of mental reservations to deal with conflict situations where telling the truth might be harmful.

The problem of needing to conceal the truth from someone who has no right to it or was going to abuse it occasioned a rethinking of the criterion of the malice of lying. The faculty of speech should not be isolated and considered in itself but rather seen as part of the human person who is related to other human persons. The malice of lying consists in the violation of my neighbour's right to truth. But if the neighbour has no right to truth then one may speak a falsehood which is not a lie. The 'physical' falsehood is not always a moral lie. The example not only illustrates the fact that the moral reality differs from the physical reality but underscores the problem with a moral criterion based on the nature and purpose of the faculty as seen in isolation from the person and the person's relationship with other persons.

The official Catholic teaching on sexuality also employs an approach based on the nature and purpose of the sexual faculty or power. Human sexuality exists for the twofold purpose of love union and procreation and consequently every sexual act must be both open to procreation and expressive of love union. Such an understanding grounds the condemnation of artificial contraception for spouses.

A word of caution is in order. Sometimes the physical and the moral are the same. The only human beings we know are physical and bodily human beings. However, one cannot *a priori* identify the human and the moral with the physical. The physical is only one aspect of the human and the moral. The ultimate moral or human judgement (I am using these two terms synonymously) must be inclusive of all aspects – the physical, the psychological, the social, the eugenic, the hygienic, and so forth. The moral or human judgement is the ultimate judgement which must balance off all the particular aspects of the human act such as the physical or the biological. Human nature cannot be reduced only to the physical or the biological.

Two other significant factors have lately affected the understanding of both human nature and human reason and have influenced the realization that concrete, specific, unqualified, absolute norms are hard to justify and ground – historicity and historical consciousness on the one hand and also the turn to the subject.

The emphasis on history contrasts with the emphasis on the givenness of nature which is basically the same throughout history and in all parts of the world. Historicity is much more aware of pluralism and diversity with regard to human beings. Historical consciousness grounded in such historicity tends to see the human in terms of the particular, the individual, the contingent and the developing. An older classicism understood the human more in terms of the immutable, the eternal, the unchanging, and often began its considerations with the essential definition of the reality that was always and everywhere true. Historical consciousness employs a more inductive methodology than the one-sided deductive approach of classicism. However, historical consciousness recognizes both continuity and discontinuity and rejects a total relativism or existentialism which emphasizes the present with no connection to the past and future and no relationships to others in the present. One can readily see how historicity and historical consciousness would make it more difficult to speak about unqualified, specific, absolute norms that are obliging in all cultures, times and circumstances.

The turn to the subject emphasizes the person not just as an object or nature but as a true subject of one's own existence. The person is a self-conscious subject who makes and shapes himself or herself in the course of history. Although limited by nature the subject is not totally determined by it. However, at times the person as subject and agent can interfere with the physical act or the physical purpose of the faculty for the good of the total person as such.

The two shifts to historical consciousness and to a greater focus on the subject have affected all ethical endeavours. These factors undergird the critical approach to the Scriptures which has already been discussed. Philosophical ethics, the vast field which bases ethics only on human reason, has also been affected by these two shifts. Three current developments in philosophical ethics which also influence moral theology or Christian ethics will be addressed – the very possibility of a universal morality, foundationalism, and the contemporary debate between deontological and teleological approaches.

First, in the light of historicity, greater pluralism, and growing diversity, some philosophers maintain that ethics are bound to a particular tradition and community and not necessarily universal. However, the mainstream Christian tradition with its emphasis on universality as illustrated in its understanding of God as the Creator of all and of

Charles E. Curran

Christian love as reaching out to all generally cannot accept such an approach denying any universality to morality.

Second, many philosophers today reject what they call foundationalism which claims there is one source or basis from which our understanding of ethics as well as our specific norms can be derived. Catholic natural law theory furnishes one illustration of foundationalism because it derives its total ethical theory about the human being as well as absolute norms from human nature. However, many who reject foundationalism still oppose relativism and accept some universal moral realities as true for all. These approaches use a more inductive methodology to arrive at some moral realities binding on all.

Third, in philosophical ethics as well as in theological ethics today many refer to the differences between the two principal methodologies concerning human actions which are described as deontological or teleological approaches. Deontology sees the moral life primarily in terms of duty, law and obligation. This position then is often associated with absolute norms. On the other hand, teleology understands the moral life in terms of ends or goals to be attained. One extreme form of teleology is consequentialism which bases morality only on the total consequences of a particular action. Such a total consequentialism maintains that good consequences could make exceptions in all moral norms. For example, infanticide or even incest might be morally acceptable in some rare circumstances because of the good consequences. However, the differences between these two approaches are not as great as first sight seems to indicate. On the one hand, many teleologists reject a total consequentialism and even some total consequentialists recognize the need for some rules or norms based on consequentialism. (A great debate exists in philosophical ethics between rule utilitarians and act utilitarians.) On the other hand, the vast majority of deontologists today who see duty or obligation as the primary consideration in morality stress that they are speaking about *prima facie* obligations which are open to some exceptions. However, many deontologists would be willing to recognize absolute norms which are of a more general or broad nature. Thus, there is no sharp opposition between deontologists insisting that all norms are absolute as opposed to consequentialists who are not willing to admit any kinds of norms.

Within Roman Catholicism at the present time one can identify three generic approaches to the question of absolute norms dealing with concrete, material behaviour. The official hierarchical teaching continues to employ the natural law approach with its emphasis on the purpose of the faculty in matters of sexuality. On this basis the hierarchical teaching authority continues to support the well-known teachings opposed to contraception, direct sterilization, artificial insemination, and *direct* killing. A second approach identified with Germain Grisez and John Finnis develops a different natural law approach based on human flourishing or integral human fulfilment. According to this approach there are certain basic human goods which human beings can never directly go against. While the theory disagrees with the emphasis on the nature of the faculty in the natural law theory of the hierarchical magisterium it comes to the same basic conclusions in practice.

A third approach, often called revisionist or proportionalist, disagrees to some extent with both the theory and the conclusions of the natural law theory proposed by the hierarchical magisterium. This theory distinguishes between moral evil and premoral (or physical or ontic) evil thus trying to avoid the danger of physicalism that seems to be present in the official hierarchical teaching. One can never intend premoral evil as an end but one can intend and do premoral evil as a means to an end provided there is a proportionate reason. Much discussion has ensued about the exact meaning of proportionate reason. Proponents of Catholic revisionism maintain they avoid the dangers of physicalism on the one hand and of total consequentialism on the other. I personally accept the Catholic revisionist position.

In conclusion the question of absolute moral norms is not the most important question for basic Christian ethics. Law in my judgement is not the most significant moral category. Morality should never be seen primarily in terms of a legal model but rather in terms of a relationality–responsibility model which sees the individual human person in multiple relationships with God, neighbour, world and self. In the context of this model great emphasis is given to the conversion or basic change of heart of the individual person together with the virtues or attitudes that should direct the Christian in daily life. Values constitute an important consideration in Christian ethics and laws should exist to protect these values. Law thus should never play the primary role in basic Christian ethics or in the moral life but laws do have a necessary place. Some laws will admit of exception while others are absolute. For example, most Christians recognize there are circumstances when the obligation of promise keeping is no longer morally required while the Christian community generally maintains an absolute prohibition of adultery.

The previous considerations have laid the groundwork for an understanding of absolute moral norms in moral theology. On a more general level there exist absolute moral values or principles or norms but as one becomes more specific the possibility of absolute, specific, unqualified norms decreases. Such a general understanding coheres with generally accepted understandings of logic. The greater the complexity and the specificity, the more difficult it is to claim that one moral value will not conflict with another. Confidentiality, for example, is a very important value based on a promise and a relationship to others. Physicians, for example, owe confidentiality to their patients. However, sometimes this obligation in specific instances can be overturned – for example, the demands of the common good or the good of another person such as the sexual partner of a person with AIDS. On the other hand, churches that celebrate the sacrament of penance insist on an absolute obligation of confidentiality on the part of the priest in order to protect the most important relationship of all – the penitent's relationship through the priest with a saving God.

In the thirteenth century in the Catholic tradition Thomas Aquinas made the same basic point about the move from the general to the more specific and complex. Thomas Aquinas makes an important distinction between the first principles of the natural law and the secondary principles. The first principles oblige always and everywhere, but Thomas usually refers to these first principles only as one is to act according to right reason and to do good and avoid evil. I do not think that any reasonable person would disagree with Aquinas. However, the conclusions of practical reason or the secondary principles of the natural law oblige *ut in pluribus* – as generally occurs but not always. Thomas Aquinas gives the example of the principle that deposits or something entrusted to another for safe-keeping must always be returned to the rightful owner. However, in some circumstances returning a deposit to the rightful owner may be irrational and even harmful. One should not return a sword to a drunk who is threatening to kill others. The basic reason proposed by Aquinas is that the more specific something becomes the more other circumstances are able to enter in and change what ordinarily should be done.

This section has tried to show both the need for some absolute norms in Christian ethics and also the reason why in the last decades many have questioned some of the existing absolute norms that have been traditionally held in some Christian churches. As pointed out, some Christians have challenged the absolute norm condemning homosexual acts between homosexual persons; many Catholics question the absolute norm condemning contraception for married couples. On the other hand, most Christians today still maintain that adultery is wrong. It might help to briefly indicate the reasons why adultery is wrong. Strong scriptural and traditional warrants exist for this condemnation. The experience of the Christian community today indicates strong support for the immorality of adultery. Reason points out the manifold bases and grounds for the condemnation of adultery since adultery involves an injury to one's spouse, a violation of one's own marriage commitment, and results in deleterious effects on the important institution of marriage. The second part of this book will discuss the question of absolute norms in the area of marriage, sexuality, divorce, truth, confidentiality, and euthanasia.

Social context

The discussion about absolute norms generally occurs only in the context of personal morality. But one must also consider here the context of social morality with the realization that no absolute dichotomy should exist between the personal and the social.

The Christian tradition in general and the Roman Catholic approach in particular have emphasized the importance of the common good. Human beings are not just isolated individuals but are social beings called to live together in civic and political community. The common good refers to shared or public values and interests which ultimately redound to the good of all the members of the community.

Such an understanding of society is opposed to individualism which sees the society as the sum total of individuals and also to collectivism which denies the legitimate needs and rights of individuals who are submerged in the collectivity. Individualism constitutes the major problem today.

Individualists pursue their own individual good or success (often understood in monetary terms) and have no concern for the common or public good of the community. I should be free to do my own thing and you should be free to do your own thing. The dangers of such an approach are obvious. Either civil society will be torn asunder or the strong and the fortunate will prevail.

Any theory of the common good asserts that a shared understanding of the requirements of justice and human rights is necessary for community and society. We must provide justice for all and ensure the basic human rights of all. But here too one must make sure that justice and human rights are not understood in a totally individualistic manner.

Human rights are both political or civil on the one hand, and economic or social on the other. Political and civil rights stress freedom from – the freedom of individuals from outside forces that are trying to restrict or restrain them. Thus we have freedom of religion, of the press, of association, of speech. But there are also social or economic rights. Every individual has the right to a basic minimum necessary for truly human existence – a right to food, clothing, shelter, and a basic level of health care. Both types of rights are necessary.

These basic human rights or common values will by definition tend to be somewhat broad and general. Likewise there will be much discussion about what such values or rights entail in practice. However, even the many particular disagreements within a given society on such issues indicate that a basic type of shared broad agreement still exists.

Some recent developments in Christian theological ethics, however, might seem at first sight to argue against any absolute norms of justice and rights in a given political community. Liberationist and feminist theologies point out there is no neutral, objective, universal reason but all of us are human subjects who are coming from different historical and social locations. Every human being brings with himself or herself their own experiences, to say nothing of that person's finitude, limitations and prejudices. The Western world and our understanding of it have been shaped by white males of an upper-class background. Consequently, not enough attention has been given to women or to those of other races and economic classes. The United States with its strong declaration of inalienable and fundamental human rights did not recognize the rights of African Americans and accepted slavery and second-class citizenship for Blacks for most of its history. Patriarchy dominated the Western world, relegating women to a subordinate role in society. The poor have been made invisible. Universal, neutral, objective reason does not really exist.

Liberation theologies begin with the location and experience of the oppressed – the poor, people of colour, and women – and take their subjective strivings for liberation seriously. In this light God is not an objective, detached observer of the human scene but God too is prejudiced and partial – in favour of the oppressed. In the liberationist perspective truth is not an abstract reality which is applied to particular issues. Rather, theology and ethics insist on the importance of praxis and reflection on praxis. Truth emerges from the experience of people striving for liberation and does not exist primarily as an abstract, objective reality.

In the light of the emphasis found in various liberation theologies one might conclude there is no possibility for any universality. But the vast majority of liberation theologians and ethicists while emphasizing social location and the experience of the oppressed do not want to deny universality. Liberation theologians in Latin America speak about a preferential option for the poor which is not exclusive but merely shows a preference. Feminist ethicists generally do not plead for an exclusive feminist society but recognize the need for all to be equal and share in the life of society.

Yes, social location and the recognition that we are not neutral, value-free, objective observers of the human scene are important insights in contemporary ethics of all kinds. However, most thinkers who start from a particular social location also recognize the need for some common morality and universal norms of justice and rights within the society. Without such commonly accepted principles of justice and rights there can be no true political community. Today we are much more conscious of the pluralism and diversity within political society. In addition, our world has witnessed the breakup of some political unities because of the diversity of language, ethnicity and culture. In the light of the greater diversity existing in most political societies today and in the light of an over-emphasis on individualism it is harder to recognize and agree on the common good of all. But without a common good involving absolute norms of justice and fundamental human rights there can be no political society.

Often the issue of norms and absolute norms or laws in basic Christian ethics has been emphasized and distorted. Norms of any type are not the primary concern of the discipline but they do have a place and a role. This chapter has attempted to explain both the need for norms in basic Christian ethics and the reasons why some absolute moral norms previously held in Christian communities have recently been challenged.

Select bibliography

Charles E. Curran and Richard A. McCormick (eds), *Readings in Moral Theology*, no. 7: *Natural Law and Theology* (New York: Paulist Press, 1991).

Germain Grisez and Russell Shaw, *Fulfillment in Christ: A Summary of Christian Moral Principles* (Notre Dame, IN: University of Notre Dame Press, 1991).

Bernard Hoose, *Proportionalism: The American Debate and Its European Roots* (Washington, DC: Georgetown University Press, 1987).

Richard J. Mouw, *The God Who Commands* (Notre Dame, IN: University of Notre Dame Press, 1990).

Jeffrey S. Siker, *Scripture and Ethics: Twentieth-Century Portraits* (New York: Oxford University Press, 1997).

5

Virtue ethics

James F. Keenan

Renewed interest in virtue ethics arises from a dissatisfaction with the way we do ethics today. Most discussions about ethics today consider major controversial actions: abortion, gay marriages, nuclear war, gene therapy, and so forth. These discussions basically dominate contemporary ethics. Many writers in this volume, in fact, belong to a variety of different schools of thought that measure whether a controversial human action is right or wrong.[1]

Virtue ethicists are different. We are not primarily interested in particular actions. We do not ask 'Is this action right?' 'What are the circumstances around an action?' or 'What are the consequences of an action?' We are simply interested in persons.

We believe that the real discussion of ethics is not the question 'What should I do?' but 'Who should I become?' In fact, virtue ethicists expand that question into three key, related ones: 'Who am I?' 'Who ought I to become?' 'How am I to get there?'[2]

Who am I?

No question is more central for ethics than 'Who am I?' It is the foundational question.[3] When we know who we are, we know where we need to improve. To the virtue ethicist, the question ethically, then, is the same as 'How virtuous am I?' This is because, as Thomas Aquinas writes, every moral question can be reduced to the consideration of the virtues.[4]

The answer is found by two major considerations. First, 'What standards am I to measure myself against?' Second, 'How will I know whether I am measuring fairly?' For the first question, two of the most important works in ethics attempt to assist us by naming the basic virtues. In the *Nicomachean Ethics*, Aristotle gives us eleven different virtues that are necessary for helpful citizens of whatever society we belong to. Friendship, magnanimity, practical wisdom are some of these. In Part II of the *Summa Theologiae*, Thomas Aquinas takes from Plato, Cicero, Ambrose, Gregory and Augustine the four cardinal virtues: prudence, justice, temperance and fortitude or bravery. Together with these he adds the three theological virtues. He states that the first four we can acquire through deliberately willed and enjoyed habitual right action; the latter three are gifts from God.

If we follow Aquinas's outline then we can say that the fundamental question is 'Am I just, temperate, brave and prudent?' For centuries we have recommended that people ask themselves this. More recently, because we equate ethics with particular major actions, we have forgotten this question for self-examination. Nonetheless, even in recent times we have had important writers reminding us of the centrality of these cardinal virtues.[5]

But how can I know how virtuous I am? To answer that question Aristotle suggests that we can know ourselves by considering how we act in spontaneous situations: we reveal ourselves to ourselves when we act in the unplanned world of ordinary life. We may believe that we are particularly brave or cowardly, but that assessment is only correct if it conforms to how we actually behave in the unanticipated concrete situation. Self-knowledge is key, therefore, but a self-knowledge that is critical and honest, not one based on wishful thinking.

Who ought I to become?

The second question embodies a vision of the type of person we ought to become. Though we use Thomas's four cardinal virtues to find out how virtuous we actually are, we should use those same four virtues to determine who we ought to become. For certainly, if we are honest in answering the first question, then some virtues are not as fully acquired by us as are others. In fact, for the honest person the virtues are not what we acquire in life; they are what we pursue.

We use the virtues, therefore, to set the personal goals that we encourage one another to seek. Thomas and others call this goal the end. That is, the middle question sets an end that we should seek. That end is a type of person with the cardinal virtues.

Setting this end means that the fundamental task of the moral life is to develop a vision and to strive to attain it. Inasmuch as that vision is who we ought to become, then, the key insight is that we should always aim to grow. As a person-oriented ethics, virtue ethics insists that without growth, we cannot become more moral.

Setting such an end describes, then, another way that virtue ethicists are different from other ethicists. Rather than examining actions and asking whether we should perform them or not, virtue ethicists say that persons ought to set ends for the type of people they wish to become and pursue them.

I have always thought that parents think this way. Parents are not primarily concerned with what action Johnny is doing. Rather, they want to understand how Johnny is growing. Certainly there are times when with young children, parents talk like deontologists: 'Don't ever talk to strangers', 'Don't ever talk back to another person', 'Don't ever cross the street unless the traffic light says so'. But behind all their judgements is a more basic concern about how Johnny is turning out.

If Johnny needs to become more sensitive to other people, his parents may pick one neighbourhood to live in with more children rather than another with fewer; if Mary should become more studious, her parents will look for the school that successfully helps students to acquire right study habits; if Tommy is insecure, his parents will try to find ways that as a family they can help Tommy to grow in confidence. Generally, parents' judgements about their children focus on what type of people their children are becoming and whether they can help their child become more fully integrated. That is, parents ask both 'Who is my child?' and 'How can he or she grow well?'

Likewise, we do well when we parent ourselves. When we begin to examine ourselves, we see which weaknesses we can respond to and which strengths we can develop. When we are pro-active and anticipate a variety of situations where we can be more open-minded, more generous, more forgiving, more assertive, we are trying to develop the virtues within us.[6]

As a matter of fact, we often act this way. For instance, if I were to ask you to take a piece of paper and write down three ethical issues, what would you write down? Poverty, war, sexual matters, gender equality, and so forth. But if I asked you to turn the paper over and write down three things about yourself that you woke up this morning thinking about, I believe that you would write about bettering a relationship, learning to work better, taking better care of your health, or becoming more conscious of your neighbour. Virtue ethicists think of the second side of the paper as the real issues of ethics. We believe that when we start thinking that way, then we can address those big controversial issues on the first side having promoted first a virtuous life for ourselves individually and communally.

To the extent that we are examining our lives and seeking ways of improving ourselves for the betterment of ourselves and others, we are engaging in virtue ethics.

How do I get to the end?

In order to get to the end, one needs prudence. For many years prudence has had a terrible reputation, being thought of as caution or self-interest. Be prudent meant: Don't get caught. Be extra careful. Watch out!

For Aristotle and Thomas prudence is not simply caution. Prudence is rather the virtue of a person whose feet are on the ground and who thinks both practically and realistically. Prudence belongs to the person who not only sets realistic ends, but sets out to attain them. The prudent person is precisely the person who knows how to grow.[7]

Being prudent is no easy task. From the medieval period until today, we believe that it is easier to get something wrong than to get it right. For today we still assert that if only one component of an action is wrong, the whole action is wrong. Think for instance of cooking. In order for something to come out right, every ingredient has to be measured exactly, prepared correctly and cooked properly. How many of us have had a terrible meal because it was too salty, overcooked, too spicy or too bland? Only when everything comes out right can we say that the meal tasted well.

Prudence is even more complicated when we try to work out the appropriate way of becoming more virtuous. It must be attentive to detail, anticipate difficulties and measure rightly. Moreover, as any one who has watched children knows, we are not born with prudence. Actually we acquire it through a very long process.

The first sign of real prudence is finding the right person to give us advice. When I taught at Fordham University in the Bronx, I lived in the student dorms and noted how often university students went to one another for advice. These students, away from home for the first time, were looking for advice no longer from their parents, but instead from their peers. Often they looked to people like themselves for advice; in fact, the groups with which they associated collectively were similar to themselves individually. Studious students stayed together, as did hard workers, athletes, snobs, shy people, excessive party-goers, and so forth. When they asked for advice they usually were not hearing anything new.

On occasion someone from outside the group might raise a question. For instance, one might say to the excessive drinker that he was drinking too much. Inevitably he sought out advice about the charge and went to his alcoholic drinking buddy to ask if he was drinking too much and his buddy would calm his friend's anxiety with denial. After a while, however, the drinker would ask someone else, usually someone from the exact opposite group, someone who thought drinking was always wrong. What the student was looking for was advice, but he went from one extreme to the other.

Finding prudence is finding the middle point. Unlike the student here, prudence guides us to moderation, where we are not at either end of an extreme. The student who drinks excessively will only get good advice when he meets someone who is able to recognize the difference between moderate and excessive drinking.

As prudence looks for the moderating advisor, it does so because it realizes that all of prudence is precisely getting to the middle point or the mean between extremes. As Aquinas says, virtue is the mean.

Getting the mean is not always easy. I remember a friend who was afraid of heights. In order to grow, he needed to face his fear, but he had to do it prudentially. That is, he needed to set a realistic goal that he could attain. But that goal had to be the mean between extremes for him. For instance, if he went too high, say if he went to the observation deck of the World Trade Center, he would feel no confidence at all, only anxiety. But if he only went to the second-storey balcony of an apartment building, he would not feel sufficient tension. Prudence helps then find the mean where there is adequate tension for growth, neither too little nor too much.

That mean is not fixed. For me to get over my fear of heights requires me to go to the height where I feel sufficient tension, a height that may not be the same as for another with a similar fear. The mean of virtue then is not something set in stone: rather, it is the mean by which only a specific person can grow. This is another reason why prudence is so difficult: no two means are the same.

But parents again know this. Though their children always cry 'Foul' or 'That's unfair' whenever a parent treats one child differently from another, still if a parent treated each child the same, then only one child would grow adequately. Instead, parents appreciate the uniqueness of each child and try to address each child as unique.

Finding the mean of the right tension depends on who the person is. Just as in weight-lifting, one needs to determine what is the right tension by considering the lifter's abilities, so too in most matters that pertain to a person's growth, we cannot give prudential advice unless we have a clear idea of who the agent is. In a manner of speaking, a virtue ought to fit a person the way a glove fits one's hand. There is a certain tailor-made feel to a virtue, which prompts Aquinas to call virtue one's second nature.

Virtue ethics is, therefore, a pro-active system of ethics. It invites all people to see themselves as they really are, to assess themselves and see who they can actually become. In order both to estimate oneself and to set desired goals it proffers the virtues for both. Moreover, it invites all people to see that they set the agenda not only of the end, but also of the means to accomplish that end. Virtuous actions, like temperate drinking or courageously facing one's fear of heights, are the prudential means for achieving the end of becoming a more virtuous person. And we see those means as moderate or prudential ones.

Virtue ethics encompasses one's entire life. It sees every moment as the possibility for acquiring or developing a virtue. To underline this point, Aquinas said that every human action is a moral action.[8] That is, any action that I knowingly perform is a moral action because it affects me as a moral person. Whatever I do makes me become what I do. If I drive to work and use that time to reflect on the day that lies before me, over time I can become a person with a developed sense of foresight. If I drive to work both aggressively and speedily, I eventually arrive at my office with the same manic personality that brought me there. If I correct everyone's mistakes at every opportunity, I am becoming more and more of a control freak. And though my corrections may hurt a few around me, they are basically making me progressively more and more trapped by this disposition. While others may be affected by some of my actions, I am the first person affected by all of my actions.

Thomas saw every human action as an exercise. The way I take breakfast, the way I leave home, the way I drive to work, the way I greet people in the morning are all exercises that affect me. My morning exercises make me in part the person I will be for the rest of the day. They make me become what I do. Though some of us go through life never examining the habits we engage, Thomas suggests to us that we ought to examine our ways of acting and ask ourselves 'Are these ways making us more just, prudent, temperate and brave?' If they are, they are virtuous exercises.

When we think of exercise we think of athletics. The person who exercises by running eventually becomes a runner just as the one who dances becomes a dancer. From that insight Thomas, like Aristotle before him, sees that intended, habitual activity in the sports arena is no different from any other arena of life. If we can develop ourselves physically we can develop ourselves morally by intended, habitual activity.

Virtue ethics sees, therefore, the ordinary as the terrain on which the moral life moves. Thus, while most ethics make their considerations about rather controversial material (genetics, abortion, war, and so forth), virtue ethics often engages the commonplace. It is concerned with what we teach our children and how; with the way we relate with friends, families, and neighbours; with the way we live our lives. Moreover, it is concerned not only with whether a physician maintains professional ethics, for instance, whether she keeps professional secrets or observes informed consent with her patients. It is equally concerned with her private life, with whether she knows how to respect her friends' confidences or whether she respects her family members' privacy. In a word, before the physician is a physician she is a person. It is her life as a person with which virtue ethics is specifically concerned.

As opposed to dilemma-based ethics, virtue ethics is pro-active, concerned with the ordinary and all-encompassing. Dilemma-based ethics, which captures so much of our time, imagination and energy, presents ethics as an emergency room in which suddenly a previously unknown person arrives in a catastrophic state: needing an organ transplant, assisted suicide or an abortion. In that made-for-TV ethics, the agent is little more than a reactor to other people's dilemmas.

Virtue ethics looks at the world from an entirely different vantage point, moving ahead with less glamour and drama, but always seeing the agent, not as reactor, but as actor: knowing oneself, setting the agenda of personal ends and means in both the ordinary and the professional life.

Virtue ethics: yesterday, today and tomorrow

While we are retrieving virtue ethics today we realize that we cannot return to the early Athens of Aristotle or the thirteenth-century Italy of Thomas. Moreover, we recognize that there are some concerns about virtue ethics being raised by a variety of people. First and foremost is the argument that virtue ethics cannot deal with practical issues. Because virtue is concerned with persons, some argue, it cannot adequately deal with human action.[9] Though one can equally ask these objectors how effective their ethical systems have been,[10] or more importantly, whether their ethical systems for all their clarity have ever helped people to become more ethical,[11] still virtue ethics must show how practical it can be. Here, it is noteworthy that nursing ethics in particular is making great headway in showing how a relationally-based concern for agents as persons is a more constructive ethics than any present rule or code-based ethics.[12] In fact, the application of virtue to medical ethics has raised several issues about the delivery of health care that other ethical systems never asked.[13] While virtue ethics is at times introspective, the complaint that it needs to be more extroverted and practical has prompted a variety of writers to demonstrate that it can give specific advice, that it can improve our ability to know the right and to do it, that it can give us new issues to address, and above all that it can make us better and our actions morally right.

Two other issues prompt us to refine our understanding of virtue. In a brilliant book, Owen Flanagan warns against preconceiving of a definitively moral person and imposing that image on others. He argues that the possibilities for moral excellence are as unlimited both as the individual is complex and as human experience is original. A discussion of great saints and heroes helps make the point that no single portrait of a moral saint or hero has ever provided a definitive expression of what a human person ought to be; St Elizabeth was not Mahatma Gandhi, St John the Baptizer was not the Little Flower. The Christian community sustains this insight: the communion of saints demonstrates the enormous variety of ways that the holy is incarnated or as Flanagan beautifully puts it, 'the deep truth that persons find their good in many different ways'.[14] He insists then that people can only become morally excellent persons by being themselves. The saint has always been an original; never an imitation.

Flanagan rightly warns us that in asking 'Who ought I to become' we understand that we are not trying to become clones. Rather we are seeking to understand how we as individuals can actually become virtuous. Thus, though we may each believe that we should become just and prudent, we must be sure that we preserve our own identities as we pursue the virtues.

Flanagan is not the only one who warns us that we cannot ask our three questions in a vacuum. Alasdair MacIntyre reminds us[15] that our local communities determine our understanding of the virtues. Justice in Aristotle's Athens is not the same as it was in the seventeenth-century pioneering Wild West or the late twentieth-century urban New York. MacIntyre's claims concern not only history but also geography. Justice is expressed differently in Congo, Malaysia, France or Brazil. Likewise, what constitutes prudence in London, Birmingham, York or Liverpool is different.

Both writers warn against any artificial designs for answering the question of who we ought to become. We each ought to strive to become the person that God made us to be and we each must recognize how our societies have contributed to our own understanding of what it means to be moral. But we should recognize that at least minimally there are some virtues that each of us ought to have, regardless of where or when we live or who we are.[16] We should not say much about the content of each of these virtues, for history, geography and the individual fill out their practical meaning. But we can say to every child, adolescent and adult there are ways of living about which every virtuous person is rightly concerned. This was what Plato, Cicero, Ambrose, Augustine, Gregory, Thomas and others meant by the cardinal virtues.

We conclude our consideration of the virtues asking then a final question: 'Are the four cardinal virtues that they offered in antiquity adequate for today?' For several reasons, I think they are inadequate and in their place I propose another set of cardinal virtues.[17]

First Thomas's cardinal virtues basically describe one type of person:

the just person. Temperance and bravery exist in order to help a person to be just; they are effectively auxiliary. Likewise prudence functions to determine the concrete mean for justice, temperance and courage. For Thomas then the just person is the virtuous person. The other virtues help the person to be just.

Today, however, the image of the just person is insufficient. Almost everyone writing on the virtues today recognizes that whereas one must be just, that is, that one must treat everyone equally, still one must also attend to the immediate needs of friends, family and community. Writers like Reinhold Niebuhr,[18] Margaret Farley[19] and Carol Gilligan[20] insist that the moral person cannot only be just: the demands to care for a loved one may conflict with the call to be fair to everyone.

Paul Ricoeur adds that it is important that justice is challenged by the affection we have for another. Rather than reducing the two claims to one, he places them in a 'tension between two distinct and sometimes opposed claims'.[21] This insight that the virtues are distinct and at times opposing stands in contrast with Thomas' strategy of the cardinal virtues where justice is supported by fortitude and temperance and none contradicts, opposes, or challenges the claims of justice.

Furthermore we recognize another difference with Thomas. Thomas argues that virtues perfect or make better our own dispositions; each virtue perfects a particular power in us. Justice perfects our will, prudence our reasoning, courage and temperance perfect particular emotions. But today we think of the person as fundamentally relational. Virtues perfect not individual powers, but rather the ways we relate with one another.[22]

In this relational light let us call the two competitive demands that we have been discussing, justice and fidelity. If justice urges us to treat all people equally, then fidelity makes different claims. Fidelity is the virtue that nurtures and sustains the bonds of those special relationships that we enjoy whether by blood, marriage, love or sacrament. Fidelity requires that we treat with special care those who are closer to us.[23] If justice rests on impartiality and universality, fidelity rests on partiality and particularity.[24]

But these two are not enough; we also must perfect the unique relationship that we have with ourselves. Thomas, through the order of charity, demonstrates the virtuous love for self.[25] Following him, Stephen Pope[26] and Edward Vacek[27] argue that we have a primary task to take care of ourselves: affectively, mentally, physically, and spiritually.

For these reasons, then, I conclude by proposing that we conceive of ourselves as relational in three ways: generally, specifically and uniquely, and each of these relational ways of being demands a cardinal virtue: as a relational being in general, we are called to justice and to treat all people fairly; as a relational being specifically, we are called to fidelity and to sustain the specific relationships that we enjoy; as a relational being uniquely, we are called to self-care that no one else can provide.

These three virtues are cardinal. Unlike Thomas's structure, none is necessarily always more important than the other: they each have equally urgent claims and they should be pursued as ends in themselves. Thus we are not called to be faithful and self-caring in order to be just, nor are we called to be self-caring and just in order to be faithful. None is auxiliary to the others. They are distinctive virtues with none being a subset or subcategory of the other. They are cardinal.

The fourth cardinal virtue is prudence, which determines what constitutes the just, faithful and self-caring way of life for an individual. It also negotiates how the cardinal virtues should interact and which one should override the others in a particular situation, and when and to what degree. Of course, this is no easy matter, but working this out requires another essay.

Notes

1 James F. Keenan, 'Virtue ethics: making a case as it comes of age', *Thought* 67 (1992), pp. 115–27; Joseph Kotva, *The Christian Case for Virtue Ethics* (Washington, DC: Georgetown University Press, 1996); Gilbert Meilaender, *The Theory and Practice of Virtue* (Notre Dame, IN: University of Notre Dame Press, 1984).

2 These questions appear in Alasdair MacIntyre, *After Virtue: A Study in Moral Theory* (Notre Dame, IN: University of Notre Dame Press, 1981).

3 John Kekes, *The Examined Life* (Lewisburg, PA: Bucknell University Press, 1988).

4 *Summa Theologiae*, Prologue, II-II, *Sic igitur tota materia morali ad considerationem virtutum reducta*.

5 See Josef Pieper, *The Four Cardinal Virtues* (Notre Dame, IN: University of Notre Dame Press, 1966); Jean Porter, *The Recovery of Virtue* (Louisville, KY: Westminster, 1990).

6 Along with essays on growth and ordinariness, see my 'Parenting and the virtue of prudence' in *Virtues for Ordinary Christians* (Kansas City, MO: Sheed and Ward, 1996).

7 Daniel Mark Nelson, *The Priority of Prudence* (University Park, PA: Pennysylvania State University, 1992).

8 See my 'Ten reasons why Thomas Aquinas is important for ethics today', *New Blackfriars* 75 (1994), pp. 354–63.

9 See for instance, the essays by Tom Beauchamp and Robert Veatch in E. Shelp (ed.), *Virtue and Medicine* (Boston: Reidel, 1984).

10 David Solomon, 'Internal objections to virtue ethics' in Peter A. French *et al.* (eds), *Midwest Studies in Philosophy* 13: *Ethical Theory: Character and Virtue* (Notre Dame, IN: University of Notre Dame Press, 1988), pp. 428–41.

11 See Leon Kass, 'Practicing ethics: where's the action?', *Hastings Center Report* 20.1 (1990), pp. 5–12.

12 See Martin Benjamin and Joy Curtis, 'Virtue and the practice of nursing' in *Virtue and Medicine*, pp. 257–74.

13 For example, James Drane, 'Character and the moral life: a virtue approach in biomedical ethics' in Edwin DuBose *et al.* (eds), *A Matter of Principles?* (Park Ridge: Trinity Press, 1994), pp. 284–309; Michael Green, 'What (if anything) is wrong with residency overwork?', *Annals of Internal Medicine* 123 (1995), pp. 512–17; James F. Keenan, 'What's morally new in genetic engineering', *Human Gene Therapy* 1 (1990), pp. 289–98; William Stempsey, 'Special report: the virtuous pathologist', *American Journal of Clinical Pathology* 91.6 (1989), pp. 730–8.

14 Owen Flanagan, *Varieties of Moral Personality: Ethics and Psychological Realism* (Cambridge, MA: Harvard University Press, 1991), p. 158.

15 Alasdair MacIntyre in both *After Virtue* and *Whose Justice? Which Rationality?* (Notre Dame, IN: Notre Dame University Press, 1988).

16 Martha Nussbaum offers a helpful response to MacIntyre's warnings in 'Non-relative virtues: an Aristotelian approach' in *Midwest Studies* 13, pp. 32–53.

17 I develop this at length in 'Proposing cardinal virtues', *Theological Studies* 56.4 (1995), pp. 709–29.

18 Reinhold Niebuhr, *Love and Justice: Selections from the Shorter Writings of Reinhold Niebuhr*, ed. D. B. Robertson (Louisville, KY: Westminster, 1957).

19 Margaret Farley, *Personal Commitments: Beginning, Keeping, Changing* (San Francisco: Harper and Row, 1990).

20 Carol Gilligan, *In a Different Voice: Psychological Theory and Women's Development* (Cambridge, MA: Harvard University Press, 1982).

21 Paul Ricoeur, 'Love and justice' in Werner G. Jeanrond and Jennifer L. Rike (eds), *Radical Pluralism and Truth: David Tracy and the Hermeneutics of Religion* (New York: Crossroad, 1991), pp. 187–202, at p. 196.

22 See Paul Lauritzen, 'The self and its discontents', *Journal of Religious Ethics* 22.1 (1994), pp. 189–210.

23 In *Virtues for Ordinary Christians* I treat each of these.

24 See a similar insight in William Spohn, 'The return of virtue ethics', *Theological Studies* 53 (1992), pp. 60–75, at p. 72.

25 The concern for self-care runs throughout the *Summa*, from I, 5.1c and 48.1 which describes how all nature seeks its own perfection to I-II, 27.3 that insists that it is natural to prefer oneself over others and 29.4 that it is impossible to hate oneself. In II-II, Aquinas argues that though inordinate self-love is the source of sin (25.4, 28.4 ad 1), self-love belongs to the order of charity and is prior to neighbour love (25.12, 26.4). He adds that charity is the source of peace which aims at ending conflict not only with others but also within oneself (29.1). By introducing self-care into the constellation of the cardinal virtues I believe that I am developing Thomas's own thoughts.

26 Stephen Pope, *The Evolution of Altruism and the Ordering of Love* (Washington, DC: Georgetown University Press, 1994).

27 Edward Vacek, *Love, Human and Divine: The Heart of Christian Ethics* (Washington, DC: Georgetown University Press, 1994), pp. 239–73.

6

The human person

Joseph Selling

Any system of moral reflection, including those which some people might like to label 'relativistic', ultimately must have some point of reference for defining its most fundamental terms. This remains true whether one considers morality from the subjective perspective, *the goodness or badness of moral intention*, or from the so-called objective perspective, *the rightness or wrongness of human behaviour*.

'Subjectively', for a behavioural event (act or omission) to be considered moral, it must exhibit elements of freedom and intention. Although there is a growing tendency to factor animals, and even 'nature', into our moral considerations, concepts such as 'animal rights' and 'the integrity of creation' remain passive items that are reflected *upon* rather than functioning as agents. Only human persons are considered moral agents, precisely because they are capable of self-direction (intention) and presumably because they enjoy the knowledge of and ability to make choices (freedom).

Random events, no matter how 'good' (bumper crops) or 'evil' (earthquakes) human beings might like to call them, are not of themselves moral events. Only human events are properly referred to as moral, although again it is necessary to qualify only certain kinds of human events in this way.

Tradition distinguished the *actus hominis*, such as walking, eating or sleeping, from the *actus humanus* according to whether freedom and intention are part of the entire event. Today we might suggest that merely describing the gestures or actions of a human *being* does not yet deliver us into the moral realm. Something more is needed before we can speak of human events as moral events, namely freedom and intentionality. Such events are uniquely perpetrated by the human *person*, a term that describes not a mere object or being but an active, existential phenomenon. The human person is not a static, ontological thing; the repository of a 'nature'. Rather, the human *person* is always dynamic, situated and (intentionally) engaged.

Considering morality 'subjectively', then, must always include reference to the human *person* because freedom and intention, unique characteristics of the human person, are indispensible elements of moral decisions.

Considering the 'objective' perspective of morality, we see that behavioural events are complex phenomena, consisting of acts (and omissions) that take place within the context of an entire range of circumstances. These behavioural events may, of course, be described without reference to intention or freedom. Not every *actus hominis* is an *actus humanus*. Nevertheless, for such an event to qualify as a candidate for moral analysis, it must again be related in some way to the human person.

The rightness or wrongness of human behaviour is never determined on the basis of a single, isolated component of a behavioural event, but rather on the basis of several, interrelated components which, together, render a description of an event sufficient to demonstrate its relevance to moral analysis, that is, an event that exhibits a complex and ambiguous conglomeration of (ontic, pre-moral) good and evil. In turn, the evaluation of these components, rendered by assigning the adjectives 'good' or 'evil', begs the question of how we are to determine what constitutes the meaning of these adjectives.

On what basis do we label the components of human behaviour good or evil? Several answers to this question are possible, ranging from authority (commandment)[1] to statistics (nature)[2] to the anticipation of pleasure or pain.[3] A personalist view of morality suggests that the answer to this question is founded upon *observation*: the shared, interpreted experience of the human community through time. True personalism, then, is always phenomenological.[4] Further, personalist morality (mores) is always elaborated within a community and supported by consensus. What is 'good' is always considered 'good-for-persons'; what is 'evil' is 'evil-for-persons'.[5]

No matter which criterion one subscribes to for analysing the components of human behaviour, some notion of person will constitute a necessary element of performing moral decision-making; for without the freedom and intention exercised by the person, we are not speaking in moral terms. If one opts for a 'personalist' kind of morality, then the notion of the person functions not only on the subjective pole but on the objective pole as well, forming the reference point for the determination of good and evil, and subsequently right(ness) and wrong(ness).

The centrality of the human person for moral reasoning

Person constitutes a concept, a working hypothesis constructed through the consensus of an interpretative community. As a concept, neither is it reducible to a single individual, person is always person-in-community, nor can it be adequately described without considering the multi-dimensionality of being human.

From an explicitly phenomenological point of view, we observe that an adequate and integral understanding of the human person recognizes that person is always person-in-relation. The human person stands in relation to everything, one could even say to the 'totality of reality'. In one sense, this observation might be said to constitute the core meaning of personhood, for it indicates the engagement of every facet of our experience. We stand in relation to reality not merely physically but intellectually, emotionally, socially and spiritually as well. We relate through physical presence but also through our imagination. We use symbols to represent, language to communicate, and a whole host of learned mechanisms to interpret the meaning of internal and external stimuli.

Ultimately, nothing will be strange or completely foreign to the human person, for it is our fundamental belief that through encounter we experience relationship. This does not mean that every single individual is open to each and every possible relationship, it means that the phenomenon we are calling 'person' is relational, open to the totality of reality on every level.

A morally sensitive person will spontaneously recognize the congruence between the expressions 'being human' and 'being moral'. Humanists refer to the realization of human identity or fulfilment, a calling that transcends any particular individual. Any person who seeks 'the meaning of life' is searching for a dimension of being human that is accessible to all while simultaneously transcending each individual. Even the fatalist recognizes something called 'destiny' into which we are all taken up, even if the subsequent denial of freedom would undermine the possibility of such a position ever becoming truly moral.

The theist will have no difficulty in seeing here an indication of what is commonly called God, that which transcends even the totality of reality itself. Every human person stands in relation to God. Those who share a faith in a 'personal God' immediately recognize that this is a personal relationship, one that is made understandable through the gratuitous gift of a loving Creator. Others will describe the relationship to the transcendent in terms appropriate to their belief system. Nevertheless, we can and should say that the fundamental relationality of the human person, adequately considered, is manifest in a particular way in the experience of our relationship to the totality of reality, to the transcendent, to God.

A focal point for multi-dimensionality

Although one might like to suggest that 'intentionality', the fundamentally relational characteristic of the human person, identifies the core meaning of person, such that whatever else might be said would merely constitute a detail of an otherwise comprehensive description, moral awareness demands that we distinguish and investigate the different ways in which human relationality is expressed.

For instance, observing that the human person stands in relation to the totality of reality would, of course, include the fact that person stands in relation to the material world. Nevertheless, while this dimension of being human is not independent from our relation with the transcendent, it is worth distinguishing this specific dimension for the sake of the clarity and completeness of our concept of person.

Another way of phrasing this is to observe that the human person is multi-dimensional. I suggest that we think of 'person' as a focal point, where all these dimensions converge. The person is a unity, but there are several ways of observing this unity and several dimensions to which the person is open, in relation. Each of these dimensions or aspects of the person needs to be named and brought to consciousness. Without an awareness of one or another dimension of person, we remain ignorant of that particular relational aspect of being human and will consequently fail to observe the real or potential presence of good and evil. To use the example above, a lack of sensitivity to the human person's relation to the material world can result either in the failure to reap the benefits of the world in which we live (use of resources) or in the neglect of the care that must be taken in our relation to the environment (pollution).

Simply saying that the human person stands in relation to the totality of reality, therefore, is insufficient to sensitize us to the multi-dimensional aspects that constitute moral sensitivity (i.e., awareness of the real or potential presence of good and evil). We must therefore distinguish each of those dimensions pertinent to the project of moral analysis. At present, we observe at least eight continuous dimensions of the human person that reveal important information for performing that moral analysis.[6] These dimensions are 'continuous' because they are always present, whether we are conscious of them or not. We cannot turn these aspects of our being a person on and off, as it were, because the person is a unity, not simply exhibiting but actually constituted by these dimensions. Therefore, whenever we refer to the human person we should immediately add 'adequately considered'. This will remind us to be cautious not to forget one or more of these dimensions in our analysis.

Finally, we must be careful not to rank or prioritize the various aspects of being human. Not only would this violate the unity of the person as moral agent, it would also result in a disbalanced anthropology. I have therefore been careful about the manner which I have chosen to present the eight continuous dimensions of the person. The order of presentation has no significance in the complete picture; for there is no priority of dimensions, only the unity of the person. That said, I have constructed the following pattern in a way that I hope will correct the Western bias toward exalting subjectivity as the 'most important' aspect of what it means to be human.[7]

The human person, adequately considered

The human person, adequately considered, stands in relation to everything, to the whole of reality

I have already mentioned this dimension of the person above. However, it not only bears repeating but I hope that some further reflections will lead to a better understanding of the importance of this observation.

Affirming that as intentional beings we stand in relation to all that is implies that there are human relationships that are not always obvious to the average observer. Some scientists, for instance, being aware of the relation that we have with our total environment, have expanded this to an appeal to our relation with the whole of humanity, human destiny, the human enterprise, even the cosmos. On the other hand, some spiritualists will claim that we stand in relation to an entire spirit world, be it the spirits of the trees, the land and the water or with the spirits of our ancestors. In more traditional language, religion speaks of our relation with a spirit world within, without, above, or around us. Those who prefer to use religious language speak of our relation to God. Theistic language certainly has advantages for those who have become accustomed to its usage, and among theists there are those who express the faith that God even communicates with human persons in a manner that is comprehensible for all human persons. We express this belief when we refer to a 'personal' God.

This being an exposition in the context of moral theology, we can describe this dimension of the human person in the explicitly religious language of our tradition. More specifically, in the Christian tradition, we have even less difficulty in speaking of a personal God who not only communicates but who has joined with humanity in the event that we call the incarnation. Our comfort in our tradition, however, should not make us insensitive to the fact that this language sometimes creates a wall between people rather than a bridge. From an ethical perspective, then, it is perhaps more ecumenical to speak of our relation with the transcendent, with that which is on a 'higher' (more encompassing) plane than what we would normally refer to as human experience. In our times, speaking of a 'world beyond our normal experience' is returning to popular usage, literally and especially implicitly. There is a good deal of attention paid to our human destiny or being caught up in a project that is universal and greater than any individual imagination (the cosmos, the rhythms of the 'natural' world, even socio-biology); there is literature and film about spirits, ghosts, and out-of-body experiences; there is a proliferation of science fiction images ranging from 'the Force (be with you!)' of *Star Wars* to the transient beings who people the world of the Trekkies!

Rather than demeaning this language, we should recognize it as an expression of contemporary persons to go 'beyond' their empirical, scientific, rational experience into a realm of different meaning. Theistic language, unfortunately, sometimes brings with it images that are counter-productive, making it hard to communicate the good news of the gospel. Legalistic, paternalistic, judgemental images of God have been somewhat dominant in Western culture, forcing people to abandon the images without having experienced the larger reality they so narrowly attempt to represent.

To speak of the human person, adequately considered, being in relation to all that is, may be affirmed in theistic language by referring to our relationship with God. In Christian tradition, we can elaborate upon this as our relationship with a loving, affirming, forgiving God whom we worship in thanksgiving and whose message we celebrate with joy. The privilege that our tradition grants us to do this helps us see why our relation with God is of fundamental ethical significance.

The human person, adequately considered, stands in relation to the material world

Since one might say that this borders on the obvious, it is necessary to be explicit about the material dimensions of our existence so that we do not fall into the trap of spiritualism or that of dualism. Even though we can affirm our relation with the transcendent, we simultaneously know that even our communication with God depends upon physical mediation.

Our existence in a material world is not insignificant for moral reflection. Our daily commerce with reality makes us keenly aware of the limitations that we experience with respect to our best aspirations. There is only so much to go around, only so many resources, that sometimes the challenge of poverty and deprivation appears to be beyond our capabilities.

Rather than dwelling upon these negative experiences which in themselves are obvious enough, we can just as well accent the positive aspects of our relation with the material world. For, just as there is a shortage of drinkable water in many parts of this world, there is also the beauty of a river or a waterfall, and the ability to harness moving water to produce work. Furthermore, we must remind ourselves that we do not live 'in' a world. Though the material and physical limitations that surround us may be a source of frustration, we should not forget that we are so intimately *part* of the material world that we can never conceive of being separate from it. Even those who go into space take an earthly environment with them. They would cease being human persons if they did not.

The material world of which we are so intimately a part, however, is also something to which we stand in relation. Dependent as we are on the air we breath and the water we drink, we tend to see these things as objects, apart from our existence. This is good insofar as it gives us the ability to utilize the material world, to humanize the natural world, to create a 'user friendly' environment for all persons. But we should take great care not to fall into the trap of thinking that the material world constitutes an arbitrary object for our unrestrained manipulation.

The human person, adequately considered, is cultural, that is, is always in relation to (groups of) other persons

The human person is fundamentally *related* in the sense that this pun is intended to convey an appreciation of our 'relatives'! No human person springs into existence spontaneously but is always born into a culture that consists of other human persons. We all have parents, even if these good people decided (or were driven) to use a Petri dish to achieve the fusion of gametes. We have grandparents, and ultimately we all have great-grandparents, uncles, aunts, cousins, and so forth. These people are all interrelated as well, such that every person is part of a family, a tribe, a clan, a nation.

An adequate consideration of the human person draws our attention to the observation that just about everything that we might consider necessary to specify our humanity is dependent upon our social – cultural – existence. Perhaps the most fundamental aspect of this inter-human relationality is language, the basic tool of relationality itself. Language, one may say, is arbitrary in the sense that it is *language, langue, taal* or *Sprache*. When we wish to communicate, however, we quickly learn that it is anything but arbitrary. Though a creation of a given people, language takes on a momentum, a life of its own that exhibits limits as well as possibilities.

We can affirm the fundamentally social character of the human person.

Without social relations we would never develop our potential as human persons. Contemplating this for even one moment leads to a critical assessment of the individualism that is often said to be characteristic of Western society. The irony of an individualistic attitude is its ignorance of the dependence of the individual upon the tools of social commerce to assert the very individuality that is being claimed. 'Different from' implies something from which to differ. The 'individual' springs into awareness only within the experience of contrast that is possible in a social context. Autonomy is the result of separation, which in turn is completely dependent upon identification with a group.

The social dimension of the human person pervades every aspect of our existence as human beings. The human environment consists in an incredibly complex web of interconnecting systems that make life as we know it possible, from our language to our kinship systems, from economic structures to the network of roads and highways, from social customs to the use of barter – which today we have reduced to the convenience of something we call money (plastic or paper). Even the mythological 'self-taught man' is dependent upon the goods of culture to 'teach himself'. In short, the human person, adequately considered, is a cultural reality, situated in an existence that is socially, linguistically, economically, politically specific.

These observations must lead us to contemplate the incongruity of suggesting an 'individual(istic) ethic'. Morality basically describes the way in which we live by guiding us through the complex web of human relationships. The construction of these relationships is never dictated by a single individual. Thus, morality itself must always be understood as a cultural phenomenon. To be human is to be cultural, and no amount of protestation against the bounds of cultural specificity will eliminate our need to deal with this dimension of human existence.

Also, we should not neglect the observation that culture itself is the product of human making.[8] The 'Pastoral Constitution on the Church in the Modern World', the final document to be approved and promulgated by the Second Vatican Council in 1965, *Gaudium et Spes* (*GS*), affirms the 'interdependence of person and society' (*GS*, n. 25) and takes note of the 'rightful independence of earthly affairs' (*GS*, n. 36). In para. 55 of that document we specifically read:

> In every group or nation, there is an ever-increasing number of men and women who are conscious that they themselves are the artisans and authors of the culture of their community. Throughout the world there is a similar growth in the combined sense of autonomy and responsibility. Such a development is of paramount importance for the spiritual and moral maturity of the human race. This truth shows clearer if we

consider how the world is becoming unified and how we have the duty to build a better world based upon truth and justice. Thus we are witnesses of the birth of a new humanism, one in which man is defined first of all by his responsibility toward his brothers and toward history.[9]

The human person, adequately considered, is historical

Following directly upon the quotation above, we must simultaneously affirm the historical dimension of human existence. In a sense, we live 'in history'. However, such a statement may be misleading if it implies that history is something 'outside' of us. Unfortunately, the study of history in schools often gives us precisely that impression, especially when history is related as a series of (large) 'events' effected by (important) personages.

History in the truly human sense focuses upon the present which derives its meaning both from the past and toward the future. From the past we inherit our culture and achieve our personal, even individual, identity. Toward the future we describe the meaning of our present decisions and activities. 'History', then, is always in the making, culturally and socially. This extends to morality as well. We inherit the wisdom of the past as well as the tools to perform moral analysis and to reach moral decisions. There is no need to begin from 'square one', as it were, when assessing a moral question. Much has been learned from the past. At the same time, what we may call moral 'tradition' should not be looked upon as static, a forever unchanging structure that precludes further development. For it is precisely what we have learned from the past that makes it possible for us to face as yet undefined questions that may beg for new, creative responses.

Although it appears rather obvious that historicity is a fundamental dimension of the human person, it is perhaps too easy to overlook the individual dimension of being historical. Each human person is also a 'history', deriving identity in the present, built upon a past and oriented toward a future. We need to take this into account not only when considering our own well-being but especially in our dealing with other persons. How we respond to other persons has a good deal to do with who they are – their own identity built up from personal history. This identity does not *determine* our behaviour, but it would be unwise to ignore its possible relevance. One does not entrust the care of children to someone who has a history of child molestation. At the same time, we respond to persons as being future-oriented beings. Making promises, for instance, should always be done with this in mind. Human persons who make commitments to each other should realize that the nature of personal commitment involves not simply the person as they appear in the present but also as they will be in the future.

With respect to moral analysis, historicity is extremely important both in situating our relations with other persons and being aware that our moral reasoning is itself historical. We make decisions on the basis of the knowledge we have, while the heritage of human wisdom is a continuously developing source of that knowledge itself. An excellent example of this would be our concern for the integrity of the environment within which we and all of humankind – including future generations – live. It is only recently that we have become aware of the importance of protecting our environment from pollution, wastefulness and general misuse. It would be ridiculous to suggest that the human community has been sensitive to this importance throughout history. On the contrary, the plagues of the Middle Ages are a graphic example of how the human environment was dangerously polluted. At the same time, we can hardly place blame on fourteenth-century society for violating rules of hygiene of which they were unaware. At a later time, we now realize the mistakes that were made. In our own time, we are just beginning to realize the enormous importance of directing our own behaviour with a view toward the future, our future and that of the coming generations.

The human person, adequately considered, stands in relation to other persons

If the human person, adequately considered, is fundamentally relational, then the most 'personal' relation of all is that with other human persons. Our relation with culture is mediated first and foremost through other persons; we come to know our history through other persons; we create our own, personal history through relation with others; even our relationship with the transcendent is communicated to us through other persons as the continuing story of God's relation with humanity (the covenant). GS, n. 12 comments that through our 'innermost nature the person is a social being, and unless one relates self to others one can neither live nor develop one's potential'; and again, in GS, n. 24: 'humankind, who is the only creature on earth which God willed for itself, cannot fully find itself except through a sincere gift of self'.

Our 'intimate' relationships, first with family, then friends, then with loved ones with whom we may create a family of our own, are the source of the process of becoming human. Since our very survival is dependent upon the response given to us while we are still helpless infants, the more 'human' that response is, the more 'human' our survival will be.[10] The goods of culture are first mediated through other human beings who teach us language and an appreciation for the treasures of human knowledge and wisdom. It is through social interaction that we develop our specifically human potential and achieve human fulfilment. By the same token, the ambiguous term 'self-fulfilment' refers to the fulfilment *of* the self and not *by* the self.

The human person, adequately considered, becomes a conscious interiority, a subject

The 'person' is not simply a material, cultural, historical, social, relational entity but also a 'self'. We relate, exercise intentionality, because the person is also an inner self, a subject endowed with freedom and called to responsibility. Therefore, we often hear it said that the person should be treated not as an object, as a thing, but as a subject.

The most personal acts one performs are initiated in one's consciousness. The ability to reflect, upon ourselves or upon something other than ourselves, is a sign of our consciousness. The propositions that we think, we know, we feel, we decide, all depend upon an interiority as the source of these activities. Indeed one of the most noble of all human activities is sometimes referred to as conscience, 'the most secret core and sanctuary of the person . . . where one is alone with God, whose voice echoes in one's depths' (*GS*, n. 16).

It is as a conscious interiority that one experiences freedom in the most meaningful sense of the term. For although 'freedom' is sometimes used to describe the experience of having choices or options for action, the most profound form of freedom is experienced as a personal identity. At the same time, the gravest offences against human freedom are precisely those things which attack personal identity: brainwashing, the use of drugs or techniques to gain control over the person, any assault on the selfhood of the person, be it individual, social, political, through the use of violence, propaganda or deception.

According to some, our conscious interiority, the fact that the human person, adequately considered, is a subject, may be said to be the primary focal point for defining the human person itself. At the same time, it is difficult to conceive of human subjectivity without the experience that comes through growth toward maturity. One does not develop a 'self' in a vacuum, for each self is cultural, historical, situated in terms of its relation with other selves, with the world at large and with the transcendent. Identity, even in the scriptural sense, is expressed by a *name*, and that name is given to us rather than created by us. Thus, we situate the conscious interiority of the person in its proper relation with all the other dimensions of the human person, adequately considered. This does not signify an objective priority but rather an intrinsic inter-relatedness.

The human person, adequately considered, is a corporeal subject

Western philosophy has suffered from an inherent dualism, paradoxically brought about by its concentration upon the individual as subject. We often hear of the body–soul split of the person, the 'ghost in the machine' image whereby the 'real' person inhabits some interior space and uses the body for purposes that are almost considered to be neutral. This type of dualism is so imbedded in our way of thinking that we are forced to use the terms body and soul, matter and spirit, even to refute them.

What we must affirm is that every person is essentially corporeal. Metaphysically, corporeality is frequently used as a signification of individuality, a principle of individuation. Because of our dualist way of thinking, we usually equate our corporeality with our bodiliness, our physical existence. To the extent that our human experience of persons is always mediated through our body, this is a valuable notion. At the same time, we might wish to use more contemporary language and say that it is through our corporeality that we interface with the material world and with other persons. While our subjectivity is 'responsible' for our potentiality to symbolize, signify, and communicate, we are dependent upon perceptible phenonema to effect that communication.

Furthermore, the observation that we are corporeal subjects offers us many possibilities to appreciate the significance of our human activity. Even activity that is non-corporeal has interpersonal ramifications, for even the formation of our opinions and attitudes will ultimately have an effect upon the way we relate to other persons. That relation, subtle as it may be, is always communicated bodily. Finally, even our relation 'with ourselves' cannot ignore our corporeality. We have an obligation to consider physical health, the strength to do our work, the ability to carry out our tasks, all of which depend upon a proper care of our physical body.

Every human person is unique

Almost by definition, the individual human person, *adequately* considered, is a totally unique, one-time occurrence. We can speak, for instance, of a 'personality' in the sense of particular characteristics that belong to the unique individual. Further, each person has their own talents, abilities, skills, perspective. These may not be equally valued in every social context, but they nonetheless constitute the value(ableness) of the person. The virtually infinite variety of personal characteristics are the result of unique combinations of 'nature and nurture' that will never be repeated. Therefore, we are justified in the observation that each person should be treated as a unique individual.

At the same time, however, we are aware of the danger of 'valuing' persons as such, ranking them in a hierarchy. Most social structures have a tendency to 'value' or reward certain personal characteristics that happen to be advantageous for that structure. A technologically advanced society, for instance, will tend to reward persons who exhibit technological skills, giving the impression that these persons are more valuable than those without the same skills.

It is more than democratic instincts that prompt us to recoil against a hierarchy of persons. I would suggest that the recognition of the uniqueness of every person ultimately leads us to a fundamentally ethical question: must we accept the maxim that all human persons are fundamentally equal? Simple as this may sound, it becomes one of the most difficult 'observations' about the human person to elaborate and to defend. The more common vocabulary on this topic usually speaks of the equal *dignity* or equal *value* of all human persons, not their fundamental *equality* as such.

Christians have always claimed that the human person – each and every human person – is created in the image and likeness of God. On the basis of this creation in God's image alone, the human person enjoys dignity and is worthy of respect. Even when Christians lived in and accepted hierarchically structured societies – think for example of the period of scholasticism that rose to its climax in the context of feudalism – they still maintained the dignity of each individual, even if an individual might be guilty of heinous crimes.

Perhaps the most fundamental challenge of contemporary (social) ethics is coming to terms with an affirmation of the dignity of each and every human person. A proliferation of 'movements' claiming recognition, liberation or equal rights appears to be a sign of this sensitivity to the dignity of the individual. Unfortunately, these 'banners' are sometimes used to attack the rights of others, paradoxically calling into question the foundation of their own claims.

The concept of the human person, adequately considered, represents the description of a multidimensional but unified being. In order to carry out a moral analysis with a view toward taking responsible decisions, it is incumbent upon us to be constantly aware of all the dimensions of the person, even and especially when one or more of those dimensions may not appear to be immediately pertinent. To ignore one or more dimension of the person is to neglect a source of moral responsibility. Ironically, it is frequently in the name of that moral responsibility that one concentrates so strongly on one dimension (e.g., medical practitioners concentrate on human corporeality, political leaders on the socio-cultural dimensions of person and church leaders on our relationship to God) that one loses sight of the person as a whole. I sometimes suspect that these disproportionate concentrations on one or another dimension of the person to the neglect of a view of the person as an integrated unity constitute a greater source of (ontic) evil than the malicious intent of wrongdoers.

Notes

1 This is the kind of moral methodology predominant in *Veritatis Splendor*, the encyclical letter of John Paul II on moral theology, promulgated on 6 August 1993. See Joseph A. Selling, '*Veritatis Splendor* and the sources of morality', *Louvain Studies* 19 (1994), pp. 3–17.

2 See Cynthia S. W. Crysdale, 'Revisioning natural law: from the classicist paradigm to emergent probability', *Theological Studies* 56 (1995), pp. 464–84.

3 When such a criterion is used individually, one usually refers to 'hedonism'; when it is used collectively, one sometimes refers to 'utilitarianism'.

4 See Kenan Osborne, 'A phenomenology of the human person: a theo-anthropology', Presidential address delivered to the Catholic Theological Society of America in 1979, *Proceedings of the Thirty-Fourth Annual Convention of the CTSA* (1979), pp. 223–33.

5 Ultimately, 'good' is that which protects, promotes or enhances the human person, adequately considered, while 'evil' is that which threatens, harms or diminishes the human person, adequately considered. See Louis Janssens, 'Ontic evil and moral evil', *Louvain Studies* 4 (1972), pp. 115–56; idem, 'Artificial insemination: ethical considerations', *Louvain Studies* 8 (1980), pp. 3–29; idem, 'Personalism in moral theology' in Charles E. Curran (ed.), *Moral Theology: Challenges for the Future – Essays in Honor of Richard A. McCormick* (New York: Paulist Press, 1990), pp. 94–107. Some authors refer to this as human fulfilment or human flourishing – again begging the question of how one might know the meaning of those terms. Such terminology is confusing without an explanation of the more basic notions of good and evil. What is good may not always contribute to 'flourishing'. See, for instance, Bernard Hoose, 'Proportionalists, deontologists and the human good', *Heythrop Journal* 33 (1992), pp. 175–91.

6 In a relatively early article, 'Personalist morals', *Louvain Studies* 3 (1970–71), pp. 5–16, Janssens had mentioned five aspects or dimensions of the human person. These were later expanded in the article referred to above on 'Artificial insemination' which discusses the eight dimensions, although in an order different from what I present here and with some variations that I have dropped or changed. Janssens' article is very useful for textually anchoring these ideas in the text of *Gaudium et Spes*. What he wrote there has been taken over by a number of authors, such as Kevin T. Kelly, *New Directions in Moral Theology: The Challenge of Being Human* (London: Geoffrey Chapman, 1992), pp. 30–60, who elaborates upon the dimensions quite extensively. At the time of 'artificial insemination', it seems that the notion of elaborating some descriptive definition of the person was needed for theology in general. See, for instance, Edward Schillebeeckx, 'God, society and human salvation' in Marc Caudron (ed.), *Faith and Society: Acta congressus internationalis theologici lovaniensis 1976* (BETL 47; Leuven: Duculot, 1978), pp. 87–99, who wrote about (five) 'anthropological constants'.

7 My experience and discussion with non-Western students, particularly Africans, has been rather enlightening. When you ask someone with this non-Western

background who they are, you are just as likely to get the answer that they are someone's relative, a member of a particular family or tribe. Self-identity, unlike the Western emphasis on conscious interiority and individuality, is frequently rendered with a reference to one's membership in a group. This experience, which has been repeated many times, over more than twenty years, has had a significant effect upon my understanding of the human person.

8 Space does not allow me to elaborate upon this idea at this point. However, I believe it is worth at least mentioning an important distinction. Objective culture refers to the goods of the human environment which are offered to and appropriated by individuals who in turn transform this into subjective culture which is personal and, again in turn, made available to the communitarian heritage of objective culture. Also in this connection, we should draw attention to the definition of the common good found in GS as 'the sum to those conditions of social life which allow social groups and their individual members relatively thorough and ready access to their own fulfilment'.

9 Walter M. Abbott (ed.), *The Documents of Vatican II* (New York: America Press, 1966), pp. 260–1.

10 Reference might be made here to the famous 'wolf children' raised by animals in the wild. Although some children raised by animals have survived, their development not only did not exhibit human characteristics, their ability to learn what most persons take for granted (language and other communication skills) was seriously impaired, even obliterated.

Select bibliography

Louis Janssens, 'Artificial insemination: ethical considerations', *Louvain Studies* 8 (1980), pp. 3–29.

Kevin T. Kelly, *New Directions in Moral Theology: The Challenge of Being Human* (London: Geoffrey Chapman, 1992).

Kenan Osborne, 'A phenomenology of the human person: a theo-anthropology', Presidential address delivered to the Catholic Theological Society of America in 1979, *Proceedings of the Thirty Fourth Annual Convention of the CTSA* (1979), pp. 223–33.

Joseph A. Selling (ed.), *Personalist Morals: Essays in Honor of Professor Louis Janssens* (BETL; Leuven: Duculot, 1988).

7

Conscience

Richard M. Gula

'Let conscience be your guide' is a reliable moral maxim. But what does it mean and what does it demand of us? Conscience is a difficult notion to understand and even more difficult to explain how it operates. Yet, we all know that we have a conscience, even if we can't explain how we got it or how it works. We know that we stand for certain things, we struggle over deciding what to do, and we feel pangs of conscience when we do something wrong, even petty matters like taking cookies from the cookie jar. Questions of conscience come up regularly and not just over the big issues like taking a stand on war, on crime and punishment, or on euthanasia. Questions of conscience also come up on very personal matters like whether to blow the whistle on a co-worker who is doing a sloppy job, or whether to reveal a brother's alcoholism to his fiancée, or whether to take more time away from the family to play another round of golf. If we are ever going to grow in our loving relationship with God and neighbour, then we need to discern what is truly loving. Conscience is our capacity for making such a discernment.

The task of this chapter is to clarify the meaning of the moral conscience. I will first distinguish the moral conscience from what it is not – its psychological cousin, the superego. Then I will sketch in greater detail the meaning of conscience in the moral tradition with added emphasis to the notion of the formation of conscience, to the relation of conscience to character and to choice, to the goal of a mature conscience, and to the requirements for acting in conscience.

Conscience/superego mixup

One way of getting at the notion of moral conscience is to distinguish it from what it is not. One of the most common errors in thinking about the moral conscience is to mistake it for what some psychologists mean when they speak of the 'superego'. Psychologists of the Freudian school tell us that we have three structures to our personality: The *id* – that unconscious reservoir of instinctual drives largely dominated by the pleasure principle; the *ego* – the conscious structure which operates on the reality principle to mediate the forces of the id, the demands of society, and the reality of the physical world; and the *superego* – the ego of another superimposed on our own to serve as an internal censor to regulate our conduct by using guilt as its powerful weapon.[1]

To understand the superego, we need to begin with childhood. As we develop through childhood, the need to be loved and approved is our basic need and drive. We fear punishment as children not for its physical pain only, but more because it represents a withdrawal of love. So we regulate our behaviour so as not to lose love and approval. As a matter of self-protection, we absorb the standards and regulations of our parents, or anyone who has authority over us. The authority figure takes up a place within us to become a kind of psychic parent or police officer keeping an eye on our behaviour and giving us commands and setting out prohibitions. Since we carry this authority with us in the unconscious structure of our mind, the voice of this authority is always and everywhere present to us. It tells us that we are good when we do what we have been told to do, and it tells us that we are bad and it makes us feel guilty when we do not do what we should.

A simplified way of thinking about the difference between superego and moral conscience is to distinguish between 'shoulds' or 'have-tos' and 'wants' as the source of the commands directing our behaviour. 'Shoulds' and 'have-tos' belong to someone else. The 'wants' of conscience (what my truest self would want to do) belong to us. Whereas the 'shoulds' and 'have-tos' of the superego look to authority, the 'wants' of conscience look to personalized and internalized values, or acquired virtues. The superego acts out of the obligation to be obedient. The moral conscience, by contrast, exercises responsible freedom – the freedom of wanting to do what we ought to do as virtuous persons because we own the values that we are expressing. When we act out of the fear of losing love, or out of our need to be accepted and approved, the superego is at work. The moral conscience, on the other hand, acts out of love for others and in response to the call to commit ourselves to value. The conscience/superego mixup helps us to understand in part what makes a person with an overly developed or overly active superego have a difficult time distinguishing between what God is calling him or her to do from what someone else in authority says he or she should do.

Although basically a principle of censorship and control, the superego still has a positive and meaningful function in our personalities. In children, the superego is a primitive but necessary stage on the way to a true moral conscience. In adults, the superego is an internalized moral legacy from our unconscious past. It functions positively when integrated into a mature conscience to relieve us from having to decide freshly in every instance those matters which are already legitimately determined by convention or custom. The difference between the working of the superego in the child and the adult is one of degree and not of kind. In concrete cases, the superego and moral conscience do not exist as pure alternatives in undiluted form. We experience them as a mixture in our efforts to decide what to do. But to be able to say that we are acting in conscience, there must be a greater influence of the internalized values that we own over the superego and the pull of social pressure to conform.

The moral conscience

Achieving clarity about the moral conscience has been complicated by the way the theological tradition has spoken of it.[2] What we understand today by conscience is rooted in the biblical notion of the 'heart'. The heart is the seat of vital decisions, for it is the centre of feeling and reason, decision and action, intention and consciousness.[3] The hope of the messianic prophecies is for the people to receive a new heart so that their inmost inclinations will be to live out of the gift of divine love which they receive in the covenant (Jer 31:31–34; Ezek 11:14–21).

In the New Testament, Jesus reflects the Hebrew understanding of the unity of the person to be centred in the heart. From a person's heart come the evil ideas which lead one to do immoral things (Mark 7:21), whereas a good person produces good from the goodness in the heart (Luke 6:45). Paul is the chief New Testament author to deal with conscience. He weaves together Hebrew and Greek thought to speak of conscience as our fundamental awareness of the difference between good and evil, as a guide to loving decisions, and as a judge for acting in ways unbecoming of a Christian (Rom 2:15; 1 Tim 1). From the biblical vision of the heart as that dimension of us which is most sensitive and open to others, especially to God's love, we can develop our theological understanding of conscience.

The medieval debates spoke of conscience as a function of the intellect (practical reasoning) or of the will (choosing). The manualist era made it a rationalistic operation that functioned in a deductive way. The Second

Vatican Council's document *Gaudium et Spes* (*GS*), The Church in the Modern World, opened us to a new era of reflecting on the nature of conscience when it taught:

> In the depths of his conscience, man detects a law which he does not impose upon himself, but which holds him to obedience. Always summoning him to love good and avoid evil, the voice of conscience can when necessary speak to his heart more specifically; do this, shun that. For man has in his heart a law written by God. To obey it is the very dignity of man; according to it he will be judged. Conscience is the most secret core and sanctuary of a man. There he is alone with God, whose voice echoes in his depths. (*GS*, n. 16)

On the inviolability of conscience, *Dignitatis Humanae* (*DH*), the Declaration on Religious Freedom of the same Council, teaches:

> In all his activity a man is bound to follow his conscience faithfully, in order that he may come to God, for whom he was created. It follows that he is not to be forced to act in a manner contrary to his conscience. Nor, on the other hand is he to be restrained from acting in accordance with his conscience, especially in matters religious. (*DH*, n. 3)

More recently, Pope John Paul II, in his encyclical on moral theology, *Veritatis Splendor* (*VS*), affirms conscience as the link between human freedom and moral truth, when he says that the relationship between freedom and God's law 'is most deeply lived out in the "heart" of the person, in his moral conscience' (*VS*, n. 54).

We can distil the wisdom of the tradition on conscience for our contemporary understanding of it by distinguishing three dimensions of conscience: a *capacity*, a *process* and a *judgement*. As a capacity, conscience is our fundamental ability to discern good and evil. Except for those who are seriously brain-damaged or emotionally traumatized, everyone seems to have this raw capacity as part of our human nature. Conscience has also been used to name the process of discovering what makes for being a good person and what particular action is morally right or wrong. This is the dimension of conscience which is subject to being formed and informed through experience and critical investigation of the sources of moral wisdom. This inquiry yields the actual judgement that concludes 'This is what I choose to do, because this is what moral truth demands'. This is the practical judgement that takes place in one's heart where we are alone with God. As *Veritatis Splendor* puts it, 'It is the judgment which applies to a concrete situation the rational conviction that one must love and do good and avoid evil' (*VS*, n. 59). This is the judgement that fulfils the maxim: let conscience be your guide. The guidance which this judgement gives us will be as reliable as the thoroughness of the homework that we did to inform it.

In light of these three dimensions of conscience, a contemporary approach to conscience focuses on the whole person. Conscience includes not only cognitive and volitional aspects, but also affective, intuitive, and somatic ones as well. We understand the moral conscience holistically as an expression of the whole self as a thinking, feeling, intuiting and willing person. *Conscience is the whole person's commitment to value and the judgement one makes in light of that commitment of who one ought to be and what one ought to do or not do.*

Many people still mistake the appeal to 'conscience' as a stand for individual freedom and against authority. In short, they think conscience is a freedom from authority. This notion could not be further from the truth. Conscience is not a law unto itself, nor is it the teacher of moral doctrine. To invoke conscience means to be subject to moral truth and to make a practical judgement of what to do in light of that truth.

Traditionally, we spoke of the judgement of conscience as the 'proximate norm of personal morality'. This does *not* mean that conscience independently determines what is good and what is evil. Nor does it mean that conscience makes all morality relative to a person's own desires, or that one's moral judgement is true merely by the fact that the judgement comes from one's conscience. It *does* mean that the person's sincerely reflective judgement of what to do sets the boundary for acting with integrity, or sincerity of heart. To say 'My conscience tells me' means 'I may be wrong, but I understand this to be an objective demand of morality and so I must live by it lest I turn from the truth and betray my truest self'.

To follow one's conscience in this sense is answering to the call of God which one hears from within the depths of one's own person. If one truly believes in one's heart (i.e., with one's whole self) that this line of action rather than another is God's objective call, then that line of action is no longer simply one option among many. It becomes the morally required line of action for that person to take. In a sense, we feel within us that we really have no other choice. Martin Luther is well remembered in history for his statement witnessing to his conscience, 'Here I stand, I can do no other'. This is what we mean by saying that a person is 'bound in conscience'.

We give primacy to conscience and regard the moral claims of conscience as absolutely binding because in conscience is where we meet God's Spirit leading us. As *Veritatis Splendor* affirms, conscience does not command things on its own authority, as though the person were in dialogue with him or herself. But the command of conscience, 'Do this, shun that', comes ultimately from God's authority (*VS*, n. 58). Conscience is the place where God speaks to us. Thus, obeying conscience is giving witness to God. To transgress the command of conscience would be to act contrary to what we believe that God is calling us to do in this instance.

The formation of conscience

The obligation to follow conscience presupposes that we have properly formed our conscience. This is a function of the second dimension of conscience named above, that is, conscience as a process of discernment. This is the process of a continuous conversion to what is true and good, the search for who we ought to be and for what we ought to do in faithful response to God's call. We are morally good to the extent that we honestly try to discover what is right. We are bad if we fail to try. But trying to find out what is right is different from actually attaining it. Forming conscience is a lifelong task, an ongoing process of conversion.

The root meaning of the word 'conscience' is 'knowing together with'. This meaning underscores that moral knowledge is social. Convictions of conscience are shaped, and moral obligations are learned, within the communities that influence us. While the judgement of conscience is always made *for* oneself (what I must do), it is never formed *by* oneself. No one can ever identify moral truth entirely on one's own. We are too limited by experience and knowledge, or almost blind from being accustomed to sin to recognize moral truth all by ourselves. So we must always take counsel before acting in conscience. That means that we ought to consult the established sources of wisdom.

As humans we consult our own experience as well as the experience of family, friends, colleagues, and experts in the field which pertains to our area of judgement at hand. We analyse and test the stories, images, language, laws, rituals, actions and norms by which the various communities in which we participate live the moral life.

As Christians we turn to the testimony of Scripture, especially the words and deeds of Jesus, the religious convictions of our creeds, and the lives of moral virtuosos, and the informed judgement of theologians past and present who help to interpret the traditions of Christian life.

More specifically, Roman Catholics are expected to pay attention not only to their rich heritage of stories, images, devotional practices and spiritual disciplines. They are also to heed the moral instruction of the magisterium, the teaching office of the pope and bishops. The magisterium is charged with the mission of understanding, interpreting and applying the moral truth found in revelation and natural law to contemporary issues. This teaching office – which Catholics believe to be guided by the promise of the Spirit – carries a weight and presumption of truth for them that no other teacher can rightfully claim. They believe that the moral guidance of the magisterium helps them to check the bias of their own sinfulness and it expands their moral awareness of how they can keep the gospel alive from age to age. Given these convictions about the magisterium, Catholics are expected to include this privileged source of moral guidance in making moral choices.

Conscience and character

The proper formation of conscience uses these sources of moral wisdom not only to answer the practical moral question, 'What ought I to do?' but also the prior moral question, 'What sort of person ought I become?' The aim of forming conscience is not simply to inquire about the right thing to do by gathering information and thinking it over, but it must also include the fuller texture of a person's moral character: one's attitudes, motives, intentions, affections and perspective. The moral life is a matter of who we are as well as what and how we choose.

Character emerges from the habits we form which reflect the beliefs, ideals, and images of life that we internalize as a result of the communities in which we live, especially the people who have captured our imaginations. To form good character, we do not begin with argument. Maybe if we were disembodied spirits, abstract analysis would work. But we are embodied persons who learn through experience most of all. So we need to begin with people of good character, like Aunt Rose and Uncle Pat. The power of example is the most formative influence on shaping character. We become persons of good character by acting in the same spirit that persons of good character act.

The fuller formation of conscience, then, must pay attention not only to the rules of explicit moral instruction, but also to the communities that influence us, the images and beliefs these communities reinforce, and the people who embody the community's style of life in a way that captures our imaginations so that we would want to be like them. In the end, the decisions we make and the actions we do will be a function of the kind of character we develop and the situation in which we find ourselves. What we do ultimately both reveals and shapes our character.

Conscience and choice

Even though the moral conscience is subject to truth, is oriented to moral values, and is committed to doing what is right and to avoiding what is wrong, conscience can still err. For example, in the process of forming conscience, we can miss or distort some of the facts of the case and so be mistaken in our judgement about the right thing to do. Consider the parent who confronts a child with tough love when everyone else can see that support is most needed now. We call this acting with an erroneous conscience. This means that, even when we sincerely search for the truth, we can still miss what is truly good objectively.

The dignity and inviolability of conscience do not exempt us from making mistakes. Acting with an erroneous conscience can lead one to doing what is wrong, but it does not necessarily make one a bad person. Pope John Paul II's encyclical *Veritatis Splendor* follows a long-standing tradition when it speaks of the erroneous conscience as possibly resulting from invincible ignorance, that is, the person acting is unaware of being wrong and is unable to overcome this ignorance on his or her own. A person who does wrong as a result of invincible ignorance commits a non-culpable error of judgement. This error does not make what is wrong become right, but neither does the error compromise the dignity of conscience (*VS*, n. 62).

The dignity of conscience assures that the one who makes a sincere effort to inform conscience and then lives by it will not betray his or her integrity. It does not guarantee that one will discern what is truly good. No one can be blamed for doing something wrong if he or she sincerely tried to find out what is right. We say that that person did the best he or she knew how to do. It is those who do not even try to find out what is right that we need to worry about. As the encyclical explains, conscience compromises its dignity when it is 'culpably erroneous', that is, when we show little concern for seeking what is true and good (*VS*, n. 63). Otherwise, we must always follow the light of our conscience in good faith and leave the rest to God. Christian theology teaches that God will judge us, not on the basis of our actions being objectively right or wrong, but on the basis of the sincerity of our hearts in seeking to do what is right, even if we make a mistake.

The goal: a mature conscience

A mature conscience takes responsibility for one's own formation and judgement before God. The mature conscience is in dialogue with the various sources of moral wisdom, but it ultimately makes up one's mind *for* oneself. It does not pin its soul on another, and abdicate responsibility. Martin Buber's tale of Rabbi Zusya poignantly illustrates that the integrity of conscience is to be true to one's self. Out of our loyalty to conscience we will witness to God and be judged by God. 'The Rabbi Zusya said a short time before his death, "In the world to come, I shall not be asked,

'Why were you not Moses?' Instead, I shall be asked, 'Why were you not Zusya?'"[4]

If a person spends his or her life doing what he or she is told to do by someone in authority simply because the authority says so, or because that is the kind of behaviour expected by the group, then that person never really makes moral decisions which are his or her own. For moral maturity one must be one's own person. It is not enough to follow what one has been told. The morally mature person must be able to perceive, choose, and identify oneself with what one does. In short, we create our character and give our lives meaning by committing our freedom, not by submitting it to someone in authority. We cannot claim to be virtuous, to have strong moral character, or to give direction to our lives if we act simply on the basis that we have been told to act that way. As long as we do not direct our own activity, we are not yet free, morally mature persons.

Who can act in conscience?

This note on moral maturity leads us to ask, then, 'Who can make moral decisions of conscience?' If conscience is the whole person's commitment to value, then to act in conscience requires some degree of knowledge, freedom, and the affective capacity to care for others and to commit oneself to moral values.

Knowledge

The kind of knowledge required to act in conscience obviously includes the capacity to reason, that is, to reflect, to analyse, or to think in somewhat of a critical fashion. But knowledge for acting in conscience also requires an appreciation of moral values (we call this 'evaluative knowledge'), especially the value of persons and what contributes to their well-being. Without a heartfelt appreciation of values, but merely conceptual knowledge about them, we act more out of hearsay than we do out of conviction. To reach an appreciation of value requires experience and reflection, not just right information.

Acting in conscience also requires the capacity to be self-reflective and to have reached some degree of self-awareness that puts us in touch with what is going on inside us. The key to acting in conscience is to be self-conscious. Knowledge of the self includes knowing not only one's limits, but also one's strengths, potentials and preferences. A basic goal of Christian morality is to live according to the graces we have received. When we live out of our blessings, and do not try to run ahead of our graces, we make the moral life a continuous expression of praise and thanksgiving to God who has endowed us with different gifts or different degrees of the same gifts.

Freedom

To act in conscience one must also be able to direct one's actions according to self-chosen goals. Actions that are not under our control cannot really be considered within the realm of conscience. For example, we cannot be held responsible for a tree falling on our house in a wind storm. Such an act of nature is beyond our control. But we can be held responsible for how we respond to the destruction it brings. In our pastoral tradition we have recognized that what we ought to do implies that we can do it. It is unreasonable to demand that someone do what is beyond his or her capacity of knowledge, freedom, or emotional or moral strength.

Our basic freedom is the freedom to make someone of ourselves. As Christians, we direct our basic freedom towards becoming one with God. But since we experience God and express our relationship to God in mediated ways, our basic freedom of self-determination gets expressed through the particular choices that we make in life. (We also call this 'free will'.) Our freedom to choose must be exercised across a broad spectrum of possibilities, but within the limits of nature and nurture. What we do is at least partially up to us and not solely the result of genetics, the environment, unconscious influences, or luck. If we were strictly programmed by our genes, or blinded by social sin and other environmental conditions, then there would be no possibility for morality. If we are beyond freedom, we are beyond morality.

The biological, psychological and social sciences have certainly made us aware of how limited our freedom is. In fact, they have made us so aware that the modern-day 'out' for immoral behaviour is often the claim to being victimized by some past experience. The great temptation is to say that, whatever my failing, it is not my fault – 'Such and such happened to me and made me to be this way and to do these things; therefore, I can't be held responsible.' Such a notion of determinism has profoundly diminished our sense of responsibility and wreaked havoc on morality.

The bottom line is that, whatever has happened to us, responsibility for our action is still possible. If we were absolutely determined, then we would never feel unsettled or indecisive about our choices. Neither would we ever have to deliberate about anything if we were completely free or completely determined. Real freedom is learning to live well within limits. Those who are free do not expect to be dealt a winning hand, but to play well the hand they have been handed. The more we become aware of what limits us, the more we will be able to live freely within those limits. Our freedom to choose challenges us all the time. Each of us has to assume responsibility for what he or she does. The power to assume an attitude towards what is happening to us makes us truly free.

The freedom we have to act in conscience, then, is not a licence to do whatever we want. Rather, the freedom of a good conscience is the freedom of wanting to do what we ought to do because it is the right thing to do. Ultimately, our freedom to choose this or that, within limits, is fundamentally a freedom to choose an identity, to become a certain sort of person. We cannot do everything. Determining factors prevent that. But we can pour ourselves into what we do, make it truly our own, choose it as a genuine expression of who we are and aspire to become.

Emotions

The degree to which knowing what is right results in doing what is right can only be understood against the flow of emotions that support a good will. In other words, knowledge will influence behaviour to the extent that we care about the good and are committed to seeing it come about. For example, someone may be a whiz-kid when it comes to moral theory, but still be morally flawed because of the lack of affective awareness and a heartfelt commitment to the values at stake. Someone else, however, may do what is right spontaneously from the heart because of his or her sympathy for the values at stake, but he or she may never be able to give any theoretical justification for acting that way. Why? Because our feelings display our moral sensitivity. They drive us to act according to our convictions.

Without the capacity for an affective experience of the value of persons and what befits their well-being, we will not have the capacity for acting in good conscience. The capacity to be loving is the beginning of moral awareness. Research on the role of empathy shows how important this human feeling is in the development of conscience.[5] Empathy is experiencing what another is experiencing. When empathy is born, care is born, and with it, morality.

The capacity to experience an emotion like empathy is set in our genetic endowment, but it requires the proper environment, especially in our early years, if it is ever to emerge in full power as part of the conscience of an adult. What is missing in a psychopath, for instance, is not the knowledge of right or wrong, but caring commitment to do the right thing. The psychopath has no empathy. To pour ourselves into what we do requires an emotional capacity to care about others and to commit ourselves to ideals and standards. Thus the emotionally traumatized, the severely brain-damaged, the gravely mentally ill, and those suffering from severe pathological conditions, like the sociopath or psychopath, cannot be said to have a functioning conscience because their emotion is blunted and their self-awareness is impaired.

The effort to engage in the moral reasoning which an act of conscience demands is doomed to failure unless a person first cares enough about people and moral values to become engaged in such reflection. Without a desire to become good and do what is right, moral instruction and reflection will profit us nothing. We can give all the moral instruction we want, or provide the best moral mentors we know, and create an environment where it is easy to be good, but if the person does not care about being good, nothing will happen to produce a morally good person. Emotions are the building blocks of conscience. Emotions enable us to care enough to want to commit ourselves to what we experience by heart as valuable. Our 'reasons of the head' demonstrate in a way that can be rationally accessible to another what our 'reasons of the heart' lead us to do.

Conclusion

Conscience, then, is our fundamental capacity for moral discernment, the process of discerning, and the judgement we make in light of the truth that we discover. We all begin with the basic capacity to know good from evil. Throughout our lives, then, we search the sources of moral wisdom to become sensitive to value, to learn virtue, and to discover what is right and what is wrong. If we are to act in conscience, we need to acquire a heartfelt awareness of what helps people to live fully and what harms them. We need to take charge and give direction to our lives lest we spend our whole lives living someone else's desires for us. We can only do this if we have sufficient emotional stability to care about ourselves and others and to commit ourselves to what we know by heart is worth striving for. Upon these foundations we can build a moral life that is responding to what God is calling us to do.

Notes

1 For a succinct treatment of the Freudian model of the person, see the still valuable article by Gregory Zilboorg, 'Superego and conscience' in C. Ellis Nelson (ed.), *Conscience: Theological and Psychological Perspectives* (New York: Newman Press, 1973), pp. 210–23.

2 For a still valuable review of the ways the tradition has talked about conscience, see Bernard Häring, *The Law of Christ*, vol. 1: *General Moral Theology*, trans. Edwin G. Kaiser (Paramus: Newman Press, 1966), pp. 135–89. Also Bernard Häring, *Free*

In Good Conscience

and Faithful in Christ, vol. 1: *General Moral Theology* (New York: Seabury Press, 1978), pp. 224–301.

3 Hans Walter Wolff, *Anthropology of the Old Testament* (Philadelphia: Fortress Press, 1974), pp. 40–55.

4 Martin Buber, *The Way of Man According to the Teaching of Hasidism* (New York: Citadel Press, 1966), p. 17.

5 For a review of this research, see Sidney Callahan, *In Good Conscience* (New York: HarperCollins, 1991), pp. 186–90. See also Charles M. Shelton, *Morality of the Heart* (New York: Crossroad, 1990), pp. 33–59.

Select bibliography

Sidney Callahan, *In Good Conscience* (New York: HarperCollins, 1991).

Richard M. Gula, *Reason Informed by Faith* (New York: Paulist Press, 1989).

Bernard Häring, *Free and Faithful in Christ*, vol. 1: *General Moral Theology* (New York: Seabury Press, 1978).

Vincent MacNamara, *Love, Law, and Christian Life* (Wilmington, DE: Michael Glazier, 1988).

Daniel C. Maguire, *The Moral Choice* (Garden City, NY: Doubleday, 1978).

Timothy E. O'Connell, *Principles for a Catholic Morality* (rev. edn; San Francisco: Harper & Row, 1990).

8

The theory of the fundamental option and moral action

Thomas R. Kopfensteiner

Introduction

Moral theology, like any science, is an open-ended enterprise. Because moral theology is an ongoing affair, theologians engaged in it will find themselves at once committed to the tradition in which they work and ready to bring the tradition into conversation with other disciplines in order to transform it. This dual order of reflection can be the context in which to discuss the theory of the fundamental option. The theory of the fundamental option is the result of neo-scholasticism's conversations with personalism, transcendental philosophy and the hermeneutical sciences. The theory has provided a new context in which to analyse the moral act in a way that is freed from the inadequate essentialist categories of the tradition.

This chapter is divided into four sections. The first section will trace the origins of the theory of the fundamental option back to a theology of grace. The second section will show how the theory of the fundamental option, when transferred into the realm of moral theology, opens the way for a new relationship between person and act. The third section will discuss the role of faith in moral reasoning focusing on how the creed provides the initial sketches of a Christian anthropology. Finally, since the theory of the fundamental option and the analysis of moral action that it entails are not without controversy, the chapter will address some of the criticisms that have been recently levelled at the theory.

Thomas R. Kopfensteiner

Origins of the theory

Though most frequently utilized and discussed in the context of moral
theology, the theory of the fundamental option has its origins in dogmatic
theology. Behind the theory is the classical axiom that grace presupposes
and perfects nature. The theory of the fundamental option originated in a
psychology of grace which was meant to explain the inner operation of
grace and the experience it begets.[1] It aimed to analyse the human sphere
in which grace flourished. The theory of the fundamental option was
developed in reaction to the tendency in neo-scholastic theology to
emphasize the transcendence of grace and its utter discontinuity with
nature. This emphasis resulted in an extrinsicism where grace was
superimposed on or grafted onto nature. In reaction to neo-scholastic
theology, there emerged a greater appreciation of the reciprocity or
interpenetration that exists between the transcendence and immanence of
grace. There emerged, in other words, a better understanding of the
human dimensions of grace. Within a personalist understanding of grace,
the gracious and salvific initiative of God presupposes a receptive potential
on our part, and our inclination for union with God is perfected by God's
free and gratuitous offer of himself.

The inclination to or potency for the infinite, which is prior to any
knowing or choosing, is the basis of the theory of the fundamental option.
The theory refers to the instinct of grace that projects us toward God as
the fulfilment of all our longings. Entailed in the theory of the fundamental option, then, is the anticipation of our eternal destiny and fulfilment;
it designates our immanent and dynamic orientation to all of reality. As
such, the fundamental option goes beyond a categorical level of analysis
and casts light on the conditions that make concrete acts of knowing and
choosing possible. This means that the fundamental option is a transcendental category. It remains on a pre-reflexive or a-thematic level. The
fundamental option can only be grasped asymptotically in individual
decisions and actions. Being a transcendental category, however, does not
lessen the fundamental option's efficacy in individual decisions and actions.
It is effective in all individual choices and actions. The fundamental option
eludes a fully thematic awareness or reflexive apprehension because human
existence is finite and contingent. This is what one of the best known
proponents of the fundamental option theory, Josef Fuchs, means when he
asserts that 'the fundamental option is not itself a single act of self-
disposition, though it is always felt in particular acts of deciding'.[2] The
fundamental option remains the nucleus of all our moral decisions. Every
decision is sustained by it and every decision substantiates it.

The theory of the fundamental option is often coupled with the theory of the final option. The theory of the final option holds that at death we definitely decide for or against salvation. The theory does not mean that a life of virtue is useless; nor is it meant to imply that we cannot reject God's grace during our lifetime. Rather, the theory of the final option underlines the fact that at death the nature of a decision is most vividly manifested, and that salvation and loss do not lie on the periphery of our lives; our daily living serves as the prehistory to our eternal destiny. 'Death issues from the whole experience of life, of which it bears the stamp, but by affirming or revoking the past, gives life its definitive character.'[3]

Though the theory of the fundamental option stands in the effective history of personalism and transcendental philosophy, important insights into the theory can be gained by recent developments in the hermeneutical sciences. The appreciation of the role of prejudices in knowledge, for instance, has undermined the traditional romantic conception of hermeneutics that was determined by a thoroughly modern view of knowledge. Guided by this epistemological interest, traditional hermeneutics sought the 'determinant' meaning of a text which, it was thought, was able to be known independently of the concerns of the interpreter or reader. This endeavour was undermined in a radical way by the rehabilitation of the role of prejudices in knowledge. Taking the role of prejudices seriously means that there is no neutral or pure access to the world as in an empirical or naïve realist account of knowledge. All our knowledge of the world is conditioned, in part, by our pre-understandings or pre-judgements. Far from distorting our knowledge of reality, our pre-judgements constitute our initial bias or openness to the world. In light of the work of the German philosopher Hans-Georg Gadamer, it has become a hermeneutical axiom to assert that our prejudices, far more than our judgements, constitute our historical existence.[4] In a similar way, individual decisions are only adequately understood when they are seen as stemming from a more primordial context which directs our stance toward life as a whole. This originating context directs freedom's striving toward the good.

From a hermeneutical perspective we can say, then, that our inclination toward the good is inseparable from our pre-understandings about what constitutes the morally good life. This means that the fundamental option is inseparable from conceptions of human flourishing, or what Gibson Winter has labelled an 'ideology of human fulfilment'.[5] The ideology of human fulfilment provides a normative orientation toward the realities of the world. This normative orientation stakes out the boundaries in which moral reasoning and freedom can function in a legitimate way. From a hermeneutical perspective, this means that moral reasoning and freedom are not self-sufficient realities, but they have a relational character. Our normative orientation toward the realities of the world also becomes the filter through which a moral norm is read or interpreted.[6] The application of a moral norm cannot be known apart from the normative horizon that it is meant to protect and promote; to forget this function of a moral norm is to easily run the risk of falling into a crude voluntarism or legalism. A moral norm, then, is like any literary text; it has a hypothetical character; its meaning is ambivalent; its meaning emerges from a process of interpretation or reading. In this interpretative process, the weighing of premoral but morally relevant goods cannot be modelled on merely technical calculation, but should be seen as the final step in a strategy of action guaranteeing that our actions witness to our conception of the morally good life. In this way, in all our individual decisions about particular goods, the ideology of human fulfilment is tacitly present as the object of our striving.

Purpose of the theory

The purpose of the theory of the fundamental option is to provide a more adequate and personalist context in which to analyse the moral act. In this regard, proponents of the theory of the fundamental option stand in opposition to the tendency of neo-scholasticism's overly objective act analysis which was modelled on the certainty of a modern ideal of science. This reductive analysis of moral action was based on the unchanging essence of human nature. Instead, proponents of the theory of the fundamental option rely on a personalist understanding of human nature in which freedom assumes a more dynamic and creative potential. Within the theory of the fundamental option, moral objectivity is no longer limited by an essentialist metaphysics of human nature but is bound to the transcendental subjectivity of the person. A more adequate analysis of the moral act, then, is achieved by a greater appreciation of the subjective conditions from which the act originates.[7]

The theory of the fundamental option emerges from a better understanding of the nature of moral truth. Moral truth is a truth of meaning; it is the truth about the whither and whence of our existence. Moral truth is not a truth among others, but it penetrates our entire life project giving the directionality and anticipatory structure of our lives. Moral truth has a teleological character in that it is the object of our striving and choosing. In this context, the meaning of freedom goes beyond the ability to choose between objects to mean our ability to achieve the moral good and to create through our choices a dignified and worthy life. Entailed in a theory of action, then, is a conception of history. History is distinguished from the more primordial category of 'time' which recounts the succession of one moment to the next. History, on the other hand, results from those successive moments being assumed into and transformed by our life projects. Moral actions, in other words, do not stand juxtaposed to each other in an unrelated fashion, but they weave the story of our moral lives. History has an autobiographical character.[8]

In this personalist context, the fundamental option represents the dynamic core of our moral identities. It represents our orientation towards the moral good as such and, though prior to any one choice, it gives direction to our deliberations and knits our choices into our unique and personal histories. Though no one decision will exhaust the fundamental option, individual decisions can be seen as interpretative extensions of it. The passage between the fundamental option and individual decisions is not done in any mechanical or automatic way. The element of decision cannot be subsumed under any naive scientific explanation; such a way of thinking would belie the risks that are inherent to the moral enterprise. The moment of decision involves what Karl Rahner has called 'the logic of existential knowledge' which escapes the surety of deductive calculus.[9] Through our decisions and actions there is a slow maturation of the fundamental option as we realize ever more fully the meaning of our life projects. As we make individual decisions the contours of our moral identities take shape. All the diverse and various experiences of life become interpreted in light of the possibilities of legitimate freedom to the point that there emerges a profound consistency and transparency between our identity and our actions, between who we are and what we do. We act authentically. We develop a morally mature personality where there is found a readiness and facility to act in a virtuous way.[10]

By rooting a theory of moral action in a personalist metaphysics, an ineluctable bond is formed between the fundamental option and individual decisions. Their inseparability creates an analogous relationship between them. A family resemblance is created between the fundamental option and an individual decision and, so too, among the various decisions. To fully understand individual decisions and actions, they must be seen as embedded in and constitutive of one's fundamental option, and they must be seen as contributing to the greater whole of our moral personalities. Naturally, some individual decisions will participate in the fundamental option to a greater or lesser degree. This is no surprise when we recall that certain decisions will involve us as subjects more than others, as and when our life projects become the appropriate object of a moral decision. There is, for instance, a more profound personal investment in a vocational decision than in the peripheral choices of daily living. In this regard, there is a convergence between metaphysical and psychological categories.

As reflective of our moral identities, there is a certain stability to the fundamental option. For the Christian this means that there is a genuine and enduring orientation toward the good under the influence of grace (1 John 3:9). Nevertheless, the fundamental option can become corrupted. Theologically speaking this occurs through mortal sin. In terms of a psychology of sin, this kind of moral tragedy occurs over time. Our orientation toward the good can become dulled through repeated offences and omissions and, as we find ourselves continually failing to strive for the moral good, our actions continually fall behind our moral potential. We embark on a perilous journey through which the inner structure of the fundamental option begins to decay and rot. As we become untethered from the mainstay of our moral identities, we flounder. Because the fundamental option and individual decisions are so intimately linked, it becomes progressively more difficult and increasingly less probable that we will regain our moral equilibrium. We are beset by a progressive moral decline to the point that our orientation to fulfilment in God – still, the end of all our knowing and acting – becomes meaningless to our self-identities. We truly experience the death of our souls. While it is true to say that our separation from God occurs through mortal sin understood in terms of the traditional categories of grave matter and full knowledge and freedom, such an act would never have its disastrous consequences had it not already been prepared for and preceded by a prehistory of moral decline. By uniting the sinful act with the process which leads up to it, Klaus Demmer likens sin unto death to a whirlpool from which we will need all our strength to escape.[11] The sinful act becomes nothing other than the confirming evidence of our moral deterioration.[12]

Faith and moral decisions

There are two positions presented on the issue of when the fundamental option can become an object of reflection in life. The first position is rooted in the Church's practice of baptizing infants and holds that the fundamental option of the Christian coincides with a person's first truly responsible decision. The second position is more speculative. It holds that the fundamental option coincides with the infusion of the theological virtues by sanctifying grace; they direct the moral life of the justified person towards a life with God.

This leads to the important question as to the role of faith in moral decision-making. What is the proper role of the content of faith in moral reasoning? What is the relationship between the truths of faith and moral truth? These questions are at the centre of the debate between the proponents of an autonomous morality and an ethics of faith.[13] On the one hand, reason cannot be regarded as completely autonomous to the extent that faith is extrinsic to the reasoning process. On the other hand, it would be a distortion of both revelation and moral reasoning to reduce revelation to divine commands directly regulating moral behaviour; faith illuminates but does not replace reason. The question is, what does the creed offer to our self-understanding, to our way of viewing the world, and to our way of being-and-acting-in the world?

Pedagogically, the creed incorporates us into a believing community. By being incorporated into the community, we learn the contours of the Christian way of life. We gain a habit of mind that enables us to speak and reason about the world in a certain way. We learn, in other words, all the implications of faith which determine our freedom, structure our experience, guide our insight and animate our action. By imparting a set of basic integrative convictions, faith is not a limitation to but the condition of moral reasoning.

In the creed, we profess that every human being is created in the image and likeness of God (Gen 1:26). This is the backing for the indestructible dignity of every human being. This dignity is not merited; it is not destroyed by sin; it cannot be diminished by any quality that can otherwise distinguish us from others.

Second, we confess in the creed that Jesus became human to reconcile us with the Father and to be our model of holiness (Matt 11:29). His sacrifice of himself is the model of the new law, 'Love one another as I have loved you' (John 15:12). By living among us, Jesus has created a new communion or solidarity among us (1 Cor 12:26–27), making everyone a neighbour worthy of our charity and care.

Third, we confess that we are redeemed by Christ and called to share eternal life with him. As Christians, we face death with the confidence of our faith in him who has conquered death by his resurrection (Rom 6:3–9; Phil 3:10–11). For us, in death, life is changed, not ended.

Finally, we confess 'to wait for the resurrection of the dead and the life of the world to come'. With this belief we can confidently leave the final judgement on history to God (1 Cor 4:5). This allows moral reasoning to continually relativize 'final' judgements within human relationships and pursue avenues of dialogue in the hope of leading to reconciliation and peace.

These integrative convictions provide the initial sketch of a Christian anthropology. They emerge from faith and are further specified through moral reasoning; they function, then, as middle terms in the reasoning process.[14] Like a research programme that practitioners of a discipline continually make more specific, these integrative convictions provide the filter for the Christian experience of the world; they condition the perception and weighing of premoral but morally relevant goods; and they provide the initial criteria by which to measure the adequacy of moral insight and action.[15]

Thomas R. Kopfensteiner

Criticisms of the theory

There are persistent criticisms of the theory of the fundamental option. Criticisms of the theory may be found in the texts of the Roman Catholic magisterium and in certain theological circles. In both cases, however, there is expressed the deep-seated fear that the theory of the fundamental option is built on a dualistic anthropology which inevitably leads to an analysis of moral action which separates the fundamental option from individual decisions. The separation of person and act 'contradicts the substantial integrity or personal unity of the moral agent in his body and in his soul'. This dualism leads to an underestimation of how particular kinds of actions can impact our moral character in a negative way. The suspicion of this dualism is found in Pope John Paul's recent encyclical *Veritatis Splendor, The Splendour of Truth.* In turning explicitly to the theory of the fundamental option, the papal text reads:

> A distinction ... comes to be introduced between the fundamental option and deliberate choices of a concrete kind of behaviour. In some authors this division tends to become a separation when they expressly limit moral 'good' and 'evil' to the transcendental dimension proper to the fundamental option and describe as 'right' or 'wrong' the choices of particular 'inner-worldly' kinds of behaviour ... There thus appears to be established within human acting a clear disjunction between two levels of morality.[16]

Within the personalist metaphysics upon which the theory of the fundamental option is built, however, there is no such separation between goodness and rightness or person and act.[17] To separate the fundamental option from individual decisions is to risk falling into pure abstractions and to somehow forget that individual decisions have repercussions – in either a positive or negative sense – on the fundamental option. By failing to appreciate the interpenetration of the transcendental and categorical levels of action, sceptics of the theory of the fundamental option are open to the criticism that they remain entrapped in a reductive metaphysics of the act. This means that the criticisms of the theory of the fundamental option can be traced back to the uncritically objective metaphysics of human nature of the neo-scholastic tradition. The differences between critics and advocates of the fundamental option originate precisely on this level: the divergent metaphysical commitments with which proponents and critics of the fundamental option work provide different points of departure from which to analyse the moral act.[18]

In the neo-scholastic tradition, the analysis of the moral act was guided by an essentialist metaphysics and centred on the determination of the moral object.[19] The point of departure for the determination of the moral object was the *finis operis*, or the end of the act. This of course made sense when the determination of the moral object was made within the epistemological tradition of realism. Nevertheless, this realist tradition was restricted by a modern notion of science and the casuistic categories of jurisprudence. In such a state of affairs, the *finis operantis*, or the end of the agent, was relegated to the psychology of action. The intention of the agent was a circumstance – albeit a principal one – and could only modify the act in an accidental way.[20]

This traditional analysis of moral action had at least two important effects, both of which are undermined by the theory of the fundamental option. First, moral objectivity was attributed to the phenomenal structure of the act which, in turn, circumscribed the possible interpretations of the action. Second, while this circumspection fostered a high level of communicability, the price it exacted was the impression that moral action no longer presupposed a human subject. There was a clear line demarcating the objective and subjective spheres of reality.

The theory of the fundamental option, however, leads to a more nuanced determination of the moral object and revision of the relationship between the *finis operis* and the *finis operantis*. From a moral perspective, the phenomenal structure of the act is underdetermined and assumes its meaning in light of the fundamental option. This means that the moral object can no longer be limited to the phenomenal aspect of the act as in the stark and essentialist categories of the neo-scholastic tradition, but must be seen under the sway of the life project which predetermines freedom and insight. The fusion between the fundamental option and the phenomenal structure of the act is never done in an arbitrary way; the fusion between intention and execution is always done in a way commensurate or proportionate to the underlying normative horizon which conditions freedom and insight.[21] The moral object, then, is the result of the phenomenal structure of the act being interpreted or read in light of the ideology of human fulfilment.

The theory of the fundamental option also provides the basis from which to reconfigure the relationship between intention and execution. The *finis operantis* is no longer relegated to the psychology of action; the agent's intention is no longer merely a circumstance answering the question why one is acting. In light of the fundamental option, the *finis operantis* plays an active and constitutive role in the determination of the moral object.[22] What is done is always seen in light of why it is done. From this perspective, *finis operantis* becomes the true *finis operis* of an action.

Thomas R. Kopfensteiner

Conclusion

The theory of the fundamental option stands as a central teaching of contemporary moral theology. Not only does the theory of the fundamental option provide the immediate context in which to analyse the individual moral act, but it reflects the renewal of moral theology at its deepest foundations.

At one level, the theory of the fundamental option provides the broadest possible context in which to analyse moral action. Moral decisions and actions are not isolated entities that can be scrutinized and understood independently of ourselves. Within the theory of the fundamental option, individual decisions and actions contribute to and are reflective of our moral identities. As an integral part of a theory of moral action, the fundamental option is rooted in a thoroughly personalist understanding of moral norms.

At a deeper level, the fundamental option reflects the renewal of the neo-scholastic tradition. Through contact with other schools of thought – in particular, transcendental philosophy – neo-scholastic theology has been put on a new foundation freed from the essentialist categories that held sway over it. Keeping this in mind means that criticisms of the theory do less to cast doubt on its validity, than to underline the need of critics and advocates alike to scrutinize and justify the metaphysical commitments with which they work.

Notes

1 Piet Fransen, 'Pour une psychologie de la grâce divine', *Lumen vitae* 12 (1957), pp. 209–40.
2 Josef Fuchs, 'Good acts and good persons', *The Tablet* (6 November 1993), pp. 1444–45.
3 Jorg Splett, 'Decision' in *Sacramentum Mundi*, vol. 2 (London: Burns and Oates, 1969), p. 63. A more critical view of the theory of the final option is given by Bruno Schüller, 'Mortal sin – sin unto death?', *Theology Digest* 16 (1968), pp. 232–5.
4 Hans-Georg Gadamer, *Truth and Method*, trans. Joel Weinsheimer and Donald G. Marshall (New York: Crossroads, 1992), pp. 276–7.
5 Gibson Winter, *Liberating Creation: Foundations of Religious Social Ethics* (New York: Crossroad, 1981), p. 126.
6 Richard Gula, *What Are They Saying About Moral Norms?* (New York: Paulist Press, 1982).
7 Klaus Demmer, 'Opzione fondamentale' in *Nuovo dizionario enciclopedico di teologia morale* (Rome: Paoline, 1991), pp. 854–61.
8 This is the insight of recent retrievals of virtue. See for instance, James F. Keenan,

'Virtue ethics: making a case as it comes of age', *Thought* 67 (1992), pp. 115–27; Paul Wadell, *Friendship and the Moral Life* (South Bend, IN: Notre Dame Press, 1989).

9   Karl Rahner, 'On the question of a formal existential ethics' in *Theological Investigations*, vol. 2 (London: Darton, Longman & Todd, 1975), pp. 217–34.

10 There is a connaturality between ourselves and the good: Thomas Aquinas, *Summa Theologiae*: II-II, q. 45, ad 2.

11 Klaus Demmer, 'Optionalismus – Entscheidung und Grundentscheidung' in Dietmar Mieth (ed.), *Moraltheologie im Abseits? Antwort auf die Enziklika 'Veritatis Splendor'* (Quaestiones Disputatae 153; Freiburg: Herder, 1994), pp. 83–4.

12 The same process can be detailed in terms of the conversion of our hearts and minds. The early Church's penitential practice is based on the insight that we do not easily pass back and forth between the state of grace and state of damnation.

13 Vincent MacNamara, *Faith and Ethics: Recent Roman Catholicism* (Washington, DC: Georgetown University Press, 1985); James Walter, 'The dependence of Christian morality on faith', *Église et Théologie* 12 (1981), pp. 237–77; Josef Fuchs, 'Moral truths – truths of salvation?' in *Christian Ethics in a Secular Arena* (Washington, DC: Georgetown University Press, 1984), pp. 48–67; idem, 'Our image of God and the morality of innerworldly behaviour' in *Christian Morality: The Word Becomes Flesh* (Washington, DC: Georgetown University Press, 1987), pp. 28–49.

14 Hans Küng, *Global Responsibility: In Search of a New World Ethic* (New York: Crossroad, 1991), pp. 66–9.

15 Jean Ladriere, 'On the notion of criterion', *Concilium* 155 (1982), pp. 10–15.

16 John Paul II, Encyclical Letter *The Splendour of Truth* (Washington, DC: The United States Catholic Conference/London: Catholic Truth Society (1993), para. 65.

17 Josef Fuchs, 'Morality: person and acts' in *Christian Morality: The Word Becomes Flesh*, pp. 105–17; James F. Keenan, 'Distinguishing charity as goodness and prudence as rightness', *The Thomist* 56 (1992), pp. 389–411.

18 This is the criticism of *Veritatis Splendor* made by Demmer, 'Optionalismus – Entscheidung und Grundentscheidung', especially pp. 73–8.

19 The historical analysis is provided by Gerhard Stanke, *Die Lehre von den 'Quellen der Moralität': Darstellung und Diskussion der neuscholastischen Aussagen und neurer Ansätze* (Studien zur Geschichte der katholischen Moraltheologie 26; Regensburg: Friedrich Pustet, 1984).

20 This is evident in one of the strongest critics of the fundamental option, William E. May, *Moral Absolutes: Catholic Tradition, Current Trends and the Truth* (Milwaukee: Marquette University, 1989).

21 In this way, the theory of proportionalism can be seen as responsible for binding all the elements of moral action into a coherent whole. See the fine study of Bernard Hoose, *Proportionalism: The American Debate and Its European Roots* (Washington, DC: Georgetown University Press, 1987).

22 See for instance, Klaus Demmer, *Die Wahrheit leben. Theorie des Handelns* (Freiburg: Herder, 1991).

Select bibliography

Josef Fuchs, 'Basic freedom and morality' in *Human Values and Christian Morality* (Dublin: Gill and Macmillan, 1970), pp. 92–111.

Thomas R. Kopfensteiner

Germain Grisez, *The Way of the Lord Jesus*, vol. 1: *Christian Moral Principles* (Chicago: Franciscan Herald Press, 1983).

Bernard Häring, *Sin in the Secular Age* (New York: Doubleday, 1974).

John Paul II, The Encyclical Letter, *The Splendour of Truth* (Washington: The United States Catholic Conference/London: Catholic Truth Society, 1993).

9
Feminist ethics

Susan F. Parsons

General comments

The starting-point for a consideration of the subject of feminist ethics must surely be the recognition that the experiences and the reasoning, the lives and the conditions of women make a difference to the fundamental assumptions that we have about ethics. When women are considered, things simply do not look the same. It has been the work of feminists to demonstrate this fact, and thereby to urge those who engage in the study and the analysis of ethics to include women in. Feminists seek to provide insights from women's experiences of moral dilemmas, so that we may shed new light on methods of decision-making. They seek to use women's stories and reflections to help us understand more fully the nature of the moral life. They seek to develop women's perspectives on matters of moral concern. Much that is discussed in feminist ethics, therefore, is about the difference women make to our understanding of the moral life, to our analysis of ethical methodology, and to our consideration of substantive moral issues.

In pressing this kind of claim for the inclusion of women, there is a necessary criticism of those systems of ethics that have not taken women into account. Since feminism is a modern development, this criticism suggests that all systems of ethics which have so far been devised to provide guidance for the living of the good human life, all of these have been inadequate. In some cases, approaches to ethics have presumed that men were the only moral agents. As a result, the description of the moral life, and the analysis of the nature of ethical reasoning, are such that women are not able to find themselves within these terms. In other cases, systems of ethics have presumed the inferior nature of woman, or have recommended the confinement of her life and activity to those things chosen for her by men. As a result, the full humanity of women has been denied. In both of these ways, ethical systems have been flawed. Feminists therefore question the philosophical and the theological traditions of ethics on behalf of women.

The outcome of this critical investigation and this constructive work has been the development of feminist ethics as a subject in itself. It may be said generally that 'a feminist is one who takes most seriously the practical concerns of women's lives, the analysis and the critique of these conditions of life, and the ways in which women's lives may become more fulfilling'.[1] To address these matters, there is a considerable body of literature which may be identified and examined. There is a shared history, both of ideas and of events, which may be searched for new understanding. There are contemporary challenges arising in human life and society, to which feminist ethicists apply themselves. And there is now a diversity amongst feminists themselves. This diversity means that feminists take different approaches to ethical questions and to the project of ethics itself. In this diversity, feminist ethics shares in the complexity of ethical considerations that is characteristic of life and thought in the late twentieth century. We begin our investigation of feminist ethics by considering three of the strands that make up this diversity.

The rights of women

Because feminism has emerged during the modern period of history, it is a child of the Enlightenment. Feminism is, firstly, a political movement concerned with the rights of women. As such, it has been and is entangled with liberalism. Early feminists argued that women should be given the same rights and responsibilities in society as men were given. Their demands for equal treatment with men, throughout all the institutions of a society, were based on the liberal ideals that shaped much of the political thinking of the Western world from the late eighteenth century. These ideals involve two significant beliefs. On the one hand is the belief that a human being is a rational agent, capable of judging her own interests in the light of moral principles. In exercising this rational capacity for making decisions, human beings realize their freedom. They become self-determining and, therefore, responsible for the lives that they lead. One liberal ideal therefore is to respect the individual person, and to give her the space in which to realize her full humanness. Early feminists believed that such an understanding of the human person included women, and they pressed for the political recognition of this.

On the other hand is the belief that the moral principles used to guide human behaviour are universal. Indeed, it was important to the whole project of the Enlightenment that through the use of human reason, we could discover universal truth and universal goodness. To embark on this discovery takes the moral person beyond her own habits, and beyond the customs of the society to which she happens to belong, and beyond unthinking obedience to those with higher status or power. It requires of her an ability to detach herself from these particular things, and in her detachment, to consider what is morally right for all persons, or what ought to be the case for people everywhere. Another liberal ideal, therefore, is to think universally, a process which is itself rigorous and demanding, and as a result of that thinking, to discover the basis for a true and just society. Once again, early feminists saw that this brought huge freedom for women to ask questions about their lives. It seemed simply logical that a method of reasoning which aims for universality must include women.

Liberal thinking still exercises a great hold on the culture and the imagination and the thinking of Western societies. Much feminism today is therefore shaped by its major emphases. It has been an important contribution of this way of thinking about ethics that issues of justice have been on the political agenda. At the centre of the liberal conception of justice is the vision of a social order, in which individual persons can be free to exercise their rights – to deliberate about what they should do, to choose their course of action, and to be personally responsible for their decisions. Liberal feminists have been hopeful that their work for such justice would be a sign of the common humanity of women and men, and of their fundamental equality within the universal human community. Therefore, they have pressed for equal rights under the law, for equal citizenship and the responsibilities that entails, for equal opportunities in education and employment, for equal pay and economic status, and for equal freedom in the self-determination of their lives.

These same liberal ideals that inspired early feminists may now also be heard in a wider context, as women throughout the world gather for international discussion. For they have discovered in liberalism a shared vocabulary for consideration of a whole range of issues that are of concern for women today. Liberal feminists believe that the political movement for the rights of women is still of major significance. They believe that the vision of justice which upholds these rights is a worthy goal of moral and political action for and by women.[2]

The liberation of women

Interwoven with this story of liberalism is another strand of thinking that has also been gathered up in feminist ethics. For feminism is, secondly, a social and cultural movement concerned with the liberation of women. There are indications that in the early stages of feminism, women were engaged in serious examination and critique of the social structures in which they found themselves. Thus feminists described the social and economic pressures upon women, and the expectations that women fulfil particular roles and functions within a society. They investigated the socialization of women in institutions, like the family or the Church. They considered the language and the thought-forms available to women, by which their self-understanding is formed. The purpose of this critique was to liberate women from those structures and those practices that were oppressive, and to reshape society in ways that encouraged realization of the full creative potential of women.

Again, there are two key beliefs central to this work of liberation. On the one hand is the belief that women can be trapped by the circumstances of their lives. It is true that all persons are shaped within and by social forces. We are the persons that we are, through the formation of our lives within the human community. We are formed in relationships with those close to us, and we understand who we are and what we are to do with ourselves through the use of common language. We have choices available to us because of our social circumstances. In the midst of this shaping, or construction, of our lives, however, we may also know that we are being imprisoned and held captive by social structures, or by cultural forces, that stifle our consciousness and our fullness of life. It is this awareness which feminists express on behalf of women. Their first task in working for liberation is to name those things that oppress women. Then women may begin to speak about the deep sense of alienation in their lives.

On the other hand is an optimistic belief that these structures of oppression can be altered. All of the social and cultural factors that contribute to the shaping of our lives are historical factors. They have no intrinsic necessity about them, and are therefore subject to change. A concern for liberation points women, not so much towards participation in society as it currently is, as towards the building of a less oppressive social order. Feminists therefore work for practical structural changes that will enhance the quality of women's lives. In this work, they are sustained by the hope that social change is positive, that a future society may be better than a present one, and that human beings can work together for good in their social and cultural environments.

This kind of thinking has also been enormously influential within feminism, and still inspires work of liberation around the world. Many women find that the language of liberal ethics does not quite reach to the depths of their concerns. The growth of the social sciences and of cultural studies has given to women new ways of understanding their situation. The increasingly international and intercultural nature of feminism has brought new insights and experiences onto the feminist ethical agenda. Therefore, feminists are today concerned to investigate the structures of domination that disempower women. In some cases, these are economic structures that rely upon the availability of women, desperate to work for any pay under any conditions and at any cost to their dignity. There is evidence of increasing impoverishment of women throughout the world, and this is disempowering. In some cases, these are political structures that do not allow women participation in the ordering of public life. That women continue to find it difficult to present for public debate the needs and concerns of their lives in a serious way in their own countries is disempowering. In some cases, these are linguistic structures configured around the absence of woman as the hidden Other. Women find in every area of discourse that the language they need to use to speak of themselves and of their wisdom is not available to them, and this is disempowering. Feminists use these realizations to encourage women to recover their power. The means that may be required to regain lost power, or to exert new forms of power, constitute a major part of ethical discussion amongst feminists, who work for the liberation of women into the fullness of their potential as human persons.[3]

The distinctiveness of women

There is yet another strand which contributes to feminist ethics. Feminism is, third, a commitment to the distinctiveness of women's perspective and insight. To take up this strand is to recognize that, through their experiences and their dilemmas, women have developed particular ways of knowing and of reasoning. Feminists are concerned to stress the significance of these ways, and to encourage their further expression and development. This emphasis offers an important corrective to traditions in which women's nature has been devalued, trivialized or feared. To affirm the validity of their insights, and to take seriously their experiential wisdom, have been most important steps for women to take in their own self-acceptance. Thus, it has been recognized by feminists that women find it difficult to love themselves, to believe in themselves, or to value themselves. As a result, they have colluded in traditional depictions of their lives as frivolous, or of their natures as passive and malleable, or of their contributions as peripheral. By agreeing to these cultural constructions, women are consenting to the loss of their full humanity. They thereby remove themselves from the development of their own moral potential. Feminists are committed to the affirmation of women as distinctive moral agents.

In addition, this emphasis promises that the contributions of women's gifts and insights may be of great significance for the reshaping of our social and personal lives, as well as for the reformulation of ethics. Feminists have resisted the man-centredness of traditional approaches to ethics. They have argued that the moral emphasis upon the freedom of the individual self may reveal an anxiety about relationships which is characteristic of men. They suggest that women's knowledge of the primacy of relationships in the formation of human personhood offers a significant new approach to our understanding of humanness. Likewise, feminists have argued that notions of rationality have typically set the mind against, or over, the body, and in this dualism have revealed man's mistrust of the body's knowledge. Again, it is significant that women derive moral insight from their experiences of embodiment. Far from being some passive material upon which a mind acts, the body itself may also be a source of moral wisdom. Similarly, feminists have argued that the major thrust of ethical thinking has been towards control – of personal behaviour, of social life, of the natural world. These aims suggest a male pride in accomplishment and in domination. Women suggest that vulnerability, and compassion, and a rather untidy pragmatism may offer a different, and possibly a better, picture of the moral life.

Such emphasis upon women's distinctiveness constitutes a major point of discussion amongst feminists today. Some will argue that their distinctive gifts are the result of women's particular embodiment, of their physical capacities for bearing and for nursing children. This makes women, naturally, more empathetic towards the needs of others, more capable of caring, more sensitive to the impact of their choices upon the welfare of others. Some find that this interpretation reinforces a simplistic biological literalism, which binds women to their bodily functions and keeps them socially confined to mothering or caring roles. They argue, instead, that women's distinctive insights are the result of the activities in which they engage, and of the positions which they occupy in social structures. Thus, women have experiences of work, of suffering, of living with others, of exclusion, or of creativity, all of which provide special insights for them. By reflecting upon and learning from these experiences, women develop the values by which they shape their own lives and their relationships with others. To pay attention to the standpoint of women, therefore, is to enrich our understanding of morality. Emphasis upon the distinctiveness of women is a third major strand in feminist ethics.[4]

Feminist ethics and Christian ethics

Throughout the development of feminism in the modern period, there have been Christian women who have contributed to, as they have gained much from, these strands of feminist ethics. Early feminists believed that the emphasis upon women's rights was an expression of their faith in the Creator. That God should endow each human creature with inalienable rights seemed an appropriate way to describe what it meant to be made in the divine image. Human persons thus were given a certain dignity of being, one indication of which was the capacity for moral thinking and behaviour. Human persons were understood to be given intrinsic value as free beings. Importantly also, human persons were believed to have been made equal in the eyes of God. Therefore, a concern for inclusive justice for women was believed to be a consistent application of this theological and philosophical humanism that emerged with the Enlightenment.

Similarly, feminists who emphasize the liberation of women have believed that their work of overcoming oppression is an implication of their faith in the Redeemer. Here the compassion of God is emphasized, a compassion for humanity caught up in sin. Thus, God directs and encourages and sustains saving acts, which set people free from the effects of sin, and from the bondage of sin. The divine Redeemer is casting down the mighty from their thrones and lifting up the lowly. Christian feminists draw out the implications of this theme of salvation for the lives of women. They believe that the principalities and powers of patriarchal structures have already been overcome, and that women are to be set free for the wholeness of life intended for all creation. They share with other liberation theologians a commitment to the transformation of the present in the light of the good news of God's work of redemption.

Feminists who emphasize the distinctiveness of women may also be Christian women, who understand their concerns as an outcome of their faith in the Sanctifier. The presence of grace in human life, by which we are able to become the persons God intended us to be, is believed by these women to be the starting point of their moral lives. In receiving this grace, they are able to overcome the fear of being unworthy, the anxiety of feeling inferior, or the desperate attempt to be someone else. Then women may discover in their own natures, and in the midst of their experiences, the gifts of God to them, which are for them to lay hold of and to develop. These Christian feminists find that the spiritual dimension of morality, by which we seek to become holy, is one that speaks to their concerns for the distinctiveness of women.

Christian feminists believe that there can be, and ought to be, a fruitful sharing of interest between feminist ethics and Christian ethics. On their part, feminists have been engaged in most serious theological reflection upon women's lives and experiences. They have come to particular conclusions, and have developed important insights for women, in the midst of this faithful searching, and they challenge the Christian tradition to make appropriate response. As for Christian ethics, the fundamental theological themes with which its fabric is woven are constantly in need of examination. We reconsider them, and we restate them in every generation, and in the midst of ever new possibilities and challenges. Feminists are making their own contribution to this unfinished tapestry by weaving in the different strands of feminist ethics. Christian feminists hope to encourage the further development of this reciprocal relationship.[5]

Relationality and autonomy

One of the matters to be addressed in this developing relationship is the nature of the moral subject. Every approach to ethics relies upon some assumptions about what a human person is, and what it is about the human person which presents the possibility for moral thinking and behaving. Running through the strands of feminist ethics are differing assumptions about the human person, differing views of what it is that makes us uniquely human, and therefore differing descriptions of the subject who thinks and chooses and acts morally. To consider the nature of this moral subject is now a matter both of some confusion, and of some urgency.

The confusion stems from our present ambivalence towards the inheritance of liberal individualism. Liberalism has presented us with a particular understanding of the human person, as an autonomous individual who is fundamentally free. There are lots of ways in which I may describe myself as a person – by my relationships, by my life-story, by my location, by my work, and so on. In liberal individualism, all of this is stripped away as external to the essence of personhood. In essence, a human being is understood to be a centre of consciousness. This is, most uniquely, a human capacity for self-knowledge and for self-transcendence, for detaching oneself from particular circumstances, and for surveying and judging alternative possibilities. In the centre of the moral life, therefore, is a fundamentally unattached being, who is uniquely free to govern himself by the use of reason. I use the masculine pronoun here, because it has never been entirely clear to feminists that women have been included in this understanding of the human person. Many have insisted that women, too, be recognized as self-legislating free persons, and therefore as autonomous individuals just like men, but this has proved troublesome.

For women have claimed, from the midst of their experiences of moral reasoning, that they do not understand their fundamental personhood in quite this way. Rather, they have sought to emphasize the social nature of the human person, who is not essentially detached, but who is integrally formed within relationships. To be a moral subject is not, therefore, to strive for that centre of transcendence from which autonomous choices can be made. Rather, it is to learn how to be responsive, in the midst of the networks of relationship in which one's life is enmeshed. Relationality, therefore, defines the moral subject. What has become confusing and difficult within feminist ethics is that these differing views of human personhood may too easily lend themselves to a new dualism, such that women become responsible for, and therefore bound by, relationships, while men are free to roam autonomously around the universe alighting wherever they choose. Women become those who care for relationships, while men become those whose universal vision provides the bigger, and morally more significant, picture.

To escape this dualism, it is no surprise that many feminists have greeted the postmodern turn with some enthusiasm. They have found in postmodernism a critical dismantling of the liberal individual self with its pretence of autonomy. Such a centre of free consciousness has been exposed as the cultural production of modernism. Thus, no appeal at all can be made to this private subjectivity in matters of moral concern. Its loss, however, has been a mixed blessing for women. For they are now torn between two undesirable alternatives. On the one hand, there is the loss of a vocabulary of moral freedom, which women had not yet fully laid hold of, and which leaves them with the playfulness of unmasking false dichotomies. On the other hand, there is a new emphasis on their lives as women, determined and potentially oppressed by relationships, for which they are morally responsible. This dilemma places feminist ethics in a critical location, and makes our consideration of the nature of the moral subject a matter of some urgency.

The question is whether and in what sense Christian ethics may address this matter satisfactorily. One hopeful expression has been offered. 'An incarnational faith such as Christianity tends to avoid severe dichotomies, forced options for either/or. Neither autonomy nor relationality, alone, is the whole story. Neither the stereotypical ways of women nor the stereotypical ways of men can claim validity to represent what "human" behaviour denotes. All the qualities characterizing our kind deserve acknowledgement.'[6] What is needed, therefore, is a closer examination of the nature of autonomy and of relationality, as these are lived and known by both women and men. We need a more adequate description of the nature of the moral subject, in which both women and men may recognize themselves in their shared humanness. Much creative work is needed in this area of theological exploration.

Susan F. Parsons

Nature and history

A second matter to be addressed in this continuing dialogue has to do
with the context of the moral life. Each approach to ethics makes some
assumptions about the significant moral environment in which human life
is set. By means of these assumptions, we are helped to see the larger stage
on which the drama of our individual human lives is unfolding. In our
moral reasoning, we are then able to place what we are considering and
doing into this larger setting. This context provides a kind of objectivity
to our ethical deliberations, giving us an overall meaning, within which
what we do as moral persons makes sense. Once again, running through
the strands of feminism are differing descriptions of this moral context.
Feminists have questioned traditional understandings of this context on
behalf of women, but they have disagreed about which is the most
appropriate one to commend for women's moral lives.

Feminism has arisen in the midst of emerging historical consciousness.
There is much, therefore, in feminist thinking to suggest that history is
the important context of our moral lives. We are historical beings. We are
shaped as persons by history, as particular circumstances and places and
people and events become woven together in the fabric of our identities.
We are shaped by the movements of history, as changing patterns of ideas
and human institutions influence our lives. This kind of awareness is
important in feminist ethics, for it has given women a context in which
to take account of the real situations in which they find themselves.
Women have been encouraged to describe their own personal histories, as
well as to see themselves as part of the larger pattern of human history.
Within this description lie the places of oppression and the places of
freedom, which women may identify. Their moral thinking is directed
towards the transformation of this history in positive ways, through work
of reconciliation, through resisting structures of domination, through
common struggle for wholeness of life. In this work, they are encountering
the transforming power of God at work within history. Placing our moral
lives in the context of history is thus potentially liberating, and carries
promise for the fulfilment of women's lives, in ways that we may not now
foresee. For many feminists, this context has freed women, most especially,
from the alternative moral context of nature.

To speak of nature as the context of our moral lives has often been to
speak of something which is not historical, which does not change, which
has been established from the beginning by the will of the divine maker.
Into nature is inscribed the natural law by which each created thing is to
exist. Human creatures must therefore search their own nature, to discover
there how they are to live. In this moral context, women's lives have

traditionally been very tightly circumscribed. Forms of natural law ethics available to us have been built around a dualism of gender, whereby the nature of men is described as potentially rational and active and free, while that of women is described as passive, determined by biological necessity and physical function. Such descriptions of our different natures have presumed the man to be the complete human being, and thus he is the norm against which the nature of woman is judged inferior. Some feminists have attempted to overturn this evaluation by affirming the goodness, indeed the superiority, of women. They have argued for a form of naturalism in ethics which celebrates women's essential nature. In this context, the moral life is no longer about transformation, but about conformity to nature and thereby to the will of the Maker.

Contemporary feminists find themselves in a difficult place in this matter. On the one hand, many have celebrated the death of nature. Feminists have helped to shatter the illusion that there is some realm of nature, apart from history, that somehow underlies all that we do. They have deconstructed this so-called reality, as yet another pretentious construction of culture. It is exposed as a lie, told by the powerful to subdue and silence the powerless. They are suspicious of language which speaks of what is natural because they need to ask who says it is so, and on what authority. The attempt to establish nature as an objectively sure foundation upon which to build ethics is no longer credible for feminists. On the other hand, they too have celebrated the end of history proclaimed in postmodernism. Many feminists now find it difficult to believe that there is any purpose to history, or within history. They have questioned the human capacity for shaping history in any active or transforming way. They suspect movements of liberation as romantic illusions which, in their turn, will also repress the weak. They find it difficult to understand how a divine being might relate to or interact with this history. Today, feminism is facing the realization that, in many ways, two of the major contexts in which the moral life may be understood have been dismantled, leaving ethics without a context of meaning in which its tasks make any sense.

Feminists are looking for a way through this dilemma, within which also lies a subject of considerable importance for Christian ethics itself. For it seems that both feminist ethics and Christian ethics are in a critical location at this intersection of ideas. Our age has become sceptical about the possibility of meeting the redeeming work of God in the midst of history, as we have come to mistrust our fellow human beings to engage in liberating work for our common good. In addition, we find it difficult to discern what is 'natural' any longer, or to meet the Creator in the natural world. Descriptions of nature seem only to be a screen upon which we project our culturally limited notions. It has thus become an important question whether either of these contexts can, any longer, stand alone as an adequate context for the moral life. Once again, it may be that a fruitful way forward is to discover the ways in which they are now inextricably linked. Thus we need to recognize that deriving moral precepts from nature 'always takes place within a historical setting in which the perspectives of some will be privileged over those of others and in which the perceived need to address social and moral problems can result in distortions of ostensibly universal values'. At the same time, we need to be able to build 'an understanding of basic and shared human characteristics through reflection upon human life itself'.[7] The more adequate rendering of the context of the moral life is a further area for creative theological exploration.

Conclusion

These are difficult matters on the agenda of feminist ethics as it faces the future. A number of alternative routes lie before those involved in the subject. To understand what these are is clearly the first important task for feminists today. Disagreement about which one ought to be taken now adds further to the complexity and diversity of feminism. In making these choices, feminists are engaged in analysing their own inheritance of ideas, in assessing their commitments to the projects that have shaped feminism in the past, and in discerning the implications of each choice for the lives and the well-being of women. New wisdom is needed from feminists in this task.

Some feminists believe that a useful framework for consideration of these issues is to be found in the theological and the philosophical tradition of natural law ethics. Within its terms, there is potential for developing an inclusive understanding of our shared humanness as women and men. There is a description of the process of moral reasoning which may overcome some of the dichotomies of relationality and autonomy, of reason and emotion, of theory and practice, which have set women against men in unhelpful ways. The positive way in which natural law ethics envisions our working together for the common good of humanity, in the midst of the realities of its sufferings and its joys, may provide the needed mix of nature and of history together, as the context for the moral life. The hope which it sets before us of discovering, through dialogue and engagement with one another, not only a deeper human communion, but also the presence of the divine intermingled with the human, is a profound expression of the ultimate meaning of the moral life.[8] Feminist ethics is straining forward towards this flourishing of all creation in the fullness of the divine presence.

Notes

1 Susan F. Parsons, *Feminism and Christian Ethics* (Cambridge: Cambridge University Press, 1996), p. 8.
2 For consideration of this strand of feminist ethics, see essays by B. H. Andolsen, N. Bancroft and B. W. Harrison in B. H. Andolsen, C. E. Gudorf and M. D. Pellauer (eds), *Women's Consciousness. Women's Conscience: A Reader in Feminist Ethics* (New York: Seabury, 1985), chs 1, 2 and 8; by Mary Wollstonecraft, Simone de Beauvoir, and R. P. Petchesky in E. H. Frazer, J. Hornsby and S. Lovibond (eds), *Ethics: A Feminist Reader* (Oxford: Blackwell, 1992), chs 1, 11 and 24; and Parsons, *Feminism*, chs 2 and 3.
3 For consideration of this strand of feminist ethics, see essays by A. M. Isasi-Diaz, R. R. Ruether and E. Schüssler Fiorenza in Andolsen *et al.* (eds), *Women's Consciousness*, chs 4, 5 and 10; by C. Hamilton, M. Sanger, B. Friedan, C. Delphy, A. Kollontai and C. A. MacKinnon in Frazer *et al.* (eds), *Ethics*, chs 2, 3, 4, 5, 17 and 21; and Parsons, *Feminism*, chs 4 and 5.
4 For consideration of this strand of feminist ethics, see essays by M. D. Pellauer, T. M. Eugene, C. E. Gudorf, C. Keller and M. A. Farley in Andolsen *et al.* (eds), *Women's Consciousness*, chs 3, 9, 12, 17 and 19; by E. Goldman (× 2), V. Woolf, K. Soper and S. Ruddick in Frazer *et al.* (eds), *Ethics*, chs 9, 10, 18, 20 and 21; and Parsons, *Feminism*, chs 6 and 7.
5 These issues are discussed more fully in essays by C. S. Robb and J. O'Connor in Andolsen *et al.* (eds), *Women's Consciousness*, chs 15 and 18; and by S. F. Parsons in Frazer *et al.* (eds), *Ethics*, ch. 23.
6 Denise L. Carmody, *Christian Feminist Theology* (Oxford: Blackwell, 1995), p. 152. See the rest of ch. 6 of her book for further discussion of this matter. See also essays by R. L. Smith and C. Keller in Andolsen *et al.* (eds), *Women's Consciousness*, chs 16 and 17; and by M. O'Neill in Catherine Mowry LaCugna (ed.), *Freeing Theology: The Essentials of Theology in Feminist Perspective* (New York: HarperCollins, 1993), ch. 6.
7 Lisa Sowle Cahill, 'Feminism and Christian ethics' in LaCugna (ed.), *Freeing Theology*, p. 215. See also essay by J. L. Griscom in Andolsen *et al.* (eds), *Women's Consciousness*, ch. 7; and L. S. Cahill, *Sex. Gender and Christian Ethics* (Cambridge: Cambridge University Press, 1996), chs 2 and 3.
8 For further discussion, see Parsons, *Feminism*, ch. 10; the essay by L. S. Cahill in LaCugna (ed.), *Freeing Theology*, ch. 9; and Cahill, *Sex, Gender*, chs 2 and 3.

Select bibliography

Barbara Hilkert Andolsen, Christine E. Gudorf and Mary D. Pellauer (eds), *Women's Consciousness. Women's Conscience: A Reader in Feminist Ethics* (New York: Seabury, 1985).
Lisa Sowle Cahill, *Sex. Gender and Christian Ethics* (Cambridge: Cambridge University Press, 1996).
Denise L. Carmody, *Christian Feminist Theology* (Oxford: Blackwell, 1995).
Elizabeth Frazer, Jennifer Hornsby and Sabina Lovibond (eds), *Ethics: A Feminist Reader* (Oxford: Blackwell, 1992).

Susan F. Parsons

Catherine Mowry LaCugna (ed.), *Freeing Theology: The Essentials of Theology in Feminist Perspective* (New York: HarperCollins, 1993).

Susan F. Parsons, *Feminism and Christian Ethics* (Cambridge: Cambridge University Press, 1996).

10

The distinctiveness of Christian morality

Vincent MacNamara

The issue of the distinctiveness of Christian morality has been taken in various ways. Words like 'distinctive', 'unique' and 'specific' have been used sometimes interchangeably, sometimes with a different nuance. I propose to consider two main forms of the question. The first explores what kind of morality is congruent with Christian faith, that is, how the believing community might be expected to understand and live moral life. The second considers in what respects such a life is unique. That is, it considers the difference between Christian morality and other forms – the morality which commends itself to the humanist or to adherents of other religions. They are different but related questions. The emphasis in the first is on distinctiveness, in the second on specificity or uniqueness.

I think it is well to see the issue against the broad canvas of the relations between morality and religion. Religion and morality are formally distinct. They deal with different clusters of questions. It is perfectly possible for an explicitly non-religious person to be sensitively moral. But what happens when morally concerned people are also religious? When we bring together in religious ethics these two profound strands of our experience we can expect various kinds of interaction. Most religions have an ethical element but they view morality in quite different ways. Individual religions interpret the major religious themes differently – the nature of the deity, the creation of the world and of human beings, the meaning of human life, the origin of good and evil, the nature of salvation. This general cosmogony bears on the morality of the religion. It gives it its distinctiveness.

The relationships between the basic faith/story/myth of a religious faith, on the one hand, and its ethical expectation, on the other, are varied. One will therefore expect the question about the distinctiveness of Christian morality to be many-faceted. In general, one is asking how Christian faith bears on moral life. But that breaks down into different questions, all of them important. One might inquire whether a particular faith affects the *notion* of morality or of *moral obligation*, and that raises questions about the source of morality and the possibility of knowing its demands. One might ask how a faith *interprets* the whole moral enterprise or supports it, or offers *motivation* for it, or provides an impulse to it. One might ask about the *significance* of moral life within the faith, since the ethical strand receives a different emphasis from one religion to another. One might ask how faith colours an understanding of the kind of *conduct* that is appropriate. One might ask how these and other elements cohere to give a particular identity or *Gestalt* to a morality. It is because Christianity answers such questions in its own way that there is, in the first instance, something that can be called a Christian morality.

Not all of these matters can be pursued here: I concentrate on what seem to me to be the more significant issues. A general problem must be mentioned, however. It is this: that the subject of Christian morality encompasses many traditions. And even within any one tradition there will be change and development of doctrinal understanding. That will affect morality. What follows, therefore, must of necessity be a personal interpretation. It is written from within the Roman Catholic perspective but with an interest in other theological perspectives.

It is an axiom in the study of comparative religious ethics that one cannot understand a particular morality if one does not understand the web of beliefs or stories in which it is inserted. Religions have sets of stories but the grounding story in all of them is the nature of the deity or of the ultimate. In some religions the deity is personal and is good and benign, in others the deity is in some respects evil. In some, the deity is otiose or indifferent and creation is devoid of moral purpose, in others the deity is the guide of human history. Not all religions believe the soul to be immortal, or dependent on the deity, and not all have notions of an afterlife. If your deity is capricious or morally indifferent your religion might not give a high priority to morality.

But the Christian story is the story of a deity who is an intelligent and purposeful creator and sustainer, who has a care for the whole cosmos, who values individuals intensely and seeks their wholeness and fulfilment, whose purposes are realized in the liberating life, death and resurrection of Jesus. That is foundational. It gives a grounding, a thrust and a significance to the whole of life. So it has been rightly said that the question of who God is, is the most basic question of moral theology.[1] It is the overarching context.

There is, therefore, in the religious stories of Jews and Christians an inner impetus towards morality, towards engagement with others and with the structures in which they live. It is a trajectory towards the fulfilment of the ancient promises that God will make all things new. The awareness of this dynamic was arrived at only slowly and painfully. It had to be tenaciously insisted on by the prophets against empty cult, and came to be enshrined in the foundation document of the Decalogue. God had cared for the people and made a covenant with them: their lives were to be a service of God and of God's purposes. Religion was to be moral, and moral life religious. 'Cease to do evil, learn to do good, seek justice, rescue the oppressed, defend the orphan, plead for the widow' (Isa 1:17ff.). The lives of other peoples might reflect their gods: that of Jews was to reflect theirs.

The New Testament story intensifies the dynamic. The worship of the God of our Lord Jesus Christ is even more clearly both mystical and prophetic, both religious and ethical. The central Christian anamnesis or remembrance is the dangerous memory of the death and resurrection of Jesus as inaugurator of the reign of God, a reign of justice, peace and reconciliation. That reign of God is the end point which beckons Christian life forward and stands in judgement on every present form of life.

The Christian understands the present reality as including sin and sinful structures, which contrast starkly with the promises of peace and justice. So the Christian ethic is revealed as a liberation ethic. The love of God poured into our hearts must issue in political love, in the struggle for a condition – for structures – that will facilitate humanness. Political love then becomes the urgent form of contemporary moral life. It will be contextual. It will take its agenda from the particular inhumanity that oppresses in any situation. It will concern itself not only with the tenacity of individual selfishness but with structural causes of injustice. And in that very life and practice of the community its God is revealed as liberator, redeemer, saviour.

We are called to and caught up into this liberating movement. The salvation offered us is, among other things, a liberation from the sin of self-enclosedness to a freedom for moral commitment. It is in solidarity with our human community, in engagement in the work of liberation, that we respond to God's love. Jesus knew, as we know, that such a way of life if it is to be consistent – if we are not only to do just things but be just people – requires a profound conversion. So he preached conversion, and New Testament ethics, as we shall see, lays out for us a catalogue of dispositions and virtues that one needs for the work of liberating love.

Jesus knew too that such a way of life is possible only for one who is securely anchored in the transforming word of the kingdom message. Gospel precedes law. Joachim Jeremias put it beautifully in his piece on the Sermon on the Mount. If we read the Sermon on its own, he says, we have torn it out of its total perspective. Every word is preceded by something else, by the preaching of the kingdom of God: you are forgiven, you are a child of God, you belong to the kingdom. Because 'your sins are forgiven' (so Jeremias puts it) there now follows 'While you are still in the way with your opponent, be reconciled to him quickly'. Because 'your sins are forgiven' there now follows 'Love your enemies and pray for those who persecute you'. And so on.[2]

Whatever else the revelation might or might not say about morality – and there can be argument about morality's source, content and binding force – there is no doubt that it sees moral commitment as the logic of faith. The Christian religion, C. H. Dodd wrote, 'is an ethical religion in the specific sense that it recognises no ultimate separation between the service of God and social behaviour'.[3] So closely are the two, faith and morals, linked in the New Testament that it is difficult at times to know whether the tradition is speaking of love of God or love of others. What is not in doubt is that one involves the other. Not to recognize the Word or not to love others, John's writings tell us, is to be in the dark. To respond to the other is to respond to the offer of God's personal love to us. There is an organic relationship between them.

So moral life is transfigured by Christian faith. It is theologal. Christian morality has been called a covenant morality, a eucharistic morality, a service of God, an obedience, a sharing in the mission of Christ. The Anglican–Roman Catholic Agreed Statement characterizes it as 'the fruit of faith in God's Word, the grace of the sacraments, and the appropriation, in a life of forgiveness, of the gifts of the Spirit for work in God's service'.[4] Faith declares the source of moral goodness – the love of God is poured into our hearts; the Spirit is given to us. It interprets its movement towards the final reign of God. It shows its ultimate significance: 'as long as you did it to one of these you did it to me'. Faith offers moral life a hope. That hope is the promise that, as goodness has a transcendent origin, in the end, goodness, however foolish it may sometimes appear, however defeated, will not finally be defeated. And this is because God is the deepest mystery, the heart and soul, of every truly human liberation.

All this says something about the distinctiveness of Christian morality. One might call it the distinctive context: the contrast is with the notion of content. The word 'context' is a useful one. It situates morality within the community's web of beliefs. It says something of the consciousness of Christians as they live their moral life and reflect on it ethically. But it leaves untouched other matters that must concern us. Two matters in particular require attention: the source of the moral claim, and the content of the moral call. However significantly religious considerations shape Christian moral consciousness, it remains that the source of the moral claim is something that is distinguishable from such considerations. Morality has a certain autonomy. By that I mean that religious faith is not necessary in order to experience and recognize the moral point of view:

that is something that is a demand of our humanness or rationality. The very existence of others itself makes a claim on us. It is the claim to respect their worth as persons, to recognize, as Outka puts it, that the human being *qua* human existent is irreducibly valuable.[5] It is a claim that does not arise as some kind of reciprocal arrangement but is founded in the sacredness of the person.

Being moral, for the Christian as for anybody else, is essentially recognizing this claim. But Christians do not split themselves into religious and moral compartments. Their religious story informs, enriches and shapes this basic perception. It suggests a fuller understanding of the indefeasible value of the other. Christians know that each individual is made in the image of God. They know that God dwells in each, that the Spirit has been given to each. They know that each is held in a covenant of love by God and that the final destiny of each one is union with God. Their story gives a deeper dimension to evaluation of the other and gives some point to the popular language of seeing Christ in others or loving others in God. And, like every other primordial story, it necessarily has a viewpoint on how the content – the main lines – of response to the other is to be filled in.

What then of the content of Christian moral life? What is distinctive Christian behaviour? And what of that is specific? The distinctiveness question asks how a community or an individual shaped by the Christian story reads the moral landscape. The specific question asks if that morality, or some elements of it, is foreign to and may not even commend itself to those who do not share that faith or world-view. We have seen something of Christian context. That is the matrix of discernment. Moral judgements are not made in a vacuum. They are made by people who see life in a particular way. Beliefs about the way things are – one's general philosophical or religious cosmogony – shape consciousness and bear on moral judgement. Like all basic myths, the Christian story gives us our stance towards the world and its creation, towards the value and significance of the human person, towards body, matter, spirit, towards the meaning and significance of history, towards life and death, towards what constitutes flourishing or perfection, towards success and failure. These are matters which in subtle ways colour understanding of the moral response.

Religious faith is then seen as forming or having the potential to form a particular kind of character. One thinks of the Christian community as having a character which has been shaped by its stories of what God has done for it in Christ – stories of creation, deliverance, covenant, incarnation, salvation, death and resurrection – and therefore as having its own moral demands and ideals. The perspective of faith leads to perspectives about living. 'All whose faith had drawn them together held everything in common: they would sell their property and possessions and make a general distribution as the need of each required. With one mind they kept up their daily attendance at the temple, and, breaking bread in private houses, shared their meals with unaffected joy, as they praised God and enjoyed the favour of the whole people' (Acts 2:44ff.). There is a dynamic relationship between the liturgical recital of the good news and moral expectations. So every liturgical celebration is a challenge to realize the enterprise of Christ's life and mission.

James Gustafson put the question thus: 'What relationships are claimed or assumed between religious beliefs and life grounded in Jesus Christ, on the one hand, and the morality of the people who hold these beliefs and share that life, on the other?'[6] One could hardly hope to delineate all such relationships: Christian engagement in the world is richly varied. Negatively, one can say that there are certain kinds of acts, intentions, dispositions and purposes that run entirely contrary to Christian sensibility. Positively, one has to say that the only total model of life is Christ Jesus as inaugurator of the reign of God. That does not mean simply imitating him. It means seeking to take on his core moral sensibility, which will express itself in our struggle to realize his humanizing purposes for society.

About this, there is a tradition. We are not the first who have sought to discover the way: our ancestors in the faith have asked the same question as we ask today. The Bible is the classic of that tradition. What it gives us are impressions of the original community's experience of the inbreak of the kingdom in Jesus and how that issued in a way of life – the logic of faith. Moral discernment calls for dialogue between faith today and the complex faith of the apostolic community. That is not a simple task. The ethical material of the Bible is diverse. Its mode is indicative, imperative, parabolic, mystical. It is more story than history, more wisdom than law. It says what it has to say in a bewildering profusion of forms and genres. A genuine conversation with it requires discrimination. What one seeks is to enter into the interplay of ethos and ethic in the apostolic community and allow it to shape consciousness. Not to engage it is not to know our lineage, not to know the story of who we are and how we are to be.

It would be naïve to suggest that all Christians agree on the reading of the story or on its implications. If Jesus is the key to Christian moral consciousness much will depend on one's dominant image of Jesus. There will be nuance of emphasis. But there is sufficient agreement, I think, to rule certain things in and certain things out. That is what the apostolic community did in its different forms of moral discourse. In continuity with it, Christian morality today has to insist, for example, that each human being is to be respected and loved, that life is sacred, that we are to be faithful to one another and to our promises, that life is a gift and is to be handed on, that we are to speak the truth in love, that we are to forgive, that the poor and weak are to be protected, that unjust structures are to be overcome, that we are to be respectful stewards of creation. Belief in the story of God's ways with us requires such a vision of society.

Most, perhaps all, of that will be assented to by people of good will generally – religious or not. But the distinctiveness of Christian moral life goes beyond this. The ethico-religious vision of the early community came to express itself – most notably in the Sermon on the Mount – as an ethic that has suggestions about true flourishing and success, about losing and finding one's life, about poverty of life and spirit, about making decisions in trust in God, about seeking the interests of others and not one's own, about giving to everyone who asks, about forgiving, about washing one another's feet, about bearing the cross, about being prepared to lay down one's life for others. About love, joy, peace, patience, kindness, goodness, fidelity, gentleness and self-control (Gal 5:22). These are ideals and, again, some of them will be shared by other traditions. That is not the point at the moment. The point is that such ideals cohere with the faith-story and provide a *continuo* to the moral journey. In Christ they have been given a vital expression, so that he remains a living norm and challenge for all time.

What then of specificity? If it is true that one's world-view modifies how one reads the content of the moral claim, is it the case that the Christian world-view leads to ethical conclusions that do not seem justified or compelling to those who do not share that world-view? What is most crucial for Christians, of course, is distinctiveness, that they discern and live life in fidelity to their common, community-building story. But the question of specificity is important for a number of reasons and has been widely debated among theologians of the different Christian traditions. It is important, first, for Christians to understand the methodology of moral discernment. And it is important for them and for others to know what kind of agreement is possible in public affairs. In fact the issue is often raised now in the context of ethical pluralism in society.

Here are two quotations which point up the matter. The Catholic theologian Josef Fuchs in a seminal article asked of his Church: 'Was it Paul VI's intention to offer a specifically Catholic or Christian solution to the problem of birth control in his encyclical *Humanae Vitae*? A significant number of oral and written positions on this question . . . seem to answer in the affirmative. Such a view implies that there is a Catholic or Christian morality which is valid only for Catholics or other Christians and which differs from another, a non-Christian, morality.'[7] The philosopher William Frankena raised a concern from the point of view of public morality: 'If morality (and hence politics) is dependent on religion, then we must look to religion as a basis for any answer to any personal or social problem of any importance . . . If morality is dependent on religion, then we cannot hope to solve our problems, or resolve our differences of opinion about them, unless and in so far as we can achieve agreement and certainty in religion (not a lively hope).'[8]

It seems correct to say that Christian morality in terms of its overall form as a way of life – and that includes how it interprets the whole enterprise, how it is inwardly related to life in Christ, what motivations and stories support it, what significance it attaches to the good life, how the elements cohere in an overall *Gestalt* – has a specific identity. Nobody else views and lives life quite like the Christian. That is not a claim about superiority, only a claim about fidelity to one's vision. But there are Christian theologians who further insist that there is some content to Christian morality that is not open to and not regarded as morally required by those who do not share Christian faith. It is not so much a claim about additional demands as about different demands. In the above quotation from Fuchs, for example, it is a matter of how a community formed by this world-view interprets marital relations.

One would expect an ethic founded on the biblical word, especially when allied with a sharp insistence on human fallenness and a distrust of the power of reason, to favour specificity of content – to maintain that only rootedness in faith can yield a true understanding of human life. That has been generally the Protestant tradition. But, within that, the range of method and emphasis has been enormous. At one extreme is the neo-orthodox stress on the transcendence of God's command in relation to human ethics, which is expressive of 'the infinite qualitative distinction' between God and humankind. That is uncompromisingly specific. In other authors, dependence on a divine command is combined with a more overt use of concepts of natural and created orders and a greater dependence on theological and philosophical principles. At the other end of the spectrum is an almost Roman Catholic appeal to natural law. The spread of approaches arises in part from the perceived need, especially in North America, to address the body politic. That has sometimes led to an underplaying of the significance of theology in the interests of public discussion. So much so that some have recently found it necessary to make the urgent plea that theological ethics be kept theological. 'The first task, Hauerwas writes, 'is not . . . to write as though Christian commitments make no difference in the sense that they only underwrite what everyone already in principle can know, but rather to show the difference those commitments make.'[9] A specific morality therefore.

The issue of specificity is not the same as that of appeal to the Bible but they are closely related. Scripture certainly informs judgement in the Protestant tradition but how and to what extent? The two-part consensus of Birch and Rasmussen is a fair statement of the methodology. The first consensus can be stated most succinctly by saying that Christian ethics is not synonymous with biblical ethics. . . . The other part of the consensus is that for Christians the Bible is somehow normative . . . the Bible *is* the charter document that holds a place more authoritative than any other source.'[10] Much will depend then on just how it is normative. There is a wide spectrum in its use from direct appeal to revealed moral laws or ideals ('what God commands') through appeal rather to moral analogies ('what God does') as an exemplary pattern for our lives, to a use that sees it as offering not so much a revealed morality as a theological vision of reality, a framework of biblically pervasive themes, with which discernment must be in harmony. The more the biblical word is set over against the inadequacy of 'human' ethics – and some elements of the tradition grant it a theological veto on the contributions of other sources – the more likely will be the claim for specificity.

Traditionally, Roman Catholicism has been characterized as a natural law ethic. It is true that its source was said to be reason *informed by faith*. But its official position was and is that the main lines of moral life are discoverable by reason. The significance of faith is that it illumines reason, so that the moral way can be known 'easily, with certitude, and without admixture of error'. Such a basically philosophical ethic has not always commended itself. So that from time to time movements for renewal have arisen, most recently and most notably in the 1940s and 1950s. The concern was to 'Christianize' moral life and ethical thinking.

The criticism was that the ethics of the time was a minimalist mixture of philosophy and jurisprudence and that it did not breathe the spirit of Christian life as found in the Scriptures and in the early Church. In effect, that it was not – as it should be – unique or specific. The basic error, it was said, was that it sought its inspiration and method in the wrong sources – in philosophy and natural law, the assumption being that revelation should make a difference to morality and give it a different content. So the call was for a morality 'out of the middle of the revelation' (the expression is Böckle's). This movement meant to say more than that revelation is necessary to illumine an ethic that is *per se* available to reason. It sought a different content deriving from life in Christ. So there was a turn to faith-themes and particularly to the Bible as offering a revealed morality.

The project proved to be more difficult than its proponents envisaged in their first, fine, careless rapture. Misgivings of various kinds produced a reaction which came to be known as the movement for an autonomous ethic within Christianity. The central tenet of this reaction is that Christian ethics can offer no specific content. It does give, it is acknowledged, a Christian context with its specific intentionality, stories and motivations. It does give an encouragement to go beyond minimal demands to the upper reaches of generosity. But it does not give a substantive content that is unavailable to other world-views, to a sensitive and thoughtful humanist, for example. Part of the stance was to seek to rebut the claim that there is a permanently valid and specific content to biblical morality.

There are different meanings of autonomy and there were different strands in this general movement for autonomy. There was concern about a rather cavalier and uncritical appeal to Scripture in the renewal and, in particular, to the claim that Scripture gives authoritative universal and permanent moral rules. There was concern about a heteronomy in morals in the appeal to biblical norms and so accusations of 'revelation-positivism', 'theological positivism', 'obedience-morality' and so forth. These are related and relevant matters. The central concern, however, and the meaning of autonomy in these circles, as the above quotation from Fuchs indicates, was autonomy of content with respect to faith. It was the question of substantive specificity. About that a vigorous debate continues.[11]

It is well to note that neither a specific morality nor a revealed morality in any sense connotes an arbitrary morality. The issue is one of the true and full understanding of human life and of the moral way. General theological developments have modified the way the question is framed. Until the middle years of the twentieth century, Roman Catholic thinking made a sharp distinction between the natural order of the unbaptized and the Christian order of the baptized and therefore raised questions about the morality appropriate to each order. Current thinking recognizes that there is but one order, the order of grace, that all people exist in that order and that to everyone the one destiny of union with God is offered: it sees all people living in the order of graced nature. (Karl Rahner's celebrated and controversial expression 'anonymous Christians' was an attempt to make the point.) If this is so, there is only one model of all human life, Jesus Christ. The question then is: what kind of morality does life in Christ require and is the insight that is in principle available to the non-believer adequate?

Christians, as I said, have to do their morality in fidelity to their story. There need be no apology for that. That is what anyone in any tradition must do – religious or not. The general moral community then will be a dialogue of communities and traditions. Clearly, there are distinctive moral biases within the Christian community. There are values and orientations. There are purposes and ideals. They point the direction and they catch the moral imagination. They are very significant. For there are different levels of moral discourse. But the question continues to be asked whether they translate into specificity at the level of norms – and one can see its importance in public debate about issues such as abortion, marriage, or medical experimentation.

Schillebeeckx has the remark that the specific character of the ethic of Christians is 'that they do not have a distinctive [*sic*] ethic, and thus are open to the *humanum* which is sought by all men and women'.[12] If that is saying that, at the level of material norms, there is nothing that is not *per se* available to the insight of the morally sensitive non-Christian, I think I agree. But it is well to acknowledge that every person of good will – and every community – faces a formidable set of obstacles from within and from without in seeking the truth. There is great difficulty not only in doing the truth but in seeing it – the Protestant tradition has always rightly suspected any liberal optimism about that. Objectivity is not natural to humans: there is need for conversion. So we need constantly to be confronted by our Christian stories and convictions to clarify for us what we are up against in ourselves and in the world, in seeking to discern the way. However much one might want to pay rightful tribute to the sincerity and insight of the non-believer, we ought not to underestimate the significance of the faith-community. Its distinctive ethos, its shaping stories about God, humans and the cosmos, facilitate a moral sensitivity in the pursuit of norms, even if these are *per se* available outside the community.

But the issue of norms is not the whole story and perhaps not the most important part of it. Morality cannot be adequately caught in material, especially negative, norms. A community's vision enters into morality and influences choice. For morality is not only public but personal. It is not only about what one must do but what one can do. Individual choices for a way of life – what one might roughly call vocational choices – such as commitment to justice and peace-making, service of the marginalized, care of the sick and handicapped, living a Christian vision of marriage, poverty, detachment, celibacy are part of it. The judgement of faith that one is called and enabled to give one's life for another is part of it. One cannot easily separate content here from what some authors call motive: does the religious motive in the choices just mentioned not enter into the description of the act? Does it not determine just what act or purpose is being chosen? And morality is not just a matter of doing: *agape*, for example, is a virtue of attachment as well as of action and the disposition of the heart is part of the virtue. The more attention is given to such considerations the more arguable is the claim that there is a specific Christian content to morality. But how much one will want to make of that is another matter.

Vincent MacNamara

Notes

1 B. V. Johnstone, 'Methodology, moral' in J. A. Dwyer (ed.), *The New Dictionary of Catholic Social Thought* (Collegeville, MN: Liturgical Press, 1994), p. 600.
2 J. Jeremias, *The Sermon on the Mount* (Bangalore: Theological Publications, 1961), p. 42.
3 C. H. Dodd, *Gospel and Law* (New York: Columbia University Press, 1951), p. 13.
4 *Life in Christ: An Agreed Statement by the Second Anglican–Roman Catholic International Commission* (London: Church House Publishing/Catholic Truth Society, 1994), p. 4.
5 G. Outka, *Agape* (New Haven and London: Yale University Press, 1972), p. 10.
6 J. M. Gustafson, *Christ and the Moral Life* (New York: Harper and Row, 1968), p. 6.
7 J. Fuchs, 'Is there a specifically Christian morality?' in C. Curran and R. McCormick (eds), *Readings in Moral Theology*, no. 2: *The Distinctiveness of Christian Ethics* (New York: Paulist Press, 1980), pp. 3ff.
8 W. Frankena, 'Is morality logically dependent on religion?' in G. Outka and J. P. Reeder Jr (eds), *Religion and Morality* (New York: Anchor Books, 1973), p. 295.
9 S. Hauerwas, 'On keeping theological ethics theological' in S. Hauerwas and A. MacIntyre (eds), *Revisions* (Notre Dame, IN: University of Notre Dame Press, 1983), p. 36.
10 R. C. Birch and L. L. Rasmussen, *Bible and Ethics in the Christian Life* (Minneapolis: Augsburg Publishing, 1976), pp. 45–6.
11 For a fuller treatment see my *Faith and Ethics: Recent Roman Catholicism* (Dublin: Gill and Macmillan, 1985). Cf. also 'Moral life, Christian' in J. Komonchak, M. Collins and D. Lane (eds), *The New Dictionary of Theology* (Dublin: Gill and Macmillan, 1987) and 'Moral life, Christian' in Dwyer (ed.), *The New Dictionary of Catholic Social Thought*.
12 E. Schillebeeckx, *Church: The Human Story of God* (New York: Crossroad, 1990), p. 29.

Select bibliography

C. Curran and R. McCormick (eds), *Readings in Moral Theology*, no. 2: *The Distinctiveness of Christian Ethics* (New York: Paulist Press, 1980).
J. Fuchs, *Christian Morality: The Word Becomes Flesh* (Dublin: Gill and Macmillan, 1987).
J. M. Gustafson, *Can Ethics Be Christian?* (Chicago: University of Chicago Press, 1975).
S. Hauerwas, *A Community of Character* (Notre Dame, IN: University of Notre Dame Press, 1981).
V. MacNamara, *Faith and Ethics: Recent Roman Catholicism* (Dublin: Gill and Macmillan, 1995).
W. C. Spohn, *What Are They Saying About Scripture and Ethics?* (New York: Paulist Press, 1995).

PART II
Applied ethics

Social ethics

11
Justice

Karen Lebacqz

Although the injunction to 'do justice' (Mic 6:8) has been a constant in Christian tradition, understandings of what the injunction means and how to do justice are probably as numerous as the Christians who respond to that injunction. Some differences are notable. Roman Catholic traditions have generally grounded the requirements of justice in natural law, presumably accessible not only to Christians, but to all humans by virtue of their 'nature' as reasonable creatures. Protestant traditions have focused less on that which is common to all people and more on 'grace', locating justice in the 'good news' of God's saving acts and in the story of a community trying to live faithfully to that Gospel. These differences are not unimportant. Nonetheless, some common themes and threads can be found, from which a tapestry of justice with a distinctively Christian texture might be woven.

Western philosophy

Since that tapestry has intersected with Western philosophical traditions at crucial points, it is easiest to see both what is distinctive about Christian approaches to justice and what problems must be addressed in contemporary Christian views by comparing those views to notions of justice that dominate the contemporary Western philosophical tradition. This chapter will outline in brief several contemporary philosophical views, and then will turn to elucidating what is distinctive about Christian approaches to justice.

Karen Lebacqz

Liberal views

In Western philosophical traditions, the formal statement of justice is 'treat similar cases similarly' or 'give to each what is due'.[1] 'Treat similar cases similarly' implies the equality of each moral agent and prevents arbitrary discrimination. It is an empty formula, however, in that it does not specify which cases are to be considered similar or how those cases should be treated. Similarly, 'give to each what is due' does not specify whether the criterion for distribution should be need (Marx), contribution or role in society (Aristotle), the overall good (Mill), or some other criterion or combination of criteria. The history of Western philosophy is a history of debates about precisely these substantive issues.

Approaches to what is generally called distributive justice will thus differ widely. Robert Nozick argues that what is 'due' to individuals depends on the voluntary exchanges that they make and the gifts they receive.[2] Arguing explicitly against any broader notion of distributive justice in which the state or a similar entity would redistribute goods among individuals, Nozick proposes to substitute commutative justice (justice in exchange) as the sole source of 'entitlements' to goods. In this approach, there is no built-in protection for the poor or disadvantaged; gifts given and bargains made by people determine what one rightly holds as entitlements.

By contrast, John Rawls begins with the recognition that social institutions position people to be in very different starting positions; these positions impact the fairness of exchanges.[3] Rational individuals choosing under fair circumstances, he argues, would establish some shared rights and then would require that differences in income, wealth, or status must ultimately benefit the least advantaged. For Rawls, inequalities in wealth, income, status, and the like are justifiable only if (a) they attach to positions that are open to all (equal opportunity) and (b) they benefit the least advantaged in the long run, consistent with just savings for the next generation.

These two theories appear to give us very different understandings of justice. In Nozick's scheme, justice derives from the voluntariness of individual exchanges and offers no explicit protections for the poor or disadvantaged. In Rawls' scheme, justice requires structuring the basic institutions of society so that they benefit the disadvantaged over the long run. Since the position of the least advantaged would appear to differ remarkably in these two approaches, it is perhaps difficult to see how much the approaches nonetheless share.

As different as they appear at first glance, these theories share some liberal presuppositions. They both claim a Kantian base of respect for the individual and individual rights. They focus on the distribution of goods,

164

and they offer no challenge to the fundamental concept of ownership of goods that derives from Locke nor do they challenge fundamental institutions such as the patriarchal family of Western culture.

Challenges to liberalism

It is precisely these presuppositions that have come under recent attack. Communitarians such as Michael Walzer eschew the notion that an abstract, universal standard of justice can be found.[4] Further, communitarians eschew the fundamental stress on the individual that liberalism presupposes. They propose instead that communities come to their own understandings of justice, consistent with their particular histories. Justice is not abstract and universal, derived by deductive logic from minimal premises or by procedures of rational choice, but emerges out of the complex and distinctive histories of communities.

Feminists such as Iris Marion Young,[5] Susan Okin,[6] and Nancy Hirschmann[7] concur in some communitarian critiques of the liberal stress on individual autonomy and rational choice. Hirschmann points out that such views tend to reflect a male standpoint that cannot speak for all. Young contends that people are not simply individuals but are organized and oppressed as members of groups. Okin notes that if Nozick's adaptation of Lockean property rights is taken seriously, women would be said to 'own' their children, since they have 'mixed their labor' with raw materials in order to 'produce' them. Hence, for feminists, the fundamental presuppositions of liberal theory are problematic: its dependence on a limited kind of rationality renders it absurd, its neglect of the realities of oppression renders it impotent, and its blindness to its own biases renders it inadequate at best and demonic at worst.

Following Carol Gilligan[8] and Nancy Chodorow[9], many feminists have charged that the focus on justice and abstract principles misses an important ethical dimension or 'voice' — the voice of care, which is particular and contextual.[10] Thus, feminists have also raised a fundamental challenge to the adequacy of justice as the rubric under which societal arrangements should be assessed. To these communitarian and feminist voices must be added the postmodern challenge that all knowledge reflects power.[11] Hence, the liberal view of justice will be the product of hegemonic discourse, reflecting the powerful, middle-class position of the advocates of liberal theory.

In sum, numerous voices are now raised questioning the entire liberal enterprise of trying to find universal standards of justice. In the face of such criticisms, not only liberal theory but any attempt to find a theory of justice may be in trouble. It is partly for this reason that in his more recent defence of liberalism John Rawls has adopted a more modest agenda for his theory of justice, and now claims it as a political rather than a moral theory of justice.[12]

Christian views: a different 'voice'

Against this backdrop of liberal theory and its critics, we can see both the distinctiveness of and the difficulties for any contemporary Christian approach to justice. We begin with what is distinctive.

An everflowing stream

Christian approaches to justice have roots in the Hebrew Scriptures. Two words from those Scriptures are translated by our word 'justice': *mishpat* and *sedakah*. *Mishpat* are particular duties and responsibilities that embody life in covenant with God and with one another. *Sedakah* refers to God's righteousness and hence brings judgement not on particular acts but on what William Coats has called the entire 'shape of the age'.[13] While *mishpat* may bear some resonances with 'give to each what is due', *sedakah* requires a far more expansive understanding of justice. Eloquent expression is given to this expansiveness in the prophet Amos's denunciation of those who trample the heads of the poor into the ground: let justice roll down like waters and righteousness like an everflowing stream (Amos 5:24).

Christians are shaped by this understanding of fundamental covenantal responsibilities and of an overarching righteousness that offers the vision of God's reign. While Western philosophy defines justice formally as 'giving to each what is due', or 'treating similar cases similarly', and Christian tradition has sometimes adopted this more narrow view,[14] contemporary Christian theorists tend to follow the call of Amos in seeing justice as an everflowing stream that will sweep away iniquities. Justice has a much broader scope, then, than it does in the philosophical tradition.

This broad scope is both benefit and burden. Taking the broader view enables Christians to address problems of oppression and of the treatment of groups as well as of individuals. We shall return to this below. It also allows Christians to refuse the division between 'care' and justice that appears to plague contemporary philosophical feminists.[15] At the same time, taking such a broad view can dilute the power of Christian discourse to address issues with precision and clarity.

Remembrance

For philosophers, the grounding of any demands of justice generally lies either in a notion of the well-ordered society (Aristotle) or in an extension of the powers of reason (Kant). For Christians, the grounding of justice is in remembrance.[16] What is 'right' or 'just' derives from the original intentions of a loving creator and from the acts of that Creator toward the creation. As we remember those saving acts (e.g., in the Lord's Supper, the words of institution often are 'Do this in remembrance of me'), we are oriented toward God and God's intentions for the human community.

What, then, are God's intentions? We are created for *shalom*, for a harmony of wholeness, peace and justice. In Roman Catholic tradition, this divine law is understood to be reflected in natural law, which can be discerned by reason and is interpreted through the teaching function of the Church.[17] Protestants are more sceptical regarding our ability to know what is right, good, or just; they tend, therefore, to turn not to human reason but to biblical texts and tradition in order to discern what justice requires.[18] Since Vatican II, Catholics and Protestants have moved closer to each other's position, prompting James Gustafson to propose that a *rapprochement* is possible.[19] Whatever their particular *method* for discerning God's will, for both, the *grounding* of justice lies in God's creating, redeeming and sustaining acts. Justice is the human response of gratitude for these great gifts.

In Christian traditions, therefore, justice is primarily determined by God. Justice has to do with fulfilling the demands of relationship.[20] Human justice is intended to reflect divine justice and is not created solely by the human community. One can see immediately the possible conflict between such a view and the stress on individual rights that permeates contemporary liberal tradition. While rights are sometimes affirmed in Christian approaches to justice,[21] those rights are always understood within the larger framework of an emphasis on the common good.

Sin and structure

The Christian affirmation that we are 'fallen' or that 'sin' pervades the world means that the original intended *sedakah* or righteousness has been broken and violated. One of the primary manifestations of sin is injustice.[22] Because the world is permeated with injustice, justice is corrective or reparative – it is dominated by the principle of redress or setting things right.[23] To speak of justice is to focus on ways of restoring right relationship.[24]

In one sense, of course, to 'give to each what is due' might be seen as establishing right relations. Yet the rather narrow, calculating philosophical notion does not seem to capture either the sense that we begin with injustice or the sense that right relation might go beyond handing out goods in accord with some established principle of desert. Just as the prophets of the Hebrew Scriptures railed against the rich for trampling the faces of the poor into the dust, so the early Church Fathers saw the rich as 'robbers' who kept bread that belonged to the hungry.[25] Contemporary liberation theologians and feminist theologians are particularly strong in stressing how 'the personal is political' – how individual suffering and pain reflects structural injustices of the larger political, economic and social systems. A Christian approach to justice therefore begins with a recognition of structural problems and of oppression.

Power and the poor

Because of the centrality of oppression to Christian discussions of justice, the poor become the litmus test of justice.[26] The central recognition that justice has to do with how systems and structures work means that the measure of justice and injustice becomes the plight of the poor and oppressed. If some are going hungry, then there must be an injustice somewhere in the system. This is what allowed early Church Fathers to declare that the poor were being 'robbed' simply because the rich were rich. It is what underlies José Miranda's claim that the poor would never have agreed to the wages they receive that keep them locked into poverty.[27]

Further, seeing the poor as the litmus test of whether justice is being done leads contemporary liberation theologians to argue for the epistemological privilege of the oppressed. Not only is justice measured by the *plight* of the poor; it is measured *by the poor* themselves, for they have epistemological privilege – they know better than the rich what justice requires, what it would take to have 'right relationship'. Feminist theologians have also stressed the standpoint of women and others who are marginalized. A host of particular theologies reflecting ethnic and racial communities (e.g., Mujerista theology, womanist theology, 'han' theology from Korea) contend against any notion that justice is done when the poor are neglected.

From this perspective, discussions of justice are not simply about what should be distributed to whom, but are also about who has the *power* to make those decisions and to determine the standards by which justice is assessed. Justice is not simply the proper distribution of goods, but must include attention to the creation of goods, the participation of all in decision-making processes, and the rectification of historical injustices.

Dimensions of justice

Significantly, the covenantal, sweeping understanding of justice in Christian tradition yields a more complex break-down of categories than we usually find in Western philosophy, in spite of some shared Aristotelian roots. In philosophical tradition, justice is typically broken down into these categories:

- Retributive (punishment and reward);
- Reparative (restitution);
- Distributive (distribution of goods to individuals by the state);
- Commutative (fairness of exchanges between individuals).

We have already seen that Nozick would collapse distributive justice into commutative concerns, that Rawls would structure institutions to ensure that distributive patterns work toward the goal of benefiting the disadvantaged, and that Young and others would put some stress on reparative justice to correct historical injustices and oppression. All three of these receive attention in Christian approaches, but two additional dimensions of justice are added explicitly in Roman Catholic theory and implicitly in Protestant approaches.

The first dimension is called social justice in Catholic tradition. Here, the term 'social justice' must not be confused with the rather vague and general use of that term to denote justice in any social sphere. Rather, in Catholic tradition, social justice has to do with what the individual owes to the social collective. In order for people to honour their duties to the common good, the society must be organized in such a way that everyone can participate.[28] Thus, marginalization and powerlessness – two of the five 'faces' of oppression noted by Young – would be explicitly forbidden.

The second dimension is the understanding that while justice has to do with systems and structures in society, it is not simply a matter of social ethics. It is also a virtue to be cultivated within the person.[29] The discussion of justice as a virtue has been strongest in Catholic tradition and much less noted in Protestant traditions. Nonetheless, there is increasing attention to virtue and character ethics in contemporary Protestantism.

Interestingly, Joel Feinberg once raised the challenge that the typical divisions into these categories of distributive, retributive, commutative, and so on were not very helpful. A more fruitful approach, he proposed, might be to take injustice as the starting point, and to look at different types of injustice.[30] This challenge was taken up by Lebacqz, who argues – with liberation theologians – that a Christian approach must begin with the realities of injustice.[31] Such an approach stresses the reparative or corrective dimension of justice, denouncing the status quo and the injustices that are built into it. But a Christian approach always adds an annunciation: the proclamation of the reign of God in which the lion and lamb will lie down together, and peace and justice will embrace.[32] This vision of *shalom*, of a jubilee of new beginnings, of the perfect harmony or love that moves justice forward offers a concrete image of the goal of justice. Where contemporary liberal theory and its critics[33] draw back from substantive notions of justice and retreat into procedural approaches, the Christian vision of justice makes no such retreat into pure procedure.

The postmodern challenge

The major challenge facing contemporary Christian views, however, will be precisely how to address questions of justice in a postmodern world where there is no shared vision of the common good or of the substance of justice. As the certainty that once accompanied Western philosophical traditions fades, for example, both Roman Catholic and Protestant traditions will tend to draw on biblical insights and sources for determining what is right. But these sources will not be compelling to those from other religious traditions or who adhere to no religious tradition. In a pluralistic, fragmented world,[34] is there any hope for a universal notion of the demands of justice, or are we relegated to a kind of relativism in which Christians can speak only with and to each other? While the strength of Christian approaches lies in their substantive vision of the demands of justice, their breadth of conceptualization of the range and focus of those demands, and their attention to voices of the oppressed, the weakness of Christian approaches may lie precisely in the fact that, ultimately, a Christian understanding of justice is posited on a story shared by a faith community.[35] The vision of a world in which all is in 'right relation' is a vision that could probably be shared by many, but the particular meaning attached to that vision and the modes by which it would be brought about promise to remain contentious in a pluralistic world.

Notes

1 See Joel Feinberg, 'Noncomparative justice', p. 55 and William K. Frankena, 'Some beliefs about justice', p. 46, in Joel Feinberg and Hyman Gross (eds), *Justice: Selected Readings* (Belmont, CA: Wadsworth, 1977).
2 Robert Nozick, *Anarchy, State and Utopia* (New York: Basic Books, 1974), ch. 7.
3 John Rawls, *A Theory of Justice* (Cambridge, MA: Harvard University Press, 1971).
4 Michael Walzer, *Spheres of Justice: A Defense of Pluralism and Equality* (New York: Basic Books, 1983).
5 Iris Marion Young, *Justice and the Politics of Difference* (Princeton, NJ: Princeton University Press, 1990).
6 Susan Moller Okin, *Justice, Gender, and the Family* (New York: Basic Books, 1989).
7 Nancy Hirschmann, *Rethinking Obligation: A Feminist Method for Political Theory* (Ithaca, NY: Cornell University Press, 1992).

8 Carol Gilligan, *In a Different Voice* (Cambridge, MA: Harvard University Press, 1982).

9 Nancy Chodorow, *The Reproduction of Mothering* (Berkeley: University of California Press, 1978).

10 See, for example, the essays in Mary Jeanne Larrabee (ed.), *An Ethic of Care: Feminist and Interdisciplinary Perspectives* (New York: Routledge, 1993).

11 Michel Foucault, *Power/Knowledge: Selected Interviews and Other Writings*, ed. Colin Gordon (New York: Pantheon Press, 1980).

12 John Rawls, *Political Liberalism* (New York: Columbia University Press, 1993).

13 William Coats, *God in Public: Political Theology Beyond Niebuhr* (Grand Rapids, MI: Eerdmans, 1974).

14 Emil Brunner laments this tendency in *Justice and the Social Order* (London: Lutterworth Press, 1945), at p. 19.

15 Karen Lebacqz, 'Justice' in Letty M. Russell and J. Shannon Clarkson (eds), *Dictionary of Feminist Theologies* (Louisville, KY: Westminster John Knox Press, 1996).

16 Karen Lebacqz, *Justice in an Unjust World: Foundations for a Christian Approach to Justice* (Minneapolis: Augsburg, 1987).

17 Charles E. Curran and Richard A. McCormick (eds), *Readings in Moral Theology*, no. 7: *Natural Law and Theology* (New York: Paulist Press, 1991).

18 Stephen Charles Mott, *Biblical Ethics and Social Change* (New York: Oxford University Press, 1982).

19 James M. Gustafson, *Protestant and Roman Catholic Ethics: Prospects for Rapprochement* (Chicago: University of Chicago Press, 1978).

20 John R. Donahue, 'Biblical perspectives on justice' in John C. Haughey (ed.), *The Faith That Does Justice* (New York: Paulist Press, 1977).

21 For example, Pope John XXIII's encyclical *Pacem in Terris* (section 26) delineates a number of basic rights, such as the right to a just wage. However, those rights are posited on an understanding that we are by nature social and that we have both a duty and a right to contribute to the common good.

22 Reinhold Niebuhr, *Nature and Destiny of Man*, vol. 1: *Human Nature* (New York: Charles Scribner's Sons, 1941), ch. 7; see also Lebacqz, *Justice in an Unjust World*.

23 Mott, *Biblical Ethics and Social Change*, p. 67.

24 Carter Heyward, *The Redemption of God: A Theology of Mutual Relation* (New York: University Press of America, 1982).

25 For instance, Basil the Great queried 'Are you not a robber? You who make your own the things which you have received to distribute?': quoted in Charles Avila, *Ownership: Early Christian Teaching* (Maryknoll, NY: Orbis Books, 1983), p. 50.

26 National Conference of Catholic Bishops, *Economic Justice for All: Catholic Social Teaching and the U.S. Economy* (*Origins* 16 [24]), pp. 409–55. The letter does not use the phrase 'litmus test' but speaks consistently of our 'special obligation' to the poor.

27 José Porfirio Miranda, *Marx and the Bible: A Critique of the Philosophy of Oppression* (Maryknoll, NY: Orbis Books, 1974), ch. 1.

28 See the excellent discussion of justice in terms of mutual rights and duties in David Hollenbach, *Claims in Conflict: Retrieving and Renewing the Catholic Human Rights Tradition* (New York: Paulist Press, 1979).

29 Josef Pieper, *The Four Cardinal Virtues* (Notre Dame, IN: University of Notre Dame Press, 1966).

30 Joel Feinberg, 'Noncomparative justice' in Feinberg and Gross (eds), *Justice: Selected Readings*, at p. 55.

31 See Lebacqz, *Justice in an Unjust World*.
32 Nicholas Wolterstorff, *Until Justice and Peace Embrace* (Grand Rapids, MI: Eerdmans, 1983).
33 See, e.g., Seyla Benhabib, *Situating the Self: Gender, Community, and Postmodernism in Contemporary Ethics* (New York: Routledge, 1992).
34 Alastair MacIntyre, *After Virtue*, 2nd edn (Notre Dame, IN: University of Notre Dame Press, 1984).
35 See Gene Outka and John P. Reeder (eds), *Prospects for a Common Morality* (Princeton, NJ: Princeton University Press, 1993) for a range of views on the question of a common morality in a postmodern world.

Select bibliography

Joel Feinberg and Hyman Gross (eds), *Justice: Selected Readings* (Belmont, CA: Wadsworth, 1977).
David Hollenbach, *Claims in Conflict: Retrieving and Renewing the Catholic Human Rights Tradition* (New York: Paulist Press, 1979).
Karen Lebacqz, *Justice in an Unjust World: Foundations for a Christian Approach to Justice* (Minneapolis: Augsburg, 1987).
Karen Lebacqz, *Six Theories of Justice: Perspectives from Philosophical and Theological Ethics* (Minneapolis: Augsburg, 1986).
Iris Marion Young, *Justice and the Politics of Difference* (Princeton, NJ: Princeton University Press, 1990).

12

Property

Timothy J. Gorringe

'The idea of property', wrote J. S. Mill, 'is not some one thing, identical throughout history and incapable of alteration, but is variable, like all other creations of the human mind; at any given time it is a brief expression denoting the rights over things conferred by the law or custom of some given society at that time; but neither on this point nor on any other has the law and custom of a given time and place a claim to be stereotyped for ever.'[1] The statement needs considerable glossing but its main point is essential to any proper understanding of the theme. Ideas of property hang together with ideas of the state, of justice, and of human nature and vary with different economies. Thus property has been understood one way in a largely peasant economy where the ox plough is the principal means of production (Scripture and the early Church Fathers), another way when trade begins to burgeon (Aquinas), another way in the light of the rise of the landed gentry (Locke), another way against the background of the industrial revolution (Hegel and Marx), and another way in late capitalism (Hayek). At the same time there is a utopian strand in the discussion of property, grounded in our earliest texts, which exercises a profound gravitational pull and which is especially important at the present time. I shall first try to outline the way in which approaches to property have changed before sketching the contemporary situation and the importance of the utopian tradition.

Property in non-capitalist economies

The Bible

'Until the lions have their historians stories of hunting will always glorify the hunter', says the African proverb. When we read the Hebrew Bible we listen in to a debate, but one of the reasons this collection of books is so unusual is that we have the history of the victims, the failures, those who never came to power, rather more than of those who did. We do have the latter – look at the bombast of much of 1 Kings 1 – 8, and some of the royal psalms, for example. But we have far more critique, much of which centres on property. When the tribes of Israel demand a king to help them meet the Philistine threat Samuel warns them that he will take, and take, and take again (1 Sam 8). The fiercely told story of Ahab and Naboth, with its bloody denouement, is a critique of the view that royal power can override the property rights of ordinary citizens (1 Kgs 21; 2 Kgs 9).

The background of this critique, as of the positive teaching on property in the Hebrew Bible, is the belief that in pre-monarchical Israel things were done differently. Norman Gottwald has argued that in the period of the Judges there was, for about two hundred years, an egalitarian society, where each family tilled its land and kept its flocks, which formed a benchmark for all later understandings of property.[2] These were theorized and set down, above all in Deuteronomy and Leviticus, during and after the exile (587–538 BCE). Here, against the bitter background of the collapse of the monarchy, certain crucial principles were laid down. The practical vision was always that of a free and independent peasantry, where each family contributed to the common good through its husbanding of the land, and where the king was 'one from amongst your brethren' (Deut 17:15) who was not permitted to amass huge property. This vision was theologically grounded above all in the understanding that, in the opening words of Psalm 24, 'The earth is the Lord's, and all that is in it'. As in the great vision of Genesis 2 human beings are stewards and park-keepers on behalf of the divine owner. They have no absolute ownership rights themselves. Creation is gift: it is not there for anyone to corner or monopolize or, as in the peculiarly British vice, to label with 'Private, keep out'. The committees who put Leviticus together wanted, if we may be excused the phrase, a 'stakeholder economy'. The land was God's and every family had its own stake in it, to dwell in peace 'under its vine and under its fig tree'. Were they to lose the land by falling into debt slavery their plot was to be restored in the year of remission, the Jubilee year – every fiftieth year according to Leviticus (ch. 25), or every seven according to the left-wingers behind Deuteronomy (ch. 15). Meanwhile draconian legislation sought to dissuade the local bully boys from moving the landmarks which staked out each family plot, thus enlarging their own estates and squeezing out the poor. This was treated as a matter of the utmost seriousness because care of the family patch of land was a sign of one's membership of the covenant people, so alienating the land was an attack on Israel's religious basis. It was also a practical measure designed to guarantee the economic viability of each family so that 'there shall be no poor amongst you' (Deut 15:4).[3] There is scholarly disagreement over the extent to which these laws might have been operative during the monarchy. If they are post-exilic it seems probable they were always impossible to execute owing to Israel's incorporation into successive world empires. This was, of course, the situation which marked Jesus' lifetime.

The process which the post-exilic legislators had sought to prevent was well advanced by the first century CE. Many smallholdings had been swallowed up in great estates. Since there were taxes to pay both to Caesar, to Herod and to the religious authorities it was easier than ever for debt slavery to arise. Instead of a free peasantry many were now wage labourers, selling their labour in the marketplace if there were any buyers. In this situation Jesus began his ministry, acording to Luke, by proclaiming the Jubilee, the 'year of the Lord's favour' (Luke 4:18). Questions of property come up again and again in Jesus' teaching. He warned again and again that putting it in the centre barred the road to discipleship (e.g., Matt 6:19ff.; 6:24; 13:22; 19:16ff.; Luke 16:1ff.; 16:14, 16:19ff.). His own practice in 'having nowhere to lay his head', and the instructions for the disciples' mission, when they were strictly forbidden to take money or any of the usual means of support, illustrate the absolute seriousness of his belief that it was quite impossible to serve both God and 'Mammon' – where by Mammon we can understand all forms of private property. What was important was God's rule and God's righteousness (Matt 6:33).

The first community, in Jerusalem, shaped itself around these imperatives and disowned private property altogether (Acts 4:32). Paul, in the rather different environment of the Hellenistic world, found it necessary to insist that an ethic of sharing and of waiting for God's decisive intervention did not license welfare scrounging. 'If people refuse to work', he said, 'they can do without food' (2 Thess 3:10). His positive effort, however, was bound up with the need for the members of the new humanity (*ecclesia*, church) to support one another materially as in every other way (this is the overall argument of 2 Corinthians).

Aristotle

Whilst these developments took place in Palestine the Greek city states, and above all Athens, rose and fell. Just past their apogee one of Plato's pupils, and the tutor of Alexander the Great, was giving lectures of seminal importance on politics and economics. Aristotle (384–322 BCE) taught, of course, in the Greek city state in which sea trade was important, but the backbone of the economy was still agriculture. Aristotle considers in detail his teacher's proposals (in *The Republic*) for common ownership. Plato is always worth reading, he notes, 'but perfection in everything can hardly be expected'. Anticipating many later critiques of the welfare state he believes that common ownership leads to neglect; people only really lavish care on what is their own. Community of wives would not work for the same reason. There is an immeasurable pleasure in owning something, and it allows us to exercise liberality, something which Plato's proposals would rule out. Several people had made practical proposals for equalizing property. Phaleas of Chalcedon thought it could be done by insisting that only the rich gave dowries and only the poor received them. In the *Laws* Plato proposed that differences of wealth within the state should never exceed a factor of five. His pupil was sceptical. If someone has too many children the law will have to be broken and besides, men of ruined fortunes are sure to stir up revolution (1266b10). His own solution is that 'property should be private, but the use of it common' (1263a38). At the heart of Aristotle's ethic is moderation: 'the amount of property which is needed for a good life is not unlimited' (1256b31). True, desire is unlimited and 'most men live only for the gratification of it' but what this teaches us is that our educational system and our laws have to target desire, rather than property in itself. 'It is not the possessions but the desires of humankind which require to be equalized, and this is impossible, unless a sufficient education is provided by the laws' (1266b30).

The Church Fathers

Aristotle's emphasis on moderation was shared, and indeed underlined, by most of the Greek philosophical schools. Puritanism does not begin with Christianity. Stoicism especially emphasized the need to be detached from material possessions. These two streams, the biblical and the Greek, come together in the Church Fathers, who without exception take the strictest line on private property. From Ambrose (333–397), bishop of Milan, and Chrysostom (347–407), bishop of Constantinople, we have thunderings worthy of the Hebrew prophets, which have continued to echo down succeeding centuries. 'How far, you rich people, do you push your mad desires? "Shall you alone dwell upon the earth" (Isa 5:8)? Why do you cast out the fellow sharers of nature and claim it all for yourselves? The earth was made in common for all.' That is Ambrose preaching on Naboth's vineyard. '"Mine" and "thine" – those chilly words which introduce innumerable wars into the world – should be eliminated from the Church ... The poor would not envy the rich, because there would be no rich ... All things would be in common.' That is Chrysostom, preaching to the wealthy congregation who first lionized him, and then exiled him, in Constantinople. The only partial exception amongst the early Church Fathers was Clement of Alexandria, who published a pamphlet on the rich man's salvation, but his sermons would provide very cold comfort to the advocates of a contemporary 'blessings theology'. Preaching on Luke 16:9 he says: 'all possessions are by nature unrighteous, when a person possesses them for personal advantage as being entirely his own, and does not bring them into the common stock for those in need'. The word 'unrighteous' is *adika* – wicked. He emphasizes, like his Greek teachers, the need for a moderation which today we would call austerity, and the need to use property for the common good.[4]

The monastic movement represented an attempt to deal evangelically with property. It was either renounced altogether or, as in the case of the Benedictine rule, held in common.

Aquinas

The need for brevity condenses the teaching of a five-hundred-year period into one figure, and that of the thirteenth century. Thomas Aquinas (1225–74), however, had a genius for synthesis, bringing together Aristotle, Scripture, and the neo-platonism of Augustine, which has made him one of the greatest of all teachers of the Church. We discern a shift in his teaching from that we have just reviewed and the expansion of trade and of markets, which was a major feature of his day, is certainly part of the reason for this. He deals with property as the presupposition of his treatment of theft. There are no absolute rights to ownership, but there are rights to use (*Summa Theologiae*, II–II, q. 66.1). Private property is necessary because we care better for our own property, things are more orderly if each looks after their own, and this situation is more conducive to peace. However, common use always has priority if there are those in need (66.2). What people have in superabundance is due by natural law to the poor. In extreme cases of need we have a right to meet that need by taking property from another either openly or secretly and this is not to be considered theft (66.7).

In *Religion and the Rise of Capitalism* R. H. Tawney has rehearsed how these pious certainties dissolved as the market economy grew. Luther, in his rage against usury, is still pre-modern. Calvin issues a cautious endorsement. When it comes to property, however, the first truly modern voice is that of John Locke.

Property in the bourgeois revolution

John Locke

The upshot of the English civil war was the consolidation of power in the hands of the landed and mercantile gentry. Locke (1632–1704) is their spokesman. He is a transitional figure because the Christian tradition is still something he has to reckon with. We learn from Scripture that the earth was given to humankind in common. Whence then came private property? In seeking an answer he formulates a new justification of property of fundamental importance. Though the earth and all its creatures are common to all 'yet every Man has a Property in his own Person. This no Body has any right to but himself. The Labour of his Body, and the Work of his Hands, we may say, are properly his. Whatsoever then he removes out of the State that Nature hath provided . . . he hath mixed his Labour with . . . and thereby makes it his Property.'[5] This was a potentially revolutionary argument. Locke was sixteen when Winstanley and the Diggers challenged Cromwell on English property ownership and began digging on St George's Hill. On his arguments they should have had possession, and changed the face of England for ever. But Locke, whose circle included many great landowners, hesitates. Are there limits to property? Yes, for 'The same Law of Nature, that does . . . give us Property, does also bound that Property too'.[6] Having granted that, in regard to the fruits of the earth, he at once becomes uncertain with regard to land. God gave the world to men in common but did not intend it to remain common and uncultivated. 'He gave it to the use of the Industrious and Rational . . . not to the Fancy or Covetousness of the Quarrelsome and Contentious.' He sees that the introduction of money as a medium of exchange crucially affects his principle. Without money property is limited to what a person can till. Now money is introduced by 'tacit and voluntary consent' and so 'Men have agreed to disproportionate and unequal Possession of the Earth'.[7] America, understood as a vast tract of uninhabited virgin territory, is constantly in the background. Even now, Locke argues, there is land in plenty for all. But Locke has other considerations about property, equally momentous. In his view property (i.e., a landowning gentry) is the surest defence against tyranny. The reason men enter society, he says, is the preservation of property and we have laws 'to limit the Power and moderate the Dominion of every Part and Member of the Society'. It is the attempt to take away property which at once mobilizes resistance against tyranny.[8] Locke talks about 'the People' establishing a Legislative, but of course only a tiny percentage of the English population had the vote at the time. Whatever his intentions, it is scarcely surprising that, after his death, his arguments were read as support for the reigning oligarchy.

Rousseau

Rousseau (1712–78), like the other *philosophes*, learned from Locke, but drew almost opposite conclusions as to property. In a famous apostrophe in his *Discourse on the Origin of Inequality* he described the first man who enclosed a piece of land and proclaimed it his as the founder of civil society. 'From how many crimes, wars and murders, from how many horrors and misfortunes might not any one have saved mankind, by pulling up the stakes . . . and crying to his fellows, "Beware of listening to this impostor; you are undone if you once forget that the fruits of the earth belong to us all, and the earth itself to nobody".'[9] Implicitly contesting Aquinas's suggestion that private property is the surest ground for peace and order he argues that it generates perpetual conflict, a situation resolved through the institution of law, an ideological ruse for the maintenance of private property. Had he inspected the work of his contemporary Blackstone this view would surely have been confirmed. The essay concludes with what is, in effect, a call to revolutionary action, which was precisely how it was understood in 1789.

Property in the capitalist era

Hegel

The great changes in production we call the 'industrial revolution' led to the erosion of the small rooted communities in which human beings had lived for millennia and the growth, for the first time in history, of truly great cities. The cult of the individual was, in part, a response to this development and the individual stands at the heart of Hegel's account of property. Property, for Hegel (1770–1831), is 'the *embodiment* of personality'. A person has to translate their freedom into an external sphere in order to exist as Idea.[10] To forbid private property, as Plato did, is to 'violate the right of personality'.[11] All notion of the priority of common ownership is now abandoned, on metaphysical grounds. 'The demand sometimes made for an equal division of land, and other resources too, is an intellectualism all the more empty and superficial in that at the heart of particular differences there lies . . . the whole compass of mind (Geist), endlessly particularized and differentiated, and the rationality of mind developed into an organism.'[12] In Hegel's system Absolute Spirit (*Geist*), like human spirit, realizes itself through embodiment. In this argument property is the most concrete instantiation of this principle. To challenge property rights, then, is to challenge the divine.

Simply theorizing about property will not do. To become persons we must take possession of things. I can grasp a thing physically and 'mechanical forces, weapons, tools, extend the range of my power. Connexions between my property and something else may be regarded as making it more easily possible for me than for another owner . . . to take possession of something or to make use of it. Instances of such connexions are that my land may be on the seashore, or on a river bank.'[13] Let us not lay at Hegel's door the responsibility for imperialism and wars of aggression. Nevertheless it is quite impossible to read these paragraphs without knowing what had happened in Prussia during the War of Austrian Succession (the annexation of Silesia), nor what was happening as Hegel wrote in India and the United States.

Marx

Mill, in our opening quotation, thinks of property in terms of things, a tendency common to most of the tradition preceding him. Marx (1818–83), on the other hand, from the start thinks in terms of relationships. 'An isolated individual could no more have property in land and soil than he could speak. He could, of course, live off it as substance, as do the animals. The relation to the earth as property is always mediated through . . . the tribe, the commune . . . The individual can never appear here in the dot-like isolation in which he appears as mere free worker.'[14] This is his great difference from the 'bourgeois economists', who think always of what he calls ironically 'Robinson Crusoe on his island'. One of the reasons Marx wished to transcend capitalism was that, developing ideas Hegel had worked out, he saw how the opposition of those who buy and those who sell labour produces a multiply alienated society. Furthermore he saw that labour itself was a form of property, a commodity. Earlier societies had rested on social inter-dependence. When the capitalist acquires ownership of the means of production this is transformed into the individual dependence of each worker on the capitalist. According to Locke rights to property rested on a person's labour. 'Now, however, property turns out to be the right, on the part of the capitalist, to appropriate the unpaid labour of others or its product, and to be the impossibility, on the part of the labourer, of appropriating his own product.'[15] All social relations are mediated by money which, Marx saw even in 1844, creates inhuman and imaginary appetites. 'Private property does not know how to turn crude need into human need.'[16] Marx believed that Luther, whom he quoted at length in his *Theory of Surplus Value*, had a greater insight into the true nature of capital than most later commentators. The answer to this problem Marx believed to be the socialization – common ownership – of the means of production, the recovery of human community.[17] Freedom will consist in the fact that 'socialized humanity, the associated producers, regulate their interchange with nature rationally, bring it under their common control, instead of being ruled by it as by some blind power'.[18] In this society it will be, as Marx put it in his *Critique of the Gotha Programme* (1875), 'from each according to his ability to each according to his needs'.

Property in the age of ecological crisis

Without attempting to offer a survey, it would probably be fair to say that defences of private property amongst philosophers are more vigorous than they have ever been.[19] Liberal theorists appeal broadly to the range of arguments we have already seen: that labour creates value, that property is essential for liberty, and that private property is essential to human realization. These arguments date largely from the late seventeenth century on and are bound up with the growth of the capitalist economy, an economy which collapses without growth. They mark a substantial rupture with earlier views of property. Broadly put, the change is from use to exchange, from community to individual, from moderation to excess. Capitalist economics in some shape or form, and thus defences of private property, form the overwhelming main stream in the West. An increasing volume of environmental and Third World critique, however, insists that present arrangements are both unjust and unsustainable. If this is the case, and I believe that it is, then a fresh look at the wisdom of our ancestors may stand us in good stead.

The heart of the argument that present trends are unsustainable hinges on the twin concerns of population growth and ecological damage, both of which are expanding exponentially. The world population has doubled since mid-century and now stands at nearly six billion. Eleven billion is a plausible prognosis for the second decade of the next century. The percentage of global income going to the richest 20 per cent of the world's population has increased from 70.2 in 1960 to 82.7 in 1989, and decreased from 2.3 to 1.4 per cent for the poorest 20 per cent in the same period.[20] This gap continues to grow. Advocates of free market capitalism like Michael Novak insist, in the teeth of the evidence, that human beings will always find a way of dealing with the situation.[21] Behind this insistence is another one, that, as President Bush put it at the Rio Summit, 'the American Way of life is non-negotiable'. It is this way of life which is putting colossal pressure on the world's ecosystems. 'The average resident of an industrial country consumes 3 times as much fresh water, 10 times as much energy, and 19 times as much aluminium as someone in a developing country.'[22] The richest 10 per cent of Americans put 11 tons of carbon dioxide, the principal greenhouse gas, into the atmosphere, compared with the tenth of a ton of those Third World poor who use fossil fuels for heating and cooking. In 1992 more than 1,600 scientists, including 102 Nobel laureates, issued a 'Warning to Humanity': 'No more than one or a few decades remain before the chance to avert the threats we now confront will be lost and the prospects for humanity immeasurably diminished ... A new ethic is required – a new attitude towards discharging our responsibility for caring for ourselves and for the earth.'[23] The economist Herman Daly has compared the earth to a ship with a Plimsoll line. We are on the Plimsoll line right now: the danger of sinking is real. This could mean one of two things. It could well be that processes of global warming are now so advanced that massive loss of territory, including whole countries, like Bangladesh, is inevitable. Meanwhile prominent spokesmen in the United States like Garret Hardin have warned that we must view the earth as a lifeboat, with the Third World poor in the water. Since our lifestyle is non-negotiable, and we cannot keep that up if they come on board, we have to let them sink. The possibility of systematic aggression against the burgeoning populations of the Third World can also by no means be ruled out. There is little to show that we have learned anything but lessons in technique from the Holocaust. Rosa Luxemburg's stark alternative of socialism or barbarism has already been realized many times over. The difference now is that it could be both global and final.

The alternative to these dark prognoses is, in Sandra Postel's words, 'a global effort to lighten humanity's load on the earth'.[24] This has to be in terms of addressing the gross disparities of wealth, of turning from a consumption to a recycling economy, and tackling population growth. As is well known, reaching a certain level of prosperity is the key to the latter. As the Union of Concerned Scientists emphasized, however, a new ethic is also crucial, and a changed attitude to property is part and parcel of this. In the light of the present situation liberal teaching on property since Locke is dangerous and irresponsible, an 'arid intellectualism' (to use Hegel's phrase) if ever there was one. Let me take four points from the founding property ethics of Western culture as an alternative.

The earth is the Lord's and all that is in it

The foundation of a property ethic cannot be either labour, security or self-realization. The foundation of a property ethic which can sustain us and not destroy us is the acknowledgement of all that we have as *gift*. Alongside Weber's elective affinity between Protestantism and capitalism we might put the fact that the aggressive property ethic of the West is the product of Protestant thinkers with their logocentric worship. Perhaps one reason for the relative resistance of Catholic social teaching to this trend is that the Eucharist, the acknowledgement of gift, was always at the heart of it. If everything we have we have as gift from the Creator and Lover of all, we cannot hang on to it, fence it round, keep it from all others.

Every family under its vine and fig tree

The legislators of post-monarchical Israel thought in terms of a fundamental equality. They recognized the need for leadership, but leaders could only be first among equals. The rights of every family flow from God's lordship. But this extends to every family on earth. A situation where, as at present, there are 202 billionaires, 3 million millionaires and 100 million homeless people who live on roadsides, in rubbish dumps and under bridges is morally unacceptable. Morally there is a case for every human community to have access to the goods of the earth. This leaves us, argues Alan Thein Durning, with a conundrum. We cannot limit the lifestyle we enjoy only to ourselves, but extending the lifestyle to the whole human family would ruin the biosphere.[25] Finding more energy-efficient technologies can take us some of the way. Developing recycling economies can take us further. Beyond that is the need for a fundamental recognition that enough is enough. Aristotle already addressed this problem. His generation, which had not lost its myths, knew, through the Midas story, that making an idol of consumption is a recipe for death. From every strand of our pre-capitalist wisdom comes the imperative: live simply that others may simply live.

Property does not consist of things but exists in relationships

This also is taught us by the Eucharist, but it was Marx who made it most explicit. The atomization of life which Marx diagnosed has increased a thousandfold with the advent of suburbanization, the private car, television. The liberal property owner is the individual, beholden to none. Such a being is a fantasy: we are all sustained by vast intricate webs of farmers, sewage workers, academics, engineers. Our property, far from being our moat and drawbridge, all signals that interdependence. Privacy, an unheard-of luxury to most of the world's population, is a key aspect of our property, along with 'freedom' (i.e., the right to do what *I* want when I want how I want – a pathetic fixation at psychological age three). By all means let us have our privacy and our freedom, but let us have it *in relation*, and not at the expense of others.

Property can become a fetish. To be free we must de-fetishize it

Both Jesus and Marx taught the fetishization of commodities. Marx's doctrine is, after all, an analysis of what happens when we decide to serve Mammon. The doctrine of late capitalism is that you are what you have, you are not a citizen but a consumer, you no longer have services but a market. The 1996 Audi advertisment has only one word: 'Worship' – but this is only to make explicit the subtext of most advertising.

Jesus' teaching about the birds of the air and the lilies of the field is not, as generations have taken it, an outline doctrine of providence. It is part of his satirical attack on Mammon – putting property in its place. A much later attack on the same lines runs:

> In place of the wealth and poverty of political economy, come the rich human being and the rich human need. The rich human being is simultaneously the human being in need of a totality of human manifestations of life – the person in whom their own realisation exists as an inner necessity, as need. Not only wealth, but likewise the poverty of a person – under the assumption of socialism – receives in equal measure a human and therefore social significance. Poverty is the passive bond which causes the human being to experience the need of the greatest wealth – viz, the other human being.[26]

'For freedom Christ has set us free' (Gal 5:1), but that freedom is illusory whilst we are bound by chains to Property/Mammon. A whole line of Christians before us saw that and sought freedom in their own way. We have to seek it in ours, but in a changed situation, and with much greater urgency. '"Watchman, what of the night?" The watchman says: "Morning comes, and also the night. If you will inquire, inquire; come back again"' (Isa 21:11–12).

Notes

1 J. S. Mill, 'Chapters on Socialism' in *Collected Works* (Toronto: University of Toronto Press, 1963), vol. 5, p. 753.
2 N. Gottwald, *The Tribes of Yahweh* (London: SCM Press, 1979).
3 C. Wright, *God's People in God's Land: Family, Land and Property in the Old Testament* (Grand Rapids, MI: Eerdmans, 1990), p. 140.
4 There is a splendid collection of Patristic teaching on property, from which these extracts are taken, in C. Avila, *Ownership: Early Christian Teaching* (Maryknoll, NY: Orbis, 1983).
5 J. Locke, *Two Treatises on Civil Government*, II.27.
6 Locke, *Two Treatises*, II.31.
7 Locke, *Two Treatises*, II.50.
8 Locke, *Two Treatises*, II.222.
9 J. J. Rousseau, *A Discourse on the Origin of Inequality* (1754), second part.
10 G. W. F. Hegel, *Philosophy of Right*, trans. T. M. Knox (London: Oxford University Press, 1952), para. 41.
11 Hegel, *Philosophy of Right*, para. 46.
12 Hegel, *Philosophy of Right*, para. 44.
13 Hegel, *Philosophy of Right*, para. 55.

14 K. Marx, *Grundrisse* (Harmondsworth: Penguin, 1973), p. 485.
15 K. Marx, *Capital*, vol. 1 (Moscow: Progress Publishers, 1961), p. 583.
16 K. Marx, *Economic and Philosophical Manuscripts*, *Collected Works*, vol. 3 (Moscow: Progress, 1975), p. 307.
17 K. Marx and F. Engels, *The German Ideology*, Pt 1 section 1, *Collected Works*, vol. 5 (Moscow: Progress, 1976).
18 K. Marx, *Capital*, vol. III (Moscow: Progress, 1959), p. 820.
19 For such a survey see L. Becker, *Property Rights* (London: Routledge, 1977).
20 *Human Development Report 1992* (Oxford: Oxford University Press, 1992).
21 In private conversation with Peter Selby.
22 A. T. Durning, *How Much Is Enough?* (London: Earthscan, 1992), p. 51.
23 Quoted in *State of the World 1994* (London: Worldwatch, 1994), p. 19.
24 S. Postel, 'Carrying capacity: earth's bottom line' in *State of the World 1994*, p. 19.
25 Durning, *How Much Is Enough?*, p. 25.
26 K. Marx, *Economic and Political Mss*, *Collected Works*, vol. 3, p. 304.

Select bibliography

C. Avila, *Ownership: Early Christian Teaching* (Maryknoll, NY: Orbis, 1983).
Friedrich Engels, *The Origin of the Family, Private Property and the State* (London: Lawrence and Wishart, 1972).
John Paul II, *Laborem Exercens* (London: Catholic Truth Society, 1981).
L. Johnson, *Sharing Possessions* (London: SCM, 1986).
John Locke, *Two Treatises on Civil Government* (1689; Cambridge: Cambridge University Press, 1988).
R. Mullin, *The Wealth of Christians* (Exeter: Paternoster, 1983).

13

Morality and law

Patrick Hannon

Our lives are shaped by two forces of which often we are hardly aware: the moral code to which we subscribe and the law of the society of which we are part. We keep promises, or at least generally believe we ought to, we pay our debts, respect the person and property of others; we refrain from deceiving people, or injuring their good name, or taking what does not belong to us. We think it 'right' to act, or refrain from acting, in such ways, 'wrong' to deviate from the path which they mark out. We believe that on the whole it is for our 'good' and the good of others that we should live according to the prescriptions and proscriptions of morality and of law.

And on the whole we don't pay much attention, nor do we need to, to the question whether the rules by which we live are moral rules or legal. One reason for this is that often they are both: murder is prohibited by the moral law as well as the law of the land, as are perjury, theft and selling defective goods. It is morally as well as legally wrong to drive at speed on the road in front of a school playground from which a child might emerge as we are passing. Inciting to racial hatred is an offence against both morality and the law. The law enforces the keeping of some of our promises, as when we sign a contract to buy or sell a house, or to do some job or render a service.

But there are times when we become aware that, for all their similarities and their overlap, law and morality are different fields of experience. There are some requirements of morality which are not enjoined by the law: there is no law which says that we ought to give to people who are in need, or show compassion for a drug addict, or speak a kind word to someone who is in pain. No law forbids the unilateral ending of a long-term relationship between partners who are not married, or compels a husband to share the household chores. There is no law forbidding adultery (at any rate in most Western systems) or fornication or lying.

Moreover, in any society the law may allow choices which are contrary to the moral code of some of its members – abortion, for example, or euthanasia, or the payment of less than a fair wage. Or it may discriminate between categories or classes of people in a morally objectionable way, as when it puts them at a disadvantage merely because they are of a particular race or religion or gender, or of a different social class.

So law and morality resemble each other, and in some matters they overlap, and they are interrelated and interdependent; but they are also importantly different. And among the most important differences is the fact that the law comes as it were from outside of us. That is, law is made by decision of the legislature, and in some countries also by way of judicial interpretation, so that its source is external to those whom it binds. And law is 'enforced' on us, in that it carries the threat of some penalty should we be found in breach of it.

At first sight the same might seem to be true of the prescriptions of morality: a religious person may speak of them as given by God, or they may be thought of as coming from the moral tradition of whatever society we happen to belong to. And on a certain view of the relationship between God and morality – that God will reward the good and punish the wicked – it might appear that the source of moral obligation, as well as of its commands and prohibitions, is in the will of God, and so external to the human being in much the same way as in the case of the law of the land.

But a better view, though it cannot be argued here, is that when we use the language of law in speaking about morality in the context of religious beliefs we should follow mainline Christian thinking. This is that certain ways of behaving are commanded by God because they are, so to speak, *already* good and right – good and right in terms of what makes for the flourishing of the human being. And these commands make a claim on us, not because God happened to will that they should, but because they accord with the way he made us as free and rational beings.

Of course the rules of morality come from outside us in the sense that we learn them from parents, school, society, church. But that is not the same thing as saying that the rules are invented or decided by fiat of some external agency. And if we are true to our nature as rational and free we shall have made our moral principles our own by choice and with understanding, and our conformity with them will come from ourselves, from our own 'conscience', from our will to find out and do what is fit for a human being.

It can sometimes be necessary to sort out the relationships between law and morality, and the Oxford jurisprudent H. L. A. Hart has formulated the questions which may be put.[1] The first is whether the development of law has been influenced by morality (and vice versa), the second is whether some reference to morality is required in an adequate definition of law. The third question is whether the law is open to moral criticism, and the fourth is whether the enforcement of morality is a part of the function of law. Hart's questions furnish a starting-point for what must here be a very general approach to a dense and complex topic.

The first question is reasonably easily disposed of: it is not difficult to think of examples of the reciprocal interaction between morality and law which leads to development in one or the other. Take, for instance, laws which aim to promote equality of opportunity for employment as between men and women. Such laws are inspired by the moral insight that women and men are of equal dignity and potential, and that it is wrong to give a job to a man in preference to a woman merely because of the difference in gender.

An employer, out of prejudice, might perpetrate such a wrong, and of course such has been the pattern in what are usually now called patriarchal societies. Campaigners for women's rights have therefore sought to secure legislation which forbids discrimination on the ground of gender alone. But of course a reformer might hope that in due course equal treatment would become the norm, not just because the law insisted but because people generally came to recognize that as a matter of morality it is wrong to discriminate in this way.

One could multiply examples, from laws forbidding racial discrimination to legislation about road safety, or conditions in the workplace, or fair trading, or due care for the environment. The point in each case is that a moral insight generates a movement for legislation coercing people to act for the good in ways which, left to themselves, they may not feel at all inclined to do. But the hope is that in time they might come to the morally more mature frame of mind in which they behave rightly, not just for fear of punishment but rather because what the law lays down is also the morally right thing to do.

This idea is not a new one, and in the Christian theological tradition it was expressed by St Thomas Aquinas who saw law as having a role in educating people in virtue: 'From being accustomed to shun what is evil and discharge what is good on account of threat of punishment a man sometimes comes to continue on that course from his own taste and choice.'[2] But it gives rise to questions to which we shall have to return when we consider the issue of the enforcement of morals. For there are difficulties and dangers in the concept of the promotion of morality through the medium of law.

Hart's second question is whether an adequate definition of law must include some reference to morality. At one level this is a technical question, much discussed by legal philosophers. But it isn't a merely theoretical issue, and its practical importance may be grasped if we think of it as asking at another level whether it is necessary that a law be 'just', that is, conform to a moral standard of justice.

For if law is law merely by virtue of its emanating from the will of the legislator, and if it is *ipso facto* binding, then it might be argued that the law may oblige one to do what is morally wrong. And it was argued at the Nuremberg trials following the Second World War that the officers and others who co-operated in the extermination of six million Jews in the death camps could be convicted of no crime, since they were only obeying orders and acting under the law.

This question too has been canvassed in Christian theology. For St Augustine an unjust law was no law, and could not bind the moral conscience.[3] Aquinas spoke of it rather as a corrupt law;[4] elsewhere he said that unjust laws are 'outrages rather than laws'.[5] It followed that a ruler might not exact obedience simply because of a legislative fiat, nor could a subject excuse moral wrong-doing on the plea of acting in accordance with the law. The answer of these authors to the defence of superior orders, as the position of the defendants at Nuremberg is called, must be that legislation cannot override the moral order.

This was the tenor of a much more ancient strain of philosophical thought, illustrated in dramatic form in Sophocles' play *Antigone*. Antigone buried her brother Polynices, in defiance of an order made by Creon, king of Thebes, forbidding him honourable burial. She defends herself by appeal to a higher law.

> That order did not come from God. Justice
> That dwells with the gods below, knows no such law.
> I did not think your edicts strong enough
> To overrule the unwritten unalterable laws
> Of God and heaven, you being only a man.
> They are not of yesterday or today, but everlasting,
> Though where they came from, none of us can tell.[6]

The unwritten, unalterable laws here referred to are what came to be known in the philosophical tradition as the Natural Law, a concept which in one shape or another, and despite various sorts of criticism, has endured in Western thinking. For our purposes it may be taken to say that reason reflecting upon human experience in the world can come to at least some general conclusions as to how humans ought to live if they are to flourish. This in broad terms is the moral order, and the claim is then made that all law and politics must respect it.[7]

It follows – and here we arrive at Hart's third question – that any law is open to moral criticism. That is, legislation is always open to scrutiny so as to ensure that it is truly in aid of human flourishing. It is not enough to say that a particular course of action is allowed or enjoined simply because it is laid down by law. For a law may be unjust, and if so it may, and sometimes must, be disobeyed.

Inevitably this gives rise to problems, in principle and in practice. What is to be made of the people in the US who during the Vietnam war burnt their draft cards in protest against the war, but also against the law? How was it that the English women who took a hammer to a Hawk aircraft destined for Indonesia were exonerated? And if we find ourselves sympathetic to these protesters, what do we think of those in the US who sit in front of abortion clinics so as to impede the access of women who are seeking abortion? Or what do we say about parents who on religious grounds refuse to allow a child to be given a blood transfusion even when it is necessary to save the child's life?

Thus is raised the question of the right of a citizen to flout or ignore the law of the land in the name of conscience, that is, in the name of a moral principle which that person holds as binding on him or her. It would be strange, given that in general there is a moral obligation to obey the law, if such actions could easily be justified morally. Of course the law itself may recognise 'conscientious objection', as when pacifists are exempted from military service, or as – in a different way – in the example of the Hawk case where the women were held not guilty of what on the face of it was a breach of the law. And a critical influence in the redress of injustice in a society may be the 'civil disobedience' of some of its members, as in the US in the 1960s or in South Africa in more recent experience.

Hart's fourth question – whether or to what extent it is a function of the law to enforce morality – was the subject of a debate between himself and Sir Patrick (later Lord) Devlin, after the latter had delivered what became a famous Maccabean lecture concerning the enforcement of morals.[8] The context of Devlin's lecture was the publication in 1957 in England of the Wolfenden Report which made proposals for the reform of the law on homosexual offences and prostitution. His criticism of the Report evoked a reply from Professor Hart[9] which in turn generated further exchanges between them. In due course the debate was entered by other legal philosophers and jurisprudents, including some from the United States and other legatees of the Anglo-American tradition. For although the debate's original context was English law, the issues which it raises have a universal application.

It will be useful later to sketch the general lines of the positions taken by Devlin and Hart. For now, just notice that at the core of their debate was the question whether there is a 'private morality' which is, as Wolfenden put it, not the law's business. The expression 'private morality' was to prove troublesome, and it may be as well at this point to be clear at least about what it does *not* mean. For a start, it doesn't make sense to think of it as referring simply to the morality of acts done in private: most murders are done in private, and privacy is virtually essential to the thief; and it would be ludicrous to suggest that the law should never intervene when a man beats his wife or children at home.

Nor is it helpful to think of the term 'private morality' as referring to what is a matter of private (in the sense of personal) moral judgement. For the question whether something is properly left to the individual's conscience, or whether it is a claim of the moral order, is usually only the starting-point of a debate. So, for example, the claim that women have a moral right to choose abortion comes up against the claim that the unborn have a moral right to life from the moment of conception.

The first claim says that it is a matter for the personal conscience of a woman whether to have an abortion or not, the second maintains that the moral order precludes the directly intended taking of any innocent life. The argument cannot be settled by *asserting* the one right or the other, and there remains for the legislator the question whether either of these moral beliefs is to be 'enforced'.

Such questions are complicated nowadays by the pluralism of moral belief and practice which is a feature of so many modern societies. For it is a fact of modern life that societies are composed of people of a variety of religious traditions and of none. If the law is to reflect and promote moral values – and it must, in some sense, as we have seen – whose values? The values of the majority religious (or other) moral tradition? What then of minorities in the community: are they to be coerced into following patterns of behaviour which are contrary to conscience as they experience it, or prevented from acting according to their consciences simply because the majority subscribes to a different world-view?

One of the reasons why it is difficult to think clearly about these questions is that it is difficult to find a starting-point which has prospect of common acceptance. I shall suggest that, for all that it comes from a particular religious tradition, Roman Catholic teaching concerning religious freedom provides a starting-point, and indeed the makings of a framework, for fruitful discussion of the issues at stake. And the reason why it has prospect of a more general acceptance is that its basis is a philosophical one, of a kind which resonates with the mind of our times.[10]

The principle is to be found in the Declaration on Religious Freedom of the Second Vatican Council. Its genesis lay in modern consciousness of the dignity of the human, and the growing demand that people 'should exercise fully their own judgement and a responsible freedom in their actions, and should not be subject to the pressure of coercion but inspired by a sense of duty'.[11] A key influence in the drafting of the Declaration – many would say its principal architect – was the US Jesuit theologian

John Courtney Murray. It was of course not accidental that the principal ideas embodied in the document had their roots in the experience of the United States, pluralist in its very foundation.[12] The Council's teaching was conceived in the context of a debate about *religious* freedom, and it will be necessary to show how it may be applied to the sphere of morality as well. But first the principle and its basis.

The principle, put shortly, is that in religious matters people should not be made to act against their consciences, nor should they be prevented from acting in accordance with their consciences 'within due limits', a phrase which turns out to mean 'within the limits of the common good'. In the context what is primarily meant is that in matters of conscience the laws of a state should not attempt to coerce people, that there should be freedom of conscience in matters of religious belief and practice, that there is a right to religious freedom, within limits imposed by the requirements of 'the common good'. The meaning of this qualification is of course crucial, and we must return to it in a moment.

The right to religious freedom is based, the Council said, on the dignity of the human person and the nature of the search for truth. Human dignity consists in the twin gifts of reason and the power of choice, and it is respected to the extent that each person is given scope for the exercise of these gifts in the pursuit of truth and human fulfilment. And it is in the nature of the search for truth that it 'must be carried out in a manner that is appropriate to the dignity and social nature of the human person: that is, by free enquiry with the help of teaching or instruction, communication and dialogue'.[13]

The right here asserted is, as already mentioned, a right to *religious* freedom, and its application to the field of morality probably needs to be shown. The argument is not complicated: the dignity of the human person and the nature of the search for truth are the same whether one is thinking about religion or about morality. As gifted with reason and freedom we live up to our dignity to the extent that we freely seek moral truth, and coercion is no more at home in the quest for moral than it is for religious value.

What I am suggesting therefore is that a starting-point and a framework for a consideration of the issues involved in debates about the enforcement of morals may be found by transposing Vatican II's principle concerning religious freedom to the sphere of morality. Our starting-point then would be that in matters of moral belief and practice people should not be coerced into going against their consciences, nor should they be prevented from following their consciences. But the qualifying clause has application here too, and so we must see what is meant by 'the common good'.

This concept has its roots in classical thought and as developed by classical and Christian thinkers is rich and complex. But for present purposes it will suffice to adopt the description given in the Council's *Declaration*, a description which is familiar in Catholic social teaching. The common good, the Council says, 'consists in the sum total of those conditions of social life which enable people to achieve a fuller measure of perfection with greater ease'.[14] The core idea is that the law should be such as to facilitate the flourishing of *each person*, but in such a way that the flourishing of any person or group is not at the expense of that of others.

A mistake which is sometimes made in debates about law and morals is to conceive the common good in terms which suggest that it is somehow over against the individual's good. This happens when it is identified with the moral beliefs of a majority of citizens, so that in Britain, for example, it might be identified with the moral values of Christianity. On that premise people could argue that the right of someone from another religious tradition (say Islam) to believe and practise according to his or her lights need not be upheld by law. But this is not so. The common good is the ensemble of conditions of social living enabling *each person* to flourish to maximum potential. It *includes* individual freedoms, including freedom of religious and moral belief and practice.

Of course the exercise of any individual's freedom cannot be at the expense of the rightful freedoms of others. A right to freedom of expression cannot mean a right to say what one likes, true or untrue, about someone else in the community, and so we have defamation laws. A right to privacy or against trespass can't be invoked by someone who wishes to conceal the fact that he has bomb-making equipment in the garden shed. A right to the truth does not entail entitlement to pry into the personal business of one's next-door neighbour. The exercise of rights and freedoms of the individuals who make up a society must be harmonized, and in some matters this bespeaks regulation by the law. This is often put by saying that the exercise of individual freedom is limited by the requirements of peace, justice and public morality.

And this brings us to the question at the centre of the Hart–Devlin debate: whether or in what sense there is a 'public morality' which it is the law's business to enforce. In discussing proposed reform of the laws on prostitution and on homosexual offences Lord Wolfenden's committee had thought it useful to look for a general principle which might shape thinking on the relationship between morals and the criminal law. The committee formulated a principle as follows: the function of the criminal law is 'to preserve public order and decency, to protect the citizen from what is offensive or injurious, and to provide sufficient safeguards against exploitation and corruption of others, particularly the young, weak in body and mind, inexperienced, or in a state of special physical, official or economic dependence'.[15]

This is a version of a principle first enunciated by John Stuart Mill, who said that the only purpose for which the law can rightfully be used is to prevent harm to others.[16] Lord Devlin interpreted Wolfenden's version to mean that 'no act of immorality should be made a criminal offence unless it is accompanied by some other feature such as indecency, corruption or exploitation',[17] or, of course, if it injures someone in his/her person or property. It is features such as these which, according to Wolfenden, bring what is immoral into the public realm. And only when there is this kind of public dimension is it permissible for the law to take an interest.

Lord Devlin took issue with the Wolfenden view, arguing that there is indeed a public morality which it is the law's business to enforce. His position may be put summarily as follows. People who form a civil society do so on the basis of certain shared ideas, including ideas about right and wrong. A society's existence is threatened by deviance from the morality so shared, and it is as entitled to protect itself from moral subversion as it is from political. It is for society to say how much deviance it will tolerate, and it is entitled to use the criminal law to enforce its morality when deviance exceeds toleration's bounds. A legislator will know when this point has been reached by reference to the standard of the reasonable man, 'the man on the Clapham omnibus'.

On this view there is no private immorality in the sense envisaged by Wolfenden. The most private of acts has a social resonance, however indirectly produced: *any* immorality is capable in its nature of threatening a society's existence. In theory therefore there is no immoral act that might not be proscribed by law. But in practice a line must be drawn; there must be some scope for individual freedom, for the individual 'cannot be expected to surrender to the judgement of society the whole conduct of his life'.[18] And in deciding what to forbid, a lawmaker may be helped by some general principles.

The first of these principles – Devlin calls them 'elastic' – is that there should be the maximum freedom consistent with the integrity of society. The law should not attempt to enforce all of a society's moral code, but only those items without the enforcement of which the society would disintegrate. Second, Devlin says, the law should move slowly, for the limits of tolerance are apt to shift from time to time. Third, as far as possible privacy should be respected; he sees a value in allowing people what would nowadays be called their personal space. And the fourth elastic principle is that the law is concerned with minimum and not maximum standards of behaviour, and it should not try to do too much.

Lord Devlin's thesis was challenged by H. L. A. Hart,[19] then Professor of Jurisprudence at Oxford, whose position was essentially that of John Stuart Mill and the Wolfenden Committee. That is, Hart reaffirmed the view that there is a realm of private morality which is not the law's business. Unless conduct involves an identifiable public harm it ought not to be proscribed by the law. On this view the law should confine itself to the prohibition of conduct which would injure others in their person or property, or corrupt or exploit, or violate the public sensibility or public order.

In making his case Hart counters Devlin's arguments, and in particular he rejects the latter's concept of a public morality. The detail of their exchanges (for the debate did not end with Hart's rejoinder to the Maccabean lecture[20]) is beyond the scope of a short chapter. But it is worth drawing attention to Hart's starting-point, for it sets the tone of his contribution as a whole. And his starting-point is the contention that the question whether morals should be enforced is itself a moral question. For enforcement entails the curtailment of freedom, and the curtailment of freedom requires moral justification.

In support of this way of looking at the matter Hart points out that legal enforcement has two aspects. The first is that it involves the punishment of offenders, and this is done through depriving them of freedom of movement or of property or of association with family or friends, or the infliction of physical pain or even death. But all of these are normally regarded as evil and normally their infliction is considered wrong. If therefore it is to escape moral censure their infliction requires special justification.

The second aspect of enforcement is no less pertinent to the need for justification. It is that law restricts freedom in that it coerces conformity through threat of punishment. One's freedom is just as surely, even if differently, inhibited when one refrains from some act for fear of being put in jail as it is when one is jailed for doing the forbidden deed. And this kind of restriction also needs to be justified, for freedom is valuable both in itself and because it enables people to experiment with different ways of living.

But there is a further reason, according to Hart, why restriction of freedom requires to be justified from the standpoint of morality: 'interference with individual liberty . . . is itself the infliction of a special form of suffering – often very acute – on those whose desires are frustrated by the fear of punishment'.[21] He observes that this is especially true of laws which impose a sexual morality.

For all that there are differences, of vantage-point and of perspective, between Lord Devlin's view and that of Hart they are not without common ground. There is this much at least: that both envisage the main issue as one of reconciling individual freedom and the public interest, in some sense of that expression. Each requires advertence to a social dimension in human conduct, and to a public interest in preventing social harm;

and each is prepared to recognize a role for the criminal law in that process.

Indeed one commentator has said that 'both are recognizably liberal',[22] meaning no doubt that each puts a premium on freedom. In Hart's case this is clear even in the way he frames the main question, but it is intimated also in Devlin's assertion that 'the individual has a *locus standi* too; he cannot be expected to surrender to the judgement of society the whole conduct of his life'.[23] And this insight is made concrete in the 'elastic principles' to which Devlin would have the legislator advert, and especially in the requirements that there should be toleration of the maximum freedom consistent with the integrity of society, and that privacy must as far as possible be respected.

It could be that the principal difference between them is one of emphasis; but the difference in emphasis is critical. Devlin's interest, first and last, is in 'the integrity of society', and in that sense he is 'conservative'. Hart's concern, first and last, is with the protection of individual freedom. Devlin's way of looking at the issues will probably recommend itself to someone whose instinct is to preserve societal values, Hart's will be the more congenial for someone who is inclined to a more 'liberal' political view.

Of course, strictly speaking, the term 'enforcement of morals' is a misnomer. For the law can at best ensure only external compliance, whereas to be moral it is not enough to behave in a way which is merely externally correct.[24] From a legal point of view it does not matter with what degree of resentment I pay my taxes; all the law requires is that I pay them. But from the viewpoint of morality a bad attitude or unworthy motive or perverse intention may mar what on the face of it is a good act, as when I give money with bad grace to someone in need. Hence it seems better to say that what the law enforces is a moral code, or the part of a code which commands or prohibits observable conduct: that it cannot enforce morality 'as such'. Indeed if someone refrains from misconduct wholly out of fear of punishment it is hardly correct to speak of morality at all.

And this provides a clue, as James Mackey has recently suggested, to the truth that emerges from the Hart–Devlin debate, and it shows that each of them was partly right. 'Law does, and must always, make its business what would be morally right for people to do or refrain from doing. That is always true of law, in any form of human society which proposes to be essential to human living . . . This is the part of the truth that Devlin protected so well on his side of the debate.'[25] But it is the merit of Hart's contribution that 'he has pointed unerringly to the quite literally demoralising tendency of the apparatus of extraneous punishment and of its ever-present threat'.[26]

In the end, of course, one's response to the concrete questions which arise in regard to law and morals will reflect a political philosophy, consciously or unconsciously held, and behind that a vision of the human and of human flourishing. It is not surprising that some of the most important debate about law and morals nowadays has its context in the relationship between politics and religion.[27] The kind of analysis provided by Hart and Devlin and their commentators is of the utmost importance. But perhaps what is now needed most of all in our public debates is an articulation and a critique of our political philosophies.

Notes

1 H. L. A. Hart, *Law, Liberty and Morality* (Oxford: Oxford University Press, 1968), pp. 1–4.
2 *Summa Theologiae*, I–II, q. 92, art. 2, ad 4: Blackfriars edn, vol. 28, ed. Thomas Gilby, 101. Cf. also q. 95, art. 2. Aquinas's approach echoes Plato's but especially Aristotle's.
3 Augustine, *De Libero Arbitrio*.
4 *Summa Theologiae*, I–II, q. 95, art. 2. Gilby translates *legis corruptio* as 'spoilt law'.
5 Gilby's translation of *violentiae*: I–II, q. 96, art. 4, 96, 4.
6 Trans. E. F. Watling, *Sophocles: The Theban Plays* (Harmondsworth: Penguin Classics, 1959), p. 138.
7 An excellent account of the history of the concept of Natural Law in legal philosophy is in John M. Kelly, *A Short History of Western Legal Theory* (Oxford: Clarendon Press, 1992).
8 Patrick Devlin, *The Enforcement of Morals* (Oxford: Oxford University Press, 1965). The text of the Maccabean Lecture, entitled 'Morals and the criminal law', is in ch. 1.
9 Hart, *Law, Liberty and Morality*.
10 The argument here is developed more fully in Patrick Hannon, *Church, State, Morality and Law* (Dublin: Gill and Macmillan, 1992), ch. 7.
11 *Dignitatis Humanae*, para. 1; trans. in Austin Flannery (ed.), *Vatican Council II* (revised translation of the basic documents) (Dublin: Dominican Publications, 1996), p. 551.
12 See John Courtney Murray, *We Hold These Truths: Catholic Reflections on the American Proposition* (New York, 1960; repr. 1988).
13 *Dignitatis Humanae*, para. 3; Flannery, p. 554.
14 Ibid., para. 6; Flannery, p. 556.
15 Devlin, *The Enforcement of Morals*, p. 2.
16 J. S. Mill, *On Liberty*, ed. Gertrude Himmelfarb (Harmondsworth: Penguin Classics, 1974), p. 68.
17 Devlin, *The Enforcement of Morals*, p. 3.
18 Ibid., p. 15.
19 Hart, *Law, Liberty and Morality*.
20 See Devlin, *The Enforcement of Morals*, Preface, chs 5, 6, 7, and bibliography at pp. xiii–xiv. See further Simon Lee, *Law and Morals* (Oxford: Oxford University Press, 1986), pp. 96–8.

21 Hart, *Law, Liberty and Morality*, p. 23.
22 Basil Mitchell, *Law, Morality and Religion in a Secular Society* (Oxford: Oxford University Press, 1967), p. 18.
23 Devlin, *The Enforcement of Morals*, p. 15.
24 In this connection it is interesting to read what Aquinas has to say about the law's role in regard to virtue: *Summa Theologiae*, I–II, q. 96, art. 3. Notice also his realism concerning the use of the law in restraining vice: I–II, q. 96, art. 7.
25 James P. Mackey, *Power and Ethics* (Cambridge: Cambridge University Press 1994), p. 52
26 Ibid. Mackey's own reflections on the debate – which occur in the course of his treatment of larger themes – are illuminating: cf. pp. 45–54.
27 See for example R. McBrien, *Caesar's Coin: Religion and Politics in America* (New York: Macmillan and London: Collier Macmillan, 1987).

Select bibliography

Patrick A. Devlin, *The Enforcement of Morals* (Oxford: Oxford University Press, 1965).
Patrick Hannon, *Church, State, Morality and Law* (Dublin: Gill and Macmillan, 1992).
H. L. A. Hart, *Law, Liberty and Morality* (Oxford: Oxford University Press, 1963).
John M. Kelly, *A Short History of Western Legal Theory* (Oxford: Clarendon Press, 1992).
Simon M. Lee, *Law and Morals* (Oxford: Oxford University Press, 1986).
Richard McBrien, *Caesar's Coin: Religion and Politics in America* (New York: Macmillan and London: Collier Macmillan, 1987).
Basil Mitchell, *Law, Morality and Religion in a Secular Society* (Oxford: Oxford University Press, 1967).

14

The punishment of criminals

Bernard Hoose

In recent years the prison population of the USA has exceeded one million. In most other Western countries the figures are much smaller, but there, as in the United States, imprisonment is merely one of several penalties that can be imposed upon people who break the law. In other words, the number of people punished by agents of the state in any one year is, in most countries, considerable. Although concern has been expressed by some about the size of the prison population in the USA and elsewhere, most people, it seems, hold that, at least in principle, the punishment of criminals is justifiable activity. It is not at all clear, however, that there is general agreement among them concerning the arguments for its justification. Three such justifications are commonly offered: deterrence, retribution and reformation or rehabilitation. Some people tend to concentrate on one of them, seeing it as the only one that is valid, but it appears that most of those who investigate the subject see a role for all of them. We shall begin this chapter with a brief examination of each in turn.

Punishment as deterrent

In conversations about how to deal with criminals one often hears arguments like the following: 'Of course criminals should be punished. That is the only way in which they will be discouraged from committing such crimes again. Punishing them also has the effect of discouraging other people from committing similar misdemeanours.' Such arguments, based on what are considered to be the likely consequences of punishment, tend to be favoured by utilitarians.

Utilitarianism is, in fact, a blanket name used to describe a number of schools of thought. Here, however, we do not have space for a detailed discussion of the various nuances of thought contained in these various schools. Suffice it to say, therefore, that adherents of what may be called the basic or classical form of act utilitarianism hold that one should choose that act from among those available which will produce or result in the greatest amount of good for the greatest number of people. There can, of course, be situations in which, whatever one does or does not do, evil will result. In such cases a negative form of the utilitarian principle applies: one should choose that course of action which will result in the least amount of evil. In this scenario, the number of people involved should, of course, be kept to a minimum. Clearly, punishment is a non-moral (or pre-moral) evil inasmuch as it consists in inflicting suffering on other human beings. If, however, punishment can be shown to be the most effective way of keeping crime to a minimum, utilitarians are likely to regard it as justifiable. If they are thorough in their application of the utilitarian principle, they will compare the effectiveness of various kinds of punishment. Moreover, if, again, utilitarians are consistent, they should take the malefactor's good into account, even though that person's good might, in the end, be sacrificed for the greater good of a greater number of people. If, therefore, an alternative to capital punishment proved to be as effective as the death penalty, the death penalty could not be justified on utilitarian grounds. To take the matter further: if, in a particular kind of case, some alternative to punishment proved to be more effective in reducing crime, a utilitarian would have to opt for that alternative.

A first question to be asked, therefore, is what effect punishment really does have in reducing crime. Although some people are no doubt deterred from certain forms of criminal activity by the threat of sanctions, it is not clear that the deterrent effect of even some severe forms of punishment is anything like as successful as many proponents of the deterrence theory appear to believe. In fact, there is even evidence to suggest that, where certain forms of punishment are concerned, the result is often not deterrence at all, but rather further corruption. This can be, and many claim often is, the case, for instance, with prison sentences. Indeed, prisons in some countries have been described as schools for criminals. Moreover, studies in various countries in which capital punishment for murder has been abandoned have not revealed any significant increases in the homicide rates of those countries. Indeed, Ruth Morris reports that, in Canada, the homicide rate went down after the abolition of the death penalty.[1] Some scholars have gone so far as to suggest, moreover, that when the state resorts to extreme forms of punishment, it runs the risk of brutalizing much of the general populace. In other words, we have here another example of punishment having a corrupting rather than a deterrent effect. In this case, however, those corrupted are not those who have already committed crimes but those others whom one might have expected to be deterred from any thoughts of criminal activity through fear of receiving like punishment. There is evidence to suggest that some such brutalizing effects occurred in certain countries in the past when particularly gory executions and horrific beatings were carried out in public places, and apparently even became a source of entertainment.

A number of researchers believe that the greatest deterrent is the fear of being caught. In places where the clear-up rate of the local police force is poor, some people will undoubtedly be willing to risk even severe punishments because they believe there is little chance of being apprehended. That single fact may explain a good deal about the widespread failure to deter people from indulging in criminal activity. However, even if the deterrent system worked quite successfully (and perhaps it does in regard to certain types of criminal activity in certain parts of the world), it would still present problems of an ethical nature. Punishing a person merely in order to cause other people to be afraid of the same punishment certainly seems to amount to using that person merely as a means to an end. On the other hand, if it were possible to justify punishment in some other way, there could surely be no objections to any deterrent effect that resulted from an appropriate sanction administered in a truly proportionate manner. Such deterrence might be seen as a bonus. Another problem, however, could rear its head. If one were concerned only with the greatest good of the greatest number and not with how the good is distributed,[2] one might be tempted to convict and punish a person known to be innocent or whose guilt was seriously in doubt. This might occur if a particularly serious type of crime had become all too common in a certain place and the police had been unable to find any of the real culprits. It is worth bearing in mind that, even in countries that have well-developed legal systems, there have been recent cases in which false evidence has been produced in court and so-called 'rough justice' has been administered.

Before moving on to the next section, it is worth recalling that, even if one were a utilitarian, proof of a successful deterrent effect in one area would not be sufficient for a justification of all punishment. Research might reveal, for instance, that a certain kind of punishment has a deterrent effect on certain kinds of criminals of a certain age group who have been wont to commit certain kinds of crimes. The same kind of research might also reveal that something other than punishment (an educational project, for example) is more effective when dealing with a different group of malefactors and/or a different category of crimes. The problem is thus shown to be a very complex one. A blanket justification of punishment could not easily be argued for using deterrence theory alone.

Retributivist theory

An alternative to the theory of deterrence is that of retribution. This theory (or perhaps we should say 'group of theories', since there can be different retributivist approaches) is concerned with justice, which is the subject matter of another chapter in this book. Here we need to say only that, equating justice with that which is due to a person or group, retributivists see punishment as something owed or due. It serves the malefactor right. Here, of course, there is no question of using somebody merely as a means to the achievement of some end. This does not mean, however, that retributivist theories are without their problems.

It is one thing to say, for instance, that punishment is due to a particular person. It is quite another to say *which* punishment is due and why. Retributivists use expression like 'the punishment must fit the crime', but how are we to work out which punishment fits which crime? Even supposing, for the sake of example, that one is certain that imprisonment is the appropriate penalty for a certain kind of criminal activity, one still has to find some way of calculating the appropriate length of the prison term. How, precisely, is one supposed to do that? It is worth noting that such questions presuppose our already having addressed the problem of deciding what is to be understood by the term 'imprisonment'. What kind of building (or combination of buildings, fields, etc.) should a prison be? What facilities should or should not be available to the inmates? What limitations, if any, are to be put on visiting by people from outside the prison? All these and many other questions would need to be answered, but on what basis?

It could also be said that seeking to make the punishment fit the crime does not necessarily serve the cause of justice. In trying to determine what is due to a particular person we would surely have to bear in mind much more than a mere physical act – taking a bag of potatoes from a shop without paying, for example. Surely we would need to take the circumstances of each case into account. Was the accused person desperately hungry, for instance, and had she been unable to get help, in spite of having asked for it many times? Had she been mistakenly discharged from hospital whilst still under the influence of a drug that could cause her to act out of character? It could, of course, be claimed that, if it worked at all, a retributivist theory could be adapted so as to make the punishment fit the *person* in the particular situation in which the crime was committed, and not just the *act* considered in isolation from the person. However, it could also be claimed that proponents of retributivist theory still need to demonstrate that punishment really is due to people whenever they commit a crime. The mere fact that many people have, for many centuries, taken for granted that it is due is simply not enough. Moreover, even if retributivist arguments were thoroughly convincing in this regard, we would need to bear in mind that 'what is due to a person' should not be confined to punishment. Help in the adjustment to a new way of life after imprisonment, for instance, may also be due, although in practice, it would seem that it is often not forthcoming.

Another point to bear in mind is that, taken to extremes, retributivism could lead to a situation in which consequences are simply ignored. One way of stating that punishment is due to people who have committed criminal offences is to say it is our duty (or at least the duty of the appropriate organs of the state) to punish them. Somebody holding to this point of view might be totally unmoved by the negative consequences of such penalties. Thus we hear conversations in which the participants appear to have no common frame of reference. Some such conversations are about whether or not punishment should be employed at all in certain kinds of cases. Others are about whether or not a certain penalty should be inflicted upon perpetrators of certain types of crimes. One person argues, for instance, that custodial sentences are counterproductive where certain types of young offenders are concerned. She suggests that a better course of action would be to send them off on weekend courses. There they will learn about good citizenship and perhaps pick up one or two useful skills. The problem with these youngsters is that nobody, including their parents and teachers, has ever taken an interest in them or helped them to acquire a sense of self-worth. Her interlocutor is unmoved by such reasoning.

> 'They have committed serious offences. They must pay the price.'
> 'But giving them custodial sentences will only make matters worse. They will return to society with even bigger chips on their shoulders, and, moreover, they will be schooled in other kinds of criminal activity.'
> 'The punishment must fit the crime.'
> 'But punishing them in the way you suggest will only serve to make matters worse.'
> 'There is a principle at stake here.'

A first point to be made here is that, in some, though certainly not all, such conversations, the person claiming to be a retributivist may be moved simply by a crude desire for revenge. The very existence of a system in which organs of the state, rather than the victim(s) of the crime, are responsible for the punishment of criminals should help us to avoid some of the worst excesses of revenge. However, many of us feel a sense of outrage when we hear about certain crimes, even though we ourselves are not the victims, and this sense of outrage is often accompanied by a wish to see the perpetrators of the crimes suffer. If they are indeed made to suffer through the administration of what we see to be a suitable punishment, we may experience some satisfaction. If, however, the punishment serves to make matters worse, society in general and certain individuals in particular have to pay a high price for our small satisfaction.

In discussions about Christian ethics, we would not, of course, expect revenge to be countenanced. Let us assume, therefore, that the person claiming to be a retributivist in the above conversation is truly concerned only with justice and is able to discuss the matters in hand dispassionately. Let us also suppose that there is sufficient evidence to show that the youngsters being discussed are corrupted by terms in prison or in similar young persons' institutions. Does it make sense to say that it would be morally right to administer such punishment even though it would produce a situation far worse than that which would result from the alternative? An affirmative answer to this question would seem to be counterintuitive. Here, then, is a major problem for those who wish to isolate retributivism from the other justifications for punishment. It might, of course, be claimed that, if they were concerned with making the punishment fit the person rather than the crime, even retributivists would have to take consequences into account. To do that effectively, however, it would seem that they would have to give some attention to the reformative effects of punishment.

Reformative theory

Before taking these two aspects of rehabilitation and retribution together, it is useful to look at the question of reform in isolation. After all, some people appear to regard it as the only real justification of punishment. According to these proponents of reformative theory, punishment can be justified on the grounds that it helps (or, at least, can help) to bring about a conversion process in the person who has committed a crime. Thus we hear talk about systems of correction and rehabilitation. Here a far too simplistic comparison can be made between the disciplining of children and the punishment of criminals. One imagines that most people would consider a minimum amount of mild, non-violent punishment to be necessary when bringing up children. Such chastisement, moreover, is held (by most people, it would seem) to be formative. When comparing this with the punishment of criminals, however, one should bear in mind the fact that, ideally, children are chastised in a loving atmosphere. If that is not the case, any punishment administered to them might well be counterproductive, even seriously harmful. Now criminals, one imagines, are rarely, if ever, punished in a loving atmosphere.

We also need to bear in mind the fact that successful personal reformation can take place only when the person concerned freely embraces the means. Quite apart from the nightmare stories one hears about coercive 'treatment' involving drugs and other questionable procedures, it is documented that, at various times and in various places, attempts have been made to reform prisoners by forcing them to live in an enforced 'monastic' atmosphere involving silence and obligatory prayers. It is hardly surprising that little is heard about successes resulting from such systems. I am not suggesting, of course, that the means to help people achieve rehabilitation in society should not be made available to them. We should surely rejoice if they are, but making such means available would not normally amount to punishment. It would be something separate from or in addition to the penalty. Various educational, psychological and religious facilities may, for instance, be made available in prisons. It is the imprisonment, however, that is the punishment, not the facilities which are made available. In other words, there is no proof that, in such cases, the punishment itself is reformative. It may be necessary to seek another justification for its existence. Having said all this, moreover, it is worth calling to mind here what was said above concerning not the reformative, but the possibly corrupting effects of certain forms of punishment.

Ronald Preston notes that Christians and others who are concerned about respect for persons realize that this concern relates in certain ways to all three of the theories so far discussed, but also that it cannot be satisfied by any one of them alone. Regarding retribution, he says that, if people offend, any punishment they receive must be deserved. Afterwards, society should wipe the slate clean. He then goes on to say: 'In certain cases the common good of persons-in-community may require an element of deterrence. I state this with caution because of the inveterate tendency of the public to exaggerate the deterrent effects of punishments. In most cases we have no deterrence except community attitudes.' Turning then to the third theory, Preston says that there must be an intention actively to promote the good of the person who has offended. 'This should not mean adding a further and indeterminate length to a retributive sentence purely for rehabilitative purposes and under coercive conditions.' He suggests that rehabilitation should be available entirely on a voluntary basis. 'Those who refuse to have anything to do with it would be free to ignore it.'[3]

Moberly's theory

Some years ago, the British scholar Sir Walter Moberly suggested that punishment could be seen as a ritual which represents the moral deterioration that is taking place in the criminal. It does so by creating a crude kind of picture of that deterioration. In other words, punishment can make the person being punished aware of the battle between good and evil that is going on within, and may be able, indirectly, to influence the course of that battle. Punishment, he says, is a kind of inverted sacrament inasmuch as it is aimed at bringing to naught what it represents (moral deterioration) rather than bringing it into effect.

Moberly, however, does not limit the role of punishment to the enlightenment of the offender. A wound has been inflicted upon society, and something must be done to set matters right. Society has to rid itself of this centre of infection. In any particular case, moreover, the punishment must symbolize both aspects: what has happened to the criminal in the sense of moral deterioration and the appropriate counter stroke that society must make in order to heal the wound. Imprisonment or excommunication, for example, indicates that one is temporarily unfit for membership of society. Certain other punishments, however, may be unsatisfactory because the correspondence between them and the crimes for which they are applied is blatantly artificial. Pecuniary fining is an example that Moberly cites.[4]

Whatever one may think of the appropriateness of fines when applied to certain kinds of criminal activity, the reader will, no doubt, agree that, in most Western countries, much of the fining that goes on has little, if any, symbolic value. Some might say, however, that Moberly is asking for far too much here. What punishment, for example, is fitting (if symbolism is such an important aspect of what is fitting) where rape or arson are concerned? It could be countered, however, that crimes such as these indicate that one is unfit for society and should therefore be imprisoned. Nevertheless, acknowledging that much would not alter the fact that, in order to meet Moberly's requirements concerning symbolism, those saddled with the task of inventing punishments would have their imaginations sorely taxed.

A more serious source of difficulty in the theory is identified by Moberly himself. Punishment as portrayed in his theory is suited only in what he calls an intermediate moral region. If we were to apply a scale to both criminals and societies, we would find that at one end of it are criminals who are simply too degraded to benefit from punishment, and societies that are too amoral to be capable of imposing it. At the other end of the scale there may be people who simply do not need it for their re-education, and societies that are too advanced morally to need it as an example. Punishment, he feels, is suited only to those who are found in the intermediate regions of the scale, and only societies located in the intermediate region are capable of administering it.

We need not concern ourselves with those (individuals and societies) who are at what we might refer to as the morally advanced end of the scale. However, we do have reason to be concerned about those at the other end. A first question we need to ask is not how many societies are actually located there, but which, if any, are located in the intermediate region. If we look at the records of countries taken at random, we may come to believe that such societies are few and far between, if, indeed, they exist. A few years ago, John Langan wrote, in regard to capital punishment, that, in the USA

> it serves as an intermittent and ominous response by a society that tolerates the careless and extensive distribution of guns and the deterioration of basic living conditions for the poor, while it declines to invest in improving educational and correctional institutions and makes the unrealistic depiction of extensive and brutal violence a central part of its entertainment and its imaginative life. It is simply not credible for such a society to present its reliance on capital punishment as a sign of its deep and passionate commitment to justice.[5]

Something similar might be said in regard to other forms of punishment inflicted in the same society, and, indeed, in many others. It would seem that, in order for Moberly's theory to function, there would have to be some minimal degree of love and respect in the treatment of offenders. As we noted when comparing the punishment of criminals with the disciplining of children, however, there are reasons for doubting that such a loving atmosphere is easy to come by in most countries. In addition to the appalling conditions found in many prisons, even in so-called 'advanced countries', one of the most striking reasons for such doubt is the fact that custodial sentences are meted out too easily. This would appear to be especially so in the United States and, to a lesser degree, in the United Kingdom. Writing in 1987 and referring to the situation in the latter country, Preston opined:

> The evidence suggests that as many as 80 per cent of those in prison at present ought not to be there. It does not protect the public and it actually harms rather than improves those imprisoned. The system is unfair and inefficient, indeed monstrous. It will not be easy to shift public opinion on this, but if I were an Old Testament prophet I would feel like saying 'Thus says the Lord: cursed be a society which tolerates this prison system; away with it; it is an abomination to me.'[6]

A second problem arises concerning those at the 'wrong' end of Moberly's scale. If there are people who are too degraded to benefit from punishment, should we not expect to find among them the perpetrators of the most serious kinds of crimes? Some readers, I imagine, would refuse to brand anybody as definitively incorrigible. Such refusal, however, does not necessarily lead us to a conclusion much different from that of Moberly. It may still be the case that, in their present state, many of these people will not benefit from punishment. Indeed, punishment may merely make matters worse.

It does not follow from this, however, that we should allow such people to continue their life of crime unabated. Where persistently violent people are concerned, drastic measures may be necessary in order to ensure protection of the public. As the present writer suggested in a recent work, even if such measures might not accord with Moberly's description of justifiable punishment (given the aforementioned supposed inability of those concerned to benefit from it), they may still be justifiable.[7] The justification would be much the same as that invoked for self-defence or defence of a third party. Usually, when discussing defence, we are concerning with the morality of using violence. Here we may also be concerned with the justification of violence, at least inasmuch as it may be necessary to use it in the act of apprehending certain criminals. Quite apart from this, however, we are concerned with the justification or otherwise of taking the people concerned out of the community in which they have been living, and detaining them in a secure place from which we do not allow them to wander. Surely, whether we wish to call this punishment or something else, it can be justified in much the same way as violent defence. It is something forced upon us by those very people who are being detained. It might be described as a lesser evil, chosen in order to protect the public. It may, moreover, be necessary to keep some very dangerous people in secure places, away from the general public, for the remainder of their lives. All that, it would seem, can be justified where there is serious danger to the public. Treating such people in an inhumane way in addition to placing such limits on their freedom, however, is a very different matter.

Notes

1 Ruth Morris, *Crumbling Walls . . . Why Prisons Fail* (London: Mosaic Press, 1989), p. 110.
2 A common criticism of utilitarianism is that it cannot deal well with problems of justice. Ross wrote that justice is not concerned merely with the greatest sum of good, but rather with how the good is distributed: W. D. Ross, *Foundations of Ethics* (Oxford: Clarendon Press, 1949), p. 319.
3 Ronald H. Preston, *The Future of Christian Ethics* (London: SCM Press, 1987), pp. 231–2.
4 Sir Walter Moberly, *The Ethics of Punishment* (London, Faber and Faber, 1968), pp. 199–237.
5 John Langan, 'Capital punishment', *Theological Studies* 54 (1993), p. 123.
6 Preston, *The Future of Christian Ethics*, pp. 235–6.

7 Bernard Hoose, *Received Wisdom? Reviewing the Role of Tradition in Christian Ethics*, (London: Geoffrey Chapman, 1994), pp. 135–43.

Select bibliography

Robert M. Baird and Stuart E. Rosenbaum (eds), *Punishment and the Death Penalty: The Current Debate* (New York: Prometheus Books, 1995).

Bernard Hoose, *Received Wisdom? Reviewing the Role of Tradition in Christian Ethics* (London: Geoffrey Chapman, 1994), ch. 4.

Sir Walter Moberly, *The Ethics of Punishment* (London: Faber and Faber, 1968).

Ronald Preston, *The Future of Christian Ethics* (London: SCM Press, 1987), ch. 13.

15

Peace, violence and war

Richard G. Jones

Many people were disturbed by the dubious moral legitimacy of the Gulf War in 1991. The British Foreign Secretary, Douglas Hurd, called together a group of church leaders and went to great pains to assure them that it was indeed a 'just war' because a tyrant, Saddam Hussein, had invaded Kuwait in a flagrant act of aggression, and Britain had a duty to support the United Nations in repelling his forces. It was yet another instance of the notion that some wars can be regarded by Christians as 'just', one that has occurred throughout Christian history from about the fourth century. From that early time some Christians – probably the majority – have seen that although war is a monstrous evil and killing is an appalling offence against Jesus' teaching, nevertheless it may be more evil not to take up arms in some, but not all, wars. But in that case, which wars?

Beginning with Ambrose, strengthened by Augustine, and elaborated by Thomas Aquinas in the thirteenth century and others later, the very ancient notion of the 'just war' was steadily refined as the main tool with which Christians tried to assess the morality of wars. Despite the immense difficulty in fashioning such a tool, it remains the basic moral guide for Christian reflection to this day. The notion is in two parts, dealing with the decision to commence war (technically called the *jus ad bellum*) and then the appropriate conduct of war (the *jus in bello*). The former has five requirements:

(1) There must be some just cause (e.g., to repel an aggressor).
(2) There must be just intent (e.g., to restore peace with justice, and not to seek to devastate the other nation).
(3) The war must be a last resort, every possibility of peaceful settlement having been exhausted.

(4) The declaration of war must be by a legitimate authority (i.e., properly constituted government, and not a faction within the nation).

(5) There must be reasonable hope of justice being effected. In other words, there must be a good prospect of success. It is not right to go to war against overwhelming odds.

For the latter, there are two fairly plain requirements:

(1) The innocent must not be directly attacked, but only the armed forces of the enemy. This provision also rules out wanton destruction and atrocities against civilians.

(2) The means used must be in proportion to the ends in view. Huge destructive force should not be deployed against small opponents. But, more particularly, the harm caused by the war should not exceed the good it aims to accomplish.

Commentators frequently criticize these just war provisions as being hopelessly unrealistic. Wars usually arise from a whole tangle of reasons, so that to select one major reason as a 'just cause' is a moral fiction. The intent is often complex too, since a whole variety of national policies may be at stake. There rarely seems to have been a war coming at the end of every possible sort of negotiation, one or both sides having acted precipitately first. Nor is it likely that the outcome can readily be calculated, since wars have a terrible dynamic of their own and in no time all sorts of unpredictable factors have complicated the scene (including other nations being drawn in). Nor is war's conduct easily controlled. Combatants will inevitably use every stratagem to save their lives and kill the enemy, and very soon wars can become 'all out'. And yet, as we shall see again later, these principles are constantly cited in almost all Christian reflection.

But although most Christians see war as the lesser of two evils, there have sometimes been Christians who have believed that a specific war was good, ordered by God, and that participation in it was incumbent upon the faithful Christian. Because the classic medieval example was the Crusades, with successive popes calling upon obedient Christians to kill the infidels who were ruling in Palestine and dominating the Holy Places, such an attitude to war now has the 'crusade' label attached to it. It is not as far-fetched today as the medieval background would suggest. There has been a marked tendency for some Christians to interpret some wars as, in effect, crusades after they have begun especially if great patriotic sentiment has been evoked by them. In Britain, for example, the so-called Great War (1914–1918) was seen in this light by many eminent churchmen once it had become clear that it would not soon become settled, that the war effort required immense sacrifice from every citizen and that every possible person would be needed to bear arms.

Thus by 1915 many churchmen identified the German Kaiser as implacably evil, the British and Allied cause as that of 'The Kingdom of God', and the bearing of arms as the moral human equivalent of Christ's work for our redemption. At the Primitive Methodist Conference in 1916 a memorial service was held in which the President declared 'Never before have we thought of the Army as we think of it now. . . . Those who have died have consecrated the Army in our thinking. Let us go with them the way of the cross.'[1] In much Christian rhetoric the sacrifice of the Cross was equated with that of the dead soldier, as so many village war memorials testify to this day when they carry the solemn text 'Greater love hath no man than this, that a man lay down his life for his friends' (John 15:13), in apparent inability to notice the context in scripture, for here Jesus was obviously talking about his own imminent and unarmed death by which he was giving himself to his friends and the world for God's sake.

This tendency to dignify a war by making it into a crusade has had echoes since then but has rarely been as blatant. Christian thinking is most prone to encourage it when a huge ideological effort has been first made to demonize the opponents, as in the Cold War when the Russians had become 'The Evil Empire' to the American public and communists were the agents of Satan. Probably the horror and ineptitude of the Vietnam War did the most to purge such lofty views about war out of the general American mind-set. For the British, the Great War battles in Flanders largely disabused the public of the moral grandeur of war.

Roland Bainton[2] notes four features of the crusade – belief that the cause is God's, belief that God is directly guiding us in it, classifying our side as godly and the enemy as ungodly, and unsparing prosecution. Fundamentally, the crusader has never accepted that all our national causes are ambiguous, a patchwork of the worthy and the unworthy, and has refused to accept the humanity of the opponents who likewise are caught up in the double-sided confusions of international politics. God is never unequivocally 'on the side of' one nation, for God's righteousness transcends the self-interest of any one nation state. God's will is always permeated with the demand for mercy, and never calls for ruthless obliteration of opponents, nor the demand for unconditional surrender. Thus the crusaders' God is too small, is a nation's desires glorified and exalted up to divine pretensions, with the self-righteousness which always accompanies such arrogance.

Here too we should notice that there is some value in the statements which churches often make about the morality of wars in general – they are not 'in Christ' and cannot be. Thus the Lambeth Conference of 1930 declared that 'War as a method of settling international disputes is incompatible with the teaching and example of our Lord Jesus Christ', and successive Lambeths have repeated this. Although it may appear bland, such declaration shows at least that there cannot be a war 'ordained by Christ'.

However, in Christian history there has almost always been a third stance taken up by a few and labelled 'pacifist'. There are many shades of so-called pacifism, but central to them is the conviction that Christians must never bear arms or undertake to kill opponents because it is flat contrary to the teaching and example of Jesus.[3] He ordered his disciples not to retaliate when attacked, to bear with insult and violent assault and always to maintain a forgiving spirit. Moreover his own actions spoke more loudly than his words: he endured evil, suffered in his body the appalling results of it, and died offering forgiveness. The constant New Testament teaching that we should copy Jesus is to be taken firmly and clearly and literally.[4]

The most consistent pacifist witness has been borne by the so-called 'peace-churches', usually Protestant bodies emerging at or after the Reformation who have cherished an obedience to Christ as rigorously faithful as they can possibly make it. Many, such as the Mennonites or Moravians or Brethren, suffered years of persecution in Europe and transferred their communities to America in the nineteenth or twentieth centuries. Others set up special 'peaceable' settlements, such as the Bruderhof homes. In Britain, the Society of Friends has always maintained a strong peace witness, following the example and teaching of its founder, George Fox, who would not under any circumstances bear a sword. Many pacifists have looked to the International Fellowship of Reconciliation as the link movement. This was founded in 1914 with a firmly Christian theological basis, holding that a Christian's duty was always to seek reconciliation in the spirit and power of the cross, and never to seek to kill opponents. It seeks the enthronement of love in personal, commercial and national life.

As a counter to pacifism many Christians have been forced into a position best called 'Christian Realism'. The classic exposition of this came in 1932 from the American theologian Reinhold Niebuhr with his bombshell work *Moral Man and Immoral Society*.[5] Niebuhr argued that man's profoundly evil nature meant that all human communities exercise coercive power and have to be contained by the coercive powers of others. Although he had once been the national chairman of the Fellowship of Reconciliation he came later to see that much pacifism was a 'heresy'. He exempted many of the peace-churches since they were attempting a life of holiness by shutting themselves off from normal political life, and he saw a place for such witness. But by 1940 he was writing that 'most modern forms of Christian pacifism are heretical. . . . They have really absorbed the Renaissance faith in the goodness of man, having rejected the Christian doctrine of original sin as a bit of outmoded pessimism, have reinterpreted the Cross so that it is made to stand for the absurd idea that perfect love is guaranteed a simple victory over the world, and have rejected all other profound elements of the Christian gospel. . . .'[6] Most of the creative theologians of the twentieth century have not been pacifists but have shared Niebuhr's devastating attacks upon that stance on the grounds that it is bad theology, failing to recognize that God rules in this fallen world in part through human institutions – governments, systems of law and order – that are obliged to use coercive force and in the last resort to kill people. The result has been that much so-called pacifism has subtly changed its position. Pacifists have argued that the most effective way to resolve disputes is that of non-violent love; this is an argument about strategy, about the best way of getting things done, rather than an argument about absolute moral principle.

The initial examplar of the non-violent methods has been Mahatma Gandhi. His passive resistance to rulers in South Africa, then later to the British occupying power in India, has been seen as the ideal. Undoubtedly, his style of protest hastened the granting of independence to India and saved many lives.

But some doubt whether he was an absolutist in his pacifism; he might have used non-violence as a pragmatic device whereby he and his followers always maintained the moral high ground and always managed to make their opponents look shameful.[7] Moreover many have commented that his approach was effective against an occupier who was wanting to be relieved of the burdens of occupation anyway, as the British were in post-war India. It might have been wholly ineffective, say, against the German occupation of Europe in the Second World War.

Martin Luther King, the civil rights leader, studied Gandhi's methods and then linked them directly to the teaching of Jesus (as Gandhi did not). He saw non-violence as a way of affirming love for the oppressor, a refusal to dehumanize opponents, as well as a power to make the oppressor give way. He had also studied Niebuhr carefully, and claimed when launching a bus boycott in Montgomery that 'true pacifism is not unrealistic submission to evil power, as Niebuhr contends. It is rather a courageous confrontation of evil by the power of love, in the faith that it is better to be the recipient of violence than the inflicter of it.'[8] When his home was bombed on 30 January 1956, King was out at a meeting, but rushed back to find his wife and baby daughter safe and an infuriated crowd of his supporters gathering. He told them: 'I want you to go home and put down your weapons. We cannot solve this problem through retaliatory violence. We must meet violence with non-violence. We must remember the words of Jesus. . . . We must love our white brothers no matter what they do to us.'[9]

There is no unanimity as to whether King's methods were effective in hastening the granting of civil rights to Negroes, or whether more violent ones would have been the more effective. What is clear is that King was totally convinced of this way of countering white intransigence, as were many of his followers. Since then, pacifism has tended to move its appeal to that of the non-violent way. By the 1970s the Fellowship of Reconciliation was calling itself 'an association of Christian pacifists from many traditions and parts of the world. It exists to challenge all Christians, in response to human need of justice and truth, to reconsider the effectiveness of non-violent love.' But it has not convinced most Christians. In 1973 the Central Committee of the World Council of Churches in a report on 'Violence and non-violence in the struggle for justice' was asking its advocates: Are you taking with sufficient seriousness the tenacity of violence in the structure of society, and the social disruption its diminution is likely to require? May non-violent action emasculate effective resistance at crucial points in the struggle? In adhering to this as an absolute principle are you not in danger of giving the means (non-violence, i.e., reduced revolutionary violence) priority over the end sought (justice, i.e., reduced structural violence)? Are you more concerned with your own 'good' conscience than with the good of the oppressed?

One effect of the constant witness of pacifists has been to establish in most Western countries the right for persons to be conscientious objectors from bearing arms in war. This has been longstanding in Britain, where there were 16,500 COs in the First World War and 59,000 in the Second, mainly on religious grounds.[10] There was no such right in Germany until long after the Second World War, largely because the Lutheran tradition especially had stressed obedience to the state and the Roman Catholic had in effect argued likewise. But the latter showed a noticeable shift when the Vatican Council somewhat reluctantly admitted that 'It seems fair moreover that laws should make provision for conscientious objectors, so long as they accept some other form of service to the community'.[11] This has been much more in accord with the traditional Catholic stress upon the integrity of the person's conscience, which should not be violated by either the church or state or any other authority.

Thus there have been three main streams of Christian reflection – that of allowing there to be some just wars which Christian rulers could declare and in which Christian soldiers could fight; that of reckoning some wars to be of divine command, crusades; that which has declared all wars and participation in them to be wholly anathema to the Christian. All have experienced severe moral critique, and all appear sometimes to be unsatisfactory if not irrelevant when handling the various ways in which the problems of violence occur today. We turn now to the most pressing contemporary problems.

Nuclear war and deterrence

In the film *Crimson Tide* an American nuclear submarine encounters a strange attack, then finds its communication system faulty. The captain becomes convinced that they have been ordered to fire their missiles, and almost everything seems to suggest this. His second in command feels convinced that they are not under such awful orders; there is a tense confrontation between the two. At the last possible minute a message is obtained by the submarine showing the presumed command to fire to be an error, and the missiles are not despatched. Then the film shows the crew going into a frenzy of relief and sheer delirium, because they need not commit that most awful deed. It expresses the gut feeling that everyone has, that to commit such an outrage and start a nuclear exchange would be an unforgivable act of folly, horror and immense guilt.

That feeling finds a more noble expression in a vast number of Church statements.[12] They tend to suggest that nuclear war is in a class all of its own because of the scale of the destructiveness involved. That assumption needs caution. After all, shortly before the first atomic bomb was dropped on Hiroshima, the Americans had firebombed Tokyo and wiped out a huge tract of the city, killing about half as many civilians as died later in Hiroshima, thus demonstrating the colossal capability for destruction acquired by conventional weapons. Again, the arming of so-called 'tactical' weapons with nuclear tips shows that the use of nuclear materials does not necessarily involve the largest powers of destruction. Nevertheless, the distinction between nuclear and conventional weaponry is useful and has been widely accepted, not least because 'deterrence' needs moral assessment.

The churches and individual Christians tend to differ profoundly about the moral issues which follow: Is it right to keep nuclear weapons as a deterrent to opponents? Is it ever right to use them in a first strike? And what about a counter strike? Here we will look briefly at three major statements – that of the report presented to the Anglican Synod in 1982 and entitled *The Church and the Bomb*,[13] the Pastoral Letter of the US Catholic Bishops on *The Challenge of Peace: God's Promise and our Response* of 1983,[14] and the Pastoral Letter of the United Methodist Council of Bishops entitled *In Defense of Creation* of 1984.[15]

The Anglican report had no difficulty in declaring that nuclear warfare was immoral. It accepted that the confrontation between East and West was the major threat to world peace but argued that negotiation from strength is 'an unsatisfactory philosophy' because it leads to an arms race of leapfrogging capacity for destruction. The superpowers were already too strong. It then proposed that Britain gave up nuclear weapons in a phased manner, whilst always working for multi-lateral disarmament, and finally that all American nuclear weapons be removed from British soil. The report infuriated the British government of the time, led to huge debates within the Anglican Synod, and never succeeded in gaining agreement. The immediate upshot was the publication of a rival series of essays *The Cross and the Bomb*,[16] in which the report was subject to a sharp critique on the grounds of its lack of realism, its naïvety in regard to the way power functions in international politics and therefore its shallow theology. After some years of debate, the Synod finally passed a motion declaring that the first use of nuclear weapons was immoral, but this too was strongly opposed by a minority.

The Catholic Bishops consciously built their case with reference to previous Catholic work (e.g., the Vatican II document *Gaudium et Spes*, and a highly significant speech by Pope John Paul II to the United Nations Special Session on Disarmament in 1982 in which he had said: 'In current conditions "deterrence" based on balance, certainly not as an end in itself but as a step on the way to progressive disarmament, . . . may still be judged morally acceptable'). The Bishops expressed deep concern about the whole culture in which talk of nuclear war came so easily. They accepted the need for deterrence, but said 'not all forms of deterrence are morally acceptable' – the targeting of civilian centres, for example, and the readiness whereby nuclear threats could escalate and, in the worst case, for nuclear war therefore to escalate. They opposed any first-strike use, declared a principle of 'sufficiency' in the build-up of adequate deterring power and recommended immense energy be directed towards widespread arms reductions, strengthening of control over nuclear weapons and the building up of peace-making agencies, especially the UN. They believed that 'There is a much greater potential for response . . . in the minds and hearts of Americans than has been reflected in US policy'. Again, the report annoyed the Reagan government, but was not as widely repudiated as the Anglican one mentioned above.

The Methodist Bishops began with biblical study of the nature of God's gift of *shalom* (peace), accepted the just war tradition as far as it is helpful, but said that a 'theology of a just peace' must guide us. They cited twenty features of this, including the key just war elements, but saw their task as outlining a way of universal peace-making. They saw deterrence policy as 'idolatry'. It perpetuates 'the most distorted and most inhuman images of our "enemy"'. They attacked the 'connection between the ideology of deterrence and the existence of weapons', and declared roundly that 'deterrence must no longer receive the church's blessing, even as the temporary warrant for the maintenance of nuclear weapons'.

As these reports indicate, there are clear differences between Christians on the morality of deterrence. Some (as in the Anglican report) repudiate it altogether but, as the critics pointed out, would they have done so if they had been living in America and carrying the major burden of opposition to the Soviet Union? The Catholics accept it regretfully, but only if linked with the intention to seek arms reduction. The Methodist report went further, calling it idolatrous because it is so linked with pride in such weaponry. But all three are deeply concerned with keeping the peace, with the last two commenting on those attitudes needed to pervade the whole culture if peace-making is to flourish.

Civil war and revolutionary violence

At the time of writing there are mercifully no wars raging between nation states, although the last fifty years have seen many such conflicts. But there are numerous civil wars and wars of revolution which have been a particular concern to the worldwide Christian conscience. The Christian voice has not been united. Inevitably those who are pacifists have said that there is no place whatever for Christians to take up arms, even in what might appear to be a very legitimate cause. Those who are pacifists and are favouring a general withdrawal from the world of politics (as with many of the peace-churches) make their repudiation of violence an element of that withdrawal. But the great majority of Christians accept the obligation to work politically and socially for a just world; it is amongst them that the debates have been most vigorous.

For the twentieth century has been one of popular uprisings, of the overthrow of long-established colonial powers, of the widespread awareness amongst the simplest peoples that they have a right to determine their own existence and not be exploited by powerful oppressors. So revolution – in the limited sense of the attempt to overthrow a government and replace it with one more favourable to the poor majority, by arms if need be – has been in the air that almost all of the southern half of the world breathes. Those people have not taken kindly to established Christians in the West who have argued that it is the primary Christian duty to obey government because it has been instituted by God. Until recently this was the dominant teaching of the Catholic, Orthodox and Lutheran churches especially.

Thus a twentieth-century Lutheran (Bonhoeffer) could write in the dark days of the beginning of the Second World War: 'According to Holy Scripture there is no right to revolution; but there is a responsibility of every individual for preserving the purity of his office and mission in the polis'[17] (i.e., in the political order). Yet Luther recognized that there was ultimately some ground for the forceful removal of a tyrant ruler, and especially one who was mad.

In complete contrast to this traditional position is that which argues that God is so involved in the processes of revolution against oppressive rule that it is a Christian duty to bear arms and promote revolution. This teaching first burst upon the world scene in 1966 when the World Council of Churches gathered together a conference in Geneva on 'Christians and the Technical and Social Revolutions of Our Time'. Here there were new sharp voices from the Third World (as it was then called) calling for immediate and wholesale revolution in the name of Christ, with theological warrant being provided. Thus the American theologian Richard Shaull proclaimed

> The Christian is called to be fully involved in the revolution as it develops. It is only at its centre that we can perceive what God is doing, understand how the struggle for humanization is being defined and serve as agents of reconciliation. From within the struggle, we discover that we do not bear witness in revolution by preserving our purity in line with certain moral principles, but by freedom to be FOR MAN at every moment.[18]

The 'moral principles' he was citing were those which traditionally have made Christians reluctant to engage in revolutionary violence against the government of the day. He was claiming that such moral scruples were now obsolete.

Others were taking up arms in guerrilla wars against oppressive powers, notably the former Catholic priest Camilo Torres in Colombia, who claimed that 'As Christians we can and we must fight against tyranny . . . all genuine revolutionaries must see force as the only means left'.[19] Torres was killed in an ambush, but his example was an inspiration to many. Whilst this revolutionary fervour was gripping Latin America especially, some theologians were claiming that Jesus had been a Zealot, a revolutionary fighter, too. This contention was fuelled by some eccentric scholarship in Europe,[20] later to be firmly repudiated by the most competent New Testament scholarship, especially by the Reformed scholar Oscar Cullmann and the Lutheran scholar Martin Hengel.[21] The great classic work of liberation theology – Gustavo Gutiérrez's *A Theology of Liberation* – has a key section in which he confesses that Cullmann has persuaded him to distance Jesus from the Zealots in many significant ways, yet he is reluctant to mention the clear implications for the practice of violence that Jesus cannot be invoked to support it by classifying him as a Zealot.[22]

Others, equally committed to the immense struggle against long-standing oppression and injustice, equally committed to the liberation in the name of Christ, taught unequivocally that the Christian involvement must be non-violent. The most notable of all voices was that of Helder Câmara, the Catholic bishop of Recife, a particularly poverty-stricken region in Brazil. Câmara held that unjust social structures were a particularly awful form of 'structural violence', but that did not justify the use of arms in bringing about their overthrow. 'If violence is met by violence, the world will fall into a spiral of violence; the only true answer is to have the courage to face the injustices which constitute violence no. 1.'[23]

Catholic teaching however, whilst being constantly in favour of democratic reform and the rule of law, made one tiny concession to those advocating violent revolution. In the major papal encyclical *Populorum Progressio* (On the Progress of Peoples) in 1967, the Pope wrote that 'We know, however, that a revolutionary uprising – save where there is a manifest long-standing tyranny which would do great damage to funda-mental personal rights and great harm to the common good of the country – produces new injustices, throws more elements out of balance and brings on new disasters. A real evil should not be fought against at the cost of greater misery.' The excepting clause in this statement is actually a huge one, as many would-be revolutionaries have noticed.

Meanwhile these issues were being keenly debated in many other circles – within the emerging Black Theology of the United States, the 'political theology' in Europe, and in Southern Africa especially – with Christian opinion always affirming that violent revolution was the last option open to Christians when there was no other course of action available to them, or else refusing to sanction that ultimate desperate course and pleading that even then Christians had no other course but to suffer injustice as creatively as possible. Nelson Mandela and the African National Congress adopted the former position, Bishop Tutu the latter. The close links between the British churches and those of South Africa meant that this issue constantly featured in their reflections together. Thus the British Council of Churches affirmed in 1970 that there could be a 'just revolution',[24] and continued much study on the issue, as did the World Council of Churches. Then in 1980 the British Council published a careful study by Paul Ballard[25] in which, drawing on a magisterial survey of the issue by the theologian J. G. Davies,[26] he defined the 'just revolution' as follows:

1 It must be declared by a movement that has some reasonable claims to legitimacy, with leaders 'who have adequate support and show them-selves just in their dealings and who would therefore make good national leaders'.

2 It must be for a just cause where there is 'sufficient structural and institutional violence to make it absolutely imperative to strike back' .

3 Armed rebellion is the last resort, and involving no hatred of the oppressor.

4 There must be just goals of 'a more just order in which different groups and powers agree to live in peace reconciled to each other'.

5 The means must be just, the social fabric not having been extensively destroyed, and with respect to the set limits to what human beings may justifiably do to others (e.g., no torture).

6 There must be such hope of success that there is a realistic prospect of a just outcome.

The echoes that can be heard here of the ancient notion of the just war are all too clear. We have returned to where this chapter began. But that tradition says little about the sort of peace that Christians should be promoting. For that one must turn to the many traditions of Christian social thought. There are however some other related issues which have become important recently – for example, civil disobedience and the arms trade, both of which have led to thoughtful reports by British churches.[27] But that cannot be the last word. The Christian must always be asking what sort of church life can best promote God's peace; the church should be 'a peaceable kingdom'.[28]

Notes

1 Alan Wilkinson, *Dissent or Conform?* (London: SCM Press, 1986), p. 33.
2 Roland Bainton, *Christian Attitudes Towards War and Peace* (London: Hodder and Stoughton, 1961).
3 John H. Yoder, *Nevertheless: The Varieties of Religious Pacifism* (San Francisco: Herald, 1971), suggests at least 17 types.
4 See R. E. O. White, *The Changing Continuity of Christian Ethics* (Exeter: Paternoster, 1994), vol. I, pp. 231f. and vol. II, pp. 369–78 for the claim that the imitation of Christ is Christianity's unique contribution to ethics.
5 Reinhold Niebuhr, *Moral Man and Immoral Society* (New York: Scribners, 1932).
6 Larry Rasmussen, *Reinhold Niebuhr, Theologian of Public Life* (London: Collins, 1989), p. 239.
7 E.g., Peter Bishop in Cyril Rodd (ed.), *New Occasions Teach New Duties* (Edinburgh: T. & T. Clark, 1995), pp. 134f.
8 Kenneth Slack, *Martin Luther King* (London: SCM Press, 1970), p. 40.
9 Slack, *Martin Luther King*, p. 55.
10 Wilkinson, *Dissent or Conform?*, p. 291.
11 *Gaudium et Spes*, para. 79.
12 Listed in Mark Ellingsen, *The Cutting Edge* (Grand Rapids: Eerdmans, 1993), pp. 226–83.
13 *The Church and the Bomb* (London: Hodder and Stoughton, 1982).

Richard G. Jones

14 *The Challenge of Peace* (London: SPCK, 1983).
15 *In Defense of Creation* (Nashville, TN: Graded Press, 1986).
16 Francis Bridger (ed.), *The Cross and the Bomb* (London: Mowbray, 1983).
17 Dietrich Bonhoeffer, *Ethics* (London: Fontana, 1966), p. 351; see also Keith Clements, *A Patriotism for Today* (Bristol: Bristol Baptist College, 1984).
18 See J. C. Bennett (ed.), *Christian Ethics in a Changing World* (London: SCM Press, 1967), p. 33.
19 Richard Shaull, *Camilo Torres, Priest and Revolutionary* (London: Sheed & Ward, 1968), pp. 73 and 126.
20 E.g., S. G. F. Brandon, *Jesus & the Zealots* (Manchester: Manchester University Press, 1967).
21 O. Cullmann, *Jesus and the Revolutionaries* (New York: Harper and Row, 1970) and M. Hengel, *Victory over Violence* (London: SPCK, 1975).
22 G. Gutiérrez, *A Theology of Liberation* (Maryknoll, NY: Orbis, 1973), pp. 225–32.
23 Helder Câmara, *Spiral of Violence* (London: Sheed & Ward, 1971), p. 55.
24 British Council of Churches, *Violence in South Africa* (London: SCM Press, 1970).
25 P. Ballard, *A Christian Perspective on Violence* (London: British Council of Churches, 1980).
26 J. G. Davies, *Christians, Politics and Violent Revolution* (London: SCM Press, 1976).
27 *Accept and Resist: A Study of Civil Disobedience in Christian History and Today* (London: Methodist Publishing House, 1986) and *Responsibility in Arms Transfer Policy* (London: Church House Publishing, 1994).
28 A good example is Stanley Hauerwas, *The Peaceable Kingdom: A Primer in Christian Ethics* (London: SCM, 1983).

Select bibliography

Roland Bainton, *Christian Attitudes Towards War and Peace* (London: Hodder and Stoughton, 1961).
R. Bauckham and R. J. Elford (eds), *The Nuclear Weapons Debate* (London: SCM Press, 1989).
Norman Cohn, *The Pursuit of the Millennium* (London: Paladin, 1970).
J. G. Davies, *Christians, Politics and Violent Revolution* (London: SCM Press, 1976).
The Challenge of Peace: God's Promise and Our Response (London: SPCK, 1983).

Interpersonal and sexual ethics

16
Sex, sexuality and relationships

Gareth Moore

The modern background

Among all Christians, or among those authorized to speak officially for Christians, certain elements of sexual ethics were in the past taken for granted, and the focus was very much on the purpose of sex, what kinds of sexual act were permitted, and in what circumstances. Since sex was ordained by God for the purpose of bringing children into the world, the proper context for it was within marriage, since children needed a loving and stable environment; this was provided by marriage, which was for the raising of children and had also been instituted by God himself. From this it followed that pre-marital sex or adultery was forbidden. From the fact that God had ordained sex for procreation it also followed that any kind of sexual activity not suitable for the production of children was not only forbidden but perverted the nature of sex itself. Masturbation, contraception, bestiality and anal and oral sex were all in a deep sense contrary to the will of God, since they not only broke the law of God concerning sexual matters, but also struck at the very purpose for which God had created sex. The same was also true of all sexual acts between people of the same sex.

It seems this view was often more honoured in the breach than in the observance, that a great deal of this forbidden sexual activity went on among Christians, including the official spokesmen. There was plenty of adultery, masturbation, homosexuality, and so forth. Nevertheless, there was no widespread challenge to the official teaching which, like many other aspects of Christian doctrine, was seen as immutable, because God-given. If people acted persistently contrary to the teaching, this was a sign of the power of sin rather than of the weakness of the teaching.

Today, the old certainties are disappearing, and sex and its place in human relationships is one of the most controversial areas of modern Christian ethics. As ever, there is much sexual activity which does not conform to the traditional picture of the nature and purpose of sex. But there is also, in the West, a widespread discontent with the traditional teaching itself, which seems to many no longer to correspond to the realities of life and to the needs of people. The traditional ideals seem to many not only unattainable but also unnecessary and even harmful. While it is a normal part of human living to enter into sexual relationships – normal because of our physical and emotional makeup – there seems, again according to many people, to be no reason why these should always be lifelong or exclusive. The old argument based on the needs of children for a stable environment is no longer convincing in a world where, thanks to the availability of efficient contraception, there is no necessary link between sex and reproduction. Neither, given the rate at which world population is expanding and the limited food and water sources at our disposal, should there be regret that contraception is so readily available. There is also an increasing recognition that homosexual acts might sometimes be appropriate. While men and women who engaged in sexual activity with others of the same sex were formerly (and in many places still are) vilified and condemned as wanton perverts, it is becoming clear to more and more people that homosexuals are capable of loving devotion and self-giving in their personal relationships, including their sexual relationships, and that they, as well as everybody else, should have the chance to taste the fulfilment that such relationships can bring without having to battle social hostility and rejection by the churches.

This change in the climate of thought about sex has multiple roots. Since Freud, much public emphasis has been placed on the importance of sexuality as an element of human personality. Sex is no longer seen simply as a way of propagating the species, nor as an occasional and potentially enjoyable necessity, but as an essential and defining aspect of each person's character, having an all-pervasive influence on human behaviour and attitudes. A person's sexual history and attitudes are, it is claimed, important factors in that person's overall health, maturity and happiness.

There has also been an increasing stress on individual liberty in Western societies, and this, together with increasingly widespread education, has encouraged people to think for themselves and find their own values in sexual as in many other matters. Linked to this has been the rise of the feminist movement and the gay movement, both of which have stimulated much new thought about sex and have begun to undermine some more traditional attitudes. It is not surprising that the advent of voices from previously largely unheard sections of the community should bring to light new points of view and call into question earlier certainties; these latter are often criticized as being, not the will of God or the reflection of some eternal law, but merely the views of socially dominant heterosexual males.

Historical, sociological and anthropological research (much used in gay and feminist literature) has also had its role to play in the change of atmosphere. In earlier ages, in a culture saturated by Christianity, Christian attitudes to sex and relationships could seem universal and changeless, and therefore obvious, because there was little knowledge of how other, non-Christian, societies functioned. Modern research has made it clear that non-Christian societies, both ancient and modern, have very different sexual practices from those sanctioned in Christianity, and have very different attitudes to sex. This awareness of difference has made Christian sexual mores less self-evident, more questionable, and has even led to a relativism which sees Christian sexual ethics merely as one option, no better and no worse than any other. The work of Foucault has been particularly important here, with its emphasis on the way in which the conceptualization of sex and sexuality – the way sex and sexual relationships are conceived and talked about – not only changes with time and place but is closely linked to the social structures and wider currents of thought within each society.[1]

The advent of efficient methods of contraception has meant that the link between sex and procreation has been, if not broken, at least rendered more tenuous, so that it is possible to think of having an active (heterosexual) sex life without having children and the resulting responsibility. For the same reason, to many it no longer seems reasonable to confine sex within the bounds of marriage. Marriage may have been the natural place for sex before, when sex resulted in children who needed to be raised in a stable environment, but if, because of the use of contraception, there are no children in prospect, then it should be possible to engage in sexual activity outside marriage, or even outside any stable relationship. If care is taken to avoid conception, it is argued, casual sex is no longer the irresponsible activity it once was.

Another important factor is the development of other forms of stable relationship than marriage. Men and women openly enter into stable long-term relationships, and have children, without going through any public ceremony of commitment, either religious or secular, which would make their relationship into a marriage, and they defend their right to do so. Again, male and female homosexuals also enter into stable relationships, more or less openly, in which they claim that sex has an appropriate place, just as it has in heterosexual relationships.

Christians are on the whole integrated into the societies in which they live, and so are not immune to changing currents of attitude and belief in the wider society, and all the above factors have brought about changes of thought and practice within the Church as well as outside. Christians of most churches are happy to practise contraception, and there is increasing (if still not widespread) acceptance of homosexual partnerships and of non-marital heterosexual partnerships. This has been accompanied by changes at an official level. Thus, for example, the Church of England accepted contraception in the 1930s, and in the 1990s has come to accept the possibility of virtuous and Christian homosexual relationships.

On the other hand, there are many Christians who view these developments with horror and see them not as the legitimate adaptation of Christian teaching to modern conditions in the light of new knowledge, but as a betrayal of the clear teachings of Scripture and of Christian tradition, an abandonment of the loving will of God. The official teaching of the Catholic Church has been among the most steadfast voices in defence of traditional Christian values in this area, most notably in its opposition to contraception and homosexuality.[2]

In such a climate of controversy it is impossible to give a simple summary of Christian teaching on sex and its place in human relationships. In addition, the space available is too short to attempt a theological treatment of the many and varied human sexual practices and the arguments concerning them deployed by Christians. In what follows I will try rather to indicate some (and only some) of the questions and problems involved in any modern Christian discussion of sex. I will concentrate particularly on the difficulties of maintaining the traditional Christian approach in general, difficulties posed in large measure by the modern discoveries referred to above. Whether these difficulties can be met, and traditional attitudes rationally maintained, is a further question beyond the scope of this chapter; but that the difficulties are there and must be addressed seems to me undeniable.

Common to all Christians is a reliance on the Bible. In addition, Catholics have accorded an important place to natural reason, and arguments of a more or less philosophical nature have often found a place in Catholic treatments of sexual ethics. Since God is seen in the Catholic tradition as the author of human nature, including both human sexuality and the human capacity to think, natural reflection on sexual behaviour, even without reference to Scripture, is seen as a legitimate and indeed important activity. One important form this reasoning has taken has been to talk in terms of 'natural law'. Fidelity to God has been seen as involving the attempt to remain faithful to the nature that God has created, to the natural law. This in turn involves investigation into that nature, which is the concern not of the Bible but of our natural capacities. It is this rational investigation, notably but not exclusively as expressed in natural law theory, which according to the Catholic tradition makes Christian ethics accessible to all non-Christians, with whom we share a common humanity, and it is what gives Christian ethics the possibility of being rationally based. This type of reflection was an important element of pagan thought in the early centuries of Christianity. It was adopted also by Christians and developed a great deal in the Middle Ages. The Protestant tradition has, by contrast, tended to shun explicit appeal to human reason or natural law, seeking to base sexual morality on Scripture alone. In accordance with these two tendencies, the following remarks will be divided into observations on the use of Scripture and comments on other, non-biblical, rather more philosophical approaches to sexual ethics.

Scripture

In examining the Christian traditions on sex and relationships, it is well to bear in mind that people, Christians as well as others, tend to have strong views on questions of sexual behaviour. It is also well known that often, when people say that their views on a particular question are based on Scripture, it is unfortunately rather the case, not that they hold the views they do because they are compelled to them by scriptural evidence, but that they have sought justification in Scripture for views that they already hold independently of Scripture, while ignoring (or being ignorant of) other parts of Scripture which might support a different view. Non-scriptural values, even if unacknowledged, can be important in the selection of biblical texts and in the interpretation of those texts. When the questions concerned are sexual ones, this tendency is likely to be strong. Scriptural arguments in this area are therefore well treated with caution. While it may well be possible to support a given opinion by reference to Scripture, this should not be interpreted as meaning that that opinion reflects the consistent view of Scripture. Indeed, it is dangerous to suppose, without careful and objective reading of the texts, that Scripture has a consistent view at all on sexual matters. The scriptural books are the products of different ages and civilizations, and it would be natural to assume that writings with such diverse backgrounds have diverse viewpoints. At the very least, it should not be assumed *a priori* that this is not so, and one should be wary of attempts to speak of '*the* biblical view of sex' which do not include a careful and thorough investigation of a wide range of texts.

Questions of sex, gender and sexual activity in human relationships occupy a not inconsiderable place in Scripture. In the Old Testament there are, among other things, laws governing sexual behaviour in Israel (e.g. Exod 20:14; Lev 18:6–23), stories of rape and vengeance (Gen 34) of adultery and treachery (2 Sam 11), and advice to young men on avoiding other people's wives (Prov 6:23–29). In the New, we find Jesus teaching against men coveting other men's wives (Matt 6:27–29). We also find Paul describing same-sex passion as a punishment for idolatry (Rom 1:21–27), condemning a case of what seems to be incest (1 Cor 5:1f.), and recommending celibacy but conceding the possibility of marriage for those who cannot exercise self-control (1 Cor 7:8f.).

It used to be possible to construct a Christian sexual ethic to a large extent by simple appeal to biblical texts. Sexual ethics was largely a matter of finding out what kinds of sexual activity were permitted by God, and in what circumstances; and this could be discovered by searching through Scripture. This would normally, though not exclusively, be done by a process of elimination, for it was for the most part sexual practices which were not permissible which tended to be mentioned, with explicit or implied condemnation. The legal texts of the Old Testament were a particularly rich field here. Thus, from the sixth commandment one learned that God forbade adultery (Exod 20:14; Deut 5:18); sexual intercourse between men was forbidden as an abomination to God (Lev 18:22); and sex with animals was likewise prohibited (Lev 18:23). Incest too was forbidden (Deut 22:30; Lev 18:6–18). A young woman who marries must do so as a virgin (Deut 22:13–21). Rape is to be punished (Deut 22:23–29). From this it appeared that the only circumstances in which sexual activity with another[3] is permissible is in marriage.

Other kinds of text, in both Testaments, reinforced this picture, and in important respects went further. For example, the story of Sodom and Gomorrah (Gen 19:1–29) implied a condemnation of homosexual acts, as did Paul's remarks in Romans 1:26f. and 1 Corinthians 6:9. The story of Tobias and Sarah (Tob 6:9 – 7:18) extolled sexual purity and by implication condemned lust. The fate of Onan (Gen 38:6–10) seemed to imply divine condemnation of marital intercourse in which contraception was used. Jesus himself, in the Sermon on the Mount, forbade not only adultery but all lustful thoughts (Matt 5:27f.).

Thus, by reference to Scripture one easily arrived at many of the tenets of traditional Christian sexual morality. Sex was for married couples only, and since Jesus forbade divorce, that meant those united in a lifelong and indissoluble relationship. Within marriage, sexual activity must be chaste, and not the result of lust. It must also be open to procreation. This morality was faithful to the word of God, and therefore expressed the will of God.

This array of biblical citations (and there are numerous others that could be mentioned) is impressive, and for many Christians, especially Protestants, it remains the foundation of sexual morality. In the Catholic tradition too, while natural reason also has an important place, this testimony of Scripture is central to sexual ethics. In the past, it seemed clear that the teaching of God in Scripture was clear and unambiguous, and to many it still seems so.

Laws and relationships

From a modern viewpoint, however, such an approach to sex and Scripture is inadequate. Both Protestants and Catholics now recognize that considerable emphasis should be placed on the role of sex in human relationships. After all, a sexual act normally takes place between two people and forms part of their relationship. A legalistic approach in terms of which acts are permissible and which not is in danger of missing out this essential element. When thinking about the morality of a particular interpersonal sexual act, the central question should not be whether the act is allowed or not, but whether it contributes to the couple's relationship. One should also ask whether it contributes positively to the partners' relationships with others. Here, what counts as a positive contribution to a relationship is determined by the fundamental Christian view that human relationships should be based on love. Thus, the questions to be asked are, for example: Is this act an expression of love between the partners? Does it strengthen their love for each other? Is it compatible with love for other people outside this particular relationship? Is it likely to increase or decrease the participants' capacity to love, or will it probably have no effect at all?

Such an approach, which is common today, has the great advantage that it integrates sexual morality with the rest of Christian morality. It does not rely on special, self-justifying rules for sex, but gives full weight to the insistence of Jesus (and of Paul and other New Testament writers) on the primacy of love. The demand of Christ that all relationships be based on love (e.g. Matt 22:39; John 13:34; 15:12, 17) is allowed to apply to sexual relationships also.

The question now arises: What does this approach imply for the status of the scriptural precepts and prohibitions concerning sexual relationships referred to earlier? Particularly important here is the strong New Testament tradition that the love of neighbour sums up the law. For example, near the beginning of the Sermon on the Mount Jesus says: 'Think not that I have come to abolish the law and the prophets; I have come not to abolish them but to fulfil them' (Matt 5:17). This can sound as if he is preoccupied with the prescriptions of the law. But then, towards the end of the Sermon, he shows what he means by this insistence on the law and the prophets when he says: 'Whatever you wish that people would do to you, do so to them; for this is the law and the prophets' (Matt 7:12). The insistence here is apparently not on the importance of keeping the letter of the law (we know in any case that Jesus subordinated the letter of the law to human need[4]) but on the summing up of the demands of God (the law *and the prophets*) which makes the way a person wishes to be treated the criterion for the way that person should treat others; in other words: 'Love your neighbour as yourself.'

This teaching, that love sums up the law, is echoed in other parts of the New Testament. For example, 'He who loves his neighbour has fulfilled the law . . . Love does no wrong to a neighbour; therefore love is the fulfilling of the law' (Rom 13:8, 10); 'The whole law is fulfilled in one word: You shall love your neighbour as yourself' (Gal 5:14); 'If you really fulfil the royal law according to the scripture – You shall love your neighbour as yourself – you do well' (Jas 2:8).

The consistency and centrality of this teaching in the New Testament makes impossible any insistence that scriptural precepts and prohibitions concerning sex (or any other matter), whether from the Old Testament or from the New, be followed *simply because they are scriptural*. What Christians need to follow is not, for example, a prohibition of incest or of homosexual acts, or a command to increase and multiply, but the injunction to love. Whatever concrete commands may be found in Scripture must be subordinated to this overriding principle.

The status of the Bible

But this is not the end of the matter. It is possible to subscribe to this principle, but to react to it in one of two contrasting ways. The first is to say that the biblical utterances on sex are effectively abrogated by the commandment to love. It might be argued that we simply do not need any more (if we ever did) to consult the Bible about what to do in our sexual lives. We have instead to think hard, seriously and honestly about what love invites us to do and what it asks us not to do. The old biblical rules may or may not be justifiable according to this criterion, but they are subject to it, and are not independent sources of morality. Thus, for example, love demands that homosexual people be allowed the same opportunity to fulfil themselves in loving sexual relationships as heterosexuals have. If Leviticus 18:22 or Romans 1:26f. imply otherwise, so much the worse for them.

This approach, one could claim, does not involve abandoning the word or the will of God. Biblical rules were made by people, perhaps inspired by God, but they were made for another society in another era, a society whose ways are not ours. If they expressed the demands of love in that society, then they were the word of God to that society, but it does not follow that they remain the word of God for our society. On the other hand, if they did not express the demands of love in that society either, but tended to make it a loveless society, then they never were the word of

God, and we can thank Jesus for showing us a higher way, the way of love, which actually does correspond to the will of God.

A second and opposite possible response is to agree that love is primary, but to insist that the Bible is the word of God, and that the word of God is permanent and in important ways changeless. God's word to the Israelites of the first millennium BC is still God's word to all peoples. The Bible must therefore always remain the source for all morality, including sexual morality. Something like this position is the traditional and official position of the Catholic Church. If biblical injunctions appear to be against the law of love as preached by Jesus and the New Testament, this should be taken to show, not that the injunctions should be jettisoned, but that our grasp of what love demands is inadequate, that God's wisdom is greater than ours. Though sanctioning homosexual relationships may appear to be what love of homosexual people demands, further investigation will show that such relationships only make the people in them unhappy in the end, or endanger the overall well-being of society. There is thus a deep wisdom in the words of Scripture which justifies our continued adherence to them.

There are problems with both these approaches. The former can seem to treat the word of Scripture in too cavalier a fashion. If one can simply ignore parts of the Bible, this raises the question of the status of Scripture in the Christian faith. Why consult Scripture at all when seeking guidance on questions of sexual morality? The principle of love, biblically based though it is, seems, if erected into the sole criterion for our sexual behaviour, to render its own source obsolete. Some might accept this consequence readily, but there is surely a problem of the status of Scripture here which goes beyond its relevance to sexual ethics. Its whole status as revelation, as divinely inspired, and as the word of God is put in question. However we interpret the Bible, one might ask, does not Scripture need to retain a privileged status of some kind within Christianity if the latter is to be true to itself and to God?

The second, traditionalist approach, on the other hand, makes empirical claims which are apparently untrue. To continue using the same example, it is not clear that careful investigation does show that homosexuals in stable sexual relationships are any worse off than they would be in non-sexual relationships or alone; anecdotal evidence suggests the contrary. There is some evidence that young homosexuals tend to be less happy than their heterosexual counterparts, and this is readily understandable in the light of the general negative image of homosexuals in society; but there is none that suggests sexual activity within a stable partnership tends to make them any unhappier. Further, it is difficult to think of any plausible causal link between sexual activity in that context and a tendency to unhappiness. Still less does it appear that the existence of such relationships damages society in general. Of course, the traditionalists can claim that we do not yet have enough evidence; but such a claim wears thin after a while, especially if not backed up by a credible causal theory. (Note how here, in the discussion of an ostensibly biblical approach to ethics, non-biblical, empirical questions already intrude.)

There is a further problem in the traditionalist approach, which is that it neglects the historical nature of the biblical documents. This problem is particularly acute when it comes to sexual questions. Old Testament sexual legislation and attitudes were formed in the context of a society in which inequality between the sexes was profound and systematic, and they take their sense from that context. Contrary to what is sometimes asserted, the Old Testament does not teach the fundamental equality of the sexes. If there are traces of such a teaching, they are rare and untypical. The great mass of legislation and teaching tends in the opposite direction. Men are presented as clearly socially superior to women. Married women were practically the property of their husbands.[5] This is why a man could divorce his wife at will,[6] whereas a woman had no right of divorce. This inequality was reflected in the sexual sphere. Within certain limits a man was sexually free,[7] so long as he did not have sex with another man's wife, his neighbour's sexual property. At Numbers 5:12ff. is prescribed a ritual to determine whether a man who suspects that his wife has had sex with another man is right; there is no corresponding ritual dealing with a woman who suspects her husband of having sex with another woman. He had sexual liberty and she did not, because he fundamentally owned, whereas she was owned. A woman shown not to have been a virgin when she married was subject to stoning;[8] nowhere is it suggested that a man should be a virgin when marrying. The only women with comparable freedom were prostitutes, who were publicly despised; though there is never any criticism of their customers. And so on. This picture is partly rectified in the New Testament, with Paul's insistence that a woman has rights over a man's body as well as vice versa,[9] and by Jesus' teaching that a man is not free to dispose of his wife as of a piece of property.[10] But the reported consternation of Jesus' own disciples at this teaching – 'If such is the case of a man with his wife, it is not expedient to marry'[11] – is an indication of how strange the idea was in a Jewish context shaped by the Old Testament. Even elsewhere in the New Testament, a thorough-going subordination of women is in evidence.[12]

In the light of this it might reasonably be asked whether, in the case of sexual ethics, we should take the Bible as a guide at all. There is general perception in the modern Church, among both revisionists and traditionalists, that there is, despite the weight of biblical material to the contrary, an essential equality between men and women. This seems to be demanded by, among other things, the rule of love proclaimed by Jesus, which is surely incompatible with the property-based ethic of so much of the Bible.[13] Since the sexual attitudes of the Bible are so clearly at variance with this perception, and so deeply embedded in the social structures from which they arise, we seem compelled, in the name of Christianity, to seek some other foundation for our sexual ethics and in general to reject scriptural pronouncements on sexual behaviour as a possible guide. Considerations such as these definitely seem to favour the revisionists rather than the traditionalists.

Non-scriptural arguments

I turn now to a brief consideration of some non-biblical elements of Christian thought on sex and relationships. Because the explicit emphasis on human reason has been stronger in Catholicism than in Protestantism, the majority of what follows will perhaps have more immediate relevance to the Catholic than to the Protestant tradition.

I earlier mentioned the dangers of selectivity and partiality in the use of biblical texts to construct arguments in sexual ethics. Parallel considerations apply to natural law and other rational arguments. We can expect it to happen but rarely that a theologian adopts a particular opinion on sexual matters because he or she is driven to it by an argument that has presented itself. It tends to be the case rather that rational arguments are sought to justify an opinion which is held independently of argument. There is perhaps nothing particularly wrong with this, except that one is normally inclined to be insufficiently critical of arguments – especially one's own – advanced to support a position one holds oneself. This means that natural law arguments – one's own as well as those of others – are to be approached with an especially critical eye. This is a crucial matter in natural law, where the position in question is supposed to be based on *sound* reason. No matter how much sympathy one has with, say, a Catholic stand against contraception, if a rational argument adduced in favour of that stand is flawed, the argument fails to support it, and it fails, moreover, to support the claim that the Catholic stand against contraception is rationally based. If one tries to support the Catholic position with a bad argument, that position is left looking irrational, based on an appeal to reason which is but specious. The reader who recognizes the poor quality of the argument is left with the impression that he has not found the rational justification of the Catholic position that the argument seemed to promise, and is left moreover with the suspicion that such a justification is not to be found. This might not matter much in a world where everybody agreed that the Catholic position was right, and where the finding of arguments to support it was merely an intellectual exercise. But we do not live in such a world. In our world, opinions are sharply divided on contraception, as on many other issues in sexual ethics. In such a world, the function of argument must be to convince those who doubt or who hold a contrary opinion. A bad argument does not achieve its end; the use of a bad argument further gives the impression that a good argument is not available, and that those who hold the opinion in support of which the argument is adduced are merely confused thinkers – or worse, bigots – whose opinions cannot be rationally justified and are more likely than not to be false.

Natural law

The natural law tradition takes its rise from Hellenistic thought, especially Stoicism. There are two basic elements which converge in the Stoic attitude to sex. First, for many Hellenistic thinkers the world was a purposeful place. It was a harmonious whole in which each element fulfilled its purpose, and each element was there so as to fulfil its natural purpose. Proper human action was action which respected and was in harmony with the purposes to be found in nature; it also respected the natural purposes of human organs. The purpose of sexual activity was clearly reproduction, since not only did normal sexual intercourse often result in conception, but it was only by reference to reproduction that the existence of the sexual organs could be understood at all – it is only because people reproduce sexually that they have sexual organs in the first place. It followed that any sexual activity which was not of a kind such as to allow reproduction did not follow nature's purpose. So, for instance, all masturbation, all homosexual activity and all heterosexual intercourse where contraception was employed were against nature, and therefore bad.

Second, if somebody did not engage in sexual activity in order to have children, the alternative was that they were doing it for pleasure. There was a suspicion of pleasure in the Hellenistic world, and not only among the Stoics. To do anything simply for the sake of pleasure was, in much Greek thought, unworthy and dangerous, and it also subverted the natural order of things. It meant that a man (and it was usually specifically men rather than women who were envisaged) allowed himself to be led by his desire rather than by reason. This was contrary to nature since according to nature it was reason, which was the distinctive mark of the human, that should determine a man's behaviour. To act for pleasure was to act in a less than human way. Since sex was an area where pleasure and desire ruled, it was suspect in itself, and could only be justified by its reproductive purpose.

It was roughly this schema that was adopted into Christianity and was developed by Augustine and by medieval thinkers such as Albert the Great and Thomas Aquinas. Various arguments were found from nature which were held to show, for example, that certain positions adopted in sexual intercourse were more natural, more respectful of the nature of human beings, and therefore more acceptable, than others,[14] or that any activity which resulted in semen being deposited elsewhere than in a vagina was unnatural and therefore wrong.[15] Masturbation and contraception were unnatural because they did not respect the natural purpose of sex and because they resulted in a waste of semen. Homosexual acts were unnatural for the same reasons, but also because they did not respect the difference of sexes and the reason why the sexes existed.

Much of this could have been written by pagan philosophers. The specifically Christian element was that it was the God who had revealed himself in Scripture who was the author of nature. The order of nature was the expression of the divine will, and the purposes inherent in nature – nature in general and human nature in particular – were God's purposes. It was God who made people male and female[16] and gave them organs whose purpose was reproduction. To perform an unnatural act, therefore, was not only to offend against nature but to sin against God; it was deliberately to set oneself to act contrary to the will of God. If somebody acted against his own nature he expressed contempt for his own nature and for the God who had created him with that nature.

Natural law and happiness

It is easy to get the impression from this brief sketch that natural law thought makes human beings subservient to an alien, impersonal, almost mechanical system of rules which can be read off from nature. People seem to be caught up, like it or not, in a machine which has little regard for them and whose purposes they are bound to follow. It is true that some examples of natural law thinking are like this, but it is not a necessary feature of natural law theory in general, nor of any thought about sex based on human reason. Take Aquinas as an example. On the one hand, he can speak of natural law as 'that which nature teaches every animal';[17] in this sense, natural law seems to put impersonal biological nature at the centre of things. But he also has a second, quite different conception of natural law. He claims that only rational beings can truly follow natural law. Natural law is a participation in reason, and only beings that can think about and understand what they are doing so participate.[18] Here, natural law seems to mean little more than rational thought about human acts in the light of human nature, thinking about what is the proper end and how to attain it. But this is already a great deal; to think about and understand what one is doing is very different from acting instinctually, like an animal, and also very different from blindly obeying laws simply because they are laws.

Of course, rational thinking can be done in different ways, and it is true that when Aquinas thinks about sexual acts, he often starts from nature in the sense of what he takes to be biological or other empirical facts about human beings and other animals, 'natural law' in the first sense. But the two conceptions of natural law are not necessarily bound together in this way. Indeed, Aquinas himself sometimes takes a different, much more promising approach. He says that God, the author of human nature, desires human happiness. Therefore God made human nature in such a way as to promote human happiness. To act in accord with nature is therefore to promote one's happiness, while to act against it is to court unhappiness.[19] This approach puts human flourishing squarely at the centre of natural law; what is natural, what is in accordance with the proper end of human beings, and therefore good, is what promotes well-being and happiness, while what is unnatural, and therefore bad, what is contrary to our true end, is what is deleterious and works against happiness. On this account, the central question of natural law is not 'What do animals do?' or even 'What is the purpose of this or that human organ?' but 'What, given the type of creature we are, makes for human happiness?'

If we use this conception of natural law, natural law no longer seems to be something which imprisons people in an impersonal system. It means simply thinking about human action in such a way that considerations of human happiness, well-being and flourishing – in short, of what is good for people – are central. This is a big improvement on that style of thought which bases itself simply on the biological functions of organs.[20]

A very important aspect of this type of natural law thought, and indeed of all types, is that it is in large measure empirically based. Those who claimed, for instance, that the sexual organs have a certain function in nature did so on the basis of what they or others actually observed, or claimed to observe, about the functioning of these organs. They observed what people and animals did with them, and what resulted. They may not always have been good observers; they may have missed certain things, and their preconceptions may have prevented them from taking due note of everything they saw. But they were basically making an empirical claim, which they then incorporated into an argument which led to a moral conclusion. Part of the cogency of such an argument was that it rested partly on evidence whose truth was open for all to see. Given enough observation and scientific knowledge, it was possible to *see* that the purpose of the sexual organs was reproduction (or so it seemed to those who argued in this fashion).

In the same way, to think about what makes for human happiness is to think empirically. It is observation which tells us whether, say, a particular social structure, economic system, personal relationship, eating habit or sexual habit makes those involved in it happy or unhappy. Once again, we may observe well or badly. Human life is immensely complex, and it requires a great deal of accurate observation, often over the long term, to understand any aspect of it adequately. Often, many factors combine to promote or hinder a person's flourishing, and it is difficult to isolate the role and importance of any individual factor. This is particularly true in the sexual domain, since sexual behaviour does not have a direct effect on human welfare in the same way that patterns of eating or drinking behaviour do. These latter have direct and often obvious physical effects, whereas the effect of sexual behaviour on well-being is likely to be much more subtle, and on the emotional or psychological plane, which is often more difficult to measure or evaluate than the physical.

But, even given the centrality of human happiness, and even if we can sort out the empirical complexities, moral questions, including questions of sexual ethics, cannot be solved simply by empirical observation. We may discover, for example, that some practices may make people happy in the short term, but not in the long term. We normally, in theory, privilege the long term, but it needs to be asked whether this is always necessary, whether happiness in the short term can sometimes be worth the price of eventual long-term unhappiness. This is not an empirical but a theoretical question. Again, when we speak of happiness we need to ask whose happiness we are talking about. Some economic and social systems, as well as many individual actions, purchase happiness for some people at the expense of misery for others. Here questions of justice come to the fore.

Sex, rationality and the meaning of acts

If we reflect on the nature of human beings with a view to asking what is good for us, one important consideration is that we are rational beings. Our being rational is not only what enables us to reflect on the world, on ourselves and on our behaviour, but is also an element of our nature that needs to be taken into account when we think about what fulfils that nature, makes us happy. What form our rationality takes, how we understand things, has an important bearing on our well-being.

The word 'rational' here covers a number of things which seem to be related and to distinguish us in large measure from other animals, which, we normally say, operate much more by instinct. We have the ability to understand the world, to discriminate between things, to make connections between things, to classify things, and so on. An important element of this rationality is that people are linguistic animals. If we distinguish, connect and classify, we do so most often with words, by what we say about things. Again, we think about our ends and the means we use to achieve them. If some other animals have a certain rationality, it still seems true that people can plan, expect, hope and fear in ways much more complex than those open to dogs or giraffes. We can also attach significance to actions and events in a way that goes beyond the capacities of other animals.

One of the things that we classify, that we talk, plan, hope and fear about and attach significance to, is our bodily behaviour and that of other people. At this point it is an important fact that many of our bodily gestures derive some of their significance from our sheer physical constitution. For example, the fact that we have a soft skin well supplied with nerves means that we are likely to be physically hurt and feel pain if somebody punches us on the nose. What hurts is inherently unpleasant, and we seek to avoid it. Deliberate behaviour which hurts us is aggressive. So if somebody punches us, that does not merely produce a physical sensation, but has a *meaning* for us, one which goes beyond the boundaries of our body. It signifies something about the relationship between ourselves and the person who hits us; it is an expression of hostility towards us on the part of that person. We expect everybody to be familiar with and sensitive to such gestures. It is perhaps conceivable that somebody might go around punching others without discrimination simply because this is an activity he finds enjoyable, without any aggressive intent. For him, punching would have no meaning. But such a person would, just for that reason, be regarded as asocial and defective. To be social means to be sensitive to interpersonal meaning. Similarly, there are sensations, feelings and activities which are inherently pleasant, and which we seek out. Somebody who helps us have these sensations or perform these activities shows himself well-disposed towards us. If somebody holds us to make us feel warm or cherished, or gives us food so that we can eat, this is a sign of friendship. Once again, our actions, including our bodily gestures, signify something about personal relationships.

A further fact about human beings is that physical intimacy serves as a sign of personal intimacy, of friendship. Friends freely come physically close to each other in ways that strangers and enemies do not. We permit friends to come close to us, as we do not strangers. Whereas we may welcome the close presence or touch of a friend, the proximity or touch of a stranger or an enemy strikes us as invasive and aggressive. The way we speak of friends as being *close* is testimony to this. Once again, the physical body and what we do with it functions to convey a relational significance.

It is on this basis, the recognition of the importance of meaning for human beings, that attempts have been made recently to reach certain conclusions about sexual behaviour. Sexual intercourse is one of the most intimate forms of bodily behaviour. It seems to be a natural expression, therefore, of the most intimate form of friendship. It naturally signifies a profoundly intimate personal relationship, just as a punch naturally signifies hostility. It is as if the partners in intercourse testify to each other, wordlessly, by the physical and sexual intimacy that they give and accept, to the depth of their relationship as persons, indeed to the fact that their relationship is the most profound possible. But the most intimate and profound human relationship is marriage, by which the partners commit themselves to being close to each other in all circumstances until death. Thus, by a modern route, we arrive at a traditional Christian conclusion, that the proper place for sex is within marriage.

This conclusion as to the significance of sexual intercourse fits well with the Second Vatican Council's description of sexual intercourse as an act 'proper to spouses' which signifies self-giving (*Gaudium et Spes*, n. 49). It has been developed by Pope John Paul II in his encyclical *Familiaris Consortio*. He writes:

> Sexuality, by means of which man and woman give themselves to one another through the acts which are proper and exclusive to spouses, is by no means something purely biological, but concerns the innermost being of the human person as such. It is realised in a truly human way only if it is an integral part of the love by which a man and a woman commit themselves totally to one another until death. The total physical self-giving would be a lie if it were not the sign and fruit of a total personal self-giving, in which the whole person, including the temporal dimension, is present: if the person were to withhold something or reserve the possibility of deciding otherwise in the future, by this very fact he or she would not be giving totally.[21]

In this passage we can see too the use of the idea of a sexual language, the notion that people actually *say* something by their acts. In this particular case an act of sexual intercourse is said to be a lie – a deliberately false bodily 'utterance' intended to deceive, if the partners to the act are not totally committed to each other. The meaning which sexual (as well as other) activities have is interpreted as closely akin to linguistic meaning. This idea, which has been developed by both Protestants and Catholics,[22] has several merits. It emphasizes that sex is not a mere animal act but a rational human activity, which can be (or fail to be) intelligent. It articulates the insight that sex is significant for people, that their sexual acts have, at least potentially, meaning for them, and that sex is a form of communication: one can communicate one's feelings and attitudes towards another by the way one acts sexually towards him or her.

But it is another question whether this line of thought actually does support traditional Christian views on marriage as the only legitimate place for sex, and whether it leads to the conclusion John Paul II and others think it does. If it is true that bodily proximity and bodily intimacy often signify an intimate personal relationship, it is far from true that they always do so. While friends habitually come close physically to each other, for the pleasure of being together and doing things together, all of us also come physically close to others in the course of our daily lives – when we talk with others at work, when we buy a ticket on a bus, when we buy something in a shop, when we stand squashed together in a rush-hour train, when we play team games, and so on. None of these close encounters need have any great personal significance, and normally they do not. Deliberate physical proximity is not of itself a bearer of deep relational meaning. If we number sexual encounters among the closest physical encounters, it does not follow that they naturally signify that the partners to it have an intimate personal relationship. It may well be true that sexual intercourse can be, within the context of close personal relationship, a meaningful and effective sign and expression of that relationship, but that has no tendency to show that sexual activity outside an intimate personal relationship, and which therefore does not have the significance that it would within such a relationship, is in any way illegitimate or inauthentic.

It seems more plausible to argue that sexual intercourse does not have great unitive significance in itself, but that it bears what significance it does by virtue of the context in which it takes place. An act of intercourse which takes place within a loving relationship, and as part of that relationship, surely does express physically the unity of the partners. On the other hand, an act of intercourse which takes place between strangers who intend to separate immediately afterwards may signify little beyond the minimal mutual good will needed to co-operate in a joint pleasurable activity.

The point may be made using the analogy between bodily activities or gestures and language. A word, a spoken or written sign, in a human language does not have meaning independently of the way in which it is used, including the context in which it is used. Meaning depends on use, and we distinguish different meanings of a word by distinguishing its different uses. In the same way, a human act gets its meaning from its context. If I aim a punch at your nose in the course of a heated argument, my act expresses hostility towards you. If I do the same thing in the context of a sparring match, it may express rather my willingness to help you improve your boxing technique.

This point is important for assessing the claim of John Paul II that sexual intercourse outside marriage is a lie, because it is not the self-giving that it claims to be. The idea here seems to be that sexual intercourse just *is* an act of total physical self-giving, regardless of context. But we can now see that this is inadequate; one cannot simply read off the meaning of an act from its physical properties, without looking at the interpersonal context in which the act is embedded. Neither is there any reason to describe intercourse outside marriage as a lie. In the context of a sparring match, my punch is not a 'lie'; it does not falsely express an intention to hurt you, an intention which I do not really have. Further, an intention to deceive is essential to lying. My punch does not express an intention to deceive you, since I have no such intention. If you are aware of the context, neither will you be tempted to think that I am trying to deceive you, any more than you will be tempted to think that I am hostile to you. It is clear from the context what my intention is, and there is no lying or deception involved. Similarly, if two strangers have a sexual encounter in the full knowledge that they have not given themselves to each other and that they have no intention of doing so, not only is the act not one of total physical self-giving, but nobody is pretending it is. Nobody is trying to deceive anybody else, and there is no lying involved.

Nevertheless, one might argue, there is surely something important in the approach of John Paul II and those who argue in a similar vein. Even if an act of intercourse does not, regardless of context, signify or express a profound and intimate personal relationship, and even if an act of intercourse outside such a relationship does not amount to a lie, still intercourse is, in certain circumstances, a *natural* expression of love. People who love each other tend to want – within certain limits – to have sex with each other.[23] One might say that intercourse is *apt* to express love. In this, it differs greatly from a punch on the nose. If I love you, I might want to go to bed with you, and I will want to do that *because* I love you; but I will not normally want to punch you on the nose, and if I do want to punch you on the nose it will not be as an expression of love, *because* I love you. But if I hate you, I may well be inclined to punch you on the nose. A punch on the nose is *apt* to express hostility.[24]

One might argue on the basis of this that sexual activity outside a context of love, unconnected with what it is apt to express, leads to an impoverishment of human expressive capabilities. People sometimes swear when they are angry, and if somebody swears only in situations of extreme anger, his swearing can be a powerful expression of his anger. But if somebody swears all the time, angry or not, his swearing ceases to communicate anger; the verbal gesture of swearing has, in this person's case, been evacuated of expressive power, and he can no longer express precisely *anger* by this means. In the same way, it could be argued, those who partake in sexual activities outside a context of love, if they have sex with people regardless of how, or whether, they feel about them, evacuate their sexual gestures of sense; they can no longer use sex to express love.

A man may love his wife deeply, but if he has sexual intercourse with all and sundry, his sexual activity with his wife cannot be, for him, expressive of his deep love for her; the activity has become too ordinary. In short, for an activity to be expressive it must be used selectively. The more selectively it is used, the more expressive it becomes, while the more indiscriminately it is used the less expressive it becomes.

Is it possible to argue on this basis that sexual activity should be used very selectively? It might be possible to argue that the capacity to express love bodily, through sex, is an important part of human well-being, and that its loss, through less selective use of sex, is a severe impoverishment. Those who indulge in sex other than in a context of love, one would have to say, are – for this reason – less fulfilled and less happy than those who only use sex for making love. I offer this as a possibility, but I admit I do not know how such an argument would be made convincing. It involves an empirical claim about the relative happiness of various classes of people that would be difficult to substantiate. Even if one could show that indiscriminate users of sex were less happy than very discriminating ones, one would also have to show that it is the difference in their sex lives that accounts for the difference in their happiness. Even if a successful argument could be generated along these lines, it would tend to show only that sexual activity is best confined to loving relationships, whether marital, extramarital or homosexual. While that would satisfy many Christians, it would be far from supporting the much stronger traditional Christian claim, that sex should be confined to marriage.

Reproduction and relationships

Given the stress on the relational aspect of sex in modern Protestant and Catholic thought, it might be thought that the reproductive aspect has become less important, that sex has come to be seen more as a way of relating to others and less as a way of bringing new human life into the world. This does indeed seem to be true for many Protestants, but not for official Catholic teaching. While Protestant churches have by and large accepted the use of contraception, which is meant to eliminate the procreative capacity of intercourse, the Catholic Church has stood out against contraception. It has done this partly by the use of old natural law arguments about the purpose of the sexual organs and of sexual activity, but it has also adopted a new approach, which came to prominence in the encyclical *Humanae Vitae*, in which Pope Paul VI reaffirmed Catholic opposition to all forms of birth control except those which depend on the timing of sexual intercourse so that it occurs in the infertile part of the menstrual cycle. According to this new approach, sexual intercourse has of its nature two 'meanings': the unitive, expressing the relationship of mutual self-giving of husband and wife; and the procreative, the ability to generate new life.[25] These two meanings, it is claimed, can never be separated. An act of intercourse must always have the unitive meaning proper to it, that is to say it must take place in the context of that true union of persons which is marriage. It must also always, as essentially procreative, be open to new life. This is the new claim. The question is: what reason can be given for making it – apart simply from a desire to reinforce a ban on contraception – and can it be substantiated?

The idea of these two meanings of intercourse is at first sight implausible. That an act might have a unitive meaning, signifying and expressing the unity between two people, is readily understandable, but how can an act have procreative meaning? How can an act signify or express procreation? Procreation is surely not a possible meaning of an act, but a possible effect. Talk of the two meanings of intercourse seems to confuse the realm of significance with that of cause and effect. However, this is principally a terminological problem. The doctrine does not appear to depend on the claim that procreation can be a meaning of an act. If a more neutral word, such as 'aspect', is used, the problem disappears. One could then rephrase by saying that an act of intercourse has an expressive, unitive aspect and a causal, procreative aspect, and that these two are inseparable, in the sense that it is never legitimate to perform an act of intercourse where one of these two aspects is deliberately suppressed.

But there still remains the problem of showing why we should believe this, that intercourse has these two aspects, and that they are indeed inseparable. That an act of intercourse *can* have these two aspects is clear: two people can make love in a way that expresses the deep love that unites them, and this can result in the birth of a child. But it is a much stronger claim to say that these two aspects cannot be legitimately deliberately separated.

It is not an implausible idea that a human act can have two such aspects which are closely united. For example, suppose I punch you on the nose. This is not a friendly thing to do. You will gather from it that I do not like you. It is an expression of my hostility towards you. My act has an expressive aspect. But it will also cause you pain. This is the physical effect of my knuckles coming into violent contact with your nose. My act, then, also has a causal aspect. But the two aspects are closely related. The reason why my act has a hostile significance is that it will, if successfully accomplished, hurt you. That is why I do it. It is the desire to produce the painful effect that makes my act hostile. I can of course throw a punch at you without hurting you: I can miss, or you can be wearing adequate facial protection. I can also hurt you without intending to, by waving my fists around carelessly and accidentally striking your nose. But I cannot deliberately separate these two aspects of the act. I cannot throw a punch at you without wanting to hurt you. Some intentional reference to the physical consequence of the act is essential to the very meaning of the act itself.

In the same way, it could be argued, sexual intercourse has these two aspects: an affective aspect, expressing love, and a causal aspect, the conception of a child. Of course, these two are in fact separable; it is possible to perform an act of sexual intercourse which expresses love without a child being conceived, and it is possible for a child to be conceived when the act does not express love, because there is no love in the union to be expressed, as in rape. But one cannot perform the act as an expression of love without willing the causal consequence, just as I cannot aggressively swing a punch at you without wanting to hurt you.

However, there are numerous things wrong with this line of argument. First, the conclusion is simply and obviously not true. It is not true that one person cannot make love to another without positively willing that a conception result. Few, even inside the Catholic Church, have ever made such a strong claim. The most that is normally claimed is that the partners to the act of intercourse must be *open* to the conception of a child, not actively prevent it through some form of contraception. But here, second, the analogy with my punch breaks down. If I swing a punch at you, I am not merely open to the possibility that I might hurt you; I positively desire to hurt you, and it is that positive desire that makes the swing an expression of my hostility towards you. If I do not particularly want to hurt you, but am merely open to hurting you, my act, whatever else it signifies (if anything), does not express hostility towards you (though of course you may with justice think that it does). Third, while it is clear that it is the desire to hurt that makes my punch an aggressive act, it is far from clear that it is the desire to conceive a baby with another person that makes the act of intercourse a loving act, expressive of love. There are a number of things which might make it expressive of love, such as the desire to engage in a mutually pleasurable activity, or the desire to give pleasure, within the context of a stable, loving relationship. If, for example, a woman, after thirty years of loving, committed relationship, has intercourse with her partner in order, say, to comfort him after a bad day at the office, it would be implausible to deny that this is an act expressive of love.

The insistence that the unitive and procreative aspects of intercourse are inseparable looks, therefore, confused and unconvincing. Theologians have produced arguments in its favour, but it is not surprising that these in turn fail to convince.[26] In addition, we have already seen that the unitive aspect of intercourse, its signifying the deep personal unity between the partners, is itself a problematic notion. At best, it is not a feature of the physical act itself, but depends on the relational context.

Conclusion

The considerations outlined here, with regard to both Scripture and natural reason, lead to no firm conclusion about the rights and wrongs of any particular sexual practice or about the human context or contexts in which sexual activity is appropriately situated. There are several reasons for this. One is the obvious one that I have drawn with very broad strokes indeed, omitting important details. And there are important relevant factors which I have not even had space to mention, such as the recent theological emphasis on the alleged complementarity of men and women and its significance in interpersonal and particularly sexual life; again, there is the contention that homosexual people suffer, as such, from some malady. Argument about sexual matters has become a complicated matter in the churches in recent years, and I cannot hope to have done anything like justice to the complexity of the debate. If the debate has become complex, however, this is because it is increasingly being recognized that human sexuality is a very complex thing in itself. The relatively simple formulations of traditional Christian sexual ethics can no longer be maintained, for they seem to rely on a vastly over-simplified view of human sexual life and of relationships. If it is to be possible to maintain, with any intellectual honesty, something like the old Christian norms – and it is clear to many that this is undesirable – then much work will have to be put into empirical research into sexuality and its relation to human well-being. There will also have to be theological investigation into the interpretation of Scripture and the formation of tradition. And it is possible that any such research will confirm instead the views of those working for change in Christian sexual teaching. Or it may be that the complexity of the matter is such that certainty is just not to be had, and that Christian theology must content itself with trying to say much less than in the past about sex and its place in human relationships.

Notes

1 See Michel Foucault, *The History of Sexuality*, vols 1–3 (Harmondsworth: Penguin, 1979–86).
2 See, for example, Pope Paul VI's encyclical *Humanae Vitae* (London: The Catholic Truth Society, 1968); the document of the Congregation for the Doctrine of the Faith published in English as *Letter to the Bishops of the Catholic Church on the Pastoral Care of Homosexual Persons* (London: Catholic Truth Society, 1986); and the same body's *A Declaration on Certain Questions Concerning Sexual Ethics* (London: Catholic Truth Society, 1975).

Gareth Moore

3 Solitary masturbation is nowhere mentioned in the legal texts, nor, apparently, elsewhere in scripture.

4 E.g., Matt 12:10ff.; Luke 13:14ff.; Mark 2:23ff.

5 Note, for example, how in the tenth commandment at Exod 20:17 a man's wife is listed simply as one of his possessions which it is forbidden to covet, coming second after his house. The corresponding commandment at Deut 5:21 puts the wife first.

6 Num 24:1ff.

7 He had to refrain from sex with other men (Lev 18:22), with animals (Lev 18:23) and with close relatives (Lev 18:6–18).

8 Deut 22:13–21.

9 1 Cor 7:2–4.

10 Matt 19:3–9.

11 Matt 19:10.

12 E.g., 1 Tim 2:11–15; Col 3:18f.

13 For an illuminating survey of the role of ideas of property in biblical sexual ethics, see William L. Countryman, *Dirt, Greed and Sex: Sexual Ethics in the New Testament and Their Implications for Today* (London: SCM, 1989). As the title implies, Countryman deals also with the importance of the notion of purity in the Bible, which there is not space to go into here.

14 E.g., Albert the Great, *Sentences*, 4.31.24.

15 E.g., Thomas Aquinas, *Summa Contra Gentiles*, 3.122.

16 In this use of the biblical account of creation we once again see the blending of scriptural and non-scriptural considerations. If the medievals attempted to derive sexual ethics from reason, it was rarely from pure reason unaided by Scripture. The thinking was done within a Christian context and in explication and support of Christian doctrines.

17 *Summa Theologiae*, I–II, 94,2c.

18 *Summa Theologiae*, I–II, 91,2.

19 *Summa Contra Gentiles*, 3.122.

20 Though we may still think that this approach has its shortcomings. What, we might ask, about the welfare of animals, or the flourishing and integrity of the non-animal environment?

21 *Familiaris Consortio*, n. 11.

22 For a Protestant approach see, for example, James B. Nelson, *Embodiment: An Approach to Sexuality and Christian Theology* (London: SPCK, 1979).

23 Evidently, parents can love their children and children their parents without in any way wanting to have sex together. Two adult friends can also love each other deeply without in any way wanting joint sexual activity. Much depends on circumstances, including the age, sex and sexual orientation of the people involved.

24 This is not to say that it is impossible for me to punch you as an expression of my love for you. But you have to think up a pretty complicated scenario, a very unusual context, to make sense of the idea. One does not, on the contrary, have to think of a very complicated scenario to make sense of the idea that I might want, as an expression of love, to go to bed with you.

25 *Humanae Vitae*, n. 12.

26 See for example Henry Peschke, who, in the context of an argument against the possibility of homosexual activity being an expression of love, says:

> The sexual act is apt to be an expression of love and appreciation in the last analysis because it is able to generate new human life. Every man and every

woman would like to have a child only with a partner whom they sincerely esteem. The readiness of a man and a woman to unite together in the sexual act is therefore a sign of their mutual esteem ... Sexual acts between two persons of the same sex however are never apt to procreate offspring. Therefore they can also not be the expression of a love and esteem which is based on the possibility to give life to a child. The precondition is missing which imparts to the sexual act the quality of a sign of love. (*Christian Ethics*, vol.2 [Alcester and Dublin: C. Goodliffe Neale, 1978], p. 435)

This is unconvincing for a number of reasons, not the least of which is that it relies on a simple logical mistake. Even if it were true that everybody would like to have a child only with a partner they sincerely esteem, that does not imply that you do not sincerely esteem somebody if you cannot, or even do not want to, have a child with them. Even if love were a condition for wanting to have a child, that would not make wanting to have a child a condition for love. Even if it were true that only if somebody is a Scot does he like haggis, it would not follow that somebody was a Scot only if he liked haggis.

For a more recent attempt, see Germain Grisez, *Living a Christian Life. The Way of the Lord Jesus*, vol. 2 (Quincy, IL: Franciscan Press, 1993), ch. 9, esp. pp. 634–6. Grisez's argument is too long to detail here, but it seems to me weak at many points, in particular that it depends on Grisez's highly suspect notion of marriage as 'one-flesh unity'. However, readers should, as in all cases, judge for themselves.

Selected bibliography

Lisa Cahill, *Sex, Gender and Christian Ethics* (Cambridge: Cambridge University Press, 1996). A general survey utilizing feminist insights.

L. William Countryman, *Dirt, Greed and Sex: Sexual Ethics in the New Testament and Their Implications for Today* (London: SCM, 1989). Interesting insights into biblical understandings of sexual relations.

Michel Foucault, *The History of Sexuality*, vols 1–3 (Harmondsworth: Penguin, 1979–86). Essential reading.

Gareth Moore, *The Body in Context: Sex and Catholicism* (London: SCM, 1992). A more thorough treatment of some of the questions raised in this chapter.

John T. Noonan, Jr, *Contraception: A History of Its Treatment by the Catholic Theologians and Canonists* (Cambridge, MA: Harvard University Press, 1986). Much wider in scope than its title suggests. Gives important information on traditional Christian thought on sex in general.

Adrian Thatcher, *Liberating Sex: A Christian Sexual Theology* (London: SPCK, 1993). An interesting modern Anglican view.

17

Divorce and remarriage

Kevin T. Kelly

The tragedy of divorce

In the USA today four out of ten marriages can be expected to end in divorce. This tragic phenomenon is equally evident in Britain and the rest of Europe. Moreover, it is not just the couples themselves who are involved in a divorce. In the United States the lives of one out of every two children is affected by the human tragedy of divorce. These figures need to be transposed into the human suffering involved. Part of the tragic evil of divorce is the terrible pain people, who once loved each other, now inflict on each other, often unconsciously and unintentionally. It is hard to imagine a deeper wounding of one's sense of self-esteem than to be told by someone, who once publicly declared they could not live without you, that now they cannot bear living with you! A relationship which it was hoped would bring love, affirmation and healing ends up causing injury, self-doubt and even, in some cases, mutual hostility and hatred.

The words 'plague on society', used in *The Catechism of the Catholic Church* (2385), are very appropriate, even though they would be better applied to marriage breakdown rather than to divorce. Divorce is simply a social damage-limitation procedure for dealing with marital breakdown, once it has become clear that reconciliation is no longer possible and continued cohabitation would be destructive, certainly for the couple themselves and possibly for their children too. In no way is divorce a panacea for all the suffering caused by the breakdown of a marriage. It operates on a different plane to the painful memories of the daily hurts and wounds involved in the gradual disintegration of the couple's love for each other. Sometimes it can even add to their pain when the finality of a divorce only serves to consolidate the erosion of self-esteem of one or both partners. In other cases there can be a more positive outcome from a divorce. For instance, from her experience of working in a shelter for battered women Rosemary Haughton writes:

> For many women, the moment of conversion, the true *metanoia*, has come when they reach the decision to seek a divorce ... To compare the decision to seek a divorce to the choice of discipleship may seem shocking – but that can be what it really is: the choice of life over death, spiritual freedom over bondage. It is for many the entrance into a new life ...[1]

To refer to divorce as 'a plague on society' need not imply any kind of condemnation of those whose marriages have broken down. Although plagues throughout history have often been accompanied by the persecution of scapegoats deemed responsible for them, for the Christian the authentic human response must always be positive and two-fold. It must involve care and compassion for those suffering as a result of the plague; and it must seek to discover the causes of the plague so that effective steps can be taken at the level of prevention and cure. Moreover, it must also resist any temptation to link sickness and sin together and thus attribute the spread of a plague to immorality. In reality, a plague might sometimes actually be the side-effect of a positive advance in medical science and health care.

For a Christian the response to the 'plague' of marriage breakdown must not be to condemn those who have been through this traumatic experience and who may be suffering grievously as a result of it. It will be sensitive to their pain and want to relieve it in any way possible. It must want to assure divorced people who are feeling so deeply wounded that they are still precious to God and in no way rejected by God's love. Moreover, the Christian community as a whole must embody this healing and affirming Gospel message by the way they relate, individually and communally, to those who have suffered marriage breakdown. A Christian response to marriage breakdown must also want to discover why it is that marriages are breaking down in such alarming numbers at present. In the West a major Christian prophet in this respect has been Dr Jack Dominian. His dedicated research has made an enormous contribution to our understanding of why and how many marriages come to break down (see *Bibliography*). In fact, in the light of his research it could be argued that, paradoxically, the Christian Churches' enriched teaching on sexuality and marriage has been a factor contributing indirectly to the breakdown of marriage. This is because their more personalist understanding of marriage could encourage couples to have very high expectations of their relationship. However, Jack Dominian has shown that the building up of such a profound and multi-dimensional personal relationship requires great verbal, bodily and sexual skills in listening, communicating and mutual accommodation. He has also shown that where people are coming from (experientially and socially, not just locally) is a very important ingredient in the mix. Hence, one major contributory factor as to why many marriages break down is simply because one or both of the partners did not have the capacity or necessary skills to build up the kind of marital relationship they believe in and which the Church has canonized. Though they might have been deeply committed to their marriage at the outset, they simply 'could not' (i.e. did not have the ability to) make it work.

If this analysis of the causes of marriage breakdown is at least partially correct, the Christian Churches will want to do everything possible to ensure that people are properly prepared and equipped for undertaking the challenging process involved in building this kind of personalist marriage. Although marriage preparation courses can help, perhaps even more important is the quality of human development education and experience received in home and school. Moreover, the growing demise of the extended family means that greater help and support is needed for couples in the crucial early years of their developing relationship.

There is also greater awareness nowadays that external factors can threaten the stability of a marriage – bad housing, unemployment or job insecurity, poverty, an unhealthy or destabilizing social environment, the subtle pressures of a consumer society infiltrating through the media, etc., etc. Church leaders are becoming increasingly aware of this connection and are beginning to voice their concern very forcefully. For instance, in 1995 the Roman Catholic bishops of England and Wales issued a public statement calling on the British government to address these factors as a matter of urgency:

> The bishops of England and Wales urge the Government and Parliament to take account of the following three needs whatever reforms are proposed in respect of the divorce law.
> a. Marriage needs to be strengthened, and the likelihood of divorce lessened by making adequate resources available to increase education for marriage and to bring about a change of people's attitudes and expectations regarding marital relationships and the bringing up of children. This must include helping young people to acquire the necessary social skills of communication, to deal sensibly and maturely with conflicts, and to develop an understanding of what commitment means in terms of changing and adapting within the marital relationship as the couple grow and change.
> b. Provision needs to be made for the generous funding of marriage counselling services and other organisations supportive of marriage

and family life, so that access to such services is available, especially when difficulties begin to arise in marital relationships.

c. Realistic support for marriage and the family requires a comprehensive family policy. This will have to deal with the support of families, including single parent families, through the tax and benefit system, access to adequate housing and employment, and child care facilities. A constructive debate must concentrate on all the elements required for an effective family policy.[2]

Although the US bishops have produced some epoch-making statements on social issues, they have not as yet spoken as clearly on this particular issue. Moreover, in a more recent series of recommendations for implementation at diocesan level, with reference to preaching and teaching the bishops of England and Wales have even been very insistent on the need for pastoral sensitivity in the way the divorced are spoken about: 'Sensitivity in the use of language and images about those who have experienced marital and family breakdown is often crucial for their welcome in the community. We ask the bishops to give this lead and to encourage their clergy to be as fully informed as possible.' They have gone so far as to encourage those involved in marriage preparation to explore 'the possibility of involving some of our divorced people in the preparation of others for marriage'.

Just as the more positive personalist Christian teaching on marriage has, unintentionally, been an indirect factor affecting the breakdown of marriage, so too has been another enrichment of Christian understanding. That is the growing appreciation of the full and equal dignity of women and the awareness that the relationships between men and women, at both personal and societal levels, have, for most of history, been seriously distorted by the sinful structure of patriarchy. This awareness is recognized by most churches as a major 'sign of the times' in our day. Even John Paul II has spoken strongly on this matter in some of his addresses in 1995 prior to the UN Fourth World Conference on Women in Beijing. This progress towards greater humanization has, in fact, had a temporary destabilizing effect on marriage. If the man–woman relationship is seen to be at the heart of marriage, it is not surprising that some marriages come to grief at a time when gender relationships are undergoing a process of profound re-evaluation and particularly when this process is far more advanced among women than among men. Some women are having to cope with the sudden awareness that they have been living in a relationship of great inequality and some couples are struggling with the fact that they do not share a common vision of equality and mutuality in the relationship they are setting out to build.

To say that marriage breakdown is a 'plague on society', therefore, need not imply any condemnation of those who have been through the traumatic experience of the disintegration of their marriage. On the other hand, personal sin, even grave personal sin in some cases, may be a factor which contributes to the breakdown of some marriages. The adoption of a 'no fault' procedure in divorce law does not imply theologically that marriage breakdown is always without sin. All human relationships are affected by sin. The breakdown of a marriage relationship is no exception. Hence, there is the same need for conversion and forgiveness as in the rest of life. However, to acknowledge that sin can play a part in the breakdown of a marriage is very different to saying that sin is usually the cause of a marriage breakdown. On occasion it may be. It is just as likely, however, that marriages fail through human incapacity to build a lasting relationship despite the best of intentions, rather than through human wickedness on the part of one or both partners.

Christians have always had to face the pastoral problem of marriage breakdown, though never before in such numbers. Moreover, in previous ages marriage was seen predominantly as a contract with strong patriarchal overtones. The bride was transferred from the authority of her father and his family to that of her husband and his family. Continuing the husband's lineage through male offspring and guaranteeing inheritance within the legitimate family line were key factors in such a transaction. With such priorities the growth of a deep multi-dimensional personal relationship did not figure largely in a marriage. The 'master' role of the husband and the 'mother/housekeeper' role of the wife were the main consideration. Consequently, the reasons why marriages broke down tended to focus on alleged deficiencies on the part of the wife – her failure to produce a male heir, her insubordination, her deficiencies in supervising the household, suspicions about her fidelity etc.

Against such a background the absolute prohibition of divorce by Jesus was truly good news for women. It challenged men to respect the personal dignity of their wives and not to reject them like a piece of unsatisfactory merchandise. Most contemporary scripture scholars hold that the radical teaching of Jesus on divorce needs to be interpreted as gospel rather than law. His absolute prohibition of divorce is more subversive and inspirational than law can be. He is challenging the whole mind-set described above which fails to appreciate the meaning of marriage in the mind of the Creator and which reduces it to a social device to ensure property rights and legitimacy of lineage and is prepared to accept divorce as a legal corrective measure when things go wrong. Among his Jewish hearers, these strong words of Jesus must have been particularly disturbing to men and powerfully encouraging to women.

Scholars seem to agree that the exceptions allowing divorce found in Matthew and Paul reflect the way the early Christian communities tried to face new situations in fidelity to the radical teaching of Jesus. As the post-Resurrection church began to spread, new pastoral problems arose. In the Hellenistic world, for instance, a wife could divorce her husband. So Paul made it clear that the radical teaching of Jesus applied equally to women as to men. Difficulties also arose when only one partner in a marriage embraced the Christian faith. Paul insisted that this did not give the Christian partner an automatic right to divorce, even though he also wrote that divorce, and presumably remarriage too, was acceptable whenever difference of belief made it impossible to maintain peace in the home.

A very thorough and easily accessible account of the teaching of Jesus on divorce and its pastoral adaptation to the needs of the early Christian communities is given by John R. Donahue.[3] It is worth quoting some passages from his conclusion:

> The teaching of the historical Jesus is cast in the form of such a 'moral ought', but it is not in the legal form of a declarative pronouncement about a bond which cannot be broken . . .
>
> The teaching of Jesus is also in the context of a prophetic defence of marriage in the face of easy divorce laws which prevented marriage from being that kind of life between man and woman in mutual interdependence and harmony intended by the creator. It is also a protest against the innocent victim of such divorce laws, the woman spouse in the marriage.
>
> The handing on of the tradition of Jesus in the early Church involves a twofold movement. On the one hand, the Church continues to reiterate Jesus' prophetic defence of marriage. On the other hand, in its application of this defence to concrete instances the Church mirrors the 'pastoral' concern of Jesus . . .
>
> [Paul] defends marriage against those who would force celibacy or separation upon would-be Christians and says that where separation does occur reconciliation is to take place. At the same time, he sees marriage as a dynamic process and in the case of the marriage between the unbeliever and the believer where sanctification, freedom and peace cannot arise, he allows for divorce.
>
> Both Mark and Matthew defend marriage against easy divorce, and Mark adapts this defence to a Hellenistic environment, while Matthew allows divorce to members of his community whose first marriages did not meet the demands of Jewish law.
>
> Despite disagreement on details there is a growing consensus among Catholic exegetes that Matthew and Paul present both an exception to the absolute prohibition of divorce and represent adaptation of Jesus' teaching to their own church situation. There is also consensus that

these exegetical findings should bear on church life and practice today. (Kelly, pp. 226–7)

The possibility of remarriage after divorce

One question which has exercised Christian minds from the earliest days has been the status of those whose marriages have broken down. Are they still married or are they now free to embark upon a second marriage? This question continues to be hotly debated within the Christian Churches even today. One of the most imaginative theological contributions to this debate is found in the Church of England Marriage Commission's 1978 report *Marriage and the Church's Task*. While it recognized that the marriage commitment is 'unconditional', it interpreted the Church's task as being one of facing the challenge of crafting 'a discipline which holds before those who are married, and those about to marry, the challenge of unconditional love, while offering to those who have failed in their marriage the possibility of a new beginning' (n. 266). The marriage 'bond' is subjected to careful scrutiny. The report argues that it is the 'personal bond' based on 'mutual love' which unifies the various dimensions of the marriage bond (n. 95). This personal bond can even be said to have an 'ontological character':

> The marriage bond unites two flesh-blood-and-spirit persons. It makes them the persons that they are. It binds them together, not in any casual or peripheral fashion, but at the very centre of their being. They become the persons they are through their relationship to each other. Each might say to the other: 'I am I and I am you; together you and I are we'. Since the marriage bond is in this way a bond of personal *being*, it is appropriate to speak of it as having an 'ontological' character. (n. 96)

In the eyes of the Commission, once a couple reach this level of oneness they have created a bond between them 'which, as a matter of fact, nothing can dissolve' (97). However, not every marriage reaches that level of oneness. Marriage relationships often break down, as current statistics show. The Commission interpreted such tragedies as failures in the growth process of personal commitment in marriage. Although the commitment is made when the marriage comes into being through their exchange of vows – it is 'grounded in promise and obligation' – it still remains part of the 'continuing process' of 'the making of the marriage' (n. 99). Tragically that process can break down irretrievably with the result that the couple fail to achieve the unbreakable character of their marriage bond. When this occurs, God's will for this marriage is thwarted by 'human failure and sin' even though this does not necessarily imply personal guilt on the part of the couple themselves:

> There is something radically wrong when a marriage does break down. Marriages *ought* to be indissoluble! However, most of us reject the doctrine that marriages *cannot* by definition be dissolved. It is only too possible for men and women in particular cases to break the bond which God, in principle and in general, wills to be unbreakable, and to put asunder what God, in his original purpose, has joined together. Therein lies the measure of human failure and sin. (n. 100)

For this approach, therefore, when the human bond has broken down irretrievably, the marriage is no longer in existence and the two partners are, in principle, free to embark on another union.

Although the theology and understanding undergirding it is very different, in practice this approach is very similar to that which has been developed in Eastern Christianity over the centuries. The Eastern tradition and Orthodox Churches today believe that a marriage can 'die'. Such a death is seen as tragic, but those who are left alone as a result of it can still trust in the loving care of God, the benevolent guardian of the Christian household (*oikonomos*), and may still find salvific life in the loving union of a second marriage, even though they might be entering it conscious of their need for healing and forgiveness as a result of their previous failed marriage. Bernard Häring suggests that the Roman Catholic Church might be enriched by a deeper understanding of the Eastern tradition of 'economy' and its application to remarriage after divorce (see Bibliography).

The theology and practice of the Latin Church, carried over in the tradition of the Roman Catholic Church, after an uneven pastoral practice in the early centuries has gradually hardened into a more ontological interpretation of the bond of marriage. This bond is constituted by the marriage covenant itself and is brought into existence by the couple's mutual consent. Its natural indissolubility becomes absolute in the case of a sacramental marriage since the bond now signifies the unbreakable bond between Christ and the Church. Theoretically this interpretation leaves no room for manoeuvre once the marriage bond has come into existence. However, it is significant that the Council of Trent's formulation of this seemingly absolute teaching was worded very carefully so as not to give the impression that the Council Fathers were rejecting the more benign Eastern Orthodox practice as incompatible with Christian faith. Moreover, some aspects of the Roman Catholic Church's own practice are not fully consistent with this interpretation. It is claimed, for instance, that the Pope has the power, as the vicar of Christ on earth, to dissolve the naturally indissoluble ontological bond in the case of marriages of the unbaptized, though this power is only exercised to ensure the peaceful state of the marriage of a baptized person. It is also claimed that in two specific situations the bond can actually be dissolved even in the case of the sacramental marriage of two baptized persons provided it has not been consummated. Such a marriage can be dissolved by a Papal act of dissolution. Prior to the 1983 Code it could also be dissolved when one partner, with the other's consent, wanted to be free to take religious vows. In that case, the bond was considered to be dissolved by this new act of life-long commitment which effectively terminated the marriage relationship (see Kelly, pp. 32–4).

Apart from these two anomalies the 'indissoluble bond' approach which holds sway in the Roman Catholic Church means that, in practice, any baptized person who has been truly married is not free to marry again after divorce since they are still bound by their first marriage. Consequently, the remarriage of a baptized person after divorce while the previous partner is still living is, as a rule, only feasible within Roman Catholic practice if the first marriage has been annulled. In other words, it has to be shown that the first marriage was not really a true marriage and so no indissoluble bond exists. Where that can be proved to the satisfaction of a marriage tribunal a divorced person is free to remarry.

This theology and practice has developed over the centuries. Tribunal practice continues to evolve to keep abreast of the latest findings regarding the kind of psychological and emotional freedom and maturity needed for a person to give any truly meaningful commitment to his or her marriage vows. In fact, it could perhaps be argued that, though the indissoluble bond theory still holds in theory, in practice the emphasis is moving relentlessly towards the more pastoral consideration of whether a couple had the capacity to undertake the profound personal relationship demanded by our modern Western understanding of marriage. That is why evidence regarding how a marriage actually worked out, unlike previously, is now deemed relevant in many nullity cases. Hence, the role of marriage tribunals today is becoming much more pastoral and directed towards helping people who have suffered the tragedy of marriage breakdown and divorce. Previously their prime concern was to defend the bond of marriage. An indication that this might be what is happening is found in the figures for annulment in the Roman Catholic Church. In 1968 there were 338 annulments world-wide. By 1983 this figure had risen to 52,000 and is now estimated to be something in the region of 70,000 per annum. In 1985 in the United States alone there were 52,471 annulments completed in the first instance. What is disturbing, however, is that the great majority of dioceses, especially in the developing world, do not have functioning marriage tribunals. For instance, there was not a single country from Africa or Asia among the eleven countries which accounted for 94 per cent of annulments in the first instance in 1985 (cf. Provost, pp. 600–1). Although difference of culture is certainly a partial explanation, such a lack of functioning tribunals means that there is little possibility of the development of a more culturally adapted tribunal system for these countries.

The differences between the Roman Catholic position and that of the Anglican Communion were explored in the ARCIC II Agreed Statement, *Life in Christ: Morals, Communion and the Church* (1994). ARCIC was able to conclude that 'Anglicans and Roman Catholics are at one in their understanding of the nature and meaning of marriage' (n. 77) despite the acknowledgement that some Anglicans believe that 'where a relationship of mutual love and trust has clearly ceased to exist, and there is no practical possibility of remaking it, the bond itself has also ceased to exist' (n. 75). One can understand, therefore, why the final section of this part of their Agreed Statement reads:

> We agree that marriage is sacramental, although we do not fully agree on how, and this affects our sacramental discipline. Thus, Roman Catholics recognise a special kind of sacramentality in a marriage between baptised persons, which they do not see in other marriages. Anglicans, on the other hand, recognise a sacramentality in all valid marriages. On the level of law and policy, neither the Roman Catholic nor the Anglican practice regarding divorce is free from real or apparent anomalies and ambiguities. While, therefore, there are differences between us concerning marriage after divorce, to isolate those differences from this context of far-reaching agreement and make them into an insuperable barrier would be a serious and sorry misrepresentation of the true situation. (n. 77)

Mark Ellingsen, in his World Council of Churches study *The Cutting Edge: How Churches Speak on Social Issues* (1993), adds an interesting gloss to this point.

> Because Orthodox practices converge with Protestantism while its theological commitments converge with Roman Catholicism, it follows that the disagreement it has with the Catholic Church in practice is not theologically related. Consequently, the final conclusion can only be that disagreements between the Roman Catholic and Protestant traditions on this matter, despite their distinct theological perspectives, are *not necessarily* theologically related. (p. 85, italics in original)

Remembering how the early Christian communities were able to hold in a kind of dialectical tension commitment to Jesus' absolute prohibition of divorce and the acceptance of divorce by way of pastoral accommodation in new situations in the community, it could be argued that all the

Christian churches are, in their different ways, struggling with the same dialectical tension. They are trying to give theological expression to the absolute teaching of Jesus within their wider interpretation of marriage; and, at the same time, they are to be faithful to the tradition of the early Christian communities by trying to be pastorally accommodating and creative in their pastoral care of those whose marriages no longer reflect the love, peace and justice of God's kingdom.

Issues of pastoral practice

(1) The remarriage of divorced persons in church

Divorced persons can remarry in most Christian churches today. Some, like the Church of England, do not give any formal approval of the practice and leave it to the clergy's pastoral decision to relax the normal discipline in particular circumstances. Others adopt a more positive stance. Most offer some kind of pastoral guide-lines to ensure that such marriages are entered into responsibly and in good conscience and to safeguard the officiating minister's own conscience.

The outstanding exception in this respect is the Roman Catholic Church. As has already been noted, the official teaching of the Roman Catholic Church is that a divorced person whose first marriage was valid and whose partner is still alive may not enter a second marriage. Despite his insisting that pastors 'are obliged to exercise careful discernment of situations' and his instancing the 'difference between those who have sincerely tried to save their first marriage and have been unjustly abandoned, and those who through their own grave fault have destroyed a canonically valid marriage', John Paul II is adamantly opposed to any semblance of a church celebration of a second marriage, as he states very clearly in his Apostolic Constitution *Familiaris Consortio* (1981):

> The respect due to the sacrament of Matrimony, to the couples themselves and their families, and also to the community of the faithful, forbids any pastor, for whatever reason or pretext even of a pastoral nature, to perform ceremonies of any kind for divorced people who remarry. Such ceremonies would give the impression of the celebration of a new sacramentally valid marriage, and would thus lead people into error concerning the indissolubility of a validly contracted marriage. (n. 84; for a discussion of whether this clear statement leaves any room for pastoral flexibility, see Kelly, especially pp. 79–81)

(2) *The divorced-remarried and the sacraments, especially admission to Communion: a special problem in the Roman Catholic Church*

Most Christian Churches see no problem in the divorced-remarried receiving Communion during the celebration of the Eucharist. However, within the Roman Catholic Church the prohibition of the sacraments to the divorced-remarried is an issue of major pastoral concern. The pastoral urgency of this issue is probably felt most deeply in the case of parents who see their receiving Communion as important for their children's faith-development as well as for themselves. Another pastorally hurtful occasion is when sons or daughters who have lost a parent are advised that they cannot communicate at their funeral Mass. Rarely has this concern been voiced more eloquently than by my late Archbishop, Derek Worlock, in the presence of Pope John Paul II himself at the 1990 Rome Synod on Marriage and the Family:

> Many pastors nowadays are faced with Catholics whose first marriages have perished and who have now a second and more stable (if legally only civil) union in which they seek to bring up a new family. Often such persons, especially in their desire to help their children, long for the restoration of full eucharistic communion with the Church and its Lord. Is this spirit of repentance and desire for sacramental strength to be for ever frustrated? Can they be told only that they must reject their new responsibilities as a necessary condition of forgiveness and resto-ration to sacramental life? (Fuller version of this intervention in Kelly, pp. 71–2)

The most authoritative recent statement from the Vatican on this matter is the 1994 *Letter of the Congregation for the Doctrine of the Faith (CDF) to the World's Bishops* (text in Kelly, pp. 121–7). In it they repeat the current strict teaching: 'In fidelity to the words of Jesus Christ, the Church affirms that a new union cannot be recognised as valid if the preceding marriage was valid. If the divorced are remarried civilly, they find themselves in a situation that objectively contravenes God's law. Consequently, they cannot receive Holy Communion as long as this situation persists' (n. 4). Though not explicitly stated in the text, there is no doubt that this statement was a reaction to the 1993 pastoral initiative on the part of the three bishops of the Upper Rhine Province. Examining the background to this initiative and how it eventually led up to the publication of the CDF letter may help to clarify where matters stand at present in the Roman Catholic Church with regard to the divorced-remarried and the sacraments.

In recent years there had developed a growing consensus among moral theologians and canon lawyers, both as individuals and in their professional associations, that, in certain clearly defined circumstances, divorced-remarried persons could in good conscience present themselves for sacramental absolution or Holy Communion and that, when they did so, they should not be refused by the church's minister (cf. Kelly, pp. 74–5; the generally agreed conditions for such a conscience decision are listed on pp. 77–8).

Though a priest might accompany such people in their conscientious decision-making process, in no way would he be giving any kind of formal permission or authorization. Some writers refer to this pastoral approach as the 'internal forum solution' (cf. Theodore Davey in Kelly, pp. 178–82). This can be confusing, as Cardinal Ratzinger points out in his letter in *The Tablet* replying to Davey's article. Ratzinger argues that the term 'internal forum solution' should be restricted as formerly to instances where a person may have genuine moral certainty that his or her first marriage was invalid but where, for one reason or another, it is not possible to have this ratified through a marriage tribunal (Kelly, pp. 183–5). Others prefer to speak of the 'pastoral solution'. This is preferable because of its use of the word 'pastoral'. However, it is still open to the objection that it can give the impression of some kind of formal permission, albeit at a pastoral level, on the part of the priest. In reality, what is involved in this pastoral approach is simply an informed conscientious decision on the part of the divorced-remarried person and the recognition that this decision should be respected.

This is the background to the 1993 pastoral initiative of the three German bishops. On 10 July 1993 they published a Pastoral Letter and an accompanying document ('Principles of Pastoral Care') dealing with the pastoral care of those who had suffered marriage breakdown and also of those who had remarried (full texts in Kelly, pp. 90–117 and 121–36). The bishops' guidelines included advice to their priests with regard to helping the divorced-remarried, when pastorally appropriate, to look conscientiously at their present situation to see whether or not they could feel justified in receiving the sacraments. Though the bishops did not want to promote indiscriminate admission to the sacraments, they did not rule out the possibility of a genuinely conscientious decision to receive the sacraments. Moreover, they recognized that such a decision needs the help of 'candid discussion with a wise and experienced priest', even though they pointed out very clearly that there was no question of his actually giving any kind of official permission.

> Such a decision can only be made by the individual in a personal review of his or her conscience and by no one else . . . The participation of a priest in this clarifying process is necessary because participation in the eucharist is a public and ecclesiastically significant act. Nevertheless,

the priest does not pronounce any official admission in a formal sense. (Kelly, p. 113)

To help people in this decision-making process the three bishops offer their own version of the criteria which, as mentioned earlier, had been put forward by various moral theologians and canon lawyers both as individuals and as representing professional groupings:

Only an honest accounting can lead to a responsible decision of conscience. An examination of the following criteria is therefore indispensable:

- when there is serious failure involved in the collapse of the first marriage, responsibility for it must be acknowledged and repented;
- it must be convincingly established that a return to the first partner is really impossible and that with the best will the first marriage cannot be restored;
- restitution must be made for wrongs committed and injuries done insofar as this is possible;
- in the first place this restitution includes fulfilment of obligations to the wife and children of the first marriage (cf. Code of Canon Law, canon 1071, n.1.3);
- whether or not a partner broke his or her first marriage under great public attention and possibly even scandal should be taken into consideration;
- the second marital partnership must have proved itself over a long period of time to represent a decisive and also publicly recognisable will to live permanently together and also according to the demands of marriage as a moral reality;
- whether or not fidelity to the second relationship has become a moral obligation with regard to the spouse and children should be examined;
- it ought to be sufficiently clear – though certainly not to any greater extent than with other Christians – that the partners seek truly to live according to the Christian faith and with true motives, i.e. moved by genuinely religious desires, to participate in the sacramental life of the Church. The same holds true in the children's upbringing. (Kelly, pp. 111–12)

Because of the high profile of these three bishops, the Congregation of the Doctrine of the Faith (CDF) felt obliged to intervene and invited the three bishops to a meeting in Rome. As mentioned above, subsequent to that meeting, even though the German bishops were not mentioned explicitly, the CDF sent a letter to all the bishops of the world reminding them of the current official teaching on divorce and remarriage and insisting that the current practice of non-admission to the sacraments be strictly adhered to (text in Kelly, pp. 121–7).

When the three German bishops sent out this CDF letter to their parishes, they included a letter written by themselves (text in Kelly, pp. 128–36). This gave their priests and people an account of their discussions with the CDF and explained how matters now stood. In this letter, they repeated what they had stressed in their earlier documents, namely, that 'remarriage during the lifetime of the first marital partner of a valid sacramental marriage stands in objective contradiction to the divine order as renewed by Jesus Christ' and that this, therefore, 'precludes official admission to the reception of holy communion, both generally and in the individual case' (Kelly, pp. 130–1). However, they go on to insist that this is not the end of the matter. Because of its pastoral importance it is worth quoting a long passage from this section of their letter:

> It certainly cannot be overlooked that the cases of the divorced and remarried often involve delicate and highly complex human situations in which the concrete application of the above principles becomes pastorally difficult . . . They represent a pastoral challenge which stands in urgent need of an answer.
>
> According to the traditional teaching of the Church, the general norm must in each case indeed be applied to concrete persons and their individual situations, without this doing away with the norm itself. 'Canon law can only posit a generally valid order of things; it cannot, however, regulate all individual cases, which are often very complex' (*Catholic Catechism for Adults*, published by the German Bishops' Conference, p. 395). The Church's doctrinal tradition has developed for this purpose the concept of *epikeia* (equity), while canon law has come up with the principle of canonical equity. It is not a question here of doing away with the law that is in force or the valid norm. Rather, it is a matter of applying them in difficult and complex situations according to 'justice and equity' in such a way that the uniqueness of the individual person is taken into account. This has nothing to do with a so-called 'situational pastoral practice' . . .
>
> The controversy concerning our pastoral letter and the principles was ignited above all by the question of whether the concepts of *epikeia* and canonical equity could also be applied in individual cases having a given character and under precisely circumscribed conditions to the question of the reception of communion by the divorced and remarried. In other words, the question is whether in particular cases of the divorced and remarried it is thinkable and legitimate not, indeed, that they be officially admitted to holy communion, but that such individuals, after appropriate guidance by a priest who first recalls to them the

Lord's word concerning lifelong fidelity in marriage, see themselves as justified by their truth-orientated consciences in approaching holy communion.

We saw no possibility of an official admission, but rather of an approach to the table of the Lord under precisely stated conditions, this being made possible on the basis of a reflective pronouncement by the individual's conscience. This distinction between *admission* and *approach* is fundamental for us. (Kelly, pp. 131–2)

The bishops stress that their 'disagreement' with the CDF position is not 'doctrinal' but concerns 'the question of pastoral practice in individual cases'. They believe that more recent research into Church tradition shows that there is 'room, beneath the threshold of the binding teaching, for pastoral flexibility in complex individual cases' and they insist that 'such flexibility does not stand in contradiction to the indissolubility of marriage'.

This letter is very carefully worded. While it shares the basic doctrinal position of the CDF and acknowledges that their pastoral principles 'are not accepted by the universal Church and therefore cannot be the binding norm of pastoral practice', it also recognizes that, as bishops, they are 'bound both to the generally valid doctrine of the Church and its unity as well as to people in existentially difficult situations' (Kelly, p. 134). In the penultimate paragraph of their letter, the bishops encourage their priests 'to seek for responsible solutions for individual cases in fidelity to the message of Jesus and the faith of the Church as well as in solidarity with the people involved and in communion with the entire Church' and they trust priests to 'act in a pastorally responsible way in the light of the above-cited basic principles' and to advise their people 'in a right way' (Kelly, p. 135). Despite the bishops' 'taking note' that 'certain statements' in their two documents 'are not accepted by the universal Church and therefore cannot be the binding norm of pastoral practice', I interpret their letter as a carefully worded attempt to help their people appreciate the CDF's role of doctrinal oversight for the whole Church, while continuing to recognize that bishops and priests have to honour their own pastoral responsibility both to help people with their conscientious decisions in difficult pastoral situations and to respect their decisions once made. Since they were not in the business of issuing 'binding norms of pastoral practice' (and certainly not for the universal Church) I would not interpret their letter as a withdrawal of their earlier guidance on the part of the three German bishops.

Conclusion

It is evident from what has been written above that doctrinal and pastoral disagreement about divorce and remarriage exists both between and within the Christian Churches. Nevertheless, all involved in these disagreements are trying to be faithful to the mind of Christ as evidenced in his teaching and pastoral practice. The US Catholic biblical scholar John R. Donahue expresses this beautifully, with particular reference to his own church, in the closing paragraph of his article referred to earlier:

> In a most basic sense the New Testament does sanction what is in fact church teaching and pastoral practice today. The Church stands in prophetic opposition to that divorce which destroys that love and life together which was intended by God for man and woman. At the same time through its marriage tribunals, through continued reflection on 'the pastoral solution' and through a ministry to the divorced, the Church is continuing that 'pastoral dimension' of the ministry of Jesus and the missionary practice of Matthew and Paul. While bearing in its life the prophetic teaching of Christ, the Church must also present to the world that Christ who defended the innocent victims of different forms of oppression and who was ever present to sinners and tax collectors and whose offer of love was closer to the religiously marginal than to the pious and just. Any step backwards to a simple 'adamantine opposition' to divorce without adaptation of this opposition and the questioning of its application would not be faithful to the New Testament. (Kelly, p. 228)

Notes

1 Rosemary Haughton, 'Marriage in women's new consciousness' in William P. Roberts (ed.), *Commitment to Partnership* (Rahway, NJ: Paulist Press, 1987), at pp. 149–50.
2 *Briefing* (2 December 1995), p. 7.
3 John R. Donahue, 'Divorce: New Testament perspectives', *The Month* (1981), pp. 113–20 (reprinted in Kelly, pp. 212–28).

Select bibliography

Timothy Buckley, *What Binds Marriage? Roman Catholic Theology in Practice* (London: Geoffrey Chapman, 1997).
Church of England General Synod Marriage Commission, *Marriage and the Church's Task* (London: Church Information Office, 1978).

Jack Dominian, *Marital Pathology: An Introduction for Doctors, Counsellors and Clergy* (London: Darton, Longman and Todd, 1979).

Bernard Häring, *No Way Out? Pastoral Care of the Divorced and Remarried* (Slough: St Paul Publications, 1989).

Kevin T. Kelly, *Divorce and Second Marriage: Facing the Challenge* (Kansas City, MO: Sheed & Ward, new and expanded edn, 1996).

Theodore Mackin, *Divorce and Remarriage* (New York: Paulist Press, 1984).

James H. Provost, 'Intolerable marriage situations: a second decade', *The Jurist* (1990), pp. 573–612.

18

Truth and lies

Bernard Hoose

The quest for truth

The search for truth of one kind or another permeates the whole of our life in this world. It comes to the fore when one follows courses at school or university or when one grapples with a book on elementary physics, anthropology, chemical engineering or Christian ethics, but it is in no way restricted to such academic pursuits. It is involved in our watching television news programmes, in the appreciation of art, in courtship, in marriage, in friendship and in prayer.

In spite of the ubiquity of the search, there is often something of an elusive quality about truth. This is especially the case when we are dealing with the deepest senses of the term. In saying this, I am not referring only to such matters as the truth that is God and the full meaning of that profoundest of statements emanating from the lips of Jesus in St John's Gospel: 'I am the Way, the Truth and the Life' (14:6). It is, for instance, essential that we strive to know ourselves, but the truth that is each of us is amazingly elusive. We hide a great deal about ouselves behind the masks that we wear for the various roles we have in life. This is, no doubt, partly a defence mechanism that prevents other people from getting too close and hurting us too deeply – the hurt resulting from their reaction to the discovery of truths about us that they may find unacceptable. Some years ago, John Powell, quoting an excerpt from an actual conversation, wrote: 'I am afraid to tell you who I am because, if I tell you who I am, you may not like who I am, and it's all that I have.'[1] The deceit, however, affects not only those we meet. It affects us too. Strange though it may seem, we simply do not know all that much about ourselves, and our persisting in wearing masks is just as much a barrier to us in our quest for knowledge about ourselves as it is to other people.

Given the fundamental importance of self-knowledge, it would seem that we would do well to devote some energy to finding ways of developing it. One such way is found in intimate relationships. This is because deep loving relationships (in which the beloved is accepted, warts and all) enable those involved to gradually let their masks and other defences fall away so that more and more of the truth about themselves is revealed to those who love them and, of course, to themselves. Another way lies in the kind of prayer that seeks God at the heart of one's own personality and inevitably finds truth about oneself along the way.[2]

It is particularly sad that, in hiding the truth about ourselves, we can be concealing something far more beautiful than that which we portray. To say this is not to deny the fact that many of us have skeletons in our cupboards. Nor is it to deny that probably all of us have doubts about the wisdom of trusting certain other people with even the lovelier truths about ourselves. They are among the pearls that we are loath to cast before those whom we have not learned to trust. In short, although our vocation as Christians may well involve, among other things, a search for the true self, it would seem that we all feel the need for some minimum of privacy, for keeping some truths, notably truths about ourselves, within a small confined circle of intimate friends, and, indeed, for confining some knowledge of truth to ourselves and God.

The question of lies and untruth

What we have said thus far serves to illustrate the tension that we encounter throughout our lives between the intuition that the expression of truth is, generally speaking, good, and the seemingly commonsense insights that a certain amount of secrecy is necessary, that some truth is better withheld (at least from certain people), and that even the telling of untruths may sometimes be necessary for the achievement of a greater good.

St Augustine, however, did not consider the achievement of such a greater good to be an option that is open to us. He taught that a lie could never be a morally right act, not even a lie told to save the life of another person. For him, a lie could be described as having one thing in mind and saying another, with the intention to deceive.[3] On the face of it, this might seem to be a useful working definition. We would do well, I think, to examine it in some detail.[4]

A first point worth noting is that, if we were to take the word 'saying' in the above description of a lie to indicate only the faculty of speech (a combination of lungs, vocal chords, tongue, lips, etc.), we would be ignoring numerous other ways of lying. We can also lie, for example, in writing, just as we can lie using Morse code, smoke signals, hand signs or any other kind of body language. A second point worth noting is that a difference between the facts and the literal meaning of what one says is not enough to constitute a lie – even if the person doing the communicating is fully aware of that difference. There must also be an intention to deceive. If this were not the case, much of our normal use of language would be morally wrong. Take, for instance, our use of hyperbole. We would also be acting in a way that is morally wrong in writing novels, plays, poems and songs if we knew that the words written did not coincide with known facts. This would be absurd, especially in view of the fact that fiction can be used very effectively to communicate deep truths, as can be seen very clearly in Jesus' use of parables in all four gospel accounts. A third point worth bearing in mind, moreover, is that an intention to deceive (even when accompanied by success therein) does not necessary suffice for a lie to occur. If it were sufficient, many of the games we play would be wrong in their very essence. In many ball games, for example, it is normal to try to mislead members of the opposing side into thinking you are going to execute a certain manoeuvre so that they will leave you free to execute a very different one, and thereby, perhaps, score a goal, point, try, run or whatever. Such misleading or deceiving of opponents, in accordance with the rules, is, of course, part of the game. Deceit outside those rules, as in the case of one who falls to the floor clutching an uninjured limb whilst falsely claiming that he or she has been injured in order to gain a penalty point or some other advantage, is, however, a very different matter. Now it might be claimed that the difference lies in the fact that this latter case fits Augustine's definition of a lie, whereas the former case (deceit within the rules) does not. But is it really so? In regard to such matters as feigning injury in order to gain a penalty point, we could say that cheats of the kind described have one thing in mind (in the sense that they know they have not been fouled) and are communicating something quite different with the intention to deceive. So far so good. However, it might also be claimed that somebody who acts *within* the rules when selling a dummy, or feigning a stroke, also has one thing in mind (knowledge that no such kick or stroke is to take place) whilst communicating another with the intention to deceive.

It could be objected that no real deception is involved when people play within the rules of a game. What might lead one to say this is the fact that the words 'deceit', 'deception' and 'deceive' tend to have a ring of moral wrongness about them in modern usage. In other words, we tend to use those words mostly to describe activity which we have already decided is morally wrong. In order to avoid misunderstandings, therefore, we might decide to avoid the use of these words in this context, and use other words to convey their essential meaning. If we consult a dictionary, we find that 'to deceive' means 'to lead someone to believe what is false' or 'to purposely mislead'. This, however, changes nothing in what we have said about selling dummies, and so forth in ball games. The fact remains that the person selling the dummy misleads purposely, and surely it is such misleading that we understand to be referred to in Augustine's definition – if we take it to apply to more than just the faculty of speech as described above.

It might seem, therefore, that, if we stay with this definition, we are led to conclusions that are counter-intuitive, one such being that some of the most skilful moves in ball games are unethical. Once again we need to look at the same kind of language problem as that just discussed, but in reference to a different word. This time the word is 'lie'. Here again we have a word that tends to be used almost exclusively to refer to morally wrong activity. Another such word is 'murder', which is used to refer to acts of unjustified homicide. Using the same kind of formula, we could say that a 'lie' is an unjustified untruth. We should note, however, that Augustine's definition of a lie is, in fact, a definition of a purposely misleading untruth. In other words, he appears to be saying that all communication of purposely misleading untruths is wrong. Apparently following his lead, various other Christian teachers over the centuries have claimed that the telling of such untruths cannot be justified in any circumstances. For them it matters not what the consequences may be of taking a course other than that of telling an untruth, although, in certain circumstances, the consequences could conceivably be disastrous. Thus we find a deontological norm being promulgated.[5]

Various arguments have been used to ground this norm. One, resulting from a particular kind of natural law thinking, is that the faculty of speech has been given to us by God only to communicate the truth. Even if we ignored the fact that the faculty of speech could be said to have numerous purposes (including that of entertaining other people in various ways), upholders of this argument would still have to show how it can be used in some extended form to prove the wrongness of falsehoods communicated by means of smoke signals, Morse code, and so forth. Some years ago, John Dedek noted a couple of somewhat different arguments used in a document called the *Summa Fratris Alexandri* to show why lying, unlike theft and homicide, could never be morally right under any circumstances. (The word 'lying' here, it would seem, means purposely misleading by communicating an untruth.) The first is that an evil intention is always involved. This is so because the person telling the untruth intends to deceive. A counter argument to this might be that analogous arguments could be used about other kinds of acts of which Christians generally approve. The second argument found by Dedek is that truth is more noble than life itself and that no new good could be introduced which could compensate for a defect of truth.[6] This is an amazing claim. Most people, moreover, if they reflected upon cases such as those in which a person's life could be saved by telling an untruth to a serial killer, would regard the claim as counter-intuitive. Whatever we may wish to say about the validity or otherwise of these arguments, however, some scholars are of the opinion that, in practice, the real grounding of this norm was the extraordinary authority attributed, for many centuries after his death, to the figure of Augustine.[7]

In order to overcome some of the problems that could result from keeping to a deontological norm about telling untruths, various mechanisms have been developed and adopted from time to time. Take, for instance, the case of George, who is approached by a known assassin. The assassin asks if the person he intends to kill is in George's house. The truth of the matter is that the intended victim is indeed in George's house. To tell the truth would obviously be disastrous. Now it would seem that many scholars who accepted the deontological norm about lying were also given to a certain amount of teleological thinking,[8] which they applied in cases such as this. They believed, on grounds that had nothing to do with consequences, that purposely misleading another person by telling an untruth was wrong, but they also saw, precisely by taking likely consequences into account, that one would do well to find some alternative to telling the truth in such circumstances. One of the mechanisms proposed was to maintain silence. Keeping silent in circumstances such as those just described, however, could, in effect amount to telling the truth, for the assassin could easily guess why George was not saying anything. Another mechanism proposed was that of mental reservation. Henry Davis describes what he calls 'broad' mental restriction or reservation as follows:

> Since, therefore, a lie is never permitted under any circumstances, there must be a legitimate means of guarding secrets when silence is impossible. That means is the use of a form of words which express the interior thought and could be known to express it, if the hearer were sensible, prudent, reasonable and knew the circumstances. It is precisely because the words employed can express and indeed do express the truth as it is in the mind of the speaker, and as it could be gathered from circumstances, and because the hearer could understand the words in their intended meaning if he had the sense to do so, that the speaker tells no lie. In other words, the expression used can be understood in two senses, one of which the speaker means, the second of which the hearer takes.

An example that Davis supplies is that of telling an importunate visitor that the person he or she wishes to see is not at home. The phrase 'not at home', he says, has two meanings, one being that the person concerned is physically absent from the house, and the other that he or she is not at home to this caller. The person speaking, he goes on to say, restricts the meaning to one, and the hearer is deceived, not by a lie, but by his own interpretation of the speaker's words. Davis also refers to strict mental restriction. This he describes as 'the restriction in the mind of the speaker of the sense of the words to a particular meaning which no one, however wise, could understand'. Such behaviour he describes as a lie and says it is never permissible. For the use of broad mental reservation to be legitimate, says Davis, there must be a sufficiently good reason for its use, and the person being addressed must have no right to the information.[9] Some theologians, both Protestant and Catholic, see no need to resort to such complications, which, generally speaking, are possible only if the person to whom the question is addressed is quick-witted. They hold that, if the questioner has no right to the information, it can be legitimate to tell an untruth.

Those who take a teleological approach to the subject of truth and lying would see a difference between justified and unjustified misleading of another person through the communication of an untruth. They would see this as analogous to the distinction between justified homicide and murder. In determining which of the two categories a particular episode falls into, they would take into account such matters as harm done, or likely to be done, to the person deceived and/or the person telling the untruth, and, indeed, anybody else who is likely to be affected. They would also take into account any reduction in trust that might result. In the case of the person who cheats in a ball game, it is clear that a reduction in trust is likely to occur and that harm could result for both the cheat and members of the opposing side. In the case of selling a dummy within the rules of the game, however, no harm should normally result. As for the case of the assassin, many teleologists would no doubt argue that, in view of the disastrous consequences likely to ensue upon the telling of the truth, there is sufficient reason for deceiving the murderer by telling an untruth. Indeed, they might argue that one should not resort to alternatives (such as maintaining silence) if telling an untruth is likely to be the most effective means of protecting the intended victim.

Many, perhaps most, Christian ethicists would describe themselves as neither totally teleologist nor totally deontologist. A present-day scholar who considers himself to fit into neither camp and yet believes that lying (by which he presumably means purposely misleading by communicating an untruth) is always wrong, is Germain Grisez. He sees human goodness in the fullness of human being. In order to understand what is involved in being a good person, therefore, we need to find out what are those things that fulfil humans. These he calls the basic goods, and supplies a list of them, included in which are: life, health and safety; knowledge and aesthetic experience; living at peace with others, neighbourliness and friendship; and integrity or self-integration. One of Grisez's basic tenets is that one should never turn directly against any of these basic goods, which he describes as aspects of persons. It would thus be wrong to be moved by hostility to opt for or even accept the destruction or impeding of a basic good. It would also be wrong to be moved by a stronger desire for an instance of one of the goods to act for it by destroying, damaging or impeding an instance of one of the others. If we were to choose in that way, says Grisez, we would thus determine ourselves against the impeded, damaged or destroyed good.[10] Now lying, he believes, causes damage to more than one basic good.

> Lying and other deceptions are intentional untruthfulness: they express outwardly something at odds with one's inner self and attempt to lead others to accept it. Thus, they divide the inner and outer selves of those who engage in them, contrary to their own self-integration and authenticity, while impeding or attacking the real community that truthful communication would foster, even when deception seems necessary. Therefore, lying and other deception in communication are always wrong.[11]

Grisez goes on to discuss lying in various situations, including: lying to save the life of a potential victim when speaking with a person who is intent on committing murder; lying to protect secrets; and supposedly helpful lying, as when one lies in order to hide bad news from someone who would be seriously upset by it. As one would expect, he describes all of these as wrong.[12]

Although Grisez describes the basic goods as aspects of persons and says clearly that they are not Platonic Ideas, the present author has argued that they sometimes appear to be treated as separate entities to which humans should bend the knee. Apart from this, however, there are other questions to be raised about Grisez's analysis of lying. When discussing the example of agents of a totalitarian regime asking people in charge of an institution to identify certain children who are to be sent to a death camp, he says that, objectively, it would not be right to lie. He accepts that, if it were feasible, it could be morally acceptable to use force, if necessary. He sees no paradox here. A person cannot lie, he says, without thereby choosing self-alienation, which, opposed as it is to the basic good of self-integration and authenticity, is sufficient to make lying wrong. A person can, however, use deadly force to defend others without choosing the death which, if it were intentionally chosen, would make the killing wrong (presumably because of the attack upon the basic good of life). Moreover, the use of deadly force in defence does not impede community (the basic good of neighbourliness, living at peace with others, friendship), whilst lying does.[13]

In answer to this, it might be said that one can see that there is a struggle within when one tells an untruth, but it is difficult to see that something similar is not there when one resorts to deadly violence, even in a good cause. It does not appear evident, moreover, that such a struggle within should necessarily lead to self-alienation. It may just be a sign of the fact that one hates having to harm another human being in any way. Moreover, it seems strange to claim that deadly violence does not impede the community as lying does, especially when the lying is addressed to the enemies of true community.

Truth in different situations

In chapters and articles devoted to the subjects of truth and lies, it seems customary to analyse cases of conflict such as that of the assassin discussed above. Another oft-quoted example is the use of lies (or deliberate untruths) in warfare, a specific example being the ways in which, during the Second World War, the Allies tried to mislead the Germans about when and where they would invade mainland Europe. Yet another example is that of placebos given by doctors to patients who have been led to believe that they are receiving medicine. As Dietrich Bonhoeffer wrote, however, restricting the problem of truthful speech to certain cases of conflict is superficial. Bonhoeffer also believed that 'telling the truth' means different things in different situations. We need to take into account the relationships involved in each case. He illustrates this by taking the example of parents demanding truthfulness of their children.

> The truthfulness of a child towards his parents is essentially different from that of the parents towards their child. The life of the small child lies open before the parents, and what the child says should reveal to them everything that is hidden and secret, but in the converse relationship this cannot possibly be the case. Consequently, in the matter of truthfulness, the parents' claim on the child is different from the child's claim on the parents.

Bonhoeffer goes on to say that it already emerges from this that telling the truth means different things in different situations. We need to take into account in each situation the relevant relationships. We have to ask whether and in what way a particular person is entitled to demand truthful speech of other people. 'Speech between parents and children is, in the nature of the case, different from speech between man and wife, between friends, between teacher and pupil, government and subject, friend and foe, and in each case the truth which this speech conveys is also different.'[14]

In a not entirely different vein, Bernard Häring discusses a case similar to one mentioned above. During the Nazi period in Germany, employees of the state went to hospitals and orphanages and asked for lists of children with certain hereditary diseases. Where such lists were supplied, the children concerned were sent off to the gas chambers. In many cases, those who were asked for the lists replied that they had no such children in their institution. Häring says that, to his mind, they did not lie, although an analysis of the words alone could reveal a 'false utterance'.

> But in the concrete situation, what Hitler's men were really asking went beyond the words they uttered. Their actual question was, 'How many children do you have for the gas chambers?' And the only response to that question could be 'None'. This was truthful communication or legitimate refusal of communication. Words have their meaning only within the context, and what, in abstraction, could be called 'lie' or 'false utterance' can be, in the actual situation, the proper response.[15]

It would appear, then, that there can be communications of truth which are appropriate to certain kinds of relationship or situation and not to others.

Concluding remarks

It seems incontrovertible to say that, generally speaking, there has to be a presumption against lying and in favour of truth just as there has to be a presumption against homicide and against taking the property of another person without his or her permission. It would also seem to be the case, however, that what is true in a particular situation, and, indeed, what is a lie in the same situation, are not always apparent to the one who searches only superficially. Having said all this, however, we would do well to remind ourselves of the damage that can be done to a person who lies too easily, as, perhaps, most of us do. Truthfulness is, in many ways, something that we learn. It is also a habit or virtue that we need to acquire and nourish. Too often, however, untruthfulness becomes something of a habit, at least in certain kinds of situations. Ronald Preston puts these points very succinctly.

> It seems clear that there are occasions when it is right to tell a lie, but most of the time people tell lies when they should not. The temptation comes suddenly, perhaps to get out of an awkward situation or to practice some petty fraud or deception, and they succumb. In order to

have the discernment to know when a lie is called for, one needs to be habitually truthful.[16]

Notes

1 John Powell, *Why Am I Afraid to Tell You Who I Am?* (London: Fontana/Collins, 1982), p. 12.

2 See, for instance, Teresa of Avila, *The Interior Castle*.

3 See Augustine's *De mendacio* (*On Lying*) and his later work *Contra mendacium* (*Against Lying*).

4 Sissela Bok defines a lie as 'any intentionally deceptive message which is stated': *Lying: Moral Choice in Public and Private Life* (Hassocks: Harvester Press, 1978), p. 13. Bok sees deception as a larger category, of which lying forms a part. She does, however, note that it is possible to define 'lie' in such a way that it is identical with deception. Thus, she says, we hear of a person 'living a lie' (p. 14).

5 Deontologists hold that certain acts are always right or always wrong regardless of consequences. Teleologists, on the other hand, hold that the rightness or wrongness of an act depends upon its consequences. Long after Augustine, the philosopher Immanuel Kant also spoke against lying in all circumstances.

6 John F. Dedek, 'Intrinsically evil acts: an historical study of the mind of St Thomas', *The Thomist* 43 (1979), p. 400.

7 Thus Ronald Preston writes: 'Theologians subsequent to Augustine did not like to contradict him . . .': 'Lying' in J. Macquarrie and J. Childress (eds), *A New Dictionary of Christian Ethics* (London: SCM Press, 1986), p. 363. John F. Dedek too is of the opinion that later theologians were generally unwilling to challenge Augustine's authority regarding this matter: 'Moral absolutes in the predecessors of St Thomas', *Theological Studies* 38 (1977), p. 680, and 'Intrinsically evil acts', p. 412.

8 See note 5.

9 Henry Davis, *Moral and Pastoral Theology*, vol. II (London: Sheed and Ward, 1946), pp. 413–16.

10 A simply worded presentation of Grisez's basic theory is found in *Beyond the New Morality: The Responsibilities of Freedom* (Notre Dame, IN and London: Notre Dame University Press, 1974), which he co-authored with Russell Shaw. See also his presentation of it in *The Way of The Lord Jesus*, vol. 1 (Chicago: Franciscan Herald Press, 1983).

11 Germain Grisez, *The Way of the Lord Jesus*, vol. 2 (Quincy, IL: Franciscan Herald Press, 1993), p. 405.

12 Grisez, *The Way of the Lord Jesus*, vol. 2, pp. 406–12.

13 Grisez, *The Way of the Lord Jesus*, vol. 2, p. 407.

14 Dietrich Bonhoeffer, *Ethics*, ed. Eberhard Bethge (London: Collins, 1966), pp. 363–72.

15 Bernard Häring, *Free and Faithful in Christ*, vol. 2 (Slough: St Paul Publications, 1979), p. 48.

16 Ronald Preston, 'Lying' in *A New Dictionary of Christian Ethics*, p. 363.

Bernard Hoose

Select bibliography

St Augustine, *De Mendacio* (*On Lying*) and *Contra Mendacium* (*Against Lying*).
Sissela Bok, *Lying: Moral Choice in Public and Private Life* (Hassocks: Harvester Press, 1978).
Dietrich Bonhoeffer, 'What is meant by "telling the truth"?' in *Ethics*, ed. Eberhard Bethge (London: Collins, 1966), pp. 363–72.
Bernard Häring, *Free and Faithful in Christ*, vol. 2 (Slough: St Paul Publications, 1979), ch. 1.

Medical ethics

19
Euthanasia

Richard M. Gula

Death's habit of arriving accompanied by the fear of enduring pain, of being trapped by machines without control, of losing bodily integrity and personal dignity, of costing a great deal financially and emotionally, along with other factors lends strength to the movement to secure the public endorsement of euthanasia and physician-assisted suicide. Fundamentally, the debate about euthanasia and physician-assisted suicide is more about competing moral visions and values than anything else. After clarifying the issue being debated, this chapter will identify the main features of the vision and values shaping the debate, especially those upheld by the Catholic moral tradition as recently reflected in Pope John Paul II's encyclical *Evangelium Vitae* (1995). The Catholic position has been singled out because Roman Catholic theology has long reflected on the extent of one's obligation to preserve life. This tradition of reflection, and its principles for making decisions about the care of the dying, are respected by diverse communities, and used, at times, as a foil by those arguing in favour of euthanasia.[1] This chapter will close with a suggestion for a way of responding to the euthanasia movement from the perspective of virtue.

The debate

The easiest way to skew the euthanasia debate is to see it as a 'pulling-the-plug' issue. It is not. Forgoing useless or disproportionately burdensome treatment (which is what we generally mean by 'pulling the plug') is not the same as euthanasia or assisted suicide. Standard medical, moral, and legal practices allow the competent patient, or surrogate of an incompetent patient, to weigh according to the patient's values the benefits and burdens of being treated, and then to select from alternative treatments or to refuse treatment altogether. In general, the traditional Catholic medical-moral principle of the ordinary/extraordinary means standard supports such practice as the morally proper way to care for the dying. To refuse treatment which is useless or disproportionately burdensome (i.e. extraordinary) is the morally appropriate forgoing of treatment. It is neither euthanasia nor assisted suicide (cf. *EV*, n. 65).

The debate *is* about voluntary active euthanasia and physician-assisted suicide. Voluntary active euthanasia means a deliberate intervention, by someone other than the person whose life is at stake, directly intended to end the life of the competent, terminally ill patient who makes a fully voluntary and persistent request for aid in dying. A common way to think about euthanasia is to have a physician give a lethal injection to the patient who wants to die. 'Mercy killing' is commonly used in place of euthanasia to emphasize that such an act is directly intended as an act of kindness. But as Pope John Paul II reminds us, 'euthanasia must be called a false mercy, and indeed a disturbing "perversion" of mercy' (*EV*, n. 66).

In a physician-assisted suicide, a physician helps to bring on the death of the patient by providing the means to do it or by giving the necessary information on how to do it, but the patient performs the lethal act on himself or herself. The typical procedure of assisted suicide is the patient taking a lethal dose of poison (by swallowing pills, by taking an injection, or by inhaling a gas, for example) requested of and then prescribed by the physician for that purpose. In this case, as in euthanasia, both the physician and patient play morally responsible roles in bringing about death. Physician-assisted suicide is not significantly morally different from euthanasia and so need not be distinguished for purposes of understanding the moral vision and values at stake in the present debate.

The basic line of argument supporting euthanasia and physician-assisted suicide can be summarized as follows. On the grounds of respect for autonomy, human persons should have the right to control their living and dying, and so they should be able to end their lives when they wish to terminate needless suffering. Physicians, as agents of the patient's best interests, should assist either by directly killing the patient or by assisting the patient in suicide. Euthanasia and assisted suicide are beneficent acts of relieving human suffering.

The main line of the religious argument against euthanasia and assisted suicide is as follows. Human persons are stewards of creation and so we have only limited dominion and thus limited freedom over our lives. Human life is a 'trust', and not a personal 'possession' over which we can assume full control. The sanctity of human life is conferred by God and requires reverence and protection. Taking innocent life is not a human right, but a grave moral evil. Human suffering, while not a value in itself, can have meaning when lived in faith and so need not diminish human dignity.

Vision and values

Autonomy

Autonomy is the centrepiece in the moral defence of euthanasia. In health care, autonomy has a prominent place as the guiding principle for treating the patient as a person with values, goals, and limits. But this same freedom which preserves the patient's right to refuse treatment is now being extended by advocates of euthanasia to include choosing death and the means to achieve it, even to the extent of eliciting the assistance of another if necessary and desired.[2] When defenders of euthanasia appeal to autonomy, they mean that each person has a right to control his or her body and life, including the end of it, and so ought to be given the freedom to exercise this right. When autonomy is absolutized, the sheer fact that a choice is 'my' choice becomes the sole right-making characteristic of the choice. In the United States, Jack Kevorkian is drum major for such a view: 'In my view the highest principle in medical ethics – in any kind of ethics – is personal autonomy, self-determination. What counts is what the patient wants and judges to be a benefit or a value in his or her own life. That's primary.'[3]

Autonomy underlies the familiar appeal to 'death with dignity' and the so-called 'right to die'[4] to justify euthanasia. The 'right to die' and 'death with dignity' according to this view means that each of us should be able to determine at what time, in what way, and by whose hand we will die. In other words, these expressions may be translated as something like the following: 'It's my body; it's my freedom; it's my life; it's my death. Let me have control.' While no one seems to doubt that autonomy is an important value, the question in the euthanasia debate is 'How far does it extend?'

A counter-argument to justifying euthanasia on the basis of autonomy can be made from the religious beliefs and moral philosophy of the Catholic tradition. The religious argument appeals to a combination of the principles of divine sovereignty and human stewardship and to our social responsibility for the common good.

According to Christian belief, we live in a world of grace. The first story of creation (Gen 1 – 2:4) tells us, in a symbolic way, that when humans appeared on the sixth day, all the rest of creation was already in place. This is a way of saying that everything comes to us as a gift from a totally free act of a gracious God. Human life is God's gift to us and our responsibility. The limits of our responsibility for life are enshrined in the principles of sovereignty and stewardship which assert that God has absolute dominion over life, and that we share in it only as limited creatures (Gen 2:7) who are to be 'ministers of God's plan' (EV, nn. 39, 52). Life is our own, but not only our own, 'because it is the property and gift of God the Creator and Father' (EV, n. 40). Together these principles temper destructive intrusions into life and demand the most serious of reasons to justify any action that would take life (e.g. killing in self-defence).

The second story of creation expresses in an imaginative way the limits that come with being created human and not being the sovereign Creator (Gen 2:15–17). As the story goes, the first man ('earth creature' is the better translation) was placed in the garden of Eden but forbidden to eat from the fruit of the tree of the knowledge of good and evil. To eat of that tree would impart a mastery of life and an autonomy inappropriate for being human. This story asserts a fundamental conviction of biblical faith that from the very beginning human freedom over life is limited.[5] Thus our religious beliefs in God's dominion and human stewardship already limit the extent of our freedom. Pope John Paul II affirmed as much in *Veritatis Splendor* (n. 35). In the face of death, freedom is not having absolute control but it requires submission to what cannot be controlled. We exercise such freedom in the face of death by accepting ourselves as creatures of God and by admitting to our powerlessness before death. But our freedom does not extend to bringing about death at the time and under the conditions we stipulate.

The social nature of being human also limits our freedom. The prevailing interpretation of autonomy, however, does not include any concern of how our personal desires and striving contribute to the good of society as a whole. The ethos of individualism is sceptical of there being any good beyond that which any single person takes to be good in his or her experience. As Pope John Paul II has diagnosed our culture, the individualistic concept of freedom 'exalts the isolated individual in an absolute way, and gives no place to solidarity, to openness to others and service of them' (EV, n. 19). The counter view which he endorses begins with an inherently relational view of human freedom. It contends that the individual will flourish only insofar as society as a whole flourishes. This view is in line with the Catholic social ethics tradition on the common good.

Charles Dougherty has made a compelling argument against euthanasia from the perspective of the common good.[6] He argues that there is a good for society as a whole beyond a good for each person. What we do in pursuing personal goals bears on the good of the whole society. We call this good 'the common good'. While it respects and serves the interests of individual persons, the common good ultimately upholds the collective good as more important than the good of any one individual. But as long as we continue to envision society as 'a mass of individuals placed side by side, but without any mutual bonds' (*EV*, n. 20), then we will continue to miss our responsibility for the common good. A commitment to the common good forces us to ask whether there are some things which we want for ourselves but which we ought not to pursue so that the good of the whole might better be served. To seek the common good, then, is to seek those actions and policies that would contribute to the total well-being of persons and the community.

Our responsibility for the common good has implications for the way we analyse euthanasia. One is that we must move away from the individual perspective which analyses euthanasia as a private issue and move towards the societal perspective which analyses it as a social one. Daniel Callahan has argued along these lines to claim that permitting euthanasia would be 'self-determination run amok'.[7] It cannot properly be classified, he claims, as a private matter of self-determination or as an autonomous act of managing one's private affairs. Euthanasia is a social decision. It involves the one to be killed as well as the one doing the killing, and it requires a complying society to make it acceptable. Therefore, euthanasia must be assessed for its social impact on caring for the dying and on our general attitude toward life. Autonomy must be understood within the limits of the social responsibilities for the common good. One possible impact of introducing euthanasia as a policy is that it will only fuel the fires of a 'culture of death' by negatively influencing social standards of acceptable life. The vulnerable, those with serious dementia or depression who cannot speak for themselves or defend their values, may be especially at risk of being killed. Overall, the practice of euthanasia threatens to weaken the general prohibition against killing in society and so we end up valuing life less.

Euthanasia perpetuates the illusion that we can control everything, that we can be masters of nature and of death. By drawing on its religious beliefs about God's sovereignty and the limited scope of responsible stewardship for life, as well as its social ethical tradition of advocating for the common good, the Catholic tradition recognizes limits to autonomy and so challenges its support for euthanasia.

The prohibition against killing

The distinction between killing and allowing to die is at the heart of the euthanasia debate. Killing is any action or omission intended to cause death. Allowing to die is withholding or withdrawing useless or dispro-portionately burdensome treatment so that nature may run its course, that is, so that the fatal condition may overtake a person. The Catholic tradition holds to a moral difference between, on the one hand, with-holding treatment from a dying patient when nothing more can be done to reverse significantly the progressive deterioration of life; and, on the other hand, intervening to put the patient to death. Only the latter is prohibited. The stance one takes on whether killing and allowing to die are morally different greatly affects the stance one takes in the euthanasia debate.

One extreme position holds to *no* moral difference between killing and allowing to die. This is the position represented by the Hemlock Society and philosophers such as Jonathan Glover, Peter Singer, Michael Tooley, Marvin Kohl, Helga Kuhse, James Rachels and others. For James Rachels, for example, the distinction is simply a descriptive difference.[8] Since death is the outcome in either case, there is no moral difference between killing and allowing to die. According to Rachels, our present acceptance of allowing to die ought to be extended to active killing, when such killing would be more merciful.

Others will hold that the distinction does have moral significance, but that it dissolves at a certain point in the process of dying. This position is represented by the late Paul Ramsey,[9] Robert Veatch,[10] and James Childress,[11] among others. While recognizing that killing is presump-tively wrong, in rare cases it may be justified as an expression of justice, love and kindness when the dying person has moved beyond the reach of benefiting from further care or being relieved of intractable pain.

The Catholic tradition, however, holds firm to the distinction between killing and allowing to die all the way through the dying process. Its position is grounded in the principle of the sanctity of life which affirms the sublime dignity of human life as a reflection of God (*EV*, n. 34) and that there are limits within which we must work to promote human well-being. Two obligations are enshrined by 'sanctity of life'. The first is the positive obligation to nurture and to support life. It gives rise to the duty to lead a fruitful life and to show reverence and love for the life of every person. The second is the negative obligation not to harm or to destroy life. This obligation is protected by the prohibition against directly taking innocent life, which includes the prohibitions against euthanasia and assisted suicide. In short, 'sanctity of life' directs us to foster life-affirming attitudes and to scrutinize any discussion to terminate life or to forgo life-sustaining treatment.

Two other associated principles add to the Catholic opposition to euthanasia. These are the principle of divine sovereignty and the principle expressed by the divine law, 'You shall not kill'. The principle of sovereignty in this context shows that what makes killing forbidden is that it violates the right of divine ownership. Only God is the master of life (*EV*, nn. 39, 55). For this reason, the Catholic tradition regards taking innocent human life as 'always morally evil and can never be licit either as an end in itself or as a means to a good end' (*EV*, n. 57).

The divine law prohibiting killing is found in the fifth commandment. The significance of appealing to this commandment in making a case against euthanasia is that it protects the bonds of being a covenantal community by prohibiting the arbitrary taking of life by an individual, private decision, without community sanction. On the positive side of this commandment to protect human life is the 'requirement to show reverence and love for every person and the life of every person' (*EV*, nn. 41, 54).

The distinction between killing and allowing to die finds further support from a different angle in Daniel Callahan's argument against euthanasia.[12] Callahan defends the distinction by appealing to three different perspectives on nature and human action: metaphysical, moral, and medical. The *metaphysical perspective* is based on a real difference between us and the external world, which has its own causal dynamism. As a result, we cannot have unlimited control over everything. To deny the distinction between killing and allowing to die concedes more power to human intervention than we actually have. The limitations of the body are ultimately beyond final human control. The *moral perspective* draws a line between physical causality and human responsibility. The line separates deaths caused by impersonal forces (the disease causes death) for which no one can be held responsible, and deaths caused by human action (a lethal injection causes death) for which someone can be held morally culpable. The *medical perspective* underscores the social purpose of the distinction. It protects the role of physicians as the ones who use their knowledge of the body and diseases to cure or comfort patients rather than to kill them. Physicians' power over life should be limited to curing and comforting. To extend their power to killing would violate what it means to be a physician.

These various perspectives on the distinction between killing and allowing to die are momentous for the euthanasia debate. If there is no moral distinction between killing and allowing to die, then every decision to withhold or withdraw futile or overly burdensome treatment can be construed as direct killing. If that were so, then we have greased the slide toward a general policy of euthanasia. Those who hold to the distinction under all circumstances oppose any policy on euthanasia. Even those who admit that the distinction does not hold under all circumstances, and so concede a qualified acceptance of an 'exceptional-case' euthanasia under certain conditions, do not have to conclude that justifying one act of euthanasia leads to justifying a social policy for the general practice of euthanasia. As James Childress argues, 'Whatever is said about particular acts of euthanasia, there are strong reasons to oppose a rule or practice of euthanasia because it would probably lead to abuses of the relevant moral principles, including both love and justice'.[13]

Beneficence

Closely following the argument from autonomy and the moral difference between killing and allowing to die is the argument from the desire to relieve the patient of suffering. This brings us within the scope of beneficence which includes the duty to help others in need and to avoid harm.

Three dimensions of the scope of beneficence have played a prominent role in the euthanasia debate: the 'character' of medicine as a profession; the 'suffering' that is to be relieved; and the 'mercy' that is to be shown the suffering/dying.

That we cannot reach a moral consensus on euthanasia reflects disagreement on the role of the physician and the very aim of medicine. The euthanasia debate raises the question whether killing patients is the physician's business and so fits within the aim of medicine. Dr Timothy Quill has become a prominent spokesman challenging the wisdom and tradition that 'Doctors must not kill'. His argument makes clear that physicians can use their medical skills not only to treat the medical needs of patients, but also to satisfy their value of life and their desire to live in a particular way. His justification takes him beyond the physician's traditional role of using specialized knowledge and skill to treat medical needs. It reaches into the realm of judging what kind of life is worth living.[14]

Opponents to physicians becoming killers argue on the basis of the traditional aim of medicine and the responsibilities proper to the physician's social role. Albert Jonsen, for example, has argued that 'killing a patient' has nothing to do with the social expectations and responsibilities attached to the physician's role 'to use scientific knowledge and clinical experience in making decisions and advising patients about the prevention, diagnosis, and treatment of disease and the maintenance of health'.[15] Similarly, Leon Kass argues that the role of the physician is defined by the goal of medicine – to benefit the wholeness of one who is sick. For him the physician-euthanizer is self-contradictory. Intentionally killing the patient does not fit within the physician's aim to promote healing and wholeness.[16]

Daniel Callahan also argues that physicians who euthanize or assist in suicide have moved beyond medicine's proper realm of promoting and preserving health and into the metaphysical realm of determining the value of life and what kind of lives are worth living. This broader realm of what makes for general human happiness is a matter of religion or philosophy. It does not belong to medicine's competence. Callahan holds to the conviction that, while it is the proper role of medicine to relieve the suffering caused by physical pain or psychological stressors that may accompany sickness, it does not belong to medicine to judge the kind of life worth living when a person suffers from despair in the human condition.[17]

Arguments such as those developed by Jonsen, Kass and Callahan support the moral character of medicine as a commitment to healing which is incompatible with doctors killing. For this reason, beneficence must be seen within the limits of the commitment of the medical profession to care for the sick. By wanting to license physicians to kill, advocates of euthanasia are calling into question the social expectations of the physician and the moral character of medical practice. The traditional aim of medicine to prevent disease and to restore or maintain health fits well within the Catholic tradition's limits of the scope of the prohibition against killing outlined above.

Another dimension to the argument from beneficence is the appeal to the obligation to relieve suffering. Next to the right to choose how and when we die, a fundamental claim of the euthanasia movement is the obligation we have to one another to relieve suffering, especially unnecessary and meaningless suffering.

The argument from suffering reaches beyond medicine's physical boundaries of promoting and preserving health or wholeness and into the boundless metaphysical realm of general human happiness or a 'meaningful' life. To enlist a physician in achieving release from a meaningless life of suffering presumes the physician is competent to judge what kinds of life are worth living. Perhaps this would be true if suffering had only medical causes. As Eric Cassell's analysis of suffering shows, while physical pain may be the major physical cause of suffering, the root problem of suffering and mortality is more than physical.[18] In many instances pain is unnecessary. Most pain can and ought to be alleviated by the proper use of analgesics, even if more aggressive treatments of pain are needed. The fact that pain is not relieved contributes to the drive for euthanasia.

The degree and intensity to which people suffer, and whether they find life empty or meaningless, turns less on their physical condition or pain and more on their outlook on life. Suffering is more a personal matter in the sense that it is a function of a person's attitude and framework of meaning than it is an unpleasant experience. While we should not be glorifying suffering or seeking it as an end, we can make it less overwhelming by framing it in the context of a life that has value and is supported by strong bonds of love.

The meaning of pain, suffering and death is tied to the meaning of life itself. This is fundamentally a religious question. Christian theology

Richard M. Gula

teaches that suffering, while not a value in itself but an experience of evil, can be transformed.[19] The story of the life–death–resurrection of Jesus tells us that the tragedy of suffering, dying and death cannot, and will not, be stronger than God's love. God's love, revealed in the resurrection of Jesus, gives us the courage to enter into suffering and death knowing that life ultimately triumphs. If, through suffering, the sufferer is brought nearer to God in Christ, then that person may bear it courageously because of the comfort of the spiritual experience it offers. The bonding with Christ is the means for managing the suffering well (EV, n. 67).

The scope of beneficence is ultimately about mercy, that is, about how we fulfil the demands of covenantal fidelity that we owe one another. What kind of mercy towards the dying fits the commitment first to be faithful and then to be healing whenever possible? While it may be inappropriate to speak of killing as healing, may it yet be compatible with mercy towards those who are dying in pain and find life empty, oppressive, and meaningless? Those who argue in support of euthanasia think so.

But our biblical witness of mercy and compassion points us in a different direction. In the Bible, mercy and compassion represent the way that God maintains covenantal fidelity with the chosen people. God's mercy is the fulfilment of the covenantal commitment to be with and for the chosen people in all circumstances. Mercy and compassion are the ways that God, who had covenanted with Israel, continues to love her, provides for her, and protects her from harm. In the life of Jesus, mercy and compassion led him to do works which restored the broken to wholeness. Out of mercy and compassion, he healed the blind, taught the ignorant, raised the dead, and fed the hungry.[20]

The biblical witness, then, shows us that deep personal relationships lie at the heart of mercy. What from the biblical view is a virtue of fidelity, love and care becomes for advocates of euthanasia a basis for killing. For Pope John Paul II, 'True "compassion" leads to sharing another's pain; it does not kill the person whose suffering we cannot bear' (EV, n. 66). Resorting to euthanasia is failing to embody the trust that sustains life and the commitment to be companions to one another, especially those who are helpless or those who are unable to contribute to the community. The refusal to participate in euthanasia is a reminder and an encouragement to remain committed to one another as partners who sustain each other through trust, love and care.

Character, suffering and mercy are three aspects of the scope of beneficence which are at issue in the euthanasia debate. The Catholic religious and moral tradition supports the traditional moral centre of medicine which finds killing incompatible with the commitment to heal. Faith informed by the biblical stories of covenant and the life–death–resurrection of Jesus provides a special context of meaning within which to understand suffering and mercy. In the eyes of faith, suffering need not diminish the dignity of the human person. The Christian faith invites those who suffer to grasp its deeper mystery. Faith offers a chance to transform the uselessness of suffering by identifying with the suffering of Christ and thereby coming to a closer bonding with God in Christ. Mercy fulfills the demands of covenantal fidelity by not killing but by companioning with compassion those who suffer. Mercy embodies the trust and care that supports the suffering and dying from not abandoning hope when life is hard.

A response

The euthanasia movement is as much a challenge to the depth of moral character as it is a challenge to the meaning of our moral principles. The true significance of the Catholic opposition to euthanasia ultimately rests on the kind of witness that runs ahead of and behind the convictions which we say make euthanasia untenable. In order to be a credible player in the debate, then, we have to bear convincing witness, personally and corporately, to the ways we live our lives, take care of our health, face our limits, let go of control, bear suffering, think about our relationship with others, make room for the weak and unsuccessful, care for the sick, the elderly and the dying. What kind of persons and community should we be in order to encourage people to view death as an inevitable outcome that no one needs to hasten through lethal intervention?

Many of our problems with reaching an agreement on the public policy and the morality of euthanasia stem from our positions on deeper questions about life and about the kind of person we want to be. So when we think about how we might respond to the euthanasia movement, we need to include not only the soundness of our principles but also the spiritual depths and strength of our character by developing virtues such as humility, humour, courage and hope that will enable us to live well while dying and to face those conditions of hopelessness which threaten to overwhelm us.

In addition to personal virtue, we also need to be a community of virtue that gives witness to those fundamental religious and moral convictions which shape our living and dying in ways that would make euthanasia unthinkable. Stanley Hauerwas gets to the heart of the matter when he says that Christians have no 'solution' to the evil of suffering. 'Rather, they have had a community of care that has made it possible for them to absorb the destructive terror of evil that constantly threatens to destroy all human relations.'[21] Our hospitals and parishes are uniquely situated to be this community of care that surrounds the sick and dying with support.

A virtuous community is one which provides the structures and develops the skills which will enable us to provide 'companionship, sympathy, and support in the time of trial' (*EV*, n. 67). The demand for euthanasia will increase if structures of support and skills of care do not keep pace with the demand. By facing our limits to heal, we as a community of care can do much to benefit the lives of the dying without resorting to euthanasia. We must address more effectively the 'need' for euthanasia, such as by providing adequate relief of pain, by withholding or withdrawing treatments that only prolong dying, by keeping company with those who are lonely, and by being a resource of meaning and hope for those tempted to despair.

That we will have to face experiences of pain, suffering, and death in ourselves and in others is the price of being human. While this fact is biologically determined, there is nothing fixed about how we will respond to it. What sickness and the threat of death do to us is one thing. What we make of them is another. The way we respond is a matter of character being shaped over the course of our lives, and not just in the time of crisis. People are responding differently to the euthanasia movement because they have different ideas about who we ought to be, where to find meaning in life, how much control we ought to have, what to make of suffering, and what we owe to one another. Whether we are going to rise to the occasion and alleviate those conditions of hopelessness which can make euthanasia so attractive is ultimately a matter of character, personal and corporate. Only if we can rise to the occasion with compelling witnesses to our religious convictions about life, suffering, and death will we ever have an impact on shaping public consensus toward death as an experience that we need not hasten through lethal interventions.

Notes

1 See, for example, James Rachels, *The End of Life: Euthanasia and Morality* (New York: Oxford University Press, 1986).
2 Derek Humphry, 'The case for rational suicide', *Euthanasia Review* 1 (Fall 1986), pp. 172–5; Helga Kushe, 'Voluntary euthanasia and the doctor', *Free Inquiry* 89 (Winter 1988), 17–19.
3 Jack Kevorkian, *Free Inquiry* 92 (1991), p. 14.
4 For a critical review of this concept, see Leon Kass, 'Is there a right to die?', *Hastings Center Report* 23 (January-February 1993), pp. 34–43.
5 Richard J. Clifford and Roland E. Murphy, 'Genesis' in Raymond E. Brown, Joseph A. Fitzmyer and Roland E. Murphy (eds), *The New Jerome Biblical Commentary* (Englewood Cliffs, NJ: Prentice Hall, 1990), p. 12.
6 Charles Dougherty, 'The common good, terminal illness, and euthanasia', *Issues in Law and Medicine* 9 (1993), pp. 151–66.

7 Daniel Callahan, 'When self-determination runs amok', *Hastings Center Report* 22 (March–April 1992), pp. 52–5.

8 Rachels' most sustained argument for euthanasia and against the moral significance of the distinction between killing and allowing to die is in *The End of Life*, pp. 106–28.

9 Paul Ramsey, *The Patient As Person* (New Haven, CT: Yale University Press, 1970), p. 153; also *Ethics at the Edges of Life* (New Haven, CT: Yale University Press, 1978), pp. 146–8.

10 Robert Veatch, *Death, Dying and the Biological Revolution* (rev. edn; New Haven, CT: Yale University Press, 1989), pp. 61–74.

11 James F. Childress, 'Love and justice in Christian biomedical ethics' in Earl E. Shelp (ed.), *Theology and Bioethics* (Boston: Reidel, 1985), p. 227.

12 Daniel Callahan, 'Vital distinctions, mortal questions', *Commonweal* 115 (15 July 1988), pp. 399–401. His argument is repeated in 'Can we return death to disease?' in 'Mercy, murder, and morality: perspectives on euthanasia', *Hastings Center Report* Special Supplement 19 (January/February 1989), pp. 5–6; *What Kind of Life* (New York: Simon and Schuster, 1990), pp. 221–49.

13 Childress, 'Love and justice in Christian biomedical ethics', p. 227.

14 Timothy E. Quill, 'Death and dignity: a case of individualized decision making', *New England Journal of Medicine* 324, no. 10 (7 March 1991), p. 693.

15 Albert R. Jonsen, 'Beyond the physicians' reference – the ethics of active euthanasia', *Western Journal of Medicine* 149 (August 1988), p. 196.

16 Leon Kass, 'Why doctors must not kill', *Commonweal* 118 (9 August 1991), p. 474.

17 Daniel Callahan, 'When self-determination runs amok', p. 55.

18 Eric J. Cassell, *The Nature of Suffering* (New York: Oxford University Press, 1991), pp. 30–47.

19 For a brief treatment of the meaning and transformation of suffering, see *Care of the Dying: A Catholic Perspective* (St Louis: Catholic Health Association, 1993), pp. 42–5.

20 On the biblical witness of mercy, see E. R. Achtemeier, 'Mercy, merciful; compassion; pity' in *The Interpreter's Dictionary of the Bible*, vol. 3 (Nashville: Abingdon, 1962), pp. 352–4.

21 Stanley Hauerwas, *Naming the Silences: God, Medicine, and the Problem of Suffering* (Grand Rapids: Eerdmans, 1990), p. 53.

Select bibliography

Baruch A. Brody (ed.), *Suicide and Euthanasia* (Dordrecht: Kluwer, 1989).

Daniel Callahan, *The Troubled Dream of Life* (New York: Simon and Schuster, 1993).

Ian Gentles (ed.), *Euthanasia and Assisted Suicide* (Toronto: Stoddart, 1995).

Richard M. Gula, *Euthanasia* (New York: Paulist Press, 1994).

John F. Kilner, Arlene B. Miller and Edmund D. Pellegrino (eds), *Dignity and Dying: A Christian Appraisal* (Grand Rapids: Eerdmans, 1996).

Robert M. Veatch, *Death, Dying, and the Biological Revolution* (rev. edn; New Haven, CT: Yale University Press, 1989).

20

Ethical problems arising from new reproductive techniques

Joyce Poole

The science of therapeutics could be said to have begun in 1936 when one of a group of drugs later to be known as the sulphonamides was used successfully to treat a patient with septicaemia. The pharmaceutical company May and Baker had, among others, been working on these compounds for many years and the first to be used clinically entered medical history as 'M and B 693', the number indicating how many had been tried before one was found that would attack the bacteria without harming the patient.

Until then the treatment of infections had been palliative – nourishing food and fluid with careful nursing to encourage the body's natural defences. These were often inadequate, and bacterial infections such as pneumonia were major killers of young and old. With the advent of a drug that actually killed the infecting organism came the need for clinical trials to test its effectiveness against a range of bacteria and, importantly, for any harmful side-effects. Medicine had entered the era of experiment in which research became inseparable from its clinical application.

The next few decades brought astonishing therapeutic progress. Penicillin and other antibiotics followed the sulphonamides. Advances in anaesthesia and technology brought the 'life support system', and with it the possibility of open heart surgery and organ transplantation. Some of the new drugs and vaccines proved to have unforeseen side-effects, however, and the patient's survival time after the first organ transplants was disappointingly low. It was inevitable that such dramatic advances would bring new medical dilemmas and some general disquiet among the public. If something *could* be done, did it necessarily follow that it *should* be done?

The wider ethical issues surrounding experimentation on human subjects need to be considered before we can properly address the legitimacy of reproductive techniques involving the use of human embryos.

Research on human subjects

There is no doubt that with the appalling experiments carried out in the Nazi death camps, medical research had sunk to unplumbed depths. Horror at what went on in these camps still makes many people wary of any research on human subjects, whether or not any useful knowledge might be obtained from it.

Organ transplantation was viewed at first with some suspicion by the Christian churches who feared that doctors might be 'playing God' and interfering too much with nature. Some Catholic commentators such as Pope Pius XII were uneasy about the 'mutilation' of live kidney donors but others concluded that donation of a kidney must be seen in its totality as an act of unselfish generosity. As for 'playing God' it could be said that the whole aim of medical research and treatment, whether by drugs, vaccines or surgery, is 'interfering with nature' in that it aims to keep alive people who might otherwise die.

The rate of advance in medical and surgical therapeutics made it urgently necessary that research programmes should be regulated and codified at an international level. A basic rule of medical practice dating from the time of Hippocrates, *Primum non nocere* – above all, do no harm – could no longer be strictly applied in an age when potentially effective treatment could ultimately be assessed only by trying it out on human subjects.

Clinical trials

Trials can be divided into two main categories each with a different ethical content.

A 'therapeutic trial' involves persons who are already ill. It compares current therapy (if it exists) with new so that there is a possibility of direct benefit to the patient concerned. The test may be of a new drug, or of different treatments for breast cancer which might be treated by surgery, radiotherapy or by a combination of these. To make valid statistical conclusions large numbers of patients have to be randomly selected from those willing to take part in the trials and those who, with hindsight, fall into the most or least successful groups do so by chance.

In 'non-therapeutic' trials the research aspect is paramount and volunteers, who must be in normal good health, benefit only indirectly by adding to the sum of scientific knowledge. Most see this as a worthwhile contribution to human welfare but it is, of course, essential that they should be well-informed and that their consent is freely given.

Trials involving children

The need for free consent raises serious questions about the use of children as human subjects. Some ethicists such as the Protestant Paul Ramsey and the Catholic Bernard Häring would limit parental consent strictly to what is in the best interests of the child. Others, such as Richard McCormick, believe it might be reasonable and permissible to allow minor procedures on children for experimental purposes.

The Declaration of Helsinki (1964, revised 1975) formalized this more permissive view by stating that the basic requirement for research on a human being is 'free consent after full information has been given', or in the case of a minor, 'the consent of the legal guardian'. Other national and international ethical codes drawn up since Helsinki appreciate the need for experimentation on human subjects, including children. Risk must, of course, be minimal, and proportionate to the foreseeable benefits.

For several years I worked in a surgical research unit attached to a teaching hospital. The project was related to the problem of resuscitating children in severe surgical shock, the words in this context meaning the loss of circulating blood volume by haemorrhage, for example, or extensive burns. All the important organs such as kidneys and brain suffer from oxygen lack and the condition is seriously life-threatening. Monitoring progress involved making complicated serial measurements of the blood volume in order to establish a logical intravenous fluid replacement programme, difficult in young children because their circulatory systems are easily over-loaded. Inevitably there were occasions when, in spite of our efforts, a child reached a stage of slow but irreversible deterioration. With the parents' permission, however, we continued to measure parameters such as blood volume, bio-chemical changes and renal function until the moment of death. The techniques were moderately invasive but not painful and these severely injured children were, of course, already sedated. Although it was emotionally harrowing, we did not consider that it was unethical. Sometimes a badly burned child was revived from the initial trauma only to die miserably several weeks later from skin loss and sepsis and this could produce quite serious and painful self-doubt in those of us who were involved. Since then, new techniques in skin grafting and better control of infection have enabled such children to survive. There is no doubt that the work was valuable and that those children who died contributed significantly, with their parents, to the survival of those who followed.

Research on the foetus

The undoubted value of foetal research extended the moral debate still further and the thalidomide disaster of 1962 underlined its importance. A searchlight was suddenly shone on the possibility that an apparently safe therapeutic drug given to a woman for pregnancy sickness could damage the embryo or foetus if it happened to be at a vulnerable stage in its development.

The foetus is not just an immature child; it exists in a different and enclosed environment. It is only by examining those that become available through misadventure that foetal development and mal-development can be understood.

Pre-viable foetuses become available from natural miscarriage and from therapeutic abortion, and although there is no strict legal requirement to obtain the mother's consent to use these for research purposes it is, of course, customary to respect her wishes in the matter. It is arguable that this should be enshrined in law although there is a risk that obtaining such consent may merely add to the mother's distress.

I have attended many cases of spontaneous abortion in the early weeks and have found that it is, in fact, unusual for a mother to take any interest in the disposal of the products. It is a common occurrence, especially when the foetus is developing abnormally, and a woman with several children will be likely to take the event in her stride. Another will be very distressed at the unsuccessful outcome of a much longed-for pregnancy and there is a pastoral need for the Christian churches to devise some form of liturgy which can be used to recognize and mark her bereavement.

Research on the embryo

In view of the general public tolerance for human medical research as so far discussed it may seem odd that the work of embryologists has been singled out by so many people for special ethical attention, anxiety and opprobrium.

During the early 1970s, research was being carried out on human embryos created from ova donated by women undergoing infertility treatment and fertilized *in vitro* with donated sperm. Except in the specialist medical journals, the pioneering work of Steptoe, Edwards and Purdy in England went largely unnoticed until in 1978 their work culminated in successful In Vitro Fertilization (IVF) and the birth of the first test-tube baby.[1]

The world was astounded. It was widely reported that the Patriarch of Venice, later that year to become Pope John Paul I, expressed delight at the news. The promise of new hope for infertile couples was greeted enthusiastically by other Churches' leaders and by the public at large.

The Catholic position has hardened, however, since then, and it now stands alone among other mainstream religious groups in condemning IVF outright on the grounds that to separate the marital act from the begetting of a child is an unlawful violation of a divinely established single act of procreation. This rules out IVF even in the 'simple case' of fertilizing a single ovum with the father's sperm and implanting it immediately in the mother's womb. The Catholic objection can be logically related, of course, to an extreme interpretation of the teaching of *Humanae Vitae* ten years earlier, forbidding the separation of conception from the act of coitus.

In the UK, the Abortion Act of 1967 had already provoked intense debate among theologians, philosophers and scientists regarding the moral absolute propounded by the magisterium of the Catholic Church that from the moment of conception a fertilized ovum has the rights of a human person. The development of IVF, which had of necessity been preceded by embryo experiment and disposal, only added fuel to a fire that was already raging.

Historically, most religious scholars of the mainstream Christian, Islamic and Judaic schools have subscribed to the philosophic tradition which relates animation or 'ensoulment' of the embryo–foetus to its morphological development. The Arab scholars of the ninth and tenth centuries reinforced what was known of the writings of Aristotle and the Greeks and the physician-philosopher Avicenna stated the matter simply – 'a soul comes into existence when a body suitable for it comes into existence'. Rabbinic teaching varied but the consensus leaned towards according increasing status to the foetus after the third month, when it had become recognizably human.[2]

The dualist theories of Plato identified 'soul' as the essential immaterial part of a human being, independent of, and only temporarily united with its body. In later Christian understanding of the soul, the body came to be seen almost as an encumbrance. The concept persists in the teaching and language of most religions so that it is not surprising that the idea of a soul 'entering' the foetus at a particular moment or ascending from the body at death is common to so many cultures.

Aristotle rejected Platonic dualism and it was the moral reasoning wrought by St Thomas Aquinas out of Aristotle that Catholic teaching finally endorsed. The latter's theory of *hylomorphism* – the essential coexistence of matter and form – led Aquinas to distinguish between the unanimated and animated foetus.[3] In the natural way of generation, he held, the progression is from the imperfect to the perfect; hence in the generation of man comes first a living thing, then the animal, and finally man. St Augustine had earlier drawn a distinction between the formed foetus already endowed with an immortal soul and a 'tissue' or living entity on the way to becoming a human person, and while the Church strenuously condemned abortion, the secular and canonical penalties were graded according to the development of the foetus.

Steptoe and Edwards reported that they were overawed at the sight of the cleaving embryo they had helped to create in a dish. For the first time it had been possible to observe from hour to hour the progressive stages of fertilization, not a 'moment' but a complex process taking 48 hours or more. They and their colleagues regarded their work as revealing the art and plan of a grand designer but did not consider that they were experimenting upon actual children.[4]

The rapid and indeed alarming pace of development after 1978 led to the establishment in the UK of a Departmental Committee of Enquiry into Human Fertilisation and Embryology chaired by the Oxford philosopher Lady Warnock and published in 1984. Most of the recommendations of that report were adopted by the British Parliament in the Human Fertilisation and Embryology Act of 1990.

In the presenting letter to the report which bears her name, Mary Warnock observed that the issues raised by the enquiry reflect fundamental moral and often religious questions which have taxed philosophers down the ages and which the report does not attempt to answer. It concentrated instead on practical recommendations including the establishment of a statutory body which would regulate and license national infertility services and experimentation upon human embryos. However, much public and theological debate since then has centred on the status of the human embryo during its first fourteen days, as envisaged by Warnock. The report itself is reserved over status, holding that the answers to questions of when human life or personhood begins are complex amalgams of factual and moral judgements.[5]

It accepts that once the process of fertilization has begun there is no particular stage that is more important than another but selects a limit of fourteen days for experiment because of the appearance at this time of the first recognizable feature of the embryo proper – the 'primitive streak'. It may be added that it is around the fourteenth day that, in nature, so many fertilized but unimplanted embryos are lost in the ensuing menstrual period, or, conversely, that a woman will begin to suspect that she has conceived.

There was naturally some disagreement among members of the Warnock committee on its recommendations. Three members registered dissent based on their conclusion first, that special status must be accorded to the human embryo because of its *potential* to develop to a stage at which everyone would recognize it as a human person, and second, with regard to experimentation, that it is wrong to create something that has this potential and then to destroy it.

The status of the embryo in recent history

Until 1827 when the developing ovum was first seen and recognized it was believed that the whole genetic inheritance of the offspring was contained in the male seed. Early microscopists had imagined that they saw a tiny 'homunculus' in the head of the spermatozoon. The maternal contribution was thought to be only that of providing the raw materials and environment necessary for the development of her husband's offspring. Thus Sarai, Abraham's wife, who had borne him no children, could say to her husband 'go in to my maid Hagar; it may be that *I* shall have children by her' (Gen 16:1–3).

There can be little doubt that ignorance of the human ovum and its genetic importance has contributed to the inferior status of women throughout history. Certainly it was not until after the discovery of the ovum that the equal and complementary roles of the male and female gametes were understood for the first time and the idea of a 'moment of fertilization' arose. The philosophic notion of gradual animation held since the time of the early Greeks had, however, provided a much-needed working hypothesis that aided moral judgement in the face of conflicting human claims and is still, in many ways, closely in accord with modern scientific insight.

Throughout recorded history women have sought means to end unwanted pregnancies, with or without the help of semi-skilled practitioners. Ancient pharmacological texts are full of recipes for abortifacient potions, some of them as lethal to the mother as to the foetus. With advancing medical knowledge in the nineteenth century safer and more certain methods became available. The consequent rise in the practice alarmed Pope Pius IX who in his bull *Apostolicae Sedis* in 1869 removed from the code of Canon Law the distinction between the 'ensouled' and 'unensouled' foetus. Excommunication was now pronounced on all who procured abortion *without regard* to the gestational age of the foetus, formed, unformed, animate or inanimate. Human status was to be accorded from the moment of fertilization.[6]

Without actually claiming that there *is* a human person from the moment of conception Catholic teaching holds that in the absence of proof one way or the other the fertilized ovum must be treated as *though it were* a person. In its *Declaration on Abortion* in 1974 (para. 1471) the Sacred

Congregation for the Doctrine of the Faith went further: 'it is not for the biological sciences to pass a definitive judgment on questions which are properly moral or philosophical, such as that of the moment when the human person first exists. . . . He who will be a human being is already a human being . . . neither divine law nor human reason admit the right of directly killing a human person.' In 1987 *Donum Vitae* (SCDF, 1987; para. 13) claimed 'the conclusions of science provide a valuable indication for discerning by the use of reason a personal presence from the moment of conception'.[7]

These teachings have been reinforced by Pope John Paul II in his sermons, speeches, and, of course, in encyclicals such as *Veritatis Splendor* in 1993 and in his 'Letter to the World' *Evangelium Vitae* in 1995. Both of these claim that the moral truth on this matter is clear and that the hierarchical magisterium has the authority to proclaim it, this truth being based solidly on the authority of revelation and tradition. It might reasonably be asked, however, if a specific Christian ethic that can be substantiated only by appealing to such authority is consistent with the basic rationalism that traditionally informs Catholic moral theology.[8] Many thoughtful and well-informed people of undoubted integrity are unable to accept the early embryo as a human person. Nor is the Catholic insistence on instant human status shared by other Christian denominations or by other religions who in the main do not oppose either responsible research on embryos or IVF.

Newman considered that it was not reasonable to try to discern *scientific* truths from moral and scriptural communications designed for religious purposes. Nor, of course, can the philosophical question of *person* or *personal presence* be gleaned from scientific evidence alone. Modern scientific insights may, however, require additional moral arguments over and above appeals to historical tradition.

The early embryo

The period we are concerned with here is the first fourteen days, as this is the time allowed in law in some countries for observation and manipulation. It is upon the philosophic and moral interpretation of this period of development that the ethical case for or against the new reproductive techniques basically depends.

A few words first about terminology. The word 'embryo' is used from fertilization until the end of the eighth week of its development. This is the period of basic formation of the primitive organs and it is at about the eighth week that the embryo becomes recognizably human. From the eighth week onwards the process is one of development and growth and it is referred to from now until birth as the 'foetus'.

Until embryo experimentation became a reality this stage was referred to in the textbooks as the 'pre-embryonic period' because, until the cleaving cells have differentiated into those that will form the embryo proper from those that will form the placenta and membranes, there is, strictly speaking, no embryo. Many workers in the field have since regretted that the word 'embryo' was used, first because of its inaccuracy and second, because of the emotional overtones attached to the word. Unfortunately there is no single word to describe this early period, each stage having a separate name. 'Gamete' is used for either ovum or sperm. The 'zygote' is the fertilized ovum prior to division, then 'two-cell', 'four-cell', 'eight-cell stages' and so forth, until the ball of cells resembles a tiny blackberry – the 'morula'. Further cell division and the beginning of differentiation continue, again with each stage having a separate name. If embryos are to be stored by freezing it is usually done at the four-cell stage.

Embryo experimentation, culminating in IVF, so caught the public interest and imagination, however, that a single word had to be selected for the whole period, and 'embryo' was, perhaps unfortunately, decided upon for the sake of simplicity. 'Conceptus' would have covered all the stages but lacked semantic appeal.

The process of fertilization of the ovum, from penetration of its cell membrane by the sperm until the formation of the human cell nucleus, takes about 48 hours. In the course of maturation in testis or ovary the sperm and ova have undergone the particular type of cell division called meiosis whereby they halve the number of their chromosomes from 46 to 23 after random exchange of their genetic material. By this mechanism the combination of genes carried by each gamete is different from the next.

After penetration of the ovum, the pro-nuclei from sperm and ovum must merge and their chromosomes align in pairs before the pattern of the new human cell nucleus is established. Evidence gleaned from recent research into infertility and recurrent miscarriage suggest this process may go wrong as often as three times out of four, resulting in a conceptus that is incapable of developing into a human being; a defective female nucleus, for example, may lead to the formation of what is known as a 'hydatidiform mole', a condition known from antiquity in which all 46 chromosomes have been derived from the male. Ova which are, occasionally, fertilized by more than one spermatozoon are not viable, nor are those that have more or fewer than 23 chromosome pairs.

If merging of the pronuclei is successfully accomplished, the resulting zygote divides rapidly, the first three divisions producing eight identical daughter cells which are 'totipotent', that is, they each have the ability, given the right conditions, to produce an identical embryo. It is at this stage in the IVF process that a sample cell may be removed to examine its genetic pattern and identify a single-gene defect such as Huntington's disease. This is at the cutting edge of advance in IVF technology but it seems that removal of a single cell for diagnostic purposes does not affect further development and that an embryo 'screened' in this way can be safely implanted in the uterus.

Twinning, if it arises from a single ovum, is observed most frequently between five and eight days after fertilization, while the cells are dividing rapidly but not yet differentiated. This phenomenon raises immediate questions about a 'personal presence' from the time of fertilization. Some submissions to the Warnock enquiry suggested that the potential to form monovular twins might be determined at fertilization and that two or more ensouled 'persons' might have been present, so to speak, in the mind of God. No genetic determinant has been demonstrated, however; twinning can be induced artificially, and it appears almost certainly to be caused by factors external to the conceptus itself.

Division continues rapidly with the cells becoming progressively smaller. By fourteen days the cells are visibly differentiating into those that will form the embryo – the 'primitive streak' – and those that will form the membranes and placenta.[9]

Twinning occasionally takes place as late as the fourteenth day, when two primitive streaks may appear. Incomplete separation at this stage is the cause of conjoined ('Siamese') twins in which case the number of individual 'persons' would be reckoned on the number of heads. This would accord with the views of many twentieth-century theologians – Karl Rahner and Bernard Häring among them – who have suggested that the presence of a primitive cerebral cortex should have at least some bearing on the requirements for personhood.

In the early eighteenth century, St Alphonsus Liguori, patron saint of moral theology, regarded it as *certain* that the foetus is not ensouled before it is formed, and, in 1713 the Holy Office of the Catholic Church actually issued a decree – which still applies – forbidding the baptism of a foetus before human form can be discerned. If, as the Catholic Church now maintains, science provides a valuable indication for discerning by the use of reason a personal presence from the moment of conception, questions arise not only with regard to twins but about why so many embryos should simply fail to develop or implant, or why another should develop into a tumour or a foetus so abnormally formed that no personal activity will be possible.

If the ascription of an individual soul to the early embryo leads to insoluble difficulties, then perhaps the ascription needs to be reconsidered.[10] Much of the discussion of the time of 'ensoulment' of the embryo has, in fact, a disconcertingly medieval ring, often sitting oddly with the detailed science that is called in aid. A sounder basis for scientifically informed debate would perhaps be a concept of ensoulment that regarded the soul not as a separate entity 'infused' at a moment in time, but rather, in more hylomorphic and Aristotelian terms, as the set of capabilities of a living organism; understood thus, the soul is not a separate entity but the measure of the development of the living body through which we become present to the world.

Potential

Those members of the Warnock committee who based their dissent on the *potential* of the embryo to develop into a human person were on much firmer ground than those who look to the evidence of science to support their argument for actual personhood. Although in nature relatively few fertilized ova develop into persons it is beyond dispute that all persons started life as fertilized ova. The only real question is whether the argument from potential will bear the weight that is put upon it.

Any answer to such a question has important implications for ethical practice. Can it support, for example a *right to life* for an early embryo or even a *right to respect*? Before there can be a person there must be an *individual* and there can be no individual before the conceptus has passed the stage when it might still divide into two or more embryos. It is at this point that the law dictates that experimentation must stop. If only *persons* have rights then it follows that the embryo *in vitro* has no rights. This does not, however, absolve us from our human duty to accord it respect. This duty derives not from rights possessed by the embryo by virtue of what it is, but something we owe to it through our own primary relationship with other members of the species; there is a danger that an exaggerated language of rights could eclipse this sense of duty.

Respect demands the observance of high ethical standards in laboratories and infertility clinics; it would clearly exclude, for example, the production of embryos for commercial purposes.

A duty to preserve *life* on the other hand would outlaw all forms of IVF on account of the experimental work that underpins it. This objection on the grounds of potential is logical even if it is not universally shared. Against such an objection it could, for instance, be argued that there are few other areas of life where potential is equated with actuality. The acorn cannot be said to *be* the oak-tree it may eventually become and in nature few acorns become trees just as few early embryos develop into human persons. This is more than a philosophical argument; an early miscarriage does not present a woman with the same degree of loss as a still-birth or a neo-natal death.

An absolute duty to preserve life is not, furthermore, one which is recognized in medicine or society generally. Doctors are not obliged to use all possible means to keep a patient alive when it is considered that the expected benefit would not be proportionate. A patient with advanced malignant disease, for example, is unlikely to be offered or to want renal dialysis even if it might confer a few more weeks of life. A patient beyond hope of benefit may well consent or volunteer to take part in a trial of a potentially toxic therapeutic drug for the sake of a medical advance that might benefit others.

It is difficult to keep an embryo alive even for the fourteen days allowed by Warnock and it has no potential unless it is implanted into a uterus. Spare embryos left over from IVF have themselves no future, therefore, but knowledge gained from observing and experimenting upon these during their brief span greatly improves the prospects for others. It could even be said that to use them in this way, with the consent of the parents, enhances the respect which is due to them as members of the human species.

Very strong feelings are aroused on the 'right to life' issue and must be recognized, but it cannot be denied that most members of the public do not see the early embryo in a test-tube as a human person with rights, although most would accord it respect.

Some who would not fundamentally prohibit embryo research would, out of respect for the embryo's human, if not personal, status, confine it to 'spare' embryos left over from IVF, and this is a cogent argument. Against it, however, it could be said that those who hold this view have already conceded that the early embryo does not yet have the status of a person, and that embryos created for experiment rather than implantation do not have the potential to acquire it. The success rate of IVF in the best clinics is no more than one in four and one of the commonest causes of childlessness is spontaneous abortion in the early weeks. It may well be, therefore, that reluctance to fertilize ova for the express purpose of experimentation, though arising from a desire to avoid the wastage of embryos, nevertheless puts off the day when so much natural wastage can be avoided.[11]

The basic ethical issue

Discussion on the ethics of reproductive technology can range from the morality of obtaining a sperm sample by masturbation to the morality of paying a woman to bear one's husband's baby. However, the question that lies at the heart of all such ethical debate concerns the moral status of any potential human being at any given point in its journey from unfertilized gametes to new-born child.

IVF has the central intention of overcoming the common problem of female infertility caused by blocked uterine tubes. The ovum is that of the natural mother and the sperm is that of the natural father so that the child is truly that of the parents in both the genetic and social sense. It thus presents a paradigm case against which ethical questions can be weighed.

The complex questions surrounding freezing, storing, selecting are secondary and beyond the scope of this single chapter. So also are the moral, social and biological problems raised by the possibility of donated gametes – male or female – and by surrogate motherhood.

Reproductive technology is an emotive subject. Ignorance and fear can lead to imagined 'designer babies' growing in bottles or monstrous hybrids produced from human and animal gametes. At the same time it cannot be denied that the possibilities and ramifications are serious matters and laws and professional codes must keep pace with new developments. All practitioners engaged in this work must demonstrate that they are worthy of the trust the profession has traditionally enjoyed.

In IVF we are not 'making babies' but, having ourselves been made in the image of an inventive, imaginative and compassionate God, we are allowed the dignity of co-operating with Him in the creation of a new human being. It is essential, therefore, that all those engaged in reproductive technology, doctors, lawyers, policy-makers or parents must place at the centre of the debate the interests and identity of the child that is to be born.

Notes

1 G. R. Dunstan, 'In-vitro fertilization: the ethics', *Human Reproduction* (1986), pp. 41–4.
2 G. R. Dunstan, 'The human embryo in the Western tradition', ch. 5 in G. R. Dunstan and Mary J. Seller (eds), *The Status of the Human Embryo* (London: King Edward's Hospital Fund, 1988).
3 Michael J. Coughlan, 'Mediation and St Thomas Aquinas', ch. 2 in *The Vatican, the Law and the Human Embryo* (London: Macmillan, 1990).
4 Robert Edwards, 'Ethics and embryology: the case for experimentation', ch. 3 in Anthony Dyson and John Harris (eds), *Experiments on Embryos* (London: Routledge, 1990).
5 John Mahoney, 'Warnock: a Catholic comment', *The Month* (September 1984).
6 Joyce Poole, 'The status of the embryo', ch. 6 in *The Harm We Do: A Catholic Doctor Confronts Church, Moral and Medical Teaching* (Mystic, CT: Twenty-Third Publications, 1993).
7 Some Catholics find it difficult to reconcile the passage quoted above from the Declaration with others found in the documents of the Second Vatican Council, such as 'all the faithful, clerical and lay have a just freedom of enquiry, of thought, and of humble and courageous expression in those matters in which they enjoy competence' (*GS*, 62).

8 G. J. Hughes, 'The authority of Christian tradition', ch. 1 in *Authority in Morals* (Heythrop Monograph; London, 1978).
9 Joyce Poole, 'The status of the embryo', ch. 6 in *The Harm We Do*.
10 Michael Coughlan, 'Souls and embryos', ch. 5 in *The Vatican, the Law and the Human Embryo*, p. 71.
11 G. R. Dunstan. 'In-vitro fertilization: the ethics'.

Select bibliography

Michael J. Coughlan, *The Vatican, the Law and the Human Embryo* (London: Macmillan, 1990).

G. R. Dunstan and Mary J. Seller (eds), *The Status of the Human Embryo* (London: King Edward's Hospital Fund, 1988).

Anthony Dyson and John Harris (eds), *Experiments on Embryos* (London: Routledge, 1990).

R. A. McCormick, *Corrective Vision: Explorations in Moral Theology* (Kansas City, MO: Sheed and Ward, 1994).

John Mahoney, *Bioethics and Belief* (London: Sheed and Ward, 1984).

Joyce Poole, *The Harm We Do: A Catholic Doctor Confronts Church, Moral and Medical Teaching* (Mystic, CT: Twenty-Third Publications, 1993).

21

Organ transplantation

David F. Kelly

Among topics in medical ethics organ transplantation offers an opportunity to examine areas both of methodological and of current practical interest. To get at these areas this chapter will begin with a brief look at the theological context from which Christian (mainly Roman Catholic) medical ethics has analysed transplantation. Then we will turn to an historical overview of the actual ethical judgements Catholic medical ethics has made about it. Finally we will look at some of the ethical issues of current interest.

The relationship of the Christian religion and the practice of bodily healing (medicine) has a long history. The most developed and most influential of the Christian traditions on medical ethical issues has been the Roman Catholic. Catholic scholars and pastors have developed over the centuries a complex system of principles and judgements.[1] Indeed, until the middle of the twentieth century Catholic moral theologians were virtually alone among Christian scholars in investigating the ethical issues connected with the art of healing.

This chapter will thus stress the approach taken by the Catholic tradition. However, except in certain limited areas, the Catholic position is not at variance with other Christian traditions, and all Christian churches are able to draw on the same religious themes and symbols. The contemporary Christian approach to transplantations is largely an ecumenical one.

Theological context

The central reality of Christianity is creation and salvation by a God who creates us in dignity and 'loves us to death'. That is what the cross and resurrection of Jesus means. We are of worth. That worth comes ultimately from God, which is the best foundation any dignity can have. Christian medical ethics, at least at its best, is rooted in this knowledge. And this means the worth of the whole person, not just of our 'souls', as we so often think.

It also means that we are called to be co-creators, or at least co-agents with God. We are thus *both* creatures, who owe our totality to God, *and* co-creators, who receive from God the gift and the task to share in God's creating and saving activity. This complex notion is of great importance in medical ethics. God wants us to do some things, but not all things. Our lives and our bodies are our own, but they are not totally our own.

These fundamental themes of human dignity[2] set the context for moral decision-making in the area of health care. The human person is created in God's image and is chosen and ordered to life with God through the grace of Jesus given in the Spirit. Catholic theology insists, of course, that this creation, choosing, and ordering is not primarily an individual event. Humans are social beings. Christianity, like Judaism, proposes a people of God, not just a loose collection of private individuals. This increases the dignity and supports the rights of each individual person as it also insists that each person find meaning in the interconnectedness and interdependence of human society.

Organ transplantation in Catholic medical ethics

The early debate and Bert Cunningham

The ethical issue of organ transplantation arose largely in the 1940s and 1950s. The first specific procedures to pose the question were transplantations of corneas and of ovarian tissue. By the late 1950s the procedure at issue was kidney transplantation. Blood transfusions and skin grafts, which had been the procedures common prior to this period, were not generally seen to pose a problem.

The moral issue as it arose in the Roman Catholic tradition was focused around the problem of mutilation. Could a person 'mutilate' him or herself for any purpose? The principle most commonly applied was the principle of totality. A part of the human body could be sacrificed for the good of the whole body. The principle of totality was, by the mid-twentieth century, an integral part of the moral methodology which had come to

David F. Kelly

the fore in Catholic medical ethics. For a number of reasons this methodology emphasized primarily the physical and individual aspects of right and wrong behaviour. This emphasis has been criticized in recent years, but it was then the central method for doing Catholic medical ethics.

In this methodological context the principle of totality had come to be limited to the physical good of the individual physical body. Thus a gangrenous leg might rightly be amputated. Similarly, 'indirect' sterilizations were permitted if an organ of generation was diseased so that its removal was necessary to save the physical organism. But one could not castrate himself in order to avoid temptations against chastity. Nor could one sterilize himself or herself in order to avoid children. Blood transfusions and skin grafts were usually considered non-mutilating. But if the principle of totality were to be applied in its physicalist and individualist limitation to transplantation from living donors of cornea or kidney, these procedures might well be forbidden. And indeed many Catholic moral theologians did forbid all 'mutilating' transplants. For a period of time Catholic moral theology was more apt to forbid organ transplantation than to permit it.

At this point a doctoral student at the Catholic University of America submitted as his dissertation a treatise entitled 'The morality of organic transplantation'.[3] This set off a controversy within Catholic medical ethics.

Cunningham's central thesis is that mutilations for the purpose of organ transplantation are indeed licit, and that they are licit according to the principle of totality, if this principle is extended to include not only the individual physical body from which the organ is removed but the entire Mystical Body of Christ. In this way he broke through the individualist limitations associated with the traditional principle of totality and gave it an explicitly social meaning.

Cunningham notes the negative judgement of some Catholic moralists who insisted that mutilations are allowed only if done for the physical good of the individual body, thus forbidding all transplant surgery.[4] But he disagrees, describing the scriptural and theological bases for the unity of humankind as a race created by God and as a Body redeemed by Christ. This unity serves in turn as a basis for arguing that a person may licitly mutilate him or herself for the good of a neighbour. He insists on the precept of charity and discusses how far it ought to extend.[5]

Cunningham gives examples of procedures his thesis would permit, and some of them are extreme. He does recognize that limits must be imposed by the principle of proportionality. Yet he permits operations which at the very least should cause more concern than they seem to do for Cunningham. For example, he allows for the transplantation of a cornea from a living donor, resulting in considerable loss of vision, and even the corneal transplant of one eye from a one-eyed donor, resulting in total blindness. In this last case, the donor is presented as a convict sentenced to life in prison, the eye thus 'not needed by anyone'![6] There is a clear lack of respect here for the individual person that arises from the thesis that individuals are ordinated to society as parts to the whole. But his recognition that moral method in medical ethics ought not be limited to the good of the individual or to the purely physical enabled him to allow for the possibility that organ transplantation might be morally right.

Reactions to Cunningham

Cunningham's thesis was hotly debated by Catholic moralists during the 1940s and 1950s. Many European moralists continued to oppose all organic transplantation. Most American moralists, and some Europeans, accepted Cunningham's conclusion that organ transplantation was licit, though many of them expressed hesitation at the lack of caution or proportion found in some of Cunningham's judgements. They had a moral sense, I believe, which tended toward allowing operations which seemed to do little if any harm to the donor and to be of great benefit to the recipient. Since the magisterium (the Catholic pope and bishops) had not made any pronouncements directly to the contrary, these Catholic moralists were willing to permit the procedure. They disagreed, however, about whether or not the principle of totality could be applied. Some argued that that principle must continue to apply only to the individual body; these justified organ transplantations on the basis of Christian charity. Others argued that, with proper safeguards, the principle of totality might be extended in a way similar to Cunningham's proposal. And some opposition to transplantation continued.

But by 1960 or so most Catholic moralists accepted the moral rightness of at least some organ transplants, and Catholics have now joined others in seeing in this procedure not only a morally correct act but indeed a laudable one to be supported by public policy. The 1994 'Ethical and religious directives for Catholic health care services'[7] permits living donor transplantation.

Today's questions about transplantation

To my knowledge no Christian theologian is today arguing for a general rejection of organ transplantation. But this does not mean that all the moral problems have been solved or that there is complete agreement about how to answer them.

David F. Kelly

Issues in living donor transplants

There is still some hesitation among Christian ethicists about some of the issues involved in living donor transplants. Many would be more cautious than Cunningham was and would be slow to approve his interpretation of the principle of totality which implies that the human person is merely one part of a wider whole. Catholic theology insists that the human person is both individual and social. Organ transplantation is morally right, but this is because it contributes to and is in keeping with the created and saved dignity of the donor as well as that of the recipient.

In this context, Catholic theologian Richard McCormick proposed an understanding of the principle of totality which differed from Cunningham's.[8] In his 1975 article McCormick accepts Cunningham's basic idea that the principle of totality ought to be changed so that it can be applied to organ transplantation. But McCormick wants to extend the notion of totality not so much in the direction of the whole society as in the direction of the total personal good of the donor. Organ transplantations are justified by the principle of totality since the donor may rightly subordinate his or her own physical perfection to his or her spiritual and personal perfection. The physical injury is indeed for the total good of the donor, a good which is sought by this gift of love to another. McCormick is quick to add, however, that this does not mean than any and all organ donations are morally right. There must be a correct proportionality of benefits and harms if donation is to be morally right.

Belgian Catholic theologian Louis Janssens takes a similar approach.[9] Though he does not explicitly mention the principle of totality, it is clear that he would refuse to apply it as Cunningham does, subordinating the individual to a wider corporate whole. 'The human body and its parts', says Janssens, 'are not merchandise.'[10] Living donor transplants are morally justifiable only under certain conditions. First, the recipient must be truly needy and there must be no other equally helpful treatment available. Second, the donor must give his or her free and informed consent. Third, certain objective criteria must also be met: organ donations which jeopardize the life of the donor are forbidden; any transplantation which would limit a person's consciousness would be immoral; organ donations are illicit which 'would render the donor incapable of playing his or her role in social collaboration'.[11] In all of this there is a sense of balance in the relationship of individual and society.

American Catholic moralists Benedict Ashley and Kevin O'Rourke elaborate on a distinction between anatomical integrity and functional integrity.[12] The former 'refers to the material or physical integrity of the human body' and the latter 'to the systematic efficiency of the human body'.[13] Whereas organ donations which harm anatomical integrity may be permitted, those which would cause a loss of functional integrity are forbidden. In addition, potential benefits must be weighed against actual risks. An honest assessment of the likely outcome must be a part of the decision process.

American Protestant ethicist James Nelson also insists that caution must reign.[14] He suggests an analogy to the just war theory, which he applies both to living donor and to cadaver transplants. Just as the resort to violence is sometimes justifiable, but not automatically right, so organ transplants, while right in some circumstances, require justification. There must be no better alternative (the requirement of last resort). The physician must have as his or her primary intent that of helping the patient, not that of advancing medical knowledge or personal prestige (the requirement of just intent). Informed consent is essential (the requirement of a just and open declaration of war). The rights of the donor, including the dying donor, and the recipient must be safeguarded (the requirement of noncombatant immunity). Transplant physicians should be honest with donors and recipients (the requirement of right attitudes in the conduct of war); they must try to avoid unrealistic expectations derived from the media. The good effects of the procedure and of the practice in general must outweigh the bad effects (the requirement of due proportion); this includes the issue of resource allocation. Finally, the end must be just and it must be achievable (the requirement of a just end). The analogy to the just war theory may appear bizarre, but it has the advantage of calling needed attention to the many reasons for hesitation in transplantation surgery.

The question of allocation and cost

The principal problems today do not usually concern living donors since most transplanted organs are taken from cadavers. The problem is much more apt to revolve around questions of cost and of distribution of scarce resources. This is a very difficult question. It is clear that society should spend its resources justly. We ought not spend so much on procedures that benefit only a few that we neglect doing what would benefit many. This conclusion can be drawn easily from the theological resources Christianity provides. Human beings, as created and saved by God in Christ, are not isolated individuals but are called to participate with one another in working for the common good.

But it would be arrogant for moralists to claim that easy specific conclusions can be drawn from these obvious premises. We cannot reject expensive procedures simply on the basis of cost. It may theoretically be true that the money spent on complex transplant surgery could help large numbers of the poor or the starving, but the complexities of today's global economy make such judgements questionable at the practical level. How can we know that it is expensive organ transplantations, and not educational costs, military costs, entertainment costs, church costs, or other allocations of society's resources, which deprive the poor of needed care and support? Yet the complexity of the question cannot cause us to give in to the temptation to ignore it. We do need to concern ourselves with questions like these. If we believe that humans are one in God's creative love, then we need to be concerned about all humans, not just about the ones in our own hospitals or offices.

Though there is no clear 'Christian answer' concerning specific policies in this area, Christianity does proceed from a different 'story' or 'myth' to that of much of American political and medical history as well as much of philosophical biomedical ethics. These tend to emphasize individual human rights, and often underemphasize the social networks within which people live. The Christian tradition, especially in its Roman Catholic forms, insists that individual rights be placed within the context of the common good. We simply do not have a right to everything we want; nor do we have a right to everything we need when others' needs are greater.

Though this religious ethos is not validly the basis for quick and easy answers to complex questions, it can help us approach a solution to the allocation problem. The American health care system, for example, needs major reform in the direction of justice. No perfect system is apparent, but other nations do better at this than the United States. In those nations some procedures which benefit only a few are given lower priority than treatments which benefit many. Organ transplants often fit this category.

Even as nations await the development of better systems of health care, some conclusions can be drawn which apply now. We ought to be able to argue with at least some strength that those medical procedures which are very expensive and which are at best of questionable benefit *to those who get them* should not get public funding, except as limited experimental research. We *also* ought to be able to argue with some strength that those medical procedures which are very expensive and which are at best of questionable benefit *to the specific population* at which they are aimed, even though they may help a few persons within that population, should not get public funding, except as limited experimental research. Now this seems quite reasonable, and I think it is, but when these principles are applied to specific kinds of organ transplants, the conclusions they lead to are not easily accepted.

The issue of artificial heart implants, either permanent or as bridge devices to human heart transplants, illustrates this problem. Theoretically the artificial heart would seem to be an ethical as well as a technological advance over cadaver transplants. A *permanent* artificial heart would eliminate that portion of organ scarcity which results from too few donors.

It is quite likely that the costs would decrease if more hearts were made. The problem of rejection, and thus the cost of immunosuppressant drugs, would seem to be less than with human or animal hearts. It might be easier to 'fix' and to 'do maintenance on' a human-made heart than an organic one.

But there has thus far been little success with the permanent artificial heart. Recipients are tied to machines which inhibit mobility. They suffer from consistent periods of significant incapacity. And the devices fail in a relatively short time.

In the absence of any real hope of success, experimentation with permanent artificial hearts should be strictly limited. If and when it is determined that they are not advancing vital knowledge, no more should be attempted even if patients (experimental subjects) consent to them.

But what about the *temporary* artificial heart? Unfortunately, major ethical problems arise even with the temporary artificial heart. Since this is not a substitute for, but an addition to organic heart transplantation, costs are increased. And the scarcity of organs is not alleviated; it is rather increased. Thus, as long as there are too few cadaver hearts for those who need them, the temporary artificial hearts only add to the list of the needing without adding to the list of the donors. This would change if enough human hearts became available, but for now the procedure seems to be of no benefit to heart patients as a whole. Potential recipients without artificial hearts are passed over in favour of those with them, who would otherwise already have died. Since this is done at great cost, and since it merely shifts the outcome of who will live and who will die from one group to another within patients with end-stage heart disease, it does seem to be unethical. As in the case of permanent implants, temporary implants are ethically right when performed on a restricted experimental basis in order to gain knowledge which might lead to a successful permanent device. Some recent advances support this claim.

Organ procurement and determination of death

The question of when death can be said to occur is not in itself an issue of organ transplantation. Indeed, it is morally and medically better to distinguish, even to separate the two questions as much as possible. Yet it is a fact that one of the problems connected with cadaver organ procurement is that of determining that the donor has died. In addition, there are questions arising today about anencephalic newborn infants as potential organ donors, and these concern the problem of determining the moment of death.

David F. Kelly

Organ procurement

Organ procurement involves a number of policy questions apart from the determination of death. Principal among these is the question of who controls the body of a deceased person and thus decides whether or not organs can be taken. There are a number of different policy options, and governments have adopted one or another of them. Some argue that cadaver organs ought to be considered the property of the state, or at least that the common good should require by law that they be available for transplantation regardless of the wishes of the person before death or of the relatives after death. Opposing this is the position that organs be taken only if relatives spontaneously volunteer them or if the now-dead person has made his or her wishes to donate clear during life. In between these two positions is the policy generally known as required request, a policy now adopted by a number of states in the United States. This policy requires by law that the relatives of a dying or newly dead person be asked about possible organ donation if it is medically possible. If the deceased carried an organ donor card or otherwise made his or her wish to donate known this wish is seen as valid consent.

There is not any clear Christian position on this issue. On the one hand is the importance of giving as a free gift and the freedom of choice that this entails. On the other hand, Catholic social ethics recognizes that there are times when individual choice must cede to the common good. Perhaps it is best here to support a moderate policy such as required request, which includes both the freedom necessary for giving and the valid needs of the common good.

Determination of death

Determining death has been a problem for much of human history. Today it arises in the context of medical technology which can maintain even in corpses the outward appearance of biological life. Thus it became necessary in some cases to develop criteria for determining that death had occurred, and these became known as 'brain-death' criteria. Two proposals were made. Some argued that since all real human activity requires the abilities of the 'higher brain' or cortex, the death of the cortex should be sufficient to declare that a person has died.

But the majority have thus far rejected this argument. To accept it would not only have changed the way death was diagnosed but would have changed the meaning of death as well. Cortically dead patients, such as those in persistent vegetative states, can breathe spontaneously. To declare such persons dead would mean we must be willing to bury breathing bodies, or to act directly to stop the breathing prior to burial.

Thus the generally accepted consensus is that only 'whole brain death', including the death of the brain stem, is sufficient to know that a person has died. In this way no one is declared dead, by these new diagnostic criteria, who would otherwise have been thought living. This approach has been generally adopted in the United States.

It is essential to note that none of this has any direct connection with organ transplantation. The issue of determination of death ought be studied and resolved on its own. Yet there is a connection which comes when cadaver organs are needed. Since 'fresh' organs are better than 'stale' ones, a quick means of diagnosing death is desirable. And the criteria of brain death may be involved since the best organs are often those of young persons who have died with head injuries resulting in trauma to the brain and little direct injury to the rest of the body. As we have seen, in the United States the criteria used are those which determine 'total brain' death. No organs can be taken from a patient in a persistent vegetative state or from an anencephalic infant since these are considered to be alive.

There is considerable discussion about this. Some argue that we should turn to a higher brain-death standard that would permit the taking of organs from the permanently comatose. Christian theology might be used to support either position. On the one hand, it is clear that the human person is more than mere biological life, and Catholic ethics has for a long time recognized that there is no obligation to sustain life when the benefits of doing so are outweighed by the burdens of the treatment. Catholic tradition does not require that persons in persistent vegetative states be kept alive by medical means. They may, and ought, be allowed to die. Thus Catholic and general Christian opinion might change toward permitting neo-cortical determination of death. On the other hand, Christian and Catholic theology would reject the notion that the entire human person is contained in brain functioning. So far most Catholic moralists are hesitant to say that the permanently unconscious are already dead.

There is one final aspect of this problem to be addressed. It must be repeated that the issue of determining death is not as such an issue of organ transplantation, even though that has often been its context. We ought not change laws merely in order to facilitate organ procurement. In fact, it is possible that if we do so the availability of organs will be harmed, not helped. Far too many of us already fear that physicians might not care properly for us if they need our organs. To add anencephalics or other cortically-dead bodies to the list of the legally dead would change what it means to be dead. There could be a backlash that would work to the detriment of organ transplantation. This could change in the future, of course, as people become more open to the notion of cortical death. But at least for now caution should rule.

David F. Kelly

Foetal transplantation

The question of foetal organ and tissue transplants, such as the transplantation of foetal dopamine-producing cells for treatment of Parkinson's disease, raises issues additional to those we have already developed, and leads to much controversy, especially in Roman Catholic ethics. The reason, of course, is the connection to abortion. Official Catholic teaching argues that from the moment of conception the foetus must be treated as a human person and rejects all direct abortions, even those of very early embryos. Even for some who would permit early abortion for serious reasons, it seems clearly right to oppose any attempt at 'growing' human foetuses simply in order to use their organs after abortion.

Less clear, however, is transplantation from a foetus which has been aborted. On one side of this question are those who argue that this will increase the likelihood of abortion and that it means a moral identification of the physician and the recipient with the abortion. These also question the authority of the woman to consent for the foetus. On the other side are those suggesting that once the abortion has taken place and the foetus is dead, the organs and tissue may be taken as with any other cadaver. There is a general agreement rejecting any techniques used to keep the organs viable if these techniques would further endanger the life of the woman or of the foetus, as well as an insistence that any child born alive be treated like any other person.

Conclusion

Over the years Catholic medical ethics has changed its judgement about organ transplantation. It now recognizes the contribution this remarkable procedure can make to human healing. Yet risks remain. Christian medical ethics will continue to find in organ transplantation a procedure that requires ongoing vigilance.

Acknowledgements

This chapter is in part a revision and a compilation of material written by me and previously published in the following formats.

'Religious aspects of organ transplantation: Christianity' in D. R. Cook and P. J. Davis (eds), *Anesthetic Principles for Organ Transplantation* (New York: Raven Press, 1994), pp. 349–60.

'Artificial hearts: an ethical solution to the donor shortage?', *Health Progress* 68.3 (April 1987), pp. 24–6.

'Individualism and corporatism in a personalist ethic: an analysis of organ transplants' in Joseph A. Selling (ed.), *Personalist Morals: Essays in Honor of Louis Janssens* (Louvain: Louvain University Press, 1988), pp. 147–66.

'A Roman Catholic perspective on organ transplantation' in C. Don Keyes (ed.), *New Harvest: Transplanted Body Parts and the Ethical Consequences* (Clifton, NJ: Humana Press, 1991), pp. 199–211.

Notes

1 For a complete history of this development, see David F. Kelly, *The Emergence of Roman Catholic Medical Ethics in North America* (New York: Edwin Mellen Press, 1979).

2 I have developed these themes at greater length in a special publication of the National Association of Catholic Chaplains entitled *A Theological Basis for Health Care and Health Care Ethics* (New York: National Association of Catholic Chaplains, 1985).

3 Bert Cunningham, 'The morality of organ transplantation', dissertation, Catholic University of America: *Studies in Sacred Theology*, no. 86 (Washington: Catholic University of America Press, 1944).

4 Cunningham cites the late 1930s manuals of Noldin-Schmitt and Iorio, popular and influential textbooks of that time (pp. 64–70).

5 Cunningham, pp. 87–99.

6 Cunningham, p. 106.

7 'Ethical and religious directives for Catholic health care services', *Origins* 24.27 (15 December 1994), pp. 449–58.

8 Richard A. McCormick, 'Transplantation of organs: a comment on Paul Ramsey', *Theological Studies* 36 (1975), pp. 503–9.

9 Louis Janssens, 'Transplantation d'organes', *Foi et Temps* 4 (1983), pp. 308–24.

10 Janssens, p. 318, translation mine.

11 Janssens, p. 320, translation mine.

12 Benedict M. Ashley and Kevin D. O'Rourke. *Health Care Ethics: A Theological Analysis* (2nd edn; St Louis, MO: Catholic Health Association of the United States, 1982), pp. 308–11.

13 Ashley and O'Rourke, p. 310.

14 James B. Nelson and Joanne Smith Rohricht, *Human Medicine: Ethical Perspectives on Today's Medical Issues* (rev. edn; Minneapolis, MN: Augsburg, 1984), pp. 176–99.

Select bibliography

Benedict M. Ashley and Kevin D. O'Rourke, *Health Care Ethics: A Theological Analysis* (2nd edn; St Louis, MO: Catholic Health Association of the United States, 1982).
Louis Janssens, 'Transplantation d'organes', *Foi et Temps* 4 (1983), pp. 308–24.
David F. Kelly, *The Emergence of Roman Catholic Medical Ethics in North America* (New York: Edwin Mellen Press, 1979).

David F. Kelly

David F. Kelly, *A Theological Basis for Health Care and Health Care Ethics* (New York: National Association of Catholic Chaplains, 1985).

Richard A. McCormick, 'Transplantation of organs: a comment on Paul Ramsey', *Theological Studies* 36 (1975), pp. 503–9.

James B. Nelson and Joanne Smith Rohricht, *Human Medicine: Ethical Perspectives on Today's Medical Issues* (rev. edn; Minneapolis, MN: Augsburg, 1984).

Richard C. Sparks, 'Ethical issues of fetal tissue transplantation: research, procurement, and complicity with abortion', *The Annual of the Society of Christian Ethics* (Washington, DC: Georgetown University Press, 1990).

United States Catholic Conference. 'Ethical and religious directives for Catholic health care services', *Origins* 24.27 (15 December 1994), pp. 449–58.

22

Hypnosis and general anaesthesia

Aureliano Pacciolla

Translated by Bernard Hoose

Hypnosis

When experimenting with the possibility of controlling pain through hypnosis and the conscious will, J. M. Charcot observed that some nuns could tolerate hot coals in their hands but reacted violently as soon as one touched their clothes as if to lift them. An initial interpretation of this could be that *a person in a deep hypnotic trance does not accept an act which is contrary to his or her moral standards*.

Since then many researchers into hypnosis have tried to look more deeply into the possibility of modifying conscience and moral behaviour through the use of hypnosis at various levels of trance – vigilant (or superficial), medium, and deep (or somnambulist) – for the most varied motives, ranging from the most licit and legal to those which are most immoral and most legally unacceptable. Hypnosis is based on suggestion and this distorts both perception and one's appraisal of reality. These being the bases of the decisional processes, hypnosis is regarded by some as highly manipulative, in the sense that it offers the opportunity to modify human behaviour more easily than is the case with other methods and other states of consciousness. This possibility of manipulating and changing various kinds of human behaviour through hypnosis should be considered both very dangerous and very useful, depending on the purpose for which it is used: for selfish exploitation of others or for treatment aimed at psychophysical well-being. It is precisely this seeming relative ease in altering the human person that gives rise to a great number and variety of moral problems concerning hypnosis.

In this context, the first crucial question regarding *hypnosis and moral behaviour* is: Can hypnosis also modify one's conscience? Can one act against one's moral principles in a hypnotic trance? Can hallucinations during hypnotic trance and post-hypnotic conditioning alter the morality of a person in his or her principles and behaviour?

The answer seems to be negative and is confirmed by research and experimentation. Nevertheless, there is a second question, regarding *hypnosis and immoral behaviour*: how is it that, under hypnosis, some people do what they have never done before and would never do in a vigilant conscious state (a state of normal alert consciousness)? It is important to explain some episodes reported in the media: sexual violence accepted in a state of trance; suicides or acts of self-harm through post-hypnotic suggestion; and other apparently inexplicable behaviour which is in the sphere of interest of forensic psychology and moral science.

These two questions, and their respective answers, imply very serious moral problems, and the maximum clarity is important for legislators, moralists and all those who submit themselves to hypnosis for reasons of therapy, research or entertainment. The response to both of these questions should be at the basis both of specific legislation concerning this matter and of the appraisal of hypnosis as a therapeutic instrument. In both spheres – as we shall see – we have particular moral problems.

Hypnosis and moral behaviour

A research experiment – among many – to illustrate the possibility of manipulating conscience and moral behaviour through hypnosis:

It was suggested to 24 people (the subjects of the experiment) that they take a poisonous snake in their hands (a self-harming act) and throw sulphuric acid into the researcher's face (an act harmful to others). As a precaution, the snake, the researcher and the subjects were separated by a sheet of invisible glass. The subjects were divided into four groups, each composed of six people. Under hypnotic trance, all were ordered in peremptory fashion to pick up the snake.

Of the first group, entirely made up of people who were highly susceptible to hypnosis, five tried to pick up the snake and also to throw the acid. Of the second group, made up of people who were only slightly susceptible to hypnosis, all fulfilled both orders. Of the third group, composed of people in a state of vigilance, three tried to pick up the snake and five threw the acid. Of the fourth group (the control group), made up of people in a state of vigilance, who had, however, been given to understand that they could not perform such acts, three tried to pick up the snake and one threw the acid.

How should we interpret this behaviour from a moral point of view? First of all, for a serious reflection on the problems of moral behaviour, it is important to ask what J. Piaget did in his study of the evolution of moral judgement in children and how L. Kohlberg proceeded in a similar study among adolescents. Or rather, it is not enough to observe behaviour. What is decisive is to ask why the person (the subject of the experiment) has decided in favour of that form of behaviour. It is very important that it is the subjects themselves who respond regarding the motivation of their conduct.

I should add that, in the experiment referred to above,[1] there was a discussion with the subjects of the experiment, and it is interesting to note how all the subjects affirmed that they were convinced they would not have done any harm either to themselves or to others, since they were aware of the fact that it was an experimental situation conducted by responsible people. In other words, the subjects (even those who were highly susceptible to hypnosis) expected that security measures would be taken.

From what we have seen, we can come to a provisional conclusion: the conscience is never completely suppressed.

In other research it has been shown that hypnosis cannot alter a person's moral principles or scale of values. What it is important to show here is how much can and cannot be obtained through the use of hypnosis. For example, it is relatively easy to obtain psychomotor block (of movement and language) in some subjects, as often happens in exhibitions in the theatre or in TV shows. Other behavioural operations – like, for example, those that occur in psychotherapy – are much more complex and more difficult to attain; for this one needs the conscious collaboration of the subject regarding the processes of change. Hypnosis does not make criminals out of honest folk or vice versa.

But then, how is it possible that sexual abuse occurs in hypnotic trance in subjects who would never have behaved in such a manner? The most frequent examples dealt with in courts concern the spheres of sexuality and fraud.

In the past, hypnosis has been used illicitly for bellicose aims: not just for political propaganda, but also for so-called 'brainwashing' or as a substitute for 'truth serum'. It is precisely in this last mentioned case that it has been possible to verify what has just been affirmed, that the conscience is never completely suppressed. In fact, in other research, it has been possible to confirm that one can lie even under hypnosis and that there is therefore no guarantee of the authenticity and reliability of the information obtained under hypnotic trance. Therefore, hypnosis alone cannot be used in a court of law as proof of the reconstruction of facts through eye witnesses who have lost their conscious memory of what happened. In some countries, a deposition given under hypnotic trance is accepted, but account is taken of it only if the crucial details coincide with, or are supported by, other evidence. In other words, nobody can be condemned solely on the basis of a deposition given by themselves or others in a state of hypnotic trance.

The problem of forensic deontology remains open above all in determining when a judge can have recourse to a means such as hypnosis and what the criteria should be for determining its reliability. In each case, nobody can be – legally or morally – put under hypnosis without his or her consent and without the participation of a professional doctor or psychologist who is qualified in the medical and legal use of hypnosis.

Hypnosis and immoral behaviour

During hypnosis, the behaviour of hypnotists is immoral whenever they try to modify a hypnotized person beyond the objectives of psychotherapy or of the clinical sphere (research and experimentation) in which they are qualified to work. Hypnotists do not have to ask for consent for every single therapeutic process to be put into operation, but they may not go beyond the limits of the therapeutic aims.

Patients always have a right to their privacy, even if they are regarded as criminals. Without a legally valid authorization, nobody may be hypnotized to get information or a confession, or as part of a programme of rehabilitation.

The behaviour of the person hypnotized – with or without his or her consent – could be immoral (or rather, contrary to the principles of his or her own conscience) as a consequence of a particular stimulation on the part of the hypnotist. How is it possible that a person who would never rob or who has no intention of committing suicide could do so in a hypnotic trance? And how would this accord with what was said before about the personal conscience remaining unaltered in a hypnotic trance? One answer to these questions, and to many analogous ones, comes from the possibility, in hypnotic trance, of modifying one's perception and appraisal of reality. Since we decide on the basis of how we perceive and appraise reality, that is what directs behavioural decisions. If I perceive the presence of a person close to me and judge that it is my fiancée, I can decide to direct my behaviour in an affectionate and intimate way. *The alteration of the perception and appraisal of reality in hypnotic trance can even alter moral behaviour.*

From a practical point of view, that can happen with fraud and deception. In hypnotic trance one can be made to believe that a drink is harmless (with a colour and taste that are different to the real ones) and pleasing, and the subject will drink it. This mechanism is at the basis of any apparently immoral behaviour that can be performed under hypnosis, and the more the subject is open to suggestion, the more realizable will it be. It is obvious that deception and fraud are also possible outside of hypnosis, but there is a notable difference. In the state of alert consciousness (or rather, outside of hypnotic trance) the logical-rational processes are more active, and, therefore, deception and fraud are more difficult to put into effect, whilst, in hypnotic trance, and in any other state of consciousness that is characterized by inhibition of the critical capacities, deception and fraud are easier.

In other words, subjects in hypnotic trance do what they would not do outside of the trance if (through distortion of perception and appraisal) a frame of reality is constructed around them that is acceptable or downright desirable and advantageous to them so much so as to provoke their collaboration. In this case, hypnotized people cannot be either morally or legally culpable because they are not aware of objective reality, and that is not because of an illness (such as, for example, psychotic delirium) or because of a lack of volitional control (as, for example, in drunkenness). The hypnotized person behaves coherently in the hallucinatory context. For this reason, the subjects who can most easily find themselves involved in these problems are those who have a greater facility to develop hallucinations in hypnotic trance.

Another problem

Another problem connected with hypnosis, although this time in the religious rather than the forensic sphere, concerns reincarnation. Some subjects regress, not only to a remote past, and then recall in detail experiences from their childhood. It even seems that they can regress to a preceding life, but, at this point, it would be more exact to say, to a 'presumed' preceding life. Even if some testimonies are really very surprising, so much so that, for many, there are doubts and perplexity concerning the different explanations about reincarnation, it is, nevertheless, important to point out that, up to this point in time, there has been insufficient research to prove the reliability of what is said under hypnosis. So far, the scientific literature on hypnosis and regression to presumed preceding lives has not produced evidence in favour of reincarnation. Furthermore, the methodology used in hypnotic regressions to presumed preceding lives cannot be said to be scientifically adapted, and, therefore, the results cannot be regarded as reliable. Nevertheless, research continues, even if there are now many who regard it as useless or inappropriate, given that no amount of scientific research can produce a conviction of faith.

Hypnosis and Christian moral theology

In moral theology, the problem of hypnosis is posed in terms of freedom of conscience between manipulation and free will. From the results of scientific experiments known about so far, it can be affirmed that – both during the trance and afterwards, with post-hypnotic suggestions – enough free will for self-determination stays with the hypnotized subject because the will is not subjugated, or, at least, not completely. The morality of a person also has an unconscious level: some moral principles are observed even in a state of intoxication or under the effect of some toxic substances. The sense of duty and responsibility can be on the alert even when one is in deep sleep. The fact that a mother can sleep deeply in spite of noise but can wake up as soon as her child emits a weak cry is probably due to this unconscious dimension of morality. For Christian moral theology, therefore, hypnosis in itself is licit and can be licitly used by professionals who are capable and competent in the therapeutic and/or didactic spheres. In hypnotic trance the hypnotized subject continues to maintain enough free will in regard to his or her own decisions.

Other useful clarifications regarding the use of hypnosis in accordance with the principles of Christian morality are those pertaining to the consent of patients: Is it necessary that patients explicitly express their consent to the use of hypnosis or can recourse be had to an 'implicit' consent? Does the hypnotizing therapist have to ask for such consent explicitly or can he consider it 'presumed'? One can respond to these questions holding that the therapist (physician or psychologist) 'has the moral duty, beyond the contractual obligation, to put into effect all those means which are held to be most advisable in the interest of the person being helped, without being concerned about consent for the carrying out of every single act. And only the explicit opposition of the person, if validly manifested, obliges the doctor to refrain from carrying out the act to which consent has not been given.'[2]

Another moral problem is that of the use of information which can be given in a state of trance. I can respond to this in general terms: in a hypnotic trance, extorting information without the consent of the subject is illicit, even if one intends doing it for a good end. Even a delinquent has the right to private intimacy; and, anyway, it has been confirmed that one can lie under hypnosis.

Concerning hypnosis, the Church has anticipated both official medicine and secular jurisprudence, but we should also say that some theologians have displayed a certain closure and some suspicion towards hypnotic phenomenology. However, as we shall see, it is more a matter of taking up a position in respect to a bad use of hypnosis. For example, in an old

Roman Catholic manual of moral theology there is an allusion to hypnosis among the sins against religion, but the description is up to date for its time which saw no taking up of positions against this approach.[3] The theologian who was the author of this manual demonstrated that he was very much in favour of 'waking suggestion', which today we can call 'indirect hypnosis':

> The milder form of hypnotism – without true hypnosis – employed in psycho-therapeutics as a curative agency is less dangerous. It works remarkable cures quickly and permanently, provided the patient uses his own will-power to maintain the primary beneficial effect. It is the mind and will of the patient that effect the cure. . . . There is no reason, therefore, to condemn 'waking suggestion' unless it is misinterpreted and misdirected, that is, if its use leads to ridiculous superstition, or the attribution to the healer of magic and occult powers, and if the suggestions employed are wrong.[4]

I have used this example from a Catholic manual of moral theology which predates the Second Vatican Council precisely to show that the attitude of *openness and prudence* on the part of the Catholic Church (and, indeed, other churches) in regard to hypnosis is not only a characteristic of the present theological position, but has always been there. Of course, I do not mean to say that this has been a universal attitude shared by all theologians of all times. If there have been exceptions, these have certainly been rare and lacking any doctrinal relevance. The prudential attitude also comes from the fact that many – above all in the past – confused hypnosis with spiritualism and magic.

The main concern of theologians springs from the consequences of an improper use of hypnosis, especially if the practitioners are not professionals. This means that no theologian has ever had any objections to hypnosis if it is used for therapeutic ends and if the practitioners are professionals. It can be said that this is, in substance, the position of the manuals of Christian moral theology.

General anaesthesia

In the 1950s we had the first publications concerning the possibility of remembering what was perceived during operations whilst under total anaesthesia.[5] The first explanatory response on the part of surgeons was that there was a momentary weakening of the anaesthesia which could permit the placing of some memories. Anaesthetists did not willingly accept this implicit accusation concerning their ability to appraise the quantity and quality of the anaesthesia on the bases of physiological and surgical parameters.

Whilst, on the one hand, anaesthesiology still needs to make advances in regard to both drugs and techniques, on the other, not a few anaesthetists pointed out that, even under total anaesthesia, the reticular system never completely loses contact with the surrounding reality. Furthermore, memories never referred to visual sensation, sensations of touch or olfactory ones, but only to auditory perceptions. And it is known that hearing is the last of the five external senses to abandon normal alert consciousness under total anaesthesia, in coma, and in various other states, such as preagonic ones. Therefore, from a purely theoretical point of view, it does not seem so absurd to suppose the hypothesis of auditory perception under total anaesthesia and an equally possible memorizing of these perceptions. Various patients have demonstrated that they can retrieve at the conscious level part of what they perceived under total anaesthesia.

A notable contribution to this hypothesis came from the first systematic experimental research and from the gathering of observations made by patients.[6] Nevertheless, there were not a few doctors who held that these post-operative accounts were 'hallucinations' of the patients caused by the dissociating effect of the anaesthetizing gas. In reality, patients who quoted to the letter phrases uttered during their operations were statistically very few (about 2 per cent), but there were certainly many others who felt the consequences of what they had heard whilst under total anaesthesia. For example, during an operation, the surgeon told his assistants that the patient was inoperable because of the advanced state of the invasion of cancer. Immediately after the operation, in spite of having forgotten the event and in spite of benevolent reassurances on the part of all the medical personnel, the patient was profoundly depressed. Since many analogous cases were observed, it was recommended that great caution be exercised during operations, or else the patient should be given earplugs. Anyway, the moral problem was from now on felt by many.[7]

From the scientific documentation gathered by the 1970s, one can conclude that one of the new moral problems of the medical profession concerned the manner of speaking about the patient during total anaesthesia, above all when reference is made to matters concerning his or her life and health. A possible conditioning seemed evident from all the conclusions of the research conducted up to that time.

One conclusion of noteworthy importance refers to the content of what is generally remembered. More than words *ad litteram* there are the emotions and reflexes that remain after anaesthesia. Two examples: (1) optimism or pessimism expressed about patients during total anaesthesia has a notable effect upon their mood during the post-operatory phase; (2) under total anaesthesia, the reflexes can be conditioned more or less as with post-hypnotic suggestion: 'Upon waking, when I pronounce this number . . . you will feel a tingling sensation and you will need to scratch your ear, or else your nose will feel itchy and you will scratch it.' When completely awake, almost all patients do not remember the words heard, but a significant percentage of patients, at the indicated stimulus (the number, for example . . .), reply with the reflex to which they have been conditioned (scratching their ear or nose). This percentage is even more significant if – in addition to, or together with, a reflex – the conditioning of a mood or state of mind is put in place (for example: 'You can be tranquil . . . everything is going well . . . you can be calm and go to sleep . . .').

The recovery of feelings and the putting in place of reflexes raises the possibility of real perception during total anaesthesia.[8]

In the 1980s a new moral problem presented itself, arising precisely from the possibility of conditioning a subject during general anaesthesia. Or rather, if subjects could be conditioned negatively by what they heard whilst under total anaesthesia, they could also be conditioned positively, and the state of total anaesthesia, then, becomes an excellent opportunity to use for therapeutic purposes. In concrete, subjects can be conditioned by putting in place useful reflexes in the post-operatory phase by sending them messages – during total anaesthesia – aimed at certain physiological functions in need of recovery in such spheres as peristalsis, pain control, anxiety, insomnia, urination, swallowing and other functions necessary to the functional autonomy of the patient. In the 1980s research and experimentation were developed, based precisely on this presupposition. Confirmed was the previously acquired datum that the state of anaesthesia is not a passive one from the point of view of psychological functioning and that it can be used for the person's benefit.[9] Patients who remember *ad litteram* the content of conversations that took place during their operations are still statistically very few in number, but the percentage rises considerably if we take into account the restoring of emotional states and the responses to conditioned reflexes. This percentage rises even further if the subjects are sensitized to memory recall by means of hypnotic induction before or in place of pre-anaesthesia and another hypnotic induction after the total anaesthesia.

This is one of the major goals that research will try to reach during the 1990s. It is not a question of substituting hypnotic trance for analgesics or drug-induced anaesthesia. It is rather a question of using hypnosis to make perception during total anaesthesia more sensitive and the putting in place of conditioned reflexes more effective and beneficial in the post-operatory phase.

It is often not necessary to add hypnosis to the messages imparted during total anaesthesia; these last mentioned could be enough. In neurosurgical operations lasting seven hours or more, uniting the two procedures assures better results in the post-operatory phase.

In general, post-operatory development is strictly correlative to the type of operation and to the psychic structure of the patient, so, in order that they may have maximum efficacy, the messages – heard through earphones during total anaesthesia – must be strictly personalized. This is one of the most important data: the messages that contain the patient's name are the ones that are most incisive.

I should immediately add that, in control groups in which patients did not hear personalized messages, but only relaxing music, these too displayed clinical benefits and advantages that were far superior to those of patients treated in accordance with traditional procedures (or rather, without any particular device other than the mere administering of the anaesthetic).[10]

One of the first moral problems brought to light here concerns precisely the benefits of this procedure. A patient can: (1) suffer less; (2) take fewer tranquillizers; (3) recover much sooner. If this particular procedure permits us to attain these objectives to the advantage of the patient, why not put it into practice?

Another problem: has this procedure been sufficiently studied to guarantee its validity? Patients and doctors can rest assured not only that this procedure is harmless, but that it presents a high probability of success in terms of real, consistent and durable blessings. Not to take into account these findings could amount to a serious omission in regard to the dignity of the patient.

In the future it will also be possible to extend research to another problem that is still not very clear: various psychological disturbances – especially of the phobic and/or obsessive type – seem to arise after total anaesthesia. Changes of taste and changes in behaviour in a direction that is not pathological have also been noticed, but all this is more difficult to verify because often there is no psychic profile of patients prior to the operation to compare with a later follow-up, which could confirm or deny a real change. Moreover, even after having verified a change – pathological or otherwise – it is still very difficult to demonstrate that total anaesthesia is the only or the principal factor in such changes in behaviour.

We can conclude that the state of total anaesthesia is the location of many problems in the sphere of medical ethics, hitherto unknown, and many will still have to be studied. The quality of the psychophysical well-being of very many patients depends on the solution to these problems.

Notes

1 M. T. Orme, 'The use and misuse of hypnosis in court', *International Journal of Clinical and Experimental Hypnosis* (1979), pp. 311–41; M. T. Orme *et al.*, 'Hypnotically induced testimony' in G. L. Wells and E. F. Loftus (eds), *Eyewitness Testimony: Psychological Perspectives* (New York: Cambridge University Press, 1984), pp. 171–213; P. W. Sheehan and K. M. McConkey, *Hypnosis and Experience: The Exploration of Phenomena and Process* (Hillsdale, NJ: Erlbaum, 1982); G. F. Wagstaff, *Hypnosis, Compliance and Belief* (Brighton: Harvester Press/New York: St Martin's Press, 1981); G. F. Wagstaff, 'The enhancement of witness memory by hypnosis: a review and methodological critique of the experimental literature', *British Journal of Experimental and Clinical Hypnosis* 2 (1984), pp. 3–12.

2 T. G. Formaggio, *Deontologia medica e legislazione sanitaria* (Pavia: Pavese 1958), cited by F. Granone, *Trattato di ipnosi* (Turin: Ed. UTET, 1989), p. 354.

3 H. Davis, *Moral and Pastoral Theology*, vol. II (London: Sheed and Ward, 1949), pp. 17–20.

4 Davis, *Moral and Pastoral Theology*, vol. II, pp. 19–20.

5 D. B. Cheek, 'Unconscious perception of meaningful sound during surgical anaesthesia as revealed under hypnosis', *American Journal of Clinical Hypnosis* I (1959), pp. 101–13: J. Rosen, 'Hearing tests during anaesthesia and N_2O and relaxants', *Acta Anaesthesiologica Scandinavica* 3 (1959), p. 1; Editorial, 'Consciousness during surgical operations', *British Medical Journal* 2 (1959), p. 810.

6 In chronological order: D. B. Cheek, 'What does the surgical anaesthetized patient hear?', *Rocky Mountain Medical Journal* 57 (January 1960), pp. 49–53; D. B. Cheek, 'Use of peri-operative hypnosis to protect patients from careless conversation', *American Journal of Clinical Hypnosis* 3.2 (1960), pp. 101–2; B. Hovell, 'Prevention of hearing during anaesthesia', *Anaesthesia* 35 (1960), p. 519; R. Hutchinson, 'Awareness during surgery. A study of its incidence', *British Journal of Anaesthesia* 33 (1960), p. 463; J. Parkhouse, 'Awareness during surgery', *Postgraduate Medical Journal* 36 (1960), p. 674; L. S. Wolfe and J. B. Millett, 'Control of post-operative by suggestion under general anesthesia', *American Journal of Clinical Hypnosis* 3 (1960) pp. 109–12; D. Hutchings, 'The value of suggestion given under anaesthesia: a report and evaluation of 200 consecutive cases', *American Journal of Clinical Hypnosis* 4 (1961), p. 26; E. E. Auld, 'Awareness during surgery', *Lancet* 2 (1961), p. 1394. R. Pearson, 'Response to suggestions given under general anaesthesia', *American Journal of Clinical Hypnosis* 4 (1961), p. 106; J. T. Brunn, 'The capacity to hear, to understand, to remember experiences during chemioanesthesia: a personal experience', *American Journal of Clinical Hypnosis* 6 (1963), p. 27; D. B. Cheek, 'Further evidence of persistence of hearing under chemio-anesthesia: detailed case report', *American Journal of Clinical Hypnosis* 7 (1964), p. 55; D. B. Cheek, 'Surgical memory and reaction to careless conversation', *American Journal of Clinical Hypnosis* 6 (1964), p. 237; B. W. Levinson, 'States of awareness under general anaesthesia: a case history', *Medical Proceedings* 11 (1965), p. 243; B. W. Levinson, 'States of awareness under general anaesthesia: primary communication', *British Journal of Anaesthesia* 27 (1965), p. 544; E. Werbel, *One Surgeon's Experience with Hypnosis* (New York: Pageant Press, 1965).

7 M. Abramson *et al.*, 'Response to our perception of auditory stimuli under deep surgical anesthesia', *American Journal of Obstetrics and Gynecology* 96 (1966), p. 584;

C. Bahl and S. Wadwas, 'Consciousness during apparent surgical anaesthesia', *British Journal of Anaesthesia* 40 (66), p. 289; J. McIntyre, 'Awareness during general anaesthesia: preliminary observations', *Canadian Anaesthetists' Society Journal* 13 (1966), p. 495; D. J. Waters, 'Factors causing awareness during surgery', *British Journal of Anaesthesia* 40 (1968), p. 259 F. J. Evans *et al.*, 'Sleep-induced behavioral response: relationship and susceptibility to hypnosis and laboratory sleep patterns', *Journal of Nervous and Mental Disease* 148.5 (1969), pp. 467–76; B. W. Levinson, 'An examination of state of awareness during general anaesthesia' (unpublished thesis) (1969); A. Kasasian, 'Awareness during anaesthesia', *British Medical Journal* 1 (1969), p. 507; R. Sia, 'Consciousness during general anesthesia', *Anesthesia and Analgesia* (Cleveland) 48 (1969), p. 636; L. Terrel *et al.*, 'Study of recall during anesthesia', *Anesthesia and Analgesia* (Cleveland) 48 (1969), p. 86; J. Wilson and D. Turner, 'Awareness during caesarean section under general anaesthesia', *British Medical Journal* 1 (1969), p. 281.

8 V. Bensen, 'One hundred cases of post-anesthetic suggestion in the recovery room', *American Journal of Clinical Hypnosis* 14 (1971), p. 9; S. Crawford, 'Awareness during operative obstetrics under general anaesthesia', *British Journal of Anaesthesia* 43 (1971), pp. 179–82; C. Perry *et al.*, 'Behavioral response to verbal stimuli administered and tested during REM sleep: a further investigation', *Waking and Sleeping* 2 (1978), pp. 35–42; S. Zornetzer, 'Neurotransmitter modulation and memory: a new neuropharmacological phrenology' in M. Lipton, *Psychopharmacology: A Generation in Progress* (New York: Raven Press, 1978); H. Rigter and J. Crable, 'Modulation of memory by the pituitary hormones' in *Vitamins and Hormones* (New York: Academic Press, 1979), p. 37; J. Barber *et al.*, 'The relationship between nitrous oxide, conscious sedation and the hypnotic state', *Journal of the American Dental Association* 99 (1979), pp. 624–6.

9 R. Yeoman *et al.*, 'Enflurane effects on acoustic and photic evoked responses', *Neuropharmacology* 19 (1980), pp. 481–9; D. B. Cheek, 'Awareness of meaningful sound under general anaesthesia', *Simposia Specialists* (paper presented at the 22nd Annual Scientific Meeting of the American Society of Clinical Hypnosis, San Francisco, 1979); K. Millar and N. Watkinson, 'Recognition of words presented during general anesthesia', *Ergonomics* 26 (1983), p. 585; C. Thornton *et al.*, 'Enflurane anaesthesia causes graded changes in the brainstem and early cortical auditory evoked response in man', *British Journal of Anaesthesia* 55 (1983), pp. 479–86; C. Thornton *et al.*, 'Effects of halothane or enflurane with controlled ventilation on auditory evoked potentials', *British Journal of Anaesthesia* 56 (1984), pp. 315–23; G. Lynch *et al.*, *Neurobiology of Learning and Memory* (New York: Guilford, 1984); I. Izquierdo *et al.*, 'Effects of various behavioral training procedures on brain B-endorphin-like immunoreactivity and the possible role of B-endorphin in behavioral regulation', *Psychoneuroendocrinology* 9.4 (1984), pp. 387–91; I. Izquierdo and R. Diaz, 'Involvement of A-adrenergic receptors in the amnestic and anti-amnestic action of ACTH, B-endorphin and epinephrine', *Psychoneuroendocrinology* 9.1 (1984), pp. 77–81; J. Richardson *et al.*, 'The effects of intravenous diazepam and hyoscine upon recognition memory', *Behavioral Brain Research* 14 (1984), pp. 193–9; C. Firth *et al.*, 'The effects of intravenous diazepam and hyoscine upon human memory', *Quarterly Journal of Experimental Psychology* 36A (1984), pp. 133–44; H. Bennett, 'Non-verbal response to intraoperative conversation', *Anesthesia and Analgesia* 63 (1984), p. 185, also in *British Journal of Anesthesia* 57 (1985), p. 174; P. Gold *et al.*, 'Epinephrine-induced learning under anesthesia: retention performance at several training testing intervals', *Behavioral Neuroscience* 99.4 (1985), pp. 1019–22; C. Thornton *et al.*, 'Effect of etomidate on

auditory evoked response in man', *British Journal of Anaesthesia* 57 (1985), pp. 554–61; R. Richardson *et al.*, 'State dependent retention induced by post-acquisition exposure to pentobarbital or shock stress in rats', *Animal Learning and Behavior* 14.1 (1986), pp. 73–9; B. Bonke *et al.*, 'A clinical study of so-called unconscious perception during general anaesthesia', *British Journal of Anaesthesia* 58 (1986), p. 957; L. Goldman and A. B. Levy, 'Orienting under anaesthesia', *Anaesthesia* 41 (1986), pp. 1056–7; L. Goldman, 'Awareness under general anaesthesia', thesis, University of Cambridge (1986); L. Goldman, M. V. Shah and M. W. Hebden, 'Memory of cardiac anaesthesia: psychological sequelae and operating room conversation', *Anaesthesia* 42 (1987), pp. 596–603; D. Cheek, 'Unconscious perception of meaningful sounds during surgical anesthesia' in *Mind–Body Therapy: Methods of Ideo-dynamic Healing in Hypnosis* (New York: Norton, 1988), pp. 113–30; H. Bennett, 'Perception and memory for events during adequate general anesthesia for surgical operation' in H. Pettinati (ed.), *Hypnosis and Memory* (New York: Guilford, 1988), pp. 194–5; M. Jelicic and B. Bonke, 'Auditory perception during general anaesthesia: psychological conse-quences', *Southern Medical Journal*, 82.10 (1989), pp. 1220–3; L. Goldman, 'Cognitive process under general anaesthesia' in Michael Heap (ed.), *Hypnosis: Current Clinical, Experimental and Forensic Practices* (London: Croom Helm, 1988), pp. 77–88; A. Pacciolla, 'Anestesia generale: nuove prospettive terapeutiche e morali', *L'ancora nell'unità di salute* 2 (1989), pp. 158–74.

10 McLintock *et al.*, 'Postoperative analgesic requirements in patients exposed to positive intraoperative suggestions', *British Medical Journal* 301 (1990), pp. 788–90; A. Pacciolla, 'Ricordi e riflessi condizionati in anestesia generale', *Rivista Medica Italiana di Psicoterapia ed Ipnosi* II (1990), pp. 167–83.

Index

Index

Index

Index